# IN STRUGGLE

# IN STRUGGLE

## SNCC AND THE

## BLACK AWAKENING

## OF THE 1960s

*Clayborne Carson*

1981

Harvard University Press

Cambridge, Massachusetts
and London, England

Publication of this book has been aided by a grant from the
Andrew W. Mellon Foundation.

Library of Congress Cataloging in Publication Data

Carson, Clayborne, 1944–
  In struggle.
  Includes bibliographical references and index.
  1. Afro-Americans—Civil rights—Southern States.
2. Student Nonviolent Coordinating Committee.
3. Southern States—Race relations. I. Title.
E185.92.C37 1981   323.1′196073′075      80-16540
ISBN 0-674-44725-5

*In Memory of My Brother*

*Michael Windell*

*and for Susan*

# ACKNOWLEDGMENTS

This book could not have been written without the help of many people who recognized SNCC's historical importance. I share with them the wish to preserve SNCC from the fate of obscurity or of misunderstanding that often befalls the harbingers of change. I received many different kinds of assistance, but all aid was accompanied by the qualities of generosity, openness, and sincerity that characterized SNCC itself. Mindful that I cannot thank everyone who helped, I wish at least to call attention to the collective effort that produced this book.

Since I began intensive research in the spring of 1972, the work has undergone many transformations. Helpful suggestions regarding the original dissertation, titled "Toward Freedom and Community: The Evolution of Ideas in the Student Nonviolent Coordinating Committee," were made by members of my doctoral committee at UCLA, which included Stanley Coben as chairman, Gary B. Nash, and Ralph H. Turner. I am especially grateful for Coben's continuing encouragement and advice. August Meier provided insightful comments and useful suggestions for further research. As the manuscript was revised, I greatly benefited from the comments of Barton J. Bernstein, William H. Chafe, Bruce Dancis, Estelle B. Freedman, Lawrence Goodwyn, Maulana Karenga, `Michael Kazin, Mary E. King, Nell Irwin Painter, Mary A. Rothschild, Ronald Schatz, Jean Wiley, and Howard Zinn. Douglas A. Gamble of the Highlander Center was especially generous of his time; he will find his concern amply reflected in this work. Friends and relatives who proofread the manuscript included Christopher Carson, Clayborne Carson, Sr., Alan Colón, Susan Diamondstone, Janet Gamble, R. Steven Hargrove, Joan S. Reid, and my principal typist, Richard Hazin. Additional typing was done by Mako Bockholt and Eileen Purcell. Research assistance was provided by Shelley Director, Bethany Korwin-Panowski, Gail Rogers, and Lisa Stotsky.

My wife, Susan, provided essential and insightful advice at every stage in the preparation of the manuscript, aiding in research and offering searching criticisms of the many drafts. I could not have completed the book

without her support and loving devotion to our children, both human and
literary.

Although I used numerous research collections, the book is based largely
on materials that I collected over the past fifteen years. The following indi-
viduals graciously allowed me access to SNCC materials in their possession:
Jan Hillegas, Mary E. King, Debbie Louis, Michael Miller, James R.
Prickett, Cleveland Sellers, Stanley Wise, and Howard Zinn. I received assistance from the staffs at several libraries, including the UCLA Research
Library, Stanford University Archives and Special Collections, John F.
Kennedy Library, Lyndon Baines Johnson Library, and especially the
State Historical Society of Wisconsin. I wish to thank the late Carl Braden
and his wife, Anne, for allowing me to use materials from their extensive
collection at the Wisconsin Historical Society.

I am grateful for receiving a grant from the UCLA faculty senate which
allowed me to conduct the interviews. The Dean of Graduate Studies at
Stanford provided funds for typing. The Center for the Study of Civil
Rights and Race Relations at Duke University provided a visiting fellowship that gave me time and pleasant surroundings to complete the manuscript.

Finally, I would like to thank those who consented to talk to me about
their association with SNCC. I am richer for my too short association with
A. Muhammad Ahmad (Max Stanford), Annie Pearl Avery, Ella Jo Baker,
Marion S. Barry, Fay Bellamy, Sam Block, Anne Braden, Bob Brown,
C. C. Bryant, Stokely Carmichael, Eldridge Cleaver, Kathleen Cleaver,
Virginia Collins, Courtland Cox, John M. Doar, Howard Dodson, Ivanhoe
Donaldson, St. Clair Drake, James Forman, Jimmy Garrett, Dewey
Greene, Freddie B. Greene, George Greene, Bill Hall, William Hansen, Phil
Hutchins, Tom Kahn, Maulana Karenga, Mary E. King, John Lewis,
Margaret Long, Worth Long, Allard Lowenstein, Bob Mants, Joe Martin,
Jack Minnis, Ethel Minor, Jesse Morris, Ernest Nobles, John O'Neal,
Gwen Patton, Willie Peacock, John Perdew, David Richmond, Willie
Ricks, Reginald J. Robinson, Luther Seabrook, Cleveland Sellers, Charles
Sherrod, Charles Smith, Scott B. Smith, Donald Stone, William Strick-
land, Muriel Tillinghast, Maria Varela, Bill Ware, Owusu Ware, Jean
Wiley, Johnny Wilson, Stanley Wise, Dorothy Miller Zellner, and Robert
Zellner.

# CONTENTS

Introduction    1

## Part One. Coming Together

1. Sit-ins    9
2. Getting Organized    19
3. Freedom Rides    31
4. Radical Cadre in McComb    45
5. The Albany Movement    56
6. Sustaining the Struggle    66
7. March on Washington    83
8. Planning for Confrontation    96
9. Mississippi Challenge    111

## Part Two. Looking Inward

10. Waveland Retreat    133
11. Breaking New Ground    153
12. The New Left    175
13. Racial Separatism    191

## Part Three. Falling Apart

14. Black Power    215
15. Internal Conflicts    229
16. White Repression    244
17. Seeking New Allies    265
18. Decline of Black Radicalism    287

Epilogue    305
Notes    307
Index    347

# ILLUSTRATIONS

*following*
*page*

Stokely Carmichael leaving Jackson, Mississippi, courthouse after arrest during 1961 freedom ride   *Ebony Magazine, Johnson Publishing Co.*    82

Reginald Robinson, Bill Hansen, Charles Jones, Cordell Reagon, and
Ruby Doris Robinson at SNCC workshop in Shiloh, Alabama,
1962   *Highlander Center*

Robert Moses and other SNCC workers urging black residents of
Ruleville, Mississippi, to register, ca. 1963   *Danny Lyon, Magnum Photos*

Frank Smith, Robert Moses, and Willie Peacock at SNCC office in
Greenwood, Mississippi, the day before it was gutted by fire,
1963   *Danny Lyon, Magnum Photos*

Ruby Doris Robinson, 1965   *Ebony Magazine, Johnson Publishing Co.*    152

John Lewis and James Forman, ca. 1963   *Danny Lyon, Magnum Photos*

Stokely Carmichael during voter registration drive in Lowndes
County, Alabama, 1965   *Ebony Magazine, Johnson Publishing Co.*

Julian Bond, ca. 1967   *Ebony Magazine, Johnson Publishing Co.*

Fannie Lou Hamer testifying for the Mississippi Freedom Democratic
Party at the Democratic National Convention, Atlantic City,
1964   *Ebony Magazine, Johnson Publishing Co.*

Floyd McKissick, Martin Luther King, and Stokely Carmichael leading march into Jackson, Mississippi, 1966   *Bob Fitch, Black Star*    212

Stokely Carmichael, Andrew Young, Martin Luther King, and
Lawrence Guyot planning Mississippi march, 1966   *Bob Fitch, Black
Star*

Cleveland Sellers  speaking to newsmen outside Atlanta induction
center after refusing the draft, 1967   *United Press International*

Party headquarters, Lowndes County, Alabama, 1966   *Doug Harris*    286

Election night, Lowndes County, Alabama, 1966   *Doug Harris*

H. Rap Brown speaking in Cambridge, Maryland, shortly before
being shot by police, 1967   *United Press International*

Bob Zellner, Ella Baker, and Charles Sherrod at civil rights conference in Jackson, Mississippi, 1979   *Clayborne Carson*

# IN STRUGGLE

# INTRODUCTION

The Student Nonviolent Coordinating Committee (SNCC, pronounced "snick") emerged from the seemingly sterile American political landscape of the 1950s, thrived in the midst of the mass struggles of the 1960s, and died in the arid atmosphere of repression, divisiveness, and self-absorption at the beginning of the 1970s. As racial discord and discontent broke through a facade of accommodation, and as black people attempted to end a heritage of racial subordination, SNCC's radicalism flowered, displaying the possible dimensions of personal freedom in pursuit of social change.

SNCC initially attracted southern black college students whose attitudes were confined within the narrow bounds of permissible political dissent of the Cold War era and the even narrower bounds imposed by the southern segregationist regimes. As black students became involved in the lunch counter sit-in movement that began in 1960, they acquired new perspectives for viewing American society and its prevailing cultural and political values. SNCC became a community in which a small but growing number of activists—whites as well as blacks, nonstudents and students, northerners and southerners—attempted to create more satisfying alternatives to the prevailing American middle-class way of life. Because SNCC so clearly reflected the emergent values of an expanding social struggle, it became a gathering point for idealistic young people, who saw in it a unique outlet for expressing their resentment of racial injustice.

After the uncompromising militancy of the student "freedom riders" placed the administration of President John F. Kennedy on the defensive during the spring and summer of 1961, a group of activists left campuses and careers to become full-time SNCC staff members. With few resources other than their commitment, creativity, and youthful energy, these SNCC workers led a frontal attack on the southern strongholds of racism. While mobilizing black communities, they acquired a distinctive radicalism that was shaped by their changing experiences and aspirations. At first this radicalism took the form of an insistence that the federal government act forcefully and swiftly on behalf of civil rights workers and southern blacks seeking civil rights. By the mid-1960s, however, SNCC workers began to question not only the pace but also the prevailing strategies of change in

1

American society. They observed that existing leaders did not initiate the most significant local struggles; instead, such struggles produced new indigenous leadership capable of sustaining them. By making southern blacks more confident of their capacity to overcome oppression, SNCC workers revived dormant feelings of racial consciousness and ultimately stimulated many of the movements that would transform American society.

This book is a study of the ideas that came to life inside SNCC. Its central theme is the evolution of SNCC's radicalism. This process involved conflict as well as consensus, for SNCC was not a homogeneous sect organized around a single set of beliefs. Staff members questioned not only the assumptions which underlay the status quo but also those that underlay their own rebellion against authority. They agreed that the goal of their struggle was to enhance human freedom, but they became increasingly aware of the inherent limitations of individualistic values as a guide for movements seeking collective goals. Although a belief in the emergence of new and better leaders from the militant black struggles prevailed within SNCC during most of the 1960s, an increasing number of staff members argued that strong, lasting institutions were also needed if SNCC were to move beyond the goal of civil rights reforms and change the American political structure. The uncompromising tone of SNCC's criticisms of the federal government and American liberalism obscured the vigorous debates within SNCC regarding tactics, strategy, and goals. In the course of their discussions, SNCC workers acquired insights regarding a question faced by idealistic reformers and revolutionaries throughout history: whether it is possible to help powerless people make political gains without creating new sources of oppression.

SNCC's development can be traced through three stages. In the first stage civil rights activists came together in SNCC to form a community within a social struggle. SNCC workers sought to create a rationale for activism by eclectically adopting ideas from the Grandhian independence movement and from the American traditions of pacifism and Christian idealism as formulated by the Congress of Racial Equality (CORE), Fellowship of Reconciliation (FOR), and Southern Christian Leadership Conference (SCLC). SNCC, however, was typically less willing than other civil rights groups to impose its ideas on local black leaders or to restrain southern black militancy. Viewed as the "shock troops" of the civil rights movement, SNCC activists established projects in areas such as rural Mississippi considered too dangerous by other organizations. As the thrust of SNCC's activities shifted from desegregation to political rights, its philosophical commitment to nonviolent direct action gave way to a secular, humanistic radicalism influenced by Marx, Camus, Malcolm X, and most of all by the SNCC organizers' own experiences in southern black communities. In the summer of 1964 SNCC's singular qualities came to national attention when it played a leading role in bringing hundreds of northern students to Mississippi for a decisive battle over voter registration in the main bastion of southern segregation.

The second stage of SNCC's development began after the defeat of an attempt by the Mississippi Freedom Democratic party (MFDP) to unseat the regular all-white delegation to the Democratic National Convention in August 1964. SNCC had by this time become a training ground for activists who would participate in the Free Speech Movement at Berkeley, the Vietnam War protests, and the women's struggle, but SNCC workers themselves had become more uncertain about the values guiding their work. Over the next two years, they looked inward, questioning whether the strategy they had followed could achieve the fundamental social changes they now viewed as necessary. Staff members debated whether southern black people could achieve lasting improvement in their lives while continuing to rely on appeals for white liberal support and federal intervention, and whether SNCC could continue to expand the black struggle while remaining tied to the rhetoric of interracialism and nonviolent direct action. They also questioned whether their remaining goals could best be achieved through continued confrontation with existing institutions or through the building of alternative institutions controlled by the poor and powerless.

The third phase of SNCC's development involved the members' efforts to resolve their differences by addressing the need for black power and black consciousness, by separating themselves from white people, and by building black-controlled institutions. After his election as chairman of SNCC in May 1966, Stokely Carmichael popularized the organization's new separatist orientation, but he and other workers were unable to formulate a set of ideas that could unify black people. As SNCC workers sought to increase black awareness of the range of available political and cultural alternatives, they became embroiled in bitter factional battles and failed to sustain local black movements in the South. Disagreements about the future direction of the struggles also divided black communities throughout the nation. Weakened by internal dissension, SNCC withered in the face of the same tactics of subtle co-optation and ruthless repression that stifled the entire black struggle.

As one of many black people who were profoundly influenced by SNCC, I wrote this book partly to repay a debt. I learned invaluable lessons from SNCC's achievements and from its failures. When I first encountered SNCC workers in 1963 as a freshman at the University of New Mexico, they gave me a view of the southern civil rights movement that was different from, and more compelling than, the press reports I had read about sit-ins and marches and Martin Luther King. I marveled at the intellectual audaciousness of Stokely Carmichael, who expressed thoughts that were latent in my own mind. I admired the humanity of Bob Moses, who combined intellectual understanding with selfless commitment. Not much older than myself, these two leaders had assumed important social roles and lived in ways that I found exciting and exemplary. Though I resisted the inclination to join SNCC's staff, I soon became involved in "the movement." Deciding to leave the relative isolation of New Mexico, I enrolled at the University of California at Los Angeles and established contact with civil rights activists in that city.

Not content to be simply a protester and yet not trained as a community organizer, I followed my instincts and became a journalist, writing for what was then called an underground newspaper. As a participant-observer of civil rights activities, I retained my respect for SNCC while also becoming aware of the difficulties it faced in mobilizing urban blacks. Like many other self-proclaimed militants, I watched without full comprehension the burning of large sections of Los Angeles in August 1965. Although realizing the necessity for SNCC's subsequent call for black power, I began to suspect that many SNCC workers were almost as uncertain as I about the future course of the black struggle.

As SNCC faded into the past, my earlier emotional attachment to it was replaced by an appreciation of SNCC's historical significance. Not only was my study of Afro-American history an outgrowth of the changes wrought by SNCC in my consciousness, but SNCC provided me with some of the intellectual tools for evaluating its successes and failures. SNCC's organizing efforts suggested a framework for understanding the black struggle of the 1960s not as an operation initiated and directed by leaders such as Martin Luther King or Malcolm X, but as a mass movement that produced its own leaders and ideas. Indeed, the major episodes of the decade—from the Montgomery bus boycott to the sit-ins to the violent urban rebellions—confirmed the validity of SNCC's view that people without resources and specialized skills can play decisive roles in bringing about social change.

Yet SNCC workers also recognized the difficulties resulting from the unleashing of sometimes conflicting desires for racial power and individual freedom. More telling than any of the criticisms directed at SNCC were those that came from within the organization itself. In examining these criticisms, I intend not to disparge SNCC but rather to show my deep respect for those who were willing to assume the risks of living experimentally. If SNCC staff members did not discover a means of reconciling their desire for social justice with their desire for individual freedom, neither have those of us who are able to reflect on such questions in more tranquil times. SNCC left an intellectual legacy that is crucial for any who will carry on its work and yet avoid its fate.

This book builds upon the foundations laid by SNCC partisans in their own critical examinations of the organization.[1] In seeking to go beyond these works, I encountered formidable obstacles, because SNCC workers rarely possessed the bureaucratic habits on which historians depend. Although the focus of my concern was SNCC's intellectual development, SNCC workers themselves were far more concerned with actions than with preserving a record of their thoughts. At present there are no official SNCC archives open to scholars. Although I used oral history to recreate SNCC's past, I was mindful of the limitations of memory to bridge the psychological gulf that separated former SNCC workers from the events of the 1960s. Thus, I relied mainly on traditional kinds of primary historical sources—transcripts of staff meetings, position papers, and other unpublished materials—to give a deeper understanding of a decidedly untraditional organization. These sources allow the reader to encounter problems and dilemmas as SNCC workers once did.

Much remains to be written about the civil rights movement and the black awakening of the 1960s. In the social struggles of that time, and especially in SNCC, a new awareness was born that continues to inform the progressive movements of today. By observing SNCC's tentative responses to complex dilemmas, we can perhaps gain a new sense of responsibility for our personal and collective fates. Although the SNCC workers failed to recognize problems which in retrospect appear obvious, it should always be remembered that they saw over the horizon before most other people of their generation.

# PART ONE
# COMING TOGETHER

# 1. SIT-INS

Late Monday afternoon, February 1, 1960, at a lunch counter in Greensboro, North Carolina, four black college students ignited one of the largest of all Afro-American protest movements. The initial spark of the movement was a simple, impulsive act of defiance, one that required no special skills or resources. Planned the previous night, the "sit-in"—as it would be called—was not the product of radical intellectual ferment. Rather, it grew out of "bull sessions" involving college freshmen who were, in most respects, typical southern black students of the time, politically unsophisticated and socially conventional. The four students would be influenced by the decade of social struggle that unexpectedly followed their protest far more than they affected the course of that struggle. Nonetheless, the initial sit-in contained the seeds of radicalism that would flower in SNCC, the principal organization to emerge from the black student sit-ins of 1960.

The four students, like many other young activists of the 1960s, acted on the basis of suppressed resentments that preceded the development of an ideological rationale for protest. Without an organizational structure and without a coherent set of ideas to guide their actions, the Greensboro students were determined to break with the past. Only after their isolated protest had provided the stimulus for an intense, sometimes chaotic process of political education within the southern struggle would the four students become fully aware of the significance of what they had done. In the beginning, they only spoke of a modest desire: to drink a cup of coffee, sitting down.

The initial sit-in was a tentative challenge to Jim Crow. Joseph McNeil and Izell Blair, roommates at the predominantly black North Carolina Agricultural and Technical College, along with two other students, Franklin McCain and David Richmond, purchased a few items at Greensboro's downtown F. W. Woolworth store and then sat down at the lunch counter reserved by custom for whites. They asked to be served but were refused. When a waitress asked them to leave, they explained politely that as they had bought items in other sections of the store, they should be allowed to sit on the stools rather than stand. They received no sympathy from a black woman who worked behind the counter. "You are stupid, ignorant!" she chastized them. "You're dumb! That's why we can't get anywhere today. You know you are supposed to eat at the other end." Although refused service, the four students became more confident as they observed the lack of forceful opposition by the store employees. When informed that the four students were continuing to sit at the lunch counter, the store manager merely ordered his employees to ignore them. The students had expected to be arrested, but instead they discovered a tactic that not only expressed their long-suppressed anger but also apparently did not provoke severe retaliation from whites. "Now it came to me all of a sudden," McCain remembered thinking. "Maybe they can't do anything to us. Maybe we can keep it up."[1]

They did. The four remained on the stools for almost an hour, until the store closed. After returning to campus, they contacted the student body president and recruited more students for another sit-in. The following morning a group of thirty students returned to the store and occupied the lunch counter. There were no confrontations, but the second sit-in, which lasted about two hours, attracted the attention of local reporters. A national news service carried an account of the protest, mentioning a group of "well-dressed Negro college students" who ended their sit-in with a prayer. On Wednesday morning a still larger group of students occupied most of the sixty-six seats at the lunch counter. In the afternoon three white students from Greensboro College joined them. Officials at North Carolina A. & T. resisted attempts by state officials to force them to restrict the activities of their students and by Thursday morning hundreds of black students had been drawn into the expanding protest. Many white youths had also gathered in the downtown section of Greensboro, cursing and threatening the black protesters and attempting to hold seats for white patrons. By the end of the week, after continued disruption of business activities and a telephoned bomb threat, the store manager decided to close the store. The mayor of Greensboro then called upon black students and business leaders to forgo temporarily "individual rights and financial interests" while city officials sought "a just and honorable resolution" of the controversy.[2] The demonstrators, by this time organized as the Students' Executive Committee for Justice, agreed to halt the protests for two weeks to give local leaders a chance to find a solution.

Although the Greensboro sit-ins were discontinued temporarily, students at nearby black colleges followed news accounts of the protest and quickly organized sit-ins. Over the weekend in which a sit-in moratorium was being arranged in Greensboro, more than one hundred students met in Winston-Salem to plan a protest of their own. Before they could act, however, Carl Matthews, a black college graduate working in Winston-Salem, conducted that city's first sit-in on Monday, February 8. Later in the afternoon

Matthews was joined by about twenty-five other blacks, many of them students at Winston-Salem Teachers College. The same day, seventeen students from North Carolina College and four from Duke University staged a sit-in at the Woolworth lunch counter in Durham. On Wednesday morning students in Raleigh decided to act after hearing a radio report assuring listeners that there would be no protests by college students in that locality. Two days later, when black students demonstrating at a suburban shopping center near Raleigh were arrested for trespassing, other students rushed to the scene to be arrested. In all, forty-one students were arrested and charged with trespassing in the first mass arrests of the sit-in movement. By the end of the week, more sit-ins had occurred in the North Carolina communities of Charlotte, Fayetteville, High Point, Elizabeth City, and Concord. On February 10, Hampton, Virginia, became the first community outside North Carolina to experience student sit-ins. Protests occurred soon afterward in the Virginia cities of Norfolk and Portsmouth. By the end of February, Nashville, Chattanooga, Richmond, Baltimore, Montgomery, and Lexington were among over thirty communities in seven states to experience sit-ins. The protests reached the remaining southern states by mid-April. By that time, according to one study, the movement had attracted about fifty thousand participants.[3]

Although the initial Greensboro sit-in had been peaceful and polite, the student protests gradually became more assertive, even boisterous. As demonstrations attracted increasing crowds of participants and onlookers, they came to be perceived as threats to social order. Most sit-ins by black college students were characterized by strict discipline among the protesters, but several outbreaks of violence occurred when protests involved high school students. The first serious instance of violence took place on February 16 in Portsmouth, Virginia, where hundreds of black and white high school students fought each other after a sit-in. More extensive violence, involving over a thousand people, took place in Chattanooga, Tennessee, after a demonstration on February 23. Over thirty persons, mostly whites, were arrested and police used fire hoses to end the two days of rioting.

Even in places where sit-ins were not accompanied by violence, there was an underlying current of hostility and fear among both blacks and whites. White onlookers verbally assaulted black protesters and at times only the rapid arrest of protesters by police prevented violent physical assaults. The protesters themselves, though usually peaceful, were engaging in a form of "passively aggressive behavior—stepping over the line and waiting, rather than exhibiting overtly hostile or revolutionary behavior."[4] Nonviolent tactics, particularly when accompanied by a rationale based on Christian principles, offered black students an appealing combination of rewards: a sense of moral superiority, an emotional release through militancy, and a possibility of achieving desegregation. The delicate balance between militancy and restraint produced tensions often released through humor. Popular jokes ridiculed the pretensions of white segregationalists:[5]

> A Negro goes into a restaurant and asks for "pigs' feet." "Don't serve them," the counterman answers. "Chitterlings then." "Don't serve them." "Pig's necks?" "Don't serve them." "Pig's ears?" "Don't serve them." "White man," the Negro says, "you just ain't ready for integration."

> A waitress told a pair of sit-inners, "I'm sorry but we don't serve Negroes here." "Oh, we don't eat them either," came the reply.

The sit-ins brought to the surface interracial tensions that had long been suppressed in the South, and they stimulated a process of self-realization among blacks that would continue through the decade. The goal of lunch counter desegregation certainly did not exhaust the range of black aspirations; nor did the sit-in tactic fully express the dormant emotions of southern blacks. But, as many other groups had discovered both in the United States and elsewhere, nonviolent direct action was a starting point for the emergence of a new political consciousness among oppressed people. For southern black students in the spring of 1960, it offered an almost irresistible model for social action.

Never again during the decade would the proportion of students active in protest equal the level reached at southern black colleges during the period from February to June 1960. On many campuses support for the sit-ins was almost unanimous. Over 90 percent of the students at North Carolina A. & T. and three nearby colleges took part in demonstrations or aided the movement by boycotting or picketing segregated stores. Student protesters commented that it was "like a fever. Everyone wanted to go. We were so happy."[6]

The emergence of a protest movement among black college students surprised many observers who were aware of the restrictive rules and conformist atmosphere that existed at southern black institutions. The sit-ins occurred only a few years after the publication of sociologist E. Franklin Frazier's *Black Bourgeoisie,* which painted black college students as politically apathetic, imbued with white middle-class values, and determined to achieve material success. Other observers saw the sit-in movement not as a signal for a basic shift in these attitudes and values but as an attempt to overcome the barriers that still separated black students from their white middle-class counterparts, through tactics that were in accord with prevailing American values. Thus, rather than representing a rejection of the mainstream of American life, the sit-ins were viewed as an outgrowth of racial assimilation and as an expression of the desire for further assimilation. Ruth Searles and J. Allen Williams made the point that black students had selected nonviolent protest "as an acceptable means of demonstrating their anger at barriers to first-class citizenship. Far from being alienated, the students appear to be committed to the society and its middle class leaders."[7]

This interpretation was reinforced by an extensive survey of black students carried out in the spring of 1962. John Orbell found that protest participation was strongly influenced by situational factors, such as the relative quality and type of school, the degree of urbanization, and the proportion of blacks in the college community. Students attending high-quality private black schools in urban settings with a low proportion of black residents were most likely to take part in demonstrations. Orbell concluded that these situational factors provided greater opportunities for interracial communication, and the resulting "higher awareness of the wider society" made students "more prone to develop the particular set of attitudes and perceptions that lead to protest." In short, most scholars who studied black protest during the early 1960s insisted that continued assimilation was the only realistic aspiration for blacks. "The Negro American judges his living standards, his opportunities, indeed, even judges himself," affirmed social psychologist Thomas F. Pettigrew, "in the only cultural terms he knows—those of the United States and its 'people of plenty.' "[8]

The upsurge of black militancy during the mid-1960s would undermine such assumptions. Moreover, the movement itself would become a source of new experiences and ideas that would alter the attitudes of black students. In the spring of 1960, however, few students would have disagreed with the view that they were motivated by conventional American values. In statements to reporters, student leaders often stressed the limited nature of their goals. "All I want is to come in and place my order and be served and leave a tip if I feel like it," Charles Jones asserted after leading Charlotte students in a sit-in. Like most student protesters, Jones was imbued with the anti-communist attitudes of the Cold War era. He had recently testified before the House Committee on Un-American Activities (HUAC) about his experience in 1959 as a delegate to the Seventh World Youth Festival in Vienna, which he attended to give foreign youths "a clearer understanding of the American way of doing things and show them that the racial situation wasn't as black as other delegations had painted it."[9] Similarly, Diane Nash, a student leader in Nashville, explicitly connected the student movement with the struggle against communism and added that if blacks were given equal educational opportunities in the South, "maybe some day a Negro will invent one of our missiles."[10]

Even as the scope of protest expanded to include targets other than lunch counters, students continued to justify their actions by appealing to dominant political values. Thus, shortly before launching a protest, Atlanta University students cited "the over-riding supremacy of the Federal

Law" and asserted their willingness "to use every legal and non-violent means" available "to secure full citizenship rights as members of this great Democracy of ours." During the summer, when representatives of the student movement appeared before the platform committee of the Democratic National Convention, they insisted that all Americans must "enjoy the full promise of our democratic heritage" in order to ensure that the nation fulfill "its responsibility to the free world."[11]

The students, who sincerely believed that the changes they demanded would benefit the nation, succeeded in presenting a positive image of their movement. The use of nonviolent tactics allowed black students to picture themselves as patient agents of progress pitted against obstinate, unreasoning whites. When President Dwight D. Eisenhower was asked on March 16 whether the "Gandhi-like" protests of the students were "manifestations of moral courage," he refused to endorse their sit-in tactics but nevertheless stated that he was "deeply sympathetic with the efforts of any group to enjoy the rights . . . guaranteed by the Constitution." Even James Kilpatrick, editor of the *Richmond News Leader* and a conservative white southerner, commented on the contrasting appearance of black students "in coats, white shirts, ties" and young white hecklers—"a ragtail rabble, slack-jawed, black jacketed, grinning fit to kill, and some of them . . . waving the proud and honored flag of the Southern states in the last war fought by gentlemen. Eheu!"[12]

The sit-ins, rather than emerging from radical intellectual ferment, reflected the students' general acceptance of the direction of racial reform in the United States. Although the lunch counter protests and the social struggles that followed would ultimately stimulate revolutionary ferment, initially most student protesters aspired to middle-class status and did not basically object to American society or its dominant political institutions. They protested against the pace rather than the direction of change. Few student protesters in 1960 belonged to political or civil rights organizations; of those who did, the largest number were members of youth groups affiliated with the National Association for the Advancement of Colored People (NAACP). Black nationalist groups, such as the Nation of Islam, had made few inroads into the South and almost none on black campuses prior to 1960. With the exception of a few demonstrations about cafeteria food and student regulations, no significant protest movement had taken place on black campuses since the 1920s.

Although the student sit-ins of 1960 marked the beginning of a reemergence of moribund Afro-American traditions of racial separatism and radicalism, they at first reflected the almost unchallenged dominance within Afro-American political life of leaders who concentrated on eliminating overt southern racism by portraying it as anachronistic and irrational, contrary to the American creed, and damaging to the interests of the nation.

Highly publicized Supreme Court decisions, most notably *Brown* vs. *Topeka Board of Education*, reinforced the domination of moderate civil rights leaders as did the Eisenhower administration's attempts to back court orders with federal troops in such cases as the Little Rock crisis of 1957. The ascendancy of the moderates was also a result of the persecution during the 1950s of leftist black leaders such as W. E. B. DuBois, Paul Robeson, and Benjamin Davis, as well as of the general suppression during that period of vigorous political dissent.

At a more basic level, the narrowing of the range of political alternatives available to blacks was the result of impersonal social trends which undermined the material basis of Afro-American cultural and political distinctiveness. As large numbers of blacks, even in the South, became enmeshed in urban industrial culture, with its associated institutions of mass education and mass communication, cultural traits that were rooted in the distinctive experience of black people were supplanted or absorbed by a pervasive mass culture. Because of the enormous power of white-controlled national institutions, blacks were under great pressure to seek to better their lives through assimilation and conventional political behavior. In the absence of a sustained and effective black protest movement, behavior that did not conform to the requirements of the dominant social order could only be regarded as trivial, ephemeral, or self-destructive.

Rather than indicating the existence of radicalism on black college campuses, the decision of black students to engage in protest was the outgrowth of guilt and frustration owing to their previous failure to take effective action against the humiliating Jim Crow system. Richmond recalled that, like many other blacks of his age group, he had "constantly heard about all the evils that were occurring and how black folks were mistreated and nobody was doing anything about it." The plan for the first sit-in was formulated after Richmond and three classmates denounced their own apathy and challenged each other to take action. "There were many words and few deeds," McCain remembered. "We did a good job of making each other feel bad."[13]

Many other black youths were witnessing the same events that stimulated the emotions of the Greensboro students. The highly publicized racial controversies following the Supreme Court's *Brown* decision in 1954 illustrated the need for blacks to take resolute action to assert rights that were assumed to be theirs. Cleveland Sellers, a black high school student in South Carolina at the time of the first lunch counter sit-ins, was one of many students who felt a strong sense of identification with blacks such as Daisy Bates, Rosa Parks, and Martin Luther King who had challenged segregation in Little Rock and Montgomery. "When they spoke," Sellers recalled, "they said what I was thinking. When they suffered, I suffered with them. And on those rare occasions when they managed to eke out a meager victory, I rejoiced too."[14]

During the 1950s some young blacks had even participated in civil rights demonstrations, though there was little news coverage of these isolated protests. Youth Marches for Integrated Schools, held in Washington, D.C., in 1958 and 1959, attracted thousands of participants. A few southern black students attended workshops sponsored by CORE or SCLC on the use of nonviolent tactics. There were even some instances of sit-in activity, most notably in Oklahoma City where in 1958 teenagers affiliated with the NAACP began to demand service at local restaurants.

The African independence movement, led by college-trained activists, also affected black youths. A black sociologist commented in 1960 that African students attending black colleges in the United States often reproached Afro-American students for "not being as aggressive as their counterparts in Africa." Students who later took part in the sit-in movement heard reports of the African independence struggle when attending an ecumenical religious conference held in Athens, Ohio, a few weeks before the initial Greensboro sit-in. A scholar at the conference noted that "hundreds" of southern black students "listened, discussed and evidently thought a great deal as militant African nationalists 'stole the show' with predictions of a 'new order.' " According to a journalist who visited black campuses during the spring of 1960, "even the most unintellectual black students were envious of the African independence movement and vaguely moved by it."[15]

The quickening pace of events affecting blacks in the United States and Africa contributed to what has been called "a state of psychosocial readiness to protest" among young southern blacks. "In a way," one student said, "we have been planning it all our lives." Another student explained: "It's like waiting for a bus, man. You know where you're going all the time, but you can't get there 'til the right vehicle comes along."[16] After the Greensboro students had seized the initiative, other students would claim that they had been planning sit-ins or similar protests even before February 1960. In fact, a few black students in Nashville had not only engaged in such planning, but also had schooled themselves in the philosophical doctrines of the Gandhian passive resistance movement in India. It was these Nashville activists, rather than the four Greensboro students, who had an enduring impact on the subsequent development of the southern movement.

The later lives of the four Greensboro students typified the careers of many students whose involvement in the racial struggle was only brief. Of the four, only Izell Blair attended the founding conference of SNCC, in which he never played a leadership role. After serving as student body president at North Carolina A. & T., Blair attended law school for a year, worked as a teacher in the Job Corps, and then joined a black self-help group in Boston, the Opportunity Industrialization Center. During the mid-1960s he became a member of the Nation of Islam, taking the name Jibreel Khazan. Franklin McCain moved to Charlotte after graduation and began a career as an engineer with the Celanese Corporation. David Richmond was briefly involved in voter registration work in Mississippi but returned to Greensboro, where he worked with local antipoverty programs and figured in efforts to prevent outbreaks of racial violence during the late 1960s. Joseph McNeil joined the Air Force after graduation and in 1966, while engaged in bombing missions over North Vietnam, publicly criticized the anti-war position taken by Stokely Carmichael as chairman of SNCC. McNeil was subsequently employed by International Business Machines and then took a management position with a Wall Street banking firm.

Quite inadvertently, the four students had set in motion historical forces which they and most of their fellow activists were unable to forecast or even comprehend. The southern struggle would result only gradually in a transformation of individual attitudes and beliefs. Most student activists were committed to the expressed values of the American political system, though many also began to identify with the black student movement and its own emerging values. Diane Nash remarked that the black student became a member of "a group of people suddenly proud to be called 'black,' " and in the student "was born a new awareness of himself as an individual." Another Nashville student activist, Marion Barry, noted that for "the first time in history black students sit down at the conference table with officials and are heard." Political scientist Michael Walzer was among the whites who noted the pride of black students for whom "new forms of political activity were a kind of self-testing and proving." Although white participation in protests was welcomed, he "never heard a Negro ask, or even hint, that whites should join their picket lines. It will be better for them, and for us, I was told, if *they* came unasked." Even outside the South, blacks were moved by news accounts of the student protest movement. Robert Moses, then a twenty-six-year-old high school teacher in New York, was impressed by the "sullen, angry, determined" looks on the faces of North Carolina student protesters in a newspaper photograph: "Before, the Negro in the South had always looked on the defensive, cringing. This time they were taking the initiative. They were kids my age, and I knew this had something to do with my own life. It made me realize that for a long time I had been troubled by the problem of being a Negro and at the same time being an American. This was the answer."[17]

Nash, Barry, Moses, and many other young blacks saw the sit-ins as the beginning of a new stage of black political development. The southern sit-in movement had demonstrated that black students could initiate a social

struggle without the guidance of older black leaders and existing organizations. As local white leaders gave in to the student demands, an increasingly self-confident, able, and resourceful group of young black activists
emerged as spokespersons for the local protest movements. Like the four
Greensboro pioneers, the emergent leaders discovered that their initial acts
of defiance could be sustained. Released from the guilt associated with accommodation, they eagerly sought new roles to intensify the social struggle.

Some student leaders sensed the need for a protest organization to consolidate their newly won influence. They wanted an organization that
would expand black militancy rather than restrain or control it. Many of
them believed that the movement also needed a set of guiding ideas, and
the sit-ins had spawned the notion that such ideas should come not from
the pre-existing ideologies but from the intellectual awakening that had
begun on the southern black campuses. Accordingly, in April 1960 these
students created SNCC to preserve the spontaneity and the militancy of
the sit-ins.

# 2. GETTING ORGANIZED

SNCC was born during a period of extensive student protest activity. Yet it's creation indicated the culmination of the lunch counter sit-in movement rather than the beginning of a new upsurge of student activism. SNCC exerted little control over the ad hoc protest groups throughout the South whose activities it was supposed to coordinate. Only as the spontaneous enthusiasm of the early protests waned did the new organization begin to attract support.

SNCC's founding conference, held on April 16-18, 1960, in Raleigh, North Carolina, was called by Ella Baker, executive director of SCLC. The initiating role of SCLC might have signaled the reassertion of control over the southern black struggle by Martin Luther King and the black ministers associated with him, but Baker, who understood the psychological need of student activists to remain independent of adult control, resisted efforts to subvert their autonomy. Students at the conference affirmed their commitment to the nonviolent doctrines popularized by King, yet they were drawn to these ideas not because of King's advocacy but because they provided an appropriate rationale for student protest.

SNCC's founding was an important step in the transformation of a limited student movement to desegregate lunch counters into a broad and sustained movement to achieve major social reforms. Although many of the students at the founding conference initially were reluctant to broaden the focus of their activities, the existence of a South-wide coordinating committee provided the opportunity for increasing numbers of young people to participate in a regional movement that would attack racism in all its dimensions.

Baker initiated the plan to bring sit-in protesters together at Raleigh because she recognized that many black students had little preparation for the leadership roles suddenly thrust upon them. As a product of a southern black college, Shaw University in Raleigh, she was herself aware of the limitations of southern black education and of the significance of the sit-ins as a departure from the pattern of political apathy among black students. She hoped that a meeting of student leaders would enable protesters to commu-

19

nicate with each other and to acquire the knowledge necessary to sustain their movement. After borrowing $800 from SCLC and contacting an acquaintance at Shaw to secure facilities there, she sent a note, signed by herself and King, to all major protest groups, asking them to send representatives.

Baker carefully avoided any implication that the meeting would subvert the independence of local student protest groups. Rather, student leaders were offered the opportunity "TO SHARE experience gained in recent protest demonstrations and TO HELP chart future goals for effective action." The notice lauded the leadership already shown by black students and called for "evaluation in terms of where do we go from here." The purpose of the meeting was to achieve "a more unified sense of direction for *training and action in Nonviolent Resistance.*" The letter assured students that, although "Adult Freedom Fighters" would be present "for counsel and guidance," the conference would be "youth centered."[1]

Although Baker's invitation did not suggest that the Raleigh conference would result in the formation of a lasting organization, her long career as a social reformer had convinced her of the need for a new type of protest group to stimulate mass struggle among blacks. Born in Virginia in 1905 and raised in North Carolina, Baker had hoped to become a medical missionary, but upon finding that the cost of medical training exceeded her family's means, she turned to sociology. After graduating as valedictorian of her college class, Baker went to New York and during the Depression worked as a community organizer while taking graduate courses at the New School for Social Research. During the 1940s she became a field secretary for the NAACP in New York. In January 1958 she made what was meant to be a short trip to Atlanta to help organize a series of mass meetings for the newly established SCLC; instead, she remained to organize SCLC's headquarters. Soon, however, she became restive under the cautious leadership of King and was planning to resign her post when the lunch counter sit-ins began.

During the spring of 1960, Baker commended the "inclination toward group-centered leadership" among the students. Undoubtedly referring to her experiences with King, she noted that such a trend was "refreshing" to those who bore "the scars of battle, the frustration and the disillusionment that come when the prophetic leader turns out to have heavy feet of clay." What was needed in a social movement, she later commented, was "the development of people who are interested not in being leaders as much as in developing leadership among other people."[2]

The conference called by Baker was the most successful of several gatherings of sit-in leaders to take place during the spring. It attracted more than 120 black student activists representing 56 colleges and high schools in twelve southern states and the District of Columbia. Also attending were observers from thirteen student and social reform organizations, representatives from northern and border state colleges, and a dozen southern white students. In addition to the SCLC, the organizations taking part included CORE and the Fellowship of Reconciliation (FOR), both of which had long been engaged in the use of nonviolent direct action to achieve social reform. Among the student organizations represented were the National Student Association (NSA), Students for a Democratic Society (SDS), and National Student Christian Federation.[3]

One of the largest delegations at the Raleigh conference, and the one that would subsequently provide SNCC with a disproportionate share of its leaders, was the Nashville student group. Though coming from varied backgrounds, the Nashville activists shared a commitment not simply to desegregation but also to Gandhiism and to the Christian ideal of "the beloved community." Fisk University provided a number of these protest leaders, most notably Marion Barry and Diane Nash.

Barry had spent his early years on a farm in Itta Bena, Mississippi. When he was seven years old, his family moved to Memphis, where he later earned a bachelor's degree at Le Moyne College. He once created an uproar by protesting an anti-black remark by a white Le Moyne trustee, and while working for a graduate degree in chemistry at Fisk, he risked losing his scholarship by participating in sit-ins. But if he "was not a free man," he explained, "I was not a man at all. I was only part of a man, and I felt in order to be a whole man I must be an American citizen as anybody else."[4]

Nash had grown up in Chicago and spent a year at Howard University before transferring to Fisk. Experiencing the Jim Crow system there for the first time, Nash felt "stifled and boxed in since so many areas of living were restricted." Raised as a Catholic, she viewed the desegregation movement as "applied religion" designed "to bring about a climate in which there is appreciation of the dignity of man and in which each individual is free to grow and produce to his fullest capacity." She saw the effects of southern barriers to black advancement in the South's "slow progress in industrial, political and other areas" and in "the weakening of American influence abroad as a result of race hatred."[5]

Another Nashville protest leader, John Lewis, was one of several black ministerial students at American Baptist Theological Seminary who had begun to view Christianity as a rationale of racial protest. Born in a tenant house near Troy, Alabama, and one of ten children of parents who had not attended high school, Lewis had been inspired by radio reports of the Montgomery bus boycott and its leader King, whom he saw as "a Moses, using organized religion and the emotionalism within the Negro church as an instrument, as a vehicle, toward freedom."[6] He began preaching in rural black churches near his family's farm while attending high school, and in

1957 he entered the Nashville seminary on a scholarship, where his friends included the black activists James Bevel, Bernard Lafayette, and Paul Brooks.

The most influencial of the Nashville leaders was James Lawson, who grew up in the North and attended Baldwin-Wallace College in Ohio. Expelled from the Vanderbilt School of Theology for his involvement in sit-in protests, Lawson was, of all those attending the Raleigh meeting, the most familiar with the philosophical doctrines associated with nonviolent direct action. In the early 1950s he had chosen to go to prison rather than serve in the military during the Korean War. After being paroled to the Methodist Board of Missions, he spent three years as a missionary in India, where he studied Mahatma Gandhi's use of nonviolence to achieve political change. Lawson then attended the Oberlin College School of Theology and became the first southern field secretary of FOR.

On one of his trips through the South, Lawson, along with another FOR representative, Glenn Smiley, organized a workshop on nonviolence for the Nashville Christian Leadership Council, which was held in March 1958. After enrolling as a theology student, Lawson opened a similar workshop at Vanderbilt University in Nashville in early 1959. The workshop attracted a small group of black students, including Nash, Barry, Lewis, and Bevel, who were interested in using nonviolent tactics to achieve desegregation in downtown dining facilities. During the fall of 1959, they staged test sit-ins in an unsuccessful attempt to prod Nashville businessmen to desegregate voluntarily. When in February 1960 Lawson received news of the sit-in in Greensboro, the Nashville students were prepared to lead one of the most disciplined and sustained of the early protests. More than 150 students, including Lawson, were arrested in Nashville during the spring before the city leaders finally agreed to desegregate some lunch counters.

The Nashville students maintained firm control over the protests, ensuring that they remained nonviolent. Their rules of conduct for demonstrators became a model for protest movements elsewhere in the South. Among other items, they specified: "Don't strike back or curse if abused . . . Show yourself courteous and friendly at all times . . . Report all serious incidents to your leader in a polite manner. Remember love and nonviolence."[7]


When the Raleigh conference opened, King, then thirty-one years old, was the center of attention. Indeed, his presence probably contributed to the large attendance. At a press conference before the opening session, King laid out an agenda for the students that presaged later trends within the southern struggle. In addition to suggesting a nationwide campaign of "selective buying," King advised the students to establish a permanent organization, collect a group of volunteers willing to go to jail rather than pay fines, and take the "freedom struggle" into all parts of the South to compel the intervention of the federal government. He also urged the students to learn more about the philosophy of nonviolence.[8]

Although King outlined much of the future strategy of the student movement, he had less impact on the students than did Lawson, who was then little known outside Nashville. Lawson expressed a visionary set of ideas that distinguished the student activists both from the rest of society and from more moderate civil rights leaders. He insisted that the basic issues behind the protest were neither legal, sociological, nor radical, but moral and spiritual. The nonviolent protests had forced white southerners to recognize the existence of sin. Its "radically Christian methods" had stripped the "segregationist power structure of its major weapon: the manipulation of law or law-enforcement to keep the Negro in his place." In addition, the nonviolent movement was an attempt to speed the pace of social change. "All of Africa," Lawson warned, "will be free before the American Negro attains first class citizenship. Most of us will be grandparents before we can live normal human lives." In his most controversial statement, Lawson called the sit-in tactic "a judgment upon middle-class conventional, half-way efforts to deal with radical social evil." He specifically criticized the NAACP for emphasizing "fund-raising and court action rather than developing our greatest resource, a people no longer the victims of racial evil who can act in a disciplined manner to implement the constitution."[9]

Lawson's influence was evident in the conference's general emphasis on nonviolence. When one delegate suggested that a decision be reached on the "goals, philosophy, future, and structure of the movement," Lawson insisted that the first two items be reversed and that the delegates first discuss the philosophy of nonviolence and then the goal of integration.[10] Although there was resistance on the part of some students who were more concerned with action than philosophy, Lawson secured adoption of his statement of purpose which expressed the religious underpinnings of nonviolent direct action:[11]

We affirm the philosophical or religious ideal of nonviolence as the foundation of our purpose, the presupposition of our faith, and the manner of our action. Nonviolence as it grows from Judaic-Christian traditions seeks a social order of justice permeated by love. Integration of human endeavor represents the crucial first step towards such a society.

Through nonviolence, courage displaces fear; love transforms hate. Acceptance dissipates prejudice; hope ends despair. Peace dominates war; faith reconciles doubt. Mutual regard cancels enmity. Justice for all overthrows injustice. The redemptive community supersedes systems of gross social immorality.

Love is the central motif of nonviolence. Love is the force by which God binds man to Himself and man to man. Such love goes to the extreme; it remains loving and forgiving even in the midst of hostility. It matches the capacity of evil to inflict suffering with an even more enduring capacity to absorb evil, all the while persisting in love.

By appealing to conscience and standing on the moral nature of human existence, nonviolence nurtures the atmosphere in which reconciliation and justice become actual possibilities.

Of more immediate concern to the student delegates than a statement of ideology was the possibility that the creation of a coordinating committee would lead to the absorption of the student movement into existing civil rights organizations. Howard Zinn noted a "tension" over whether the students would have official ties with SCLC. Baker recalled that forces were at work "to try to attach the young people to on-going organizations," but she thought "they had the right to direct their own affairs and even make their own mistakes." She knew from experience "how people and their ideas can be captured by those who have programs of their own." The students were willing to meet "on the basis of equality, but were intolerant of anything that smacked of manipulation or domination." Baker's views coincided with those of the black students. "She was much older in terms of age," recalled Lewis, "but I think in terms of ideas and philosophy and commitment she was one of the youngest persons in the movement."[12]

With Baker's encouragement, the students voted to establish a temporary Student Nonviolent Coordinating Committee. It would have no official ties but would cooperate with all civil rights organizations. SNCC was established on the understanding that its permanent status would be determined at a future meeting of students.

On the last day of the conference Barry, SNCC's newly elected chairman, conducted his first press conference for the few reporters covering the meeting. He outlined the "findings and recommendations" of the students, including approval of the principle of going to jail rather than accepting bail. He appealed to lawyers to refrain from charging "exorbitant prices" in sit-in cases. Then, in a gratuitous statement of the kind that would come to characterize SNCC, Barry injected the new coordinating committee into the midst of national and international politics. Reacting to news stories about a possible trip to Africa by President Eisenhower, Barry announced that "the President should lend the prestige of his office to the solution of the racial problems in this country and thus he shall be even better prepared for his visit to Africa."[13]

The Raleigh conference represented the peak of influence within SNCC for Lawson and his Nashville group. Determined to finish his theological studies, Lawson enrolled later in the spring of 1960 at Boston University, where that summer he received a Bachelor of Sacred Theology degree.

With the exception of Barry, the other participants in Lawson's workshops focused their activities on Nashville, though many later joined SNCC's staff. Barry himself resigned the chair of SNCC in the fall to return to graduate work at the University of Tennessee. As the influence of the Lawson group waned, secular influences grew in importance. Nonetheless, the rhetoric of nonviolent direct action and the moralistic orientation of the Nashville movement continued to pervade SNCC through the early 1960s.

On May 13 and 14 eleven students met in Atlanta for the first official meeting of SNCC. Although it still had no operating funds or even an office, the students apparently expected to attract support, because they voted to hire a temporary office worker to sustain the organization during the summer.[14] The establishment of a functioning organization was made possible when Baker offered SNCC a corner of the SCLC headquarters in Atlanta for use as an office and made available to the students SCLC's mailing facilities. Baker also recruited Jane Stembridge, daughter of a white Baptist minister from Virginia and a student at Union Theological Seminary, to run the SNCC office until a permanent administrative secretary could be found.

In June Stembridge and other student volunteers published the first issue of SNCC's newspaper, the *Student Voice*. Articles in that issue revealed an already wide range of concerns among the students affiliated with SNCC. They included not only Lawson's statement on nonviolence and King's advice on nonviolent tactics, but also items about raising funds for the protest movement and obtaining scholarships for students expelled as a result of protest participation. Morehouse College student Julian Bond, whose father was dean of Atlanta University's School of Education, co-authored a report on the Atlanta sit-ins and provided a poem about the increasing race consciousness of many students protesters:

> I too, hear American singing
> But from where I stand
> I can only hear Little Richard
> and Fats Domino.[15]

Although by the summer of 1960 a few black students saw SNCC as an important, independent voice for the protest movement, the survival of the new group was by no means assured. Other student and civil rights organizations encouraged SNCC's emergence as a permanent organization, since it offered them a central point of contact with southern black activists. The director of NSA's southern programs, Constance Curry, was particularly helpful in SNCC's early months, offering the use of NSA equipment and facilities in Atlanta at a time when SNCC had few resources of its own. Despite such backing, SNCC would probably not have survived its first summer had it not been for the energy and skills of Baker and Stembridge. Whereas SNCC appeared to outsiders and even to many black student leaders to be merely a clearinghouse for the exchange of information about localized protest movements, to the two women it was potentially an organization for expanding the struggle beyond its campus base to include all classes of blacks.

In July Baker and Stembridge were joined by Robert Moses, a former graduate student at Harvard University. Moses, who went to Atlanta to work on an SCLC voter registration project, found that no one at the organization had prepared for his arrival. He was therefore assigned the task of stuffing fund-raising packets, a task he accepted until he decided that more interesting work was being done by Stembridge in SNCC's corner of the SCLC office. He soon discovered that he and Stembridge had a common interest in Christian theology and mysticism and shared a skepticism regarding King's leadership. When Stembridge suggested that Moses assist SNCC by recruiting black leaders in the deep South for an October conference, he eagerly agreed to do so at his own expense.

The decision proved fateful both for Moses and for SNCC. At Baker's suggestion, he met with Amzie Moore, head of the NAACP chapter in Cleveland, Mississippi. Moore was one of a small group of people who had kept the civil rights struggle in the deep South alive despite violence and intimidation. When Moses invited Moore to attend the SNCC conference, Moore accepted but made clear that his main concern was voter registration rather than desegregation. He suggested that SNCC send students to Mississippi to assist in a voter registration drive that could ultimately result in the overthrow of the segregationist regime in that state. Impressed by Moore's vision and determination, Moses promised he would return to take part in the Mississippi effort. Although Moses was not yet even a member of SNCC's staff, this short meeting signaled the beginning of a black struggle in Mississippi that would decisively shape SNCC's future development.

Apart from Moses' trip to the deep South, the most significant of SNCC's activities during the summer occurred at the Democratic and Republican conventions. Barry and other SNCC representatives were given an opportunity to address members of the platform committees of each party, and their statements revealed the increasing concern of black student leaders with issues beyond desegregation. At the Democratic convention, for example, SNCC representatives proposed that delegates and candidates "stop playing political football with the civil rights of eighteen million Negro Americans" and take immediate action to desegregate public schools, expand job opportunities for blacks in the federal government and with federal contractors, grant self-government for the District of Columbia, and increase federal protection for blacks seeking to vote or exercise their civil rights.[16]

The few minutes allotted to SNCC representatives at both conventions did not allow for much impact; few newspapers even noted their appearances. Nonetheless, their statements indicated the beginning of a transformation of SNCC into an organization capable of competing with larger civil rights organizations on a national scale.

This transformation was also evident in a speech given by Stembridge at the NSA annual convention in August 1960. Stembridge committed SNCC to "demanding that the Congress of the United States stop using civil rights as a political springboard, that the Presidential candidates cease their double talk, and that the Federal government hear and act upon the voice of freedom." Discrimination was a problem that must be attacked nationally. Nonviolence itself was more than a technique; it could "speak to our total lives" in such areas as nuclear armament. She promised that SNCC, when made permanent, would create an "unbroken chain" of information among students across the nation, thereby helping to fulfill the two basic requirements of the movement: to "understand where it is going" and to "branch out with full force into broader areas, especially . . . into the political arena."[17]

At summer's end, the small SNCC staff could cite little evidence of their impact on the student protest movement. Edward King, a Kentucky state student who had been elected SNCC's historian at the Raleigh conference, admitted that a major problem was the organization's failure to gain the cooperation of the "highly autonomous local groups." The only major sit-in demonstrations of the summer had taken place in Greenville, South Carolina, and Jacksonville, Florida, neither of which communities had been represented at the Raleigh conference. Yet, having observed the success of student movements in desegregating lunch counters in numerous towns, members of SNCC adopted a strategy of action based on those experiences. As one observer noted, "They know the value of spontaneity and local initiative and don't want to lose it."[18] Those associated with SNCC recognized that their primary function was to stimulate further protests which would allow them to regain the momentum of the early spring.

At a fall conference in Atlanta on October 14-16, 1960, SNCC attempted to consolidate the student protest movement by establishing an organizational structure and clarifying its goals and principles. The invitation to the conference stressed that it would be "action-oriented" because SNCC leaders were "convinced that truth comes from being involved and not from observation and speculation. We are further convinced that only mass action is strong enough to force all of America to assume responsibility and that nonviolent direct action alone is strong enough to enable all of America to understand the responsibility she must assume." The invitation noted the national and international implications of the nonviolent movement—"students must look beyond the South, into the Pentagon, into Europe, and into Russia"—but also defined the movement's goals as "individual freedom and personhood."[19]

Topics to be covered in workshops included desegregation of public facilities, black political activity, discrimination in employment, and racial problems in education. Workshop leaders included black students who had been active in sit-ins—Diane Nash, Ben Brown of Clark College in Atlanta, and Charles McDew of South Carolina State College—a white southern student, Sandra Cason of the University of Texas, and Tim Jenkins from the NSA. The prominent roles taken by students in planning and directing the conference revealed their increasing self-confidence and helped to overcome the lingering suspicions of some local protest leaders that SNCC would subvert their autonomy.

About 140 delegates, alternatives, and observers from 46 protest centers attended the conference, as well as over 80 observers from northern colleges and sympathetic organizations. Unlike the Raleigh conference, which occurred during a period of extensive protest activity, the conference in Atlanta attracted only the hard core of students who remained involved in the movement after the initial level of black student activism declined. These southern student leaders came together with representatives of student and social reform organizations throughout the country who wanted to establish ties with the southern protest movement. A significant aspect of the conference was the presence of representatives from groups advocating Marxist ideas and interracial coalitions. Among the leftist groups represented were the Socialist party and its youth wing, the Young People's Socialist League, the newly formed SDS, the Southern Conference Educational Fund (SCEF), and the Highlander Folk School, a training school for labor organizers.

Although Martin Luther King spoke on "the philosophy of nonviolence," Lawson's remarks again attracted greater comment among the students. Despite the decline of his personal influence within SNCC, Lawson expressed the view of many student activists that the movement had lost its "finest hour" when the students allowed themselves to be released on bail. "Instead of letting the adults scurry around getting bail," he maintained, "we should have insisted that they scurry about to end the system which had put us in jail. If history offers us such an opportunity again, let us be prepared to seize it." This "jail, no bail" strategy, which was to become dominant in SNCC, reflected the increasingly militant orientation of many proponents of nonviolent direct action. According to Lawson, the student protests were the start of a "nonviolent revolution" to destroy "segregation, slavery, serfdom, paternalism," and "industrialization which preserves cheap labor and racial discrimination."[20]

The principal accomplishment of the conference was to create a permanent organizational structure for SNCC. The delegates established a Coordinating Committee to be composed of one representative from each southern state and the District of Columbia. Delegates nevertheless remained reluctant to give the reorganized SNCC much power. Local protest groups were allowed to remain autonomous, and all members of the committee could speak for the movement. SNCC was also authorized to raise funds and to continue to publish the *Student Voice* monthly to maintain communication among protest groups.

The only action proposal considered by the delegates was one backed by socialist representatives to stage demonstrations on election day demanding that presidential candidates John Kennedy and Richard Nixon take positive stands on civil rights issues. Although the proposal was adopted and a few election day protests were conducted, a demonstration engineered by Atlanta student activists at the end of the conference had a much greater impact on the election. By convincing King to be arrested with them in a protest against discriminatory policies at Rich's department store in Atlanta, the students put national political leaders on the spot. Highly publicized telephone calls expressing concern from John Kennedy to King's wife and from Robert Kennedy to the judge handling the case undoubtedly increased John Kennedy's black support and contributed to his narrow victory over Nixon, who chose not to involve himself.

Although socialists had some influence at the conference, most black students did not accept even moderately socialist ideas. Bayard Rustin, a leader of the League for Industrial Democracy and King's adviser, was first invited to address the conference and then the invitation was withdrawn when a union sponsoring the conference objected to Rustin's radical reputation. The decision to rescind the invitation, however, was the only significant instance in which SNCC leaders capitulated to such pressures. Julian Bond later commented that the barring of Rustin gave the students "their first lesson in the proper exercise of civil liberties"[21] Interestingly, a few years later SNCC leaders would clash with Rustin because they considered him too moderate and entrenched in the liberal establishment.

The October conference marked a turning point in the development of the student protest movement. SNCC gained permanent status, and its student leaders became increasingly confident of their ability to formulate the future course of the movement. The conference also revealed a general trend in the protest movement toward a greater emphasis on political issues rather than on the religious ideals expressed by Lawson. The influence of the Nashville group declined still further in November when McDew replaced Barry as chairman. McDew, a native of Massilon, Ohio, and a sociology major at South Carolina State College, was one of the few black student activists who had grown up outside the South. He was also exceptional for being a convert to Judaism. Although chosen to serve only until the next meeting, McDew was retained as chairman until the election of John Lewis in 1963.

Another indication of the broadening of student concerns was the visit of Edward King, SNCC's new administrative secretary, to Fayette County, Tennessee, to offer support to black tenants who had been evicted from farms for registering to vote. SNCC also supported the proposal of its affiliate, the Nonviolent Action Group (NAG) at Howard University, that the President and Congress aid blacks in Tennessee and cancel government contracts with firms which discriminated against blacks who attempted to vote. SNCC later requested that Fayette and Haywood counties be placed on the State Department's roster for technical assistance from the newly organized Peace Corps.[22]

Even as SNCC leaders began to involve themselves in activities other than the desegregation of public facilities, they still had not resolved the issue of whether SNCC should be primarily a medium of communication and coordination among protest groups or an initiator of protest activities and civil rights projects. Baker's notion of "group-centered leadership" had taken hold among student activists, and they strongly opposed any hierarchy of authority such as existed in other civil rights organizations. The guidelines adopted at the November meeting limited SNCC to a "suggestive rather than directive" role in relation to local protest groups. Furthermore, SNCC was authorized to speak for the movement only "in a cautious manner in which it is made quite clear that SNCC does not control local groups." Significantly, the Coordinating Committee decided that it could initiate action only when two-thirds of the members present supported such a course.[23]

The reluctance of the Coordinating Committee to assume a more assertive role resulted from the belief of most student activists that local autonomy was the basis of sustained militancy. Throughout its history SNCC would continue to support the notion that local community groups should determine their own direction. But the lull in protest activity since the spring of 1960 led some students by the end of the year to suspect that they, as representatives of SNCC, must take action to restore the movement. Only when SNCC workers were prepared to initiate protests outside their own communities could they begin to revive and extend the social struggle that had already become a central focus of their lives.

# 3. FREEDOM RIDES

At the end of 1960 SNCC was still a loosely organized committee of part-time student activists, uncertain of their roles in the southern struggle and generally conventional in their political orientations. Yet within months, SNCC became a cadre of full-time organizers and protestors. Its militant identity was forged during the "freedom rides," a series of assaults on southern segregation that for the first time brought student protesters into conflict with the Kennedy administration. SNCC's militancy was further sharpened by the experiences of student activists in Mississippi jails during the summer of 1961.

Tension within SNCC between the religious and political activists, which had been implicit in the gradual drift away from Lawson's religious radicalism throughout 1960, reappeared the following summer as a vigorous dispute about whether the group should encourage nonviolent direct action or voter registration. Most who viewed the struggle in moralistic terms resisted the idea of emphasizing voter registration, which, they charged with some justification, was a plot by friends of the Kennedy administration to use the promise of federal backing to redirect student militancy toward goals other than desegregation. That SNCC was able to survive its first internal crisis was due largely to the efforts of Ella Baker, who offered a compromise solution to the conflict, and of James Forman, who provided needed administrative skill and political sophistication. In addition, SNCC's survival was assured by the willingness of the proponents both of direct action and of voter registration to demonstrate their idealism by leaving school and becoming full-time SNCC "field secretaries."

SNCC's transformation began early in 1961 when the organization responded to a call for assistance from black protesters in Rock Hill, South Carolina. Students at Friendship Junior College in Rock Hill had first become involved in protest activities at a sit-in on February 12, 1960, where they encountered strong resistance, and a month later seventy students were arrested. Black residents of Rock Hill then began a boycott of segregated establishments, which continued through the summer and fall. Most of the students at Friendship belonged to local NAACP and CORE chap-

31

ters, and it was after attending a CORE workshop in December that a few students adopted the plan of remaining in jail after being arrested rather than posting bond. CORE field secretary Tom Gaither, who had led a black student movement in Orangeburg the previous spring, went to Rock Hill to offer assistance.

On January 31, 1961—the eve of the first anniversary of the Greensboro sit-in—Gaither and nine black students sat at a segregated lunch counter. The following day a judge found all ten guilty of trespassing and sentenced each to thirty days in jail or a fine of $100. Gaither and eight of the students chose to serve the sentence. When CORE appealed for outside help, SNCC confronted its first major policy question.[1]

At a SNCC meeting in early February, the fifteen students present unanimously decided to support the Rock Hill protesters. Four black activists volunteered to travel to Rock Hill and join those in jail. The four volunteers were Diane Nash, Charles Jones of John C. Smith University in Charlotte, North Carolina, Ruby Doris Smith of Spelman College in Atlanta, and Charles Sherrod of Virginia Union. As the four left for Rock Hill, SNCC's executive secretary, Ed King, issued a statement calling upon all those who shared their convictions to "join them at the lunch counters and in jail. Only by this type of action can we show that the non-violent movement against segregation is not a local issue for just the individual community, but rather a united movement of all those who believe in equality."[2]

After arriving in Rock Hill, the SNCC contingent were arrested and convicted for attempting to obtain service at a lunch counter, and they joined the group already imprisoned. For the students, the Rock Hill "jail-in" was an attempt to revive the student movement by returning to the moral principle of noncooperation with evil that was the basis of passive resistance. As Jones explained, he "could not cooperate . . . with any facet of the society—in this case the legal, judicial system—that perpetuated in any sense segregation and discrimination on the basis of color." The Rock Hill protest offered the movement a "second chance" to serve jail sentences rather than accept bond.[3]

Although the jailed activists hoped that many others would join them in Rock Hill, few students were willing to leave school for extended jail terms. After a month in jail, the activists were forced to concede that they had not achieved their objective. Despite the collapse of the Rock Hill jail-in movement, the decision of the four SNCC representatives to participate demonstrated the willingness of activists associated with SNCC to become involved whenever a confrontation with segregationist forces developed. Furthermore, the Rock Hill experience contributed to the process of building a sense of group identity among militant students. For Sherrod, as for many students later in the decade and for many radicals and revolutionaries of other times, imprisonment was a crucial learning experience. "You get ideas in jail," he remarked shortly afterward. "You talk with other young people you've never seen. Right away we recognize each other. People like yourself, getting out of the past. We're up all night, sharing creativity, planning action. You learn the truth in prison, you learn wholeness. You find out the difference between being dead and alive."[4]

Another opportunity for SNCC activists to revive the flagging spirit of student militancy came a few months later when southern whites attacked a group of freedom riders who were traveling through the south and attempting to use segregated eating facilities at southern bus terminals. The idea of the freedom ride had been conceived by CORE as a test of the jail-no bail idea and as a demonstration of the effectiveness of nonviolent direct action by disciplined adherents. Since CORE's founding in World War II, it had been the organization most closely associated with the use of nonviolent direct action to achieve civil rights goals, and in 1947 it had attempted a "journey of reconciliation" similar to the later freedom rides. But until the outbreak of the student sit-ins in 1960, CORE had attracted little support among southern blacks for its Gandhian approach.[5]

CORE selected the thirteen volunteers for the first freedom ride, most of whom came from its own members; but two of the seven blacks chosen were students who had been active in the sit-in movement: John Lewis of Nashville and Henry Thomas, Howard University's representative to SNCC. Although both students had grown up in large families in the rural South, Lewis came from a stable home environment and was intensely religious, whereas Thomas was a self-described rebel raised in insecure circumstances by a difficult stepfather. Thomas worked on road gangs and in cotton fields before entering Howard on a scholarship. He recalled that most of the boys with whom he grew up had gone to jail before they were adults— "they did their rebelling all at once. I guess I did mine in small bits all along."[6]

The first freedom riders left Washington on May 4 in two buses—with reporters on board to assure press coverage—and traveled peacefully through Virginia and North Carolina before encountering violence. On May 9 a group of whites assaulted Lewis and another rider as they attempted to enter the white waiting room at the Rock Hill bus terminal. Neither was seriously injured, and after the arrival of police the freedom riders were able to continue their journey. The next day, Thomas and Jim Peck, a white CORE veteran, were arrested in Winnsboro, South Carolina and charged with trespassing after they entered the white lunchroom together. In Georgia, the freedom riders used terminal facilities in several communities without incident, and when they arrived in Atlanta, they were welcomed by a large group of students, including Ed King of SNCC.[7]

After resuming their trip, the freedom riders entered Anniston, Alabama, where a mob attacked one of the two buses, breaking windows and slashing tires before police arrived. When the bus continued its journey, white men in cars followed and forced the bus to stop outside of Anniston. The pursuers then hurled a smoke bomb inside, and the freedom riders fled the vehicle into the hands of the waiting group of angry whites. As the bus burst into flames, the mob beat up the riders before police again arrived belatedly. Soon afterward the other bus carrying freedom riders reached Anniston. A group of whites entered it and forced the riders to the rear, beating those who resisted.

The freedom riders regrouped and continued on to Birmingham, expecting further trouble since they had heard rumors that a white mob would be waiting for them. A large crowd of whites were present when their bus entered the Birmingham terminal, and local police were conspicuously absent for a fifteen-minute period while a group of white men assaulted the freedom riders as they emerged from the bus. Peck was seriously injured, requiring fifty stitches to close the gashes in his head.[8] After this incident, no bus driver could be found to take the riders to Montgomery and the protesters decided to end the freedom ride and fly to New Orleans for a rally on May 17, the seventh anniversary of the Supreme Court's *Brown* vs. *Board of Education* decision.

Although CORE leaders chose to discontinue the freedom ride, some black student activists saw the protests as another opportunity to test their commitment and militancy. The violence in Anniston and Birmingham was widely publicized and served to revitalize the student protest movement. Howard University student Bill Mahoney recalled being "infuriated" after seeing a picture of Thomas being attacked near Anniston. Soon afterward he picketed at the White House to demand federal action and then left for Alabama to join the protesters.

Upon learning of the attacks, Diane Nash, by then coordinator of student activities for the Nashville Christian Leadership Council, and other Nashville students quickly organized a group to continue the freedom ride campaign. The group included ten students—eight blacks and two whites. The students were told that, if they continued the rides, at least one of them would be killed, but they would not be deterred. "These people faced the probability of their own deaths before they ever left Nashville," Nash recalled. "Several made out wills. A few more gave me sealed letters to be mailed if they were killed. Some told me frankly that they were afraid, but they knew this was something that they must do because freedom was worth it."[9]

On May 17 the group took a bus from Nashville to Birmingham. When they arrived in the Birmingham bus terminal, they were arrested by police and held in "protective custody." After spending a day in jail, they were escorted by Birmingham Police Chief Eugene "Bull" Conner back to the Alabama-Tennessee border. The students walked to the home of a black family and called Nash, who sent a car to take them back to Birmingham. They planned to continue the freedom ride from Birmingham, but received another setback when they were unable to find a bus driver willing to take them from there to Montgomery.[10]

As the student activists gained control over the freedom ride campaign, Kennedy's aides attempted to de-escalate their first civil rights crisis. President Kennedy and leading Justice Department officials supported the goals of the freedom rides but feared the potential for large-scale racial violence, which would require forceful federal intervention. Soon after taking office, Kennedy had decided against asking for new civil rights legislation or using the power of the federal government to achieve desegregation of public facilities. Rather, he intended to concentrate on the investigation of white interference with black voting rights, believing that such a course would not alienate white southerners and would prepare the way for other social changes in the south.[11] The assaults on the CORE freedom riders in Alabama placed administration officials in the difficult position of attempting to maintain their commitment to civil rights while also avoiding actions that would upset white southern Democrats and force changes in federal priorities.

Attorney General Robert Kennedy responded to the violence in Anniston and Birmingham by ordering the FBI to investigate the incidents while working quietly himself to ensure that Alabama officials preserved public order. The attorney general and the President also attempted to reach Alabama Governor John Patterson, who had supported President Kennedy during the election, but Patterson refused to discuss the matter over the telephone, and at a press conference he stated, with reference to the freedom riders that the state could not "guarantee the safety of fools." Only after Robert Kennedy's special assistant, John Seigenthaler, was dispatched to meet personally with the governor on May 19 did the administration receive assurances that state officials would uphold their responsibilities. Meanwhile, other Justice Department officials contacted the students to determine their intentions. After negotiations involving federal, state, and bus company officials as well as students, arrangements were completed for continuation of the Nashville students' freedom ride.[12]

Early in the morning of May 20, the freedom riders left Birmingham and traveled without incident to Montgomery. Ample police protection was provided during the trip, but no police were present when the riders arrived at the Montgomery terminal. As in Birmingham, a white mob attacked the freedom riders as they disembarked and attempted to find cabs. Lewis was beaten and left the terminal bleeding profusely from the head, Siegenthaler was also beaten as he attempted to aid one of the freedom riders outside the terminal. Another Justice Department official, John Doar, who observed the violence from a nearby building, called Burke Marshall, his superior in the Civil Rights Division, to report that the riders had been "mobbed" again.[13] Soon afterward Robert Kennedy, on orders from the President, sent federal marshals to Montgomery and obtained an injunction against the Ku Klux Klan and other groups interfering with the freedom rides.

The following night, May 21, an even more serious situation developed when freedom riders and over a thousand black residents gathered at the First Baptist Church in Montgomery to hear an address by Martin Luther King. As hundreds of whites began ominously assembling outside the church, King telephoned the attorney general to request protection for the people inside the church. When federal marshals finally appeared, rioting had already begun, and those inside the church were forced to remain there for the rest of the night. According to a student, there was no panic, because many of the people in attendance had participated in the Montgomery bus boycott and had learned how to avoid being intimidated by the threat of white violence—"the desire for freedom was so strong ... that nothing, nothing the mob could do, would stop us in any way ... We decided to make the most of our situation. We sang and the fellowship grew stronger and stronger, person to person to person."[14] Governor Patterson, faced with the fact of his authority being undermined by the intervention of federal officials, then declared martial law in Montgomery and sent eight hundred national guardsmen to the city to restore order.

On May 23, Nash and Lewis, along with King and Ralph Abernathy of SCLC and CORE leader James Farmer, held a press conference to announce that the freedom rides would continue. Still uncertain about the fate awaiting them, twelve freedom riders boarded a public bus—along with six white national guardsmen and sixteen reporters—and departed from Montgomery in a convoy of helicopters. "Obviously this is not in the nonviolent tradition," remarked James Lawson, who conducted workshops on nonviolent tactics during the journey.[15] A few hours later another bus containing freedom riders left Birmingham. When the first bus arrived in Jackson, Mississippi, police arrested the riders as they attempted to use the white rest rooms. A similar reception awaited the second bus, and at the end of the day twenty-seven protesters had been jailed for breach of the peace or refusal to obey an officer.

Although Robert Kennedy pleaded for a "cooling-off period," more volunteers for the freedom rides continued to arrive in Montgomery. A Freedom Riders Coordinating Committee was formed by representatives of SNCC, CORE, and SCLC. During the following months, more than three hundred protesters were arrested in Jackson. Choosing to stay in jail rather than pay the fines, the protesters were sent to serve their sentences in Parchman Prison and other Mississippi jails. White sympathizers in the North mobilized financial support for the campaign, and several prominent white liberals, including William Sloane Coffin, chaplain of Yale University, and Mark Lane, a New York State assemblyman, went to Montgomery to join the protests. While the Jackson protests became a rallying point for activists from every section of the nation, Justice Department officials began behind-the-scenes efforts to convince the Interstate Commerce Commission to issue a regulation prohibiting separate facilities for blacks and whites in bus and train terminals. Such a ruling was issued on September 22 and became effective on November 1, although defiance continued in many southern communities.[16]

The significance of the freedom rides was not merely that they led to desegregation of southern transportation facilities. The rides also contributed to the development of a self-consciously radical southern student movement prepared to direct its militancy toward other concerns. Unlike the widespread sit-ins of 1960, the freedom rides of 1961 directly involved only a few hundred protesters, but they had a greater impact on the nation and on the politcal consciousness of the participants, who suddenly became aware of their collective ability to provoke a crisis that would attract international publicity and compel federal intervention. The vulnerability of the new liberal administration to criticisms regarding its civil rights policies was evident throughout the spring, and in subsequent years that vulnerability would be exploited by young activists, black and white. Although most student activists realized that the Kennedy administration supported some civil rights reforms, involvement in the southern struggle had instilled in them a moralistic sense of personal commitment that made them intolerant of political expediency. SNCC too, though not directly responsible for the freedom ride campaign, was infused with the new spirit of militancy which helped to shape its emerging character.

Even before the freedom rides there had been a noticeable shift in the tone of SNCC's statements regarding the federal government. SNCC was increasingly willing to charge the government with hypocrisy for failing to act forcefully to achieve civil rights goals at home while proclaiming democratic values abroad. The March issue of the *Student Voice,* noting that two-thirds of humankind were nonwhite, remarked that the admission of thirteen new African and Asian nations to the United Nations in one day had "literally shifted the weight of international authority from white to non-white hands." Thus, the nation would be well advised to "purge itself of the rabies of racism." A few weeks later, after the attack on the freedom riders in Alabama, Ed King criticized President Kennedy for failing to condemn such assaults at a time when the nation was "telling the people of Asia, Africa, Latin America and the free world in general that we desire to be their friends."[17]

The increasing stridency of student militants was noted by Kennedy administration officials, who acknowledged the need for civil rights reforms but were disturbed by the tactics of young activists. Doar found the students in Alabama unwilling "to make any kind of accommodation on the strength of the federal government's representation of what they were going to do to correct the situation."[18] The handling of a request by Nash, as head of the Freedom Ride Coordinating Committee, for a meeting with President Kennedy revealed the ambivalent attitude of administration officials toward the student militants. Harris Wofford, a White House adviser, suggested that "it would be better for the President to see them for ten or fifteen minutes than to wait until they launch fasts in jail or encampments outside the White House asking to see him."[19]

For the freedom riders, the experiences of the spring and summer transformed their own attitudes and produced a new sense of group identity. The jails of Mississippi were the scene of a rapid process of political education for student activists who encountered persons from different backgrounds and with a variety of political beliefs. Stokely Carmichael remembered "great philosophical disagreements" among those in jail. He and fellow NAG members Hank Thomas and Bill Mahoney, who generally opposed the religious radicalism of protesters such as John Lewis and James Bevel, would even sit silently in a corner rather than join the others in prayer.[20] Despite these differences in attitudes about the philosophy of nonviolence and the need for a basic restructuring of American society, the common commitment of student activists led to the development among them of feelings of mutual respect and trust.

Rather than abandon the protest movement after enduring assaults and imprisonment during the rides, many students made even firmer commitments to remain in the struggle. Frank Holloway, a student from Atlanta, indicated that he would not have traded the experience "for anything" and that he was glad to be "a witness undergoing the suffering which Negroes endure in Mississippi," because he was helping to "bring about a new life" for Mississippi blacks. Similarly, Nashville student Lucretia Collins was "willing to do it all over again because I know a new world is opening up." And while Mahoney was singing "We Will Meet Again" with other youthful protesters who had just been released from jail, he looked round at their serious faces and suddenly "knew that we *would* meet again."[21]

Recognizing that they could not forestall the type of student militancy displayed in the freedom rides, Kennedy administration officials tried to persuade civil rights groups, including SNCC, to become more involved in voter registration work, which presumably would result in less intense white opposition. SNCC and other civil rights organizations sent representatives to a meeting with Robert Kennedy on June 16, 1961, where the attorney general suggested that the energies of the freedom ride campaign be redirected toward the goal of registering southern blacks who had been disenfranchised through violence, intimidation, and more subtle methods such as literacy tests and poll taxes. Kennedy assured the activists that financial support for such projects would be made available by private foundations.[22]

Students affiliated with SNCC were divided over whether to become involved in voter registration work. They recognized that this was an important activity, since the paucity of black voters, especially in the deep South, prevented blacks from acquiring the political power necessary to achieve civil rights goals. Nonetheless many student activists were reluctant to abandon the direct action tactics that had placed them at the forefront of the black struggle. They felt that such tactics, though well suited for assaults on segregated facilities, were probably not sufficient to register millions of black adults. Some students were also disturbed by the implication that their movement could be "bought off" by the liberal establishment. Despite these concerns, a growing number of black activists saw voter registration as a natural outgrowth of their movement. Rather than viewing liberal financial support as a restraining influence, they began to see it as an opportunity to transform small-scale, nonviolent protest activities into a massive political struggle for racial advancement.

A shift in SNCC's political orientation was signaled by the decision to send a delegation to discuss fund-raising for voter registration programs with Harry Belafonte, a personal friend of the Kennedys who was earlier involved in the discussions with Justice Department officials regarding voter registration. One of the members of the delegation was former Howard student Timothy Jenkins, the NSA representative to SNCC. He had also participated in the Justice Department meetings and, along with several other SNCC members, had become convinced that SNCC should develop political programs to attract financial support that would otherwise go to the older civil rights organizations.

Another member of the delegation, Charles Jones, shared Jenkins's belief that SNCC should accede to the urgings of administration officials. The son of a Presbyterian minister, Jones was a determined and articulate proponent of nonviolent direct action, but his political experiences, both as an NSA leader and as an anti-communist delegate to the 1959 World Youth Festival, were far broader than was the case for most southern black college students. In 1960 Jones became the North Carolina representative to SNCC and participated in the Rock Hill jail-in; however, by the summer of 1961 he was convinced that SNCC should move beyond the issue of desegregation to voter registration to become a force in the civil rights movement. According to Baker, Jenkins and Jones, when compared with the direct action proponents, were "much more articulate and had more of certain kinds of contacts."[23]

The meeting with Belafonte began on June 27. According to Jones, the group "discussed and analyzed the student movement and attempted to place it in the historical context of the total civil rights struggle in the United States." They concluded that the most urgent issue confronting blacks and the nation as a whole was the registration of disenfranchised southern blacks. To carry out the mass registration, Jones proposed a dramatic expansion of the student movement to include over a hundred thousand students.[24] The SNCC delegation left the meeting expecting that Belafonte would help them gain the necessary financial support once they convinced other SNCC members to approve a voter registration program.

Even before SNCC could meet to discuss the proposal, other events took place that increased the likelihood of the group becoming involved in voter registration. In June, Sherrod was hired as SNCC's first field secretary. This was a crucial step, since it marked the beginning of SNCC's transformation from simply a committee coordinating student protest groups to an organization of full-time staff members located throughout the South. Sherrod, although a sit-in leader, felt that SNCC should broaden its concerns and thus favored the voter registration project. Early in the summer he met with Amzie Moore in Cleveland, Mississippi, to discuss recruiting students to begin a voter registration effort there. Also involved in the Cleveland discussions was Bob Moses, who had returned from his job teaching in New York to keep his promise made the previous summer to aid Moore's voter registration work. The three concluded that SNCC should send volunteers to Cleveland.

At the next SNCC meeting, held in Baltimore on July 14–16, Jones recommended that SNCC give "top priority" to the establishment of a voter registration project, "not excluding the direct action projects," and that SNCC hire eight or ten full-time workers to initiate the project and a permanent executive secretary to administer it. But still the students were not willing to give their approval. In part, this was owing to the resistance of the direct action proponents, but other students voiced pragmatic objections, such as that SNCC was not yet prepared to initiate so ambitious a project. The organization still lacked a permanent executive secretary, because Ed King intended to resign to go to law school, and it still lacked dependable sources of funds. Instead, Jones's committee was asked to justify its recommendations in detail at the next SNCC meeting.[25]

Although the voter registration proponents had again been rebuffed, the balance had begun to tip in their favor. Soon after the July meeting, Moses broke his informal ties with SCLC to accept a position in SNCC as a volunteer field secretary in Mississippi. In addition, SNCC sent three student volunteers to work with him there.[26] Thus, even before the plan for a voter registration project had been officially approved, black students from SNCC were already involved in such a program.

Jenkins also proceeded with his efforts to turn SNCC "from an amorphous movement to an organization" by securing funds from the New World Foundation for a three-week student leadership seminar, to be held in Nashville beginning on July 30. Many student activists who had emerged as leaders during the previous year and a half were invited to attend, including McDew, Sherrod, Nash, Smith, Jones, Carmichael, Bevel, and Lewis. "We made a calculated attempt to pull the best people out of the movement," Jenkins commented, "and give them a solid academic approach to understanding the movement. What we needed now was information, not inspiration."[27]

The central theme of the seminar was "Understanding the Nature of Social Change," and among the consultants recruited were Doar of the Justice Department and scholars such as Kenneth Clark, E. Harlan Randolph, E. Franklin Frazier, C. Eric Lincoln, Rayford Logan, and Herbert Hill. By bringing together student activists with important academic and government figures, Jenkins hoped to overcome the students' "lack of comprehension of the institutional world and the way in which their programs had to plug in and manipulate those forces in the institutional world in order to succeed." In particular, he hoped to convince the students of the existence in the federal government of people willing "to smash the southern bloc" and to show them the "power of the Justice Department and its potential to help and protect us in the political revolution."[28] Although the seminar did not entirely allay the students' suspicions of the federal government, it gave them a valuable opportunity to meet together for an extended period and expanded their awareness of the historical significance of their movement.

When the students gathered on August 11 at the Highlander Folk School for the next SNCC meeting, a few direct action proponents remained opposed to the voter registration project, even to the extent of being prepared to leave SNCC if they lost. Baker, who had the respect of both sides of the controversy, recalled, "I think this was about the only time I made any special effort to influence." She mentioned the difficulties caused by reform organizations splitting, with "nobody accomplishing anything."[29] Her efforts were aided by the fact that many advocates of direct action were themselves beginning to recognize both the need for voter registration and, perhaps more important, the financial resources that could be tapped if SNCC became involved in such work. Barry, who was identified with the direct action proponents, had recently met with representatives of the Taconic Foundation regarding possible financial support for voter registration work. The advocates of voter registration were further strengthened by the fact that about a dozen participants in the Nashville leadership seminar had indicated a willingness to drop out of school to participate in the project. After three days of acrimonious debate, Baker suggested a compromise, which was accepted. SNCC would have two wings, one for direct action and one for voter registration. Nash was named head of the protest wing, while Jones became head of the voter registration wing.[30]

Although differences regarding tactics and strategy remained, SNCC at this time acquired a cohesive force in its new executive secretary, James Forman. He gained the confidence of both groups by recognizing the need both for militant protest and for increased political sophistication and financial support. Born in Chicago in 1928, Forman had spent most of his early childhood with his grandmother on a farm in Marshall County, Mississippi, before returning to Chicago for school. In high school, according to his own account, he was "greatly influenced by the call of Dr. DuBois for young black people to get an education, including higher education, for the use of their people."[31] At Roosevelt University in Chicago Forman majored in management and was elected president of the student body and head of a delegation to the 1956 NSA convention. The next year Forman began graduate work in African affairs at Boston University. As a reporter for the *Chicago Defender,* he observed the battle in 1958 to integrate Central High School in Little Rock, Arkansas. He also wrote an unpublished novel about "a movement of young people of both races which would use nonviolent techniques to usher in social change." In 1960, while teaching in a public school in Chicago, Forman worked with a CORE affiliate, the Emergency Relief Committee, to help secure housing and food for blacks who had been evicted from their farms in Fayette County, Tennessee, for attempting to vote.

Forman's personal involvement in the southern protest movement began in August 1960 in Monroe, North Carolina, where Robert F. Williams, head of the local NAACP chapter, had become the center of a national controversy because of his advocacy of armed self-defense by blacks. He actively recruited working-class blacks into the NAACP who supported not only his position on self-defense but also his demands for employment opportunities and for desegregation. Forman and a group of freedom riders went to Monroe to support Williams' desegregation campaign. Soon after their arrival Forman told a reporter, "We hope nonviolence can offer an answer to the economic problems of lower-class blacks."[32] Williams, though skeptical, asked local blacks to support the non-violent activists picketing the Monroe Courthouse on behalf of black demands that had been presented on August 15 to the Board of Aldermen.

On August 27, a mob of several thousand whites surrounded a group of demonstrators, including Forman. In the violence that followed, which Forman later described as a "moment of death," the protesters were forced to retreat to a police station to save their lives. The police arrested over twenty protesters, including Forman, and charged them with incitement to riot. During a night of racial battles, local police attempted to arrest Williams on the grounds that he had kidnapped a white couple, whom Williams claimed had remained at his home for their own protection. Williams fled Monroe and a few months later went to Cuba for a long period of exile. Forman and the other demonstrators were found guilty but received suspended sentences on condition that they not demonstrate in North Carolina for two years.

Forman returned to his teaching job in Chicago but maintained contact with student activists in the South. In September 1961 Nashville activist Paul Brooks described SNCC to Forman as the same kind of nonviolent activist group that Forman had earlier portrayed in his novel. After a short period of deliberation, Forman left his teaching job and went to work in SNCC's national headquarters in Atlanta. A week later, he agreed to become its executive secretary, replacing Ed King, who returned to college.

Someone less dedicated than Forman might have regretted the decision to join SNCC after encountering the conditions at the headquarters. He described the scene that greeted him as, "One room. Greasy walls. A faint light from a dusty plastic skylight overhead. The mustiness, the smell, the mail scattered all over the floor." The phone rang, and it was *Newsweek* wanting information that he did not have.[33] Despite misgivings, Forman decided that SNCC needed him and that he should stay. He grasped the opportunity to realize his dream of building an organization that would sustain the idealism of young blacks rather than stifle it with bureaucratic constraints and concern for respectability.

Forman provided a necessary ingredient in the development of an organizational structure for the southern student movement. By the end of the summer of 1961 SNCC had become a gathering point for southern black activists who had made the southern struggle the focus of their lives. Yet without a leader like Forman, who was prepared to assume responsibility for fund-raising and for directing the activities of a full-time staff, it is unlikely that SNCC could have become a durable organization. The freedom rides had demonstrated that the militancy of black students had not waned since the sit-in days. Indeed, it had become more intense as student riders confronted the brutal forces of racism in the deep South.

Now that impulsive, part-time student protesters had captured the national attention, it was SNCC's function to provide them with a framework to pursue the struggle full-time and to test the radical ideas that were emerging in its course.

# 4. RADICAL CADRE IN McCOMB

The freedom rides, the resulting jail terms, the Nashville leadership seminar, and the Highlander meeting had each contributed to the political development of black student activists. But the new orientation of the students was not apparent until they left the southern college campuses where the movement had begun and assumed full-time roles as a radical cadre within a southern black community removed from the mainstream of American life. Late in the summer of 1961 they established a project in McComb, Mississippi, where they were joined by northern black students as well as by white students affiliated with the emerging northern student movement.

Events in McComb soon overshadowed the previous experiences of the small group of activists who were SNCC's field secretaries. Although the disagreements that had threatened to divide SNCC were still not resolved, they lost their importance as the staff began to formulate policies through actions. In McComb, the direct action advocates attempted to demonstrate the power of nonviolence in the deep South, while the voter registration workers patiently sought to convince black residents that they should risk assault, economic retaliation, and even death in order to register. Both groups brought into the McComb struggle a long-standing moral commitment as well as a new-found political sophistication. Their experiences in McComb nonetheless forced them to reassess their previous assumptions and to begin to develop a strategy of action capable of sustaining a social struggle among black people who faced enormous obstacles with few resources.

SNCC workers began to see themselves, and were seen by others, as a unique group within the civil rights movement. They were courageous and dedicated organizers, with a revolutionary élan if not a revolutionary ideology. The staff also began to see themselves as SNCC. The Coordinating Committee had approved the McComb project, but the staff members themselves, now no longer students, would determine the future direction of SNCC. The organizational structure did not hold the staff together; rather, they were drawn together by their conviction that SNCC's structure should be subordinate to their common goals.

* * *

Bob Moses, head of the McComb project, symbolized SNCC's emerging style of radical political action, and his self-effacing personality and humanistic beliefs were important ingredients in the transformation of political consciousness in SNCC. Born in 1935, Moses had grown up in a Harlem housing project. He passed a city-wide examination to gain admittance to Stuyvesant High School, an elite public school in lower Manhattan. As one of the school's few black students, he felt the double isolation of being treated as intellectually exceptional and being confronted with racial barriers. In 1952 he won a scholarship to Hamilton College in New York, where he was active in sports and student politics. In college he was attracted to the existentialist philosophy of the French philosopher Albert Camus, which combined an individualistic moral code with a humanistic approach to social change. According to Moses, his principal lesson from Camus was the need to cease being "a victim" while at the same time not becoming "an executioner."[1]

Moses, like Lawson and Forman, began his social activism during the 1950s. At the end of his junior year at Hamilton he worked in a European summer camp sponsored by the pacifistic American Friends Service Committee, and the following year he worked at a similar camp in Japan. He did graduate work at Harvard University in philosophy, specializing in mathematical logic, and earned his master's degree in June 1957, but the following year the death of his mother and the hospitalization of his father forced him to leave graduate school and start teaching high school mathematics in New York. In 1959 Moses helped veteran black activist Bayard Rustin in organizing the second Youth March for Integrated Schools. He had his introduction to the southern protest movement in 1960 on a visit to an uncle in Virginia, where he joined a demonstration in Newport News. As he recalled, his initial involvement brought "a feeling of release" from the burden of accommodating himself to racial affronts: "My whole reaction through life to such humiliation was to avoid it, keep it down, hold it in, play it cool."[2]

At the urging of Rustin, Moses went to Atlanta to work in the SCLC office in the summer of 1960 and then traveled through the deep South, where he met Amzie Moore. The following summer Moses first planned to return to Cleveland, Mississippi, to establish a voter registration project, as he had promised Moore, but changed his mind when he learned that no equipment or meeting places were available there. Instead, he accepted the invitation of C. C. Bryant, head of the Pike County chapter of the NAACP, to establish a program in McComb, a town of about 13,000 inhabitants located in the southwestern corner of the state. Moses, not having participated in the SNCC discussions on voter registration, characteristically began making plans for a project on his own. Arriving in McComb in July, he persuaded black residents to provide housing for student voter registration workers for the month of August. Then he officially became a member of SNCC's staff and encouraged black students affiliated with SNCC to join him in McComb. First to arrive were Reginald Robinson, who had previously worked on a voter registration project run by SNCC's affiliate in Baltimore, and John Hardy, a freedom rider from Nashville who had just completed a jail term in Parchman Penitentiary. The three opened a voter registration school to train black McComb residents to take Mississippi's literacy test for voters.

Moses, along with the two other SNCC workers, walked door to door during August trying to convince black residents of McComb that "we meant business, that is, that we were serious, that we were not only young, but that we were people who were responsible." During the first few days of canvassing, the SNCC workers persuaded about a dozen black residents to attempt to register, although few were successful in convincing the white registrar that they had adequately answered the twenty-one questions on the voter registration forms. Nonetheless, these initial attempts to register led residents in two nearby rural counties, Amite and Walthall, to ask Moses to establish voter registration schools in their areas. Although recognizing that resistance in the rural countries would be even stronger than in McComb, because they contained only one registered black voter as compared to about two hundred in Pike County, Moses agreed that he and the newly arrived SNCC workers should go. His reasoning was that SNCC should not be put in the position of "turning down the tough areas," because blacks would then lose confidence in the organization.[3]

Moses' attempt to enter the rural areas led to the first confrontations between SNCC workers and Mississippi authorities. On August 15, 1961, Moses escorted three blacks to the courthouse in Liberty, Amite County, and stood by as they filled out the registration forms. While driving back to McComb, he was arrested by police and charged with interfering with the discharge of their duties.

Despite many calls made to John Doar at the Justice Department to protest this harassment, Moses was convicted, given a ninety-day suspended sustence, and fined $5. He spent two days in jail before allowing the NAACP to post bond while the conviction was under appeal. On August 22, after another registration attempt in Liberty, Moses was attacked and beaten by Billy Jack Caston, a cousin of the local sheriff. Moses pressed charges against Caston, and on August 31 a trial was held. After their testimony, SNCC workers were advised to leave the courtroom, as Moses recalled: "the sheriff came back and told us that he didn't think it was safe for us to remain there while the all-white jury gave its decision."[4] Police escorted the SNCC workers to the county line, and the next day Moses read in the newspaper that Caston had been acquitted.

Moses did not join nor encourage attempts to desegregate public facilities, but he also did not discourage other SNCC workers from testing the effectiveness of nonviolent direct action in Mississippi. Soon after the opening of the McComb office in August, Marion Barry and Charles Sherrod began to conduct workshops in the use of nonviolent tactics. They attracted many black high school students who were not content to limit their activities to canvassing prospective voters in black neighborhoods. On August 26, Hollis Watkins and Curtis Hayes, two black teenagers from Pike County who were working with SNCC, staged a sit-in at a Woolworth store and were charged with breach of the peace. A few days later three high school students, including a sixteen-year-old girl, Brenda Travis, were arrested after taking part in a sit-in at the local Greyhound bus terminal. Although the local black populace was thrown into an uproar, especially because of the continued incarceration of the young girl, the five teenagers were not released until early October.

While the direct action proponents were learning during August and September 1961 about the type of resistance to expect in the deep South, a small but growing number of SNCC voter registration workers also encountered increasing violence. On September 5, Moses and Travis Britt, a SNCC worker from New York, accompanied four blacks to the registrar in Liberty. While waiting outside the courthouse, they were surrounded by a group of white men, who asked Moses why he had come from New York to stir up trouble. Moses remained silent. One of the white men turned to Britt and, after questioning him, hit him repeatedly. Moses helped Britt escape, and the SNCC workers, along with the local blacks, quickly left town.

Two days later John Hardy, who had been working in Walthall County, accompanied two people to the registrar's office in Tylertown. The registrar argued with Hardy and then ordered him out of his office at gunpoint. As Hardy was leaving, the registrar hit him with his pistol and then called the sheriff, who charged Hardy with disorderly conduct. The Justice Department entered the case on behalf of Hardy, arguing that if he were convicted, blacks would be discouraged from registering to vote, but the arrest of Hardy and the assault on Britt further slowed the voter registration effort.

The voter registration project received a severe setback on September 25 when Herbert Lee, a black resident of Amite County who had helped Moses, was shot and killed by E. H. Hurst, a white state representative. Hurst claimed self-defense and was absolved by a coroner's jury, but a black witness to the shooting, Louis Allen, told Moses that he had lied at the inquest because of fear but would tell the truth if he were promised protection. When Moses asked for such protection from the Justice Department, officials told him that "there was no way possible to provide protection for a witness at such a hearing and that probably, in any case it didn't matter what he testified [because Hurst] would be found innocent." According to Moses, Allen was later beaten by a deputy sheriff, who had been informed by the FBI that Allen had lied to the coroner's jury. The episode was one of many that resulted in feelings of distrust among SNCC workers regarding the FBI, which worked closely with local police forces. A few years later, on January 31, 1964, as Allen prepared to leave the South, he was shot and killed outside his home by an unknown assailant.[5]

Lee's killing brought voter registration attempts to a complete halt, but the release from jail of the high school students arrested in August led to a reactivation of the nonviolent movement. On October 4, when the principal of the black high school refused to readmit two of the students, over a hundred students protested the decision, as well as the killing of Lee, by marching to McComb's city hall. Moses, Charles McDew, and Bob Zellner, then the only white SNCC field secretary, joined the students for prayers in front of city hall. As a large crowd of whites looked on, police began arresting the black youngsters. Suddenly a white man attacked Zellner. Moses and McDew tried to protect him, but other whites joined in the attack, and Zellner's eye was gouged. Police arrested the three SNCC workers along with 119 students. The protesters were charged with disturbing the peace, and those over eighteen years of age were also charged with contributing to the delinquency of minors.

After their release on bond, Moses and McDew spent the following days teaching at a "nonviolent high school" attended by students who had refused to sign a statement, demanded by the public school administration, acknowledging that they would be automatically expelled if they participated in further demonstrations. Later in the month Moses, McDew, Zellner, and nine local residents were sentenced to four months in jail and fined $200. Travis, who was on probation, was sent to a juvenile detention center, where she remained for six months. Other high school students who had taken part in the protest decided to transfer to a school in Jackson.

Although a few isolated protests occurred in McComb during November, the jailing of Moses and practically all of the local blacks who had worked closely with him temporarily ended SNCC's first voter registration project. While in jail, Moses described the efforts of the civil rights workers to maintain their spirits: "Hollis [Watkins] will lead out with a clear tenor into a freedom song, [Robert] Talbert and [Ike] Lewis will supply jokes, and McDew will discourse on the history of the black man and the Jew." Despite the bravura, Moses recognized that the protest in McComb had been only "a tremor in the middle of the iceberg." In December, after Moses and other SNCC workers were released on appeal bond, they left McComb to renew their struggle elsewhere. "We had, to put it mildly, got our feet wet," Moses commented. "We now knew something of what it took to run a voter registration campaign in Mississippi. We knew some of the obstacles we would have to face; we had some general idea of what had to be done to get such a campaign started . . . And we began to set about doing this."[6]

The McComb experience, though a setback for SNCC, provided a basis for later, more successful projects in the deep South. SNCC had quickly acquired a field staff capable of launching sustained assaults against southern racism. During the fall about a dozen student activists dropped out of college to go to McComb and work with SNCC. No longer was SNCC composed of part-time student protesters representing their local movements on the Coordinating Committee. Instead, a group of students now identified themselves as full-time SNCC field secretaries and functioned as spearheads of militant racial struggle in the deep South.

The Coordinating Committee remained the nominal policy-making body, but SNCC's policies were actually determined by the actions of its field staff. Members of the Coordinating Committee often found it difficult to resist the attractions of full-time involvement as a staff member. Thus, membership on the Coordinating Committee was in constant flux. Of the twenty-four persons listed as members in July 1961, only six had participated in SNCC's founding conference. Later in the year seven of these committee members joined SNCC's staff, and most of the rest discontinued their participation in SNCC's affairs. Whereas the black student protest movement, for which the Coordinating Committee was a representative body, was in a decline, SNCC itself was not. The SNCC staff included the most militant and dedicated leaders of the southern student movement.

Through their experiences in McComb, the newly formed SNCC staff gained a new sense of themselves as cohesive and unique. The direct action proponents, fresh from the Highlander debates over voter registration, discovered in McComb that their nonviolent tactics were not always effective and sometimes ruinous when used against a determined white establishment. They also discovered that voter registration in the deep South offered as much of a test of militancy and courage as did direct action protests. As Reginald Robinson commented, "if you went into Mississippi and talked about voter registration they're going to hit you on the side of the head and that's as direct as you can get."[7] The compromise arranged at Highlander, where Nash and Jones had been put in charge of SNCC's two wings, became meaningless when both found that they had little to administer and that influence within SNCC was determined not by organizational titles but by a willingness to become involved in the struggle.

SNCC staff members, though not a revolutionary group, possessed far more political awareness than did the southern black students who had founded SNCC. Though they had just begun to articulate radical or revolutionary ideas, they saw their methods of achieving social change as differing dramatically from those of any other reform organization. While retaining some of the liberal and Christian beliefs, they had broken away from conventional liberalism and institutional religion by asserting an unwillingness to compromise their ideals.

A measure of the new spirit of militancy among SNCC workers was their use of the term *revolutionary* as a self-description. For them the word did not imply a desire to overthrow the federal government but rather indicated a need to challenge both the segregationist social order and the more moderate civil rights organizations. The appellation also reflected an increased willingness among SNCC workers to associate themselves with a broad movement, spearheaded by young people, to achieve radical social change.

Many of the black protest leaders of the previous year, imbued with Cold War anti-communism, had once suspected anyone who seemed politically radical. According to James Forman, even Moses was initially suspect among students on grounds of being a communist. Sherrod later noted that he himself had been a "red-baiter" at college.[8] Nevertheless, as a result of their participation in the protest movement, black student activists for the first time encountered socialists who were sincerely committed to the cause of civil rights. SNCC workers in McComb, for example, cut off from previous social ties and sources of financial and legal support, gratefully accepted help from almost any source, including socialists.

SNCC's relations with SCEF illustrated the growing willingness of SNCC workers to associate with leftist groups, in addition to explaining the presence in the McComb protests of Zellner, a white activist. SCEF had long been a center of controversy, because of charges that there were communists in its ranks. An interracial organization dedicated to civil rights reform, SCEF was founded during the 1930s with the help of communists, but its supporters included many noncommunists, including Eleanor Roosevelt. During the late 1950s SCEF became a target of the southern press when one of its representatives, Carl Braden, refused to answer questions before HUAC and was later sentenced to a year in prison. Despite the controversy, SNCC leaders as early as the fall of 1960 developed close ties with Braden and his wife, Anne. SCEF's newspaper, the *Southern Patriot*, devoted considerable coverage to SNCC activities at a time when the organization received little attention elsewhere, and during 1960 and 1961 the paper contained essays written by Ella Baker and James Lawson.

The Bradens had gained the trust of SNCC workers because they understood better than most white leftists the militant mood of black activists, and they respected the desire of those in SNCC to remain independent of all outside control. Anne Braden commented in 1960 that those in SNCC were "suspicious as hell of organizations," since they believed that other groups were "out with an ax to grind and do not have the true cause at heart. They want no part of them; they want something new. Their concept of what this new thing will be is vague, but they are convinced that it has to be different from the disillusionments of the past." The southern black did not "want the participation of white people if they are to be a drag on his movement" or if their participation was to be "in the old pattern that has often prevailed even in liberal interracial organizations—that of white domination."[9]

Anne Braden was nevertheless convinced that southern whites could play important roles in the civil rights struggle, and as early as the fall of 1960 she urged SNCC to hire a white field secretary to recruit students at white colleges. In the negotiations that followed, Braden resisted the efforts of SCEF's Board of Directors to place the new organizer on SCEF's staff rather than on SNCC's, and she convinced the board to give SNCC a grant for hiring the white worker. Although Braden feared that the more cautious black student activists in SNCC, such as Jenkins and Jones, might oppose the grant, it was approved by SNCC during the summer of 1961.[10] SCEF's grant of $5000 per year, which was subsequently renewed for two years, was an important addition to SNCC's meager income. Although the money was supposed to be set aside to pay the salary of the white field secretary, it was actually used to pay other organizational expenses.

The white student hired for the position was Bob Zellner, the son of an itinerant Methodist preacher. Born in southern Alabama, Zellner had attended high school in Mobile. He became involved in the protest movement at Huntingdon College in Montgomery, where in the course of research for a sociology class he met black students involved in desegregation protests and observed a nonviolent workshop at a black church. He became deeply involved in student political activities and, at the time he applied for the position on SNCC's staff funded by the SCEF grant, was participating in summer workshops at the Highlander Folk School. Recognizing the difficulties that could result from SCEF's reputation, Zellner made clear that the source of the grant for his salary should remain unpublicized—"the less overt connection with SCEF the better."[11]

Anne Braden had hoped that Zellner could concentrate on the task of bringing southern white students into the civil rights movement, but Zellner soon decided that he could not explain "what was going on unless I myself became an integral part of it, and of course my personality make-up and psychology also tended to draw me into the area of action." Not only was he involved in the McComb demonstrations, but later in 1961 he was arrested after a freedom ride to Albany, Georgia, and he was charged with criminal anarchy after delivering protest literature to a jailed SNCC member in Baton Rouge. As his involvement with SNCC increased, he found that he was "estranged from other southern white students." In a report on his work he asked, "How do you relate to the white southern moderate or liberal and at the same time relate to a group of people who are as militant and as activist as students in [SNCC]?"[12]

For Zellner and many of the other white activists who followed him into SNCC, the southern protest movement became a magnet. White activists, like the black students in SNCC, had previously lacked a means of expressing their dissatisfaction with aspects of American society. The McComb protests, along with the many subsequent southern protests, offered the newly revived white student left a model of activism that was crucial for its own development. Thus Tom Hayden, southern field representative of SDS, came away from a September 1961 meeting of the SNCC staff in Mississippi convinced that he had witnessed the beginning of "a revolution" led by activists who did not identify with their "Negro predecessors but with the new nations around the world." Students in SNCC now recognized that "beyond lunch counter desegregations there are more serious evils which must be ripped out by any means: exploitation, socially destructive capital, evil political and legal structure, and myopic liberalism which is anti-revolutionary. Revolution permeates discussion like never before."[13]

The black-dominated southern movement had a significant effect on the white student left. Without the nonviolent tactics and organizing techniques developed by SNCC in the South, white student activism would probably not have expanded as quickly as it did. Not only did Hayden and other SDS leaders learn from their experiences in the South, but SDS, the Northern Student Movement, and other predominantly white student organizations attracted students whose initial political activities involved civil rights issues. The overlap in the membership of both movements is illustrated by the fact that during 1961 Zellner, Jim Monsonis, and Casey Hayden, recently married to Tom, were members simultaneously of SNCC's staff and of the National Executive Committee of SDS. Tim Jenkins too was a member both of the Coordinating Committee and of SDS's Executive Committee.

Hayden's view of the southern black movement, though romanticized, reflected the significant shift in SNCC's public image that occurred during the fall of 1961. Previously the organization had been dominated by activists whose manners and appearance betrayed a desire to conform to white middle-class notions of respectability. Then in McComb SNCC workers sensed that the goals for which they were struggling were too far-reaching to be won through prayer, persuasion, or appeals to the liberal conscience. McDew noted the role of the civil rights movement in promoting "a full-scale social revolution" in the United States by activating people "who feel freedom as a passion in their lives" and were "willing to make it more than an abstract concept." Lawson, who had joined the staff of SCLC, was one of many activists who asserted that, despite its limited goals, the southern nonviolent movement was "a revolutionary enterprise moving toward real revolution and total revolution."[14]

Even though SNCC activists had begun to adopt the rhetoric of revolution, their militancy remained an outgrowth of the obstinacy of the segregationist opposition in the deep South, and the staff continued to seek the aid of the Justice Department in their efforts to achieve civil rights goals. As Julian Bond remarked, the staff was still "operating on the theory that here was a problem, you expose it to the world, the world says 'How horrible!' and moves to correct it." When the McComb staff returned to Atlanta for discussions during September, Forman noted the lack of discipline or political sophistication among SNCC workers, who refused even to acknowledge the need for a program of political education: "So long as we were working on voter registration and public accommodations, there was a broad consensus under which everyone could move. It seemed important then just to do, to act, as a means of overcoming the lethargy and hopelessness of so many black people. Also, we had no adequate models for what we were doing, for how we should proceed. Rather than set up rigid definitions of goals and tactics, it seemed best then to experiment and learn and experiment some more and draw conclusions from this process."[15]

Few SNCC workers saw the need for a revolutionary ideology. Instead they assumed that the intense struggle in which they were involved would itself provide the necessary insights for their work. Unlike student radicals who had merely been exposed to revolutionary ideas, SNCC workers were now full-time activists testing ideas against the harsh realities of life for blacks in the South. In the process the staff learned more about their collective capabilities and about southern blacks of all classes. Although a gulf still existed between the recent college students on the staff and the black residents of the rural South, the staff had moved beyond the Gandhian orientation promoted by the Nashville students. They had begun to develop distinctive organizing techniques, emphasizing local leadership and brash militancy, which would enable them to mobilize entire black communities in the South for protracted struggle.

# 5. THE ALBANY MOVEMENT

While the SNCC workers tested their commitment in McComb, other members of the staff launched massive protests involving a broad cross-section of blacks in Albany, Georgia. And whereas the proponents of nonviolent direct action suffered a defeat in McComb, in Albany they were able to bring previously dormant elements of the black populace into a sustained struggle for civil rights. The SNCC workers in Albany, drawing on their previous experiences, began consciously to use militancy to overcome the psychological barriers that previously had prevented political activism among blacks in the deep South.

The Albany protests, which occurred between the fall of 1961 and the summer of 1962, demonstrated not only the appeal of SNCC's militancy to urban blacks but also the importance of Afro-American religious beliefs and institutions as a foundation for mass struggle among blacks in general. The growing confidence of SNCC activists in Albany led to their open criticism of the approaches of other civil rights groups and to their decision to expand the work into rural areas. But they also learned in Albany that even massive, sustained, and generally disciplined protests based on moral principles did not necessarily ensure immediate success and that efficient police action against demonstrators could seriously hamper their struggle.

Albany experienced little protest activity before October 1961 when SNCC field secretaries Charles Sherrod and Cordell Reagon arrived there to open a SNCC office. Students at Albany State College, a restrictive, paternalistic institution that was typical of most black schools in the deep South, had not taken part in the sit-ins of the spring. "The campus is separated from the community by a river, a dump yard and a cemetery," commented Sherrod. "And if any system of intelligence gets through all of that it is promptly stomped underfoot by men in administrative positions who refuse to think further than a new car, a bulging refrigerator and an insatiable lust for more than enough of everything we call leisure."[1]

Albany itself was a backwater city of about 60,000 inhabitants with a history of generally peaceful if unequal relations between the black minority, representing about 40 percent of the population, and the white major-

56

ity. The only significant indication of dissatisfaction had been the presentation to the city commission of a modest petition for reforms by a small group of blacks in early 1961. The petition was condemned by the staunchly segregationist *Albany Herald* and was subsequently rejected.[2]

Sherrod and Reagon were experienced activists who had already formulated a strategy for their work in Albany. Both had been freedom riders and were influenced by the religious ideas that pervaded the early student protest movement. Reagon, who was eighteen when he began work in Albany, had been active in the Nashville student movement; Sherrod, who was twenty-two, had let sit-in protests in Richmond, Virginia. Sherrod, the more articulate of the two, was also director of SNCC's southwest Georgia voter registration project, in which capacity he was able to imprint his own personality and attitudes on the activities in Albany.

Like other young blacks who participated in the sit-in movement, Sherrod was sensitive to the psychological importance of militancy for blacks. He had grown up in the slums of Petersburg, Virginia, the eldest of six children in a fatherless home. His mother, who was fourteen at the time of his birth, had only reached the eighth grade. He worked as a child, "carrying junk and shining shoes," to help support his family, which received welfare assistance. Strong-willed and earnest, Sherrod studied religion at Virginia Union University while continuing to contribute to his family's support. "I worked as hard as any two men getting through school," he commented. As a Baptist preacher, he was attracted, like John Lewis and many others, to the radical implications of Christianity. After becoming a civil rights activist, he felt a new sense of freedom and racial pride. During the spring of 1961 he expressed the desire "to go ahead in a new way— maybe not the way the whites have shown . . . We are *not* the puppets of the white man. We want a different world where *we* can speak, where *we* can communicate."[3]

Sherrod's experience in the sit-ins and freedom rides led to his decision to use nonviolent protest as a means of prompting Albany blacks to break with previous traditions of accommodation. Initially, however, he found that "the people were afraid, really afraid. Sometimes we'd walk down the streets and the little kids would call us freedom riders and the people walking in the same direction would go across the street from us." Sherrod's first objective was to remove "the mental block in the minds of those who wanted to move but were unable for fear that we were not who we said we were."[4]

Sherrod and Reagon sought the support of all segments of the black populace. As Reagon explained, they acted "like neighborhood boys," because "you don't achieve anything with the preachers, teachers and businessmen until you work with the common people first." Sherrod recalled that they talked to people "in churches, social meetings, on the streets, in the pool halls, lunch rooms and night clubs," telling them "how it feels to be . . . in jail for the cause . . . that there were worse chains than jail and prison. We referred to the system that imprisons men's minds and robs them of creativity. We mocked the system that teaches men to be good Negroes instead of good men. We gave an account of many resistances, of injustice in the courts, in employment, registration and voting . . . we started to illustrate what had happened to . . . other cities where people came together and protested against an evil system."[5]

Although Sherrod and Reagon initially focused on "the common people," they later received crucial support from the black middle class, particularly from ministers who allowed their churches to be used for meetings. According to Sherrod, "even the hypocrisy" of the black church bore the "seeds of the ultimate victory of Truth." Rather than attempting to "beat the box," Sherrod advised, one must accept the people "where they are."[6] Sherrod's own religious training helped him to gain the support of the Baptist Ministerial Alliance and the Interdenominational Alliance.

Sherrod and Reagon led nightly workshops in churches on nonviolent tactics. They drew growing numbers of young people from colleges, trade schools, high schools, and the street, who, Sherrod recounted, were "searching for a meaning in life."[7]

On November 1, 1961, their efforts led to a sit-in at a bus station by nine students to test compliance with the Interstate Commerce Commission ruling, which became effective that day, barring segregation in transportation terminals. As Sherrod recalled, many blacks gathered at the bus station, which was located in a predominantly black neighborhood, to watch the protesters, who symbolized in their eyes "the expression of years of resentment—for police brutality, for poor housing, for disenfranchisement, for inferior education, for the whole damnable system." Even though the students left as planned when threatened with arrest, in the hearts of black residents "from that moment on, segregation was dead."[8] Later the students filed affidavits with the commission charging that Albany whites were ignoring its ruling.

After the protest at the bus terminal, representatives of civil rights organizations and other black community groups met to discuss their grievances, and they formed the Albany Movement, a coalition of SNCC, NAACP, the ministerial alliances, the Federation of Women's Clubs, the Negro Voters League, and many other groups interested in racial reform. William G. Anderson, a black osteopath, was elected president, and Slater King, a black realtor, became vice-president. One of the black leaders of the Albany Movement commented: "The kids were going to do it anyway . . . they were holding their own mass meetings and making plans . . . we didn't want them to have to do it alone."[9]

A few days after the formation of the Albany Movement, three members of the NAACP Youth Council were arrested by Albany Police Chief Laurie Pritchett as they attempted to use the dining room at the Trailways bus station. Later that same day, Bertha Gober and Blanton Hall, two Albany State students who had been working with SNCC, were arrested after entering the white waiting room at the bus station. These arrests further aroused the black community and set the stage for the first mass meeting of the Albany Movement.

Held on November 25 in Mount Zion Baptist Church, the meeting revealed the depth of pent-up emotions that had been released by the student protest. "The church was packed," Sherrod reported. The students who had been arrested described their experiences in jail, and after the last speaker had finished, "there was nothing left to say. Tears filled the eyes of hard, grown men who had known personally and seen with their own eyes merciless atrocities committed by small men without conscience."[10]

Then everyone rose to sing "We Shall Overcome," which had recently been adopted as a "freedom song." As Bernice Reagon, one of the Albany student activists, recalled: "When I opened my mouth and began to sing, there was a force and power within myself I had never heard before. Somehow this music . . . released a kind of power and required a level of concentrated energy I did not know I had." Goldie Jackson, a black woman who had lost her job after allowing SNCC workers to stay in her house, remembered praying and singing in the church for the rest of the night: "Two things we knew held us together: prayer of something good to come and song that tells from the depth of the heart how we feel about our fellow man."[11]

The trial of the five students on November 27 was the scene of a mass rally to protest both their arrests and the expulsion of Gober and Hall from Albany State College. SNCC worker Charles Jones led the demonstrators on a march to a church where four hundred people signed a petition demanding the reinstatement of the students. When the *Albany Herald* condemned the march, black residents began a boycott against advertisers in the paper.

On Sunday, December 10, ten activists, including James Forman, Bob Zellner, and Norma Collins of SNCC, arrived from Atlanta to fan the flames of militancy. While several hundred Albany blacks looked on, the integrated group of protesters sat in the waiting room at the Albany train station and were quickly arrested on trespassing charges. Their arrests, which Albany mayor Asa Kelley later conceded was "our first mistake," ignited a week of mass rallies and demonstrations.[12]

On Monday, Forman addressed a mass meeting where residents planned further protests. On Tuesday, 267 black high school and college students were arrested when they refused to disperse from a protest at the trial of the train station protesters. Most of the students chose to remain in jail rather than paying bail. On Wednesday Slater King, after leading a prayer vigil at the courthouse, was arrested, and later in the day more than 200 demonstrators who had marched to City Hall were jailed for parading without a permit. As Chief Pritchett told newsmen, "We can't tolerate the NAACP or the SNCC or any other nigger organization to take over this town with mass demonstrations."[13] On Thursday, when the number of arrests had exceeded 500, the governor of Georgia sent 150 national guardsmen to Albany.

Local city officials then agreed to establish a biracial committee to discuss black demands for the integration of transportation facilities and the release of demonstrators. Anderson invited Martin Luther King to address a rally on Friday, December 15, where King told the largest gathering yet assembled at Shiloh Baptist Church: "Don't stop now. Keep moving. Don't get weary. We will wear them down with our capacity to suffer."[14] The next day after negotiations had broken down, King led a prayer march to City Hall and was arrested along with more than 250 demonstrators. When King announced that he would remain in jail and spend Christmas there, city officials again resumed negotiations in order to resolve the crisis. Two days later, King suddenly announced that he was allowing himself to be released on bail as part of a settlement which included city compliance with the Interstate Commerce Commission ruling and release of the other demonstrators.

The truce marked the end of the first stage of the Albany protests. To the dismay of SNCC workers, the momentum that had developed during December dissipated rapidly. City officials stalled on implementing the concessions they had granted and refused to seek desegregation of the city bus service, which became the target of a black boycott early in 1962. SNCC workers continued to use direct action tactics in attempts to revive the movement, but these protests received little attention. In April 1962, Jones, Reagon, and two others sat in at a lunch counter and were arrested; subsequently they were sentenced to sixty-day jail terms. And in a SNCC-led demonstration at City Hall, twenty-nine persons were arrested while protesting the April shooting by an Albany policeman of a black man for allegedly resisting arrest.

Then on July 10, 1962, the Albany Movement came alive once again when Martin Luther King and his associate, Ralph Abernathy, returned to Albany for sentencing in connection with the December protests. King and Abernathy were given jail terms of forty-five days or a fine of $178. When both announced that they would serve their sentences, Albany Movement leaders announced a mass rally for the following night. The rally was preceded by a march to City Hall, which resulted in the arrest of thirty-two persons, and that evening violent clashes took place between brick-throwing black youngsters and police outside the church where the rally was held. On July 13, the crisis atmosphere eased when King and Abernathy were released from jail after an unidentified black man paid their fines. "I've been thrown out of lots of places in my day," Abernathy later remarked, "but never before have I been thrown out of jail."[15]

Demonstrations, however, continued. Small groups of blacks led by Jones of SNCC and Wyatt T. Walker of SCLC attempted to gain admission to segregated facilities in Albany, and there were mass marches to City Hall demanding civil rights. One of these, on July 24, ended in more rock and brick throwing.

This outbreak of violence brought back national guardsmen to Albany. King responded by calling a "day of penance" while he, Abernathy, and Jones attempted to convince local black residents to remain nonviolent. A few days later King, Abernathy, and Anderson were arrested while leading a prayer pilgrimage to City Hall, and they joined hundreds of protesters already in jail. By this time, the Albany jails had been filled, and prisoners had to be moved to nearby jails.

Violence was not confined to the streets of Albany. At Camilla jail Marion King, Slater King's pregnant wife, was knocked unconscious by a deputy sheriff when she visited demonstrators there, and a few weeks later attorney C. B. King was caned by the sheriff of Dougherty County. "I wanted to let him know," the sheriff remarked, "I'm a white man and he's a damn nigger."[16]

After repeated requests by Albany black leaders for a statement of support, President Kennedy finally responded by urging Albany officials to negotiate a settlement. At a news conference on August 1 Kennedy noted that the United States government was "involved in sitting down at Geneva with the Soviet Union. I can't understand why the government of Albany, City Council of Albany, cannot do the same for American citizens."

King, Abernathy, and Anderson were convicted on August 10 of disturbing the peace and parading without a permit, but their sentences were suspended. By this time the enthusiasm of Albany blacks had been weakened by the months of fruitless appeals to the conscience of Albany's white residents. According to journalist Pat Watters, "that final despair in Albany—the losing of steam," was perhaps a profound expression "of disappointment at having found and offered so much—and being understood so little." The Albany protests were a turning point for the civil rights movement, after which, "activists in the movement to whom, from the beginning, non-violence was merely a sophisticated weapon were to gain in influence over those who were imbued in their personal lives with it as a spiritual quality." Or as SNCC worker Bill Hansen analyzed the situation: "We were naive enough to think we could fill up the jails . . . We ran out of people before [Chief Pritchett] ran out of jails."[17] Although the Albany

Movement remained in existence through the late 1960s and SNCC continued its activities in Albany for several years, the emotion and sense of hope were never recaptured.

In a purely instrumental sense, the Albany protests could be viewed as a serious setback for the civil rights movement. The initial objective of desegregation in bus and train terminals involved no more than compliance with federal rulings, and the broader civil rights goals of the movement—general desegregation of facilities and acceptance by city officials of the rights of blacks to hold peaceful demonstrations—remained in contention. Chief Pritchett had consistently crushed demonstrations through mass arrests without resorting to the kind of excessive force that would have provoked federal intervention. The lesson to those in SNCC was clear: patient suffering by nonviolent protesters was insufficient to bring about federal intervention. Yet, though the Albany Movement failed to achieve some of its objectives, it served as a training ground for many SNCC workers who learned new techniques for sustaining mass militancy for long periods and it served as a model for blacks in other southern cities where mass struggles would soon emerge. As Howard Zinn explained at the time, the black movement in Albany, though "not one of perfectly coordinated tactical efficiency," was "one of courage, passion and sacrifice, and it brought forth . . . some of the noblest qualities that human beings have shown anywhere."[18]

SNCC workers, though disappointed by the few immediate tangible gains, emerged from the Albany protests confident of being in the vanguard of a mass struggle. Sherrod observed that "the superstructure" was "being shaken to the very foundations" by the protests. Southern racial etiquette was being challenged: "It is no longer a matter-of-fact procedure for a Negro to respond in 'yes sirs' and 'no sirs.' " Blacks were beginning to "wonder if it is their right to say what they strongly believe even if this means letting the mayor or chief of police or 'bossman' know about it; *they are thinking.*"[19]

The Albany struggle convinced SNCC workers that their strategy of organizing had broad support among the black residents. They developed close ties with local black leaders and carefully avoided threatening the authority of those leaders. Jones, at a SNCC meeting in March 1962, cited Albany as an example of SNCC's unique "willingness to sacrifice" and to "form community movements, not organizations." At the same meeting, Julian Bond asserted that when SNCC left an area, it left behind "a community movement with local leadership, not a new branch of SNCC." Marion King thanked the SNCC activists for starting the movement in her town: "You have given my children something that cannot be taken away from them."[20]

SNCC workers' close ties to local residents and their deference to local leadership distinguished them from SCLC representatives who came to Albany after the protest movement had begun. Soon after Martin Luther King had visited Albany in December 1961, a reporter noted that SNCC workers held a "dominant position" among the competing civil rights groups in Albany. Sherrod was quoted as saying that "a constant war" regarding strategy took place between SNCC and SCLC. "The students," observed historian David Lewis, "were piqued by the fixation of the press and some of the older community people upon the person and utterances of [King]. SNCC had labored unheralded in the vineyards of racial protest in Albany long before 'De Lawd'—Martin's new SNCC appellation—appeared on the scene to work his miracles." SNCC workers and local black leaders resented Wyatt Walker, SCLC's executive director, who moved "about the community a little too haughtily and noisily, dispensing the patronage that the SCLC's sizable financial resources allowed." The resentments of SNCC workers against SCLC were expressed openly at a meeting in July 1962 involving King, Sherrod, Reagon, and Jones. According to Lewis, the SNCC workers "disputed with the Atlanta pastor the right of SCLC to monopolize the Movement. Martin denied any such intent on the part of his organization and attempted to extenuate the peremptory conduct of Wyatt. Until that afternoon, he had probably not been fully aware of the extent to which his chief subaltern had alienated the local leadership."[21]

By the fall of 1962, SNCC workers had firmly asserted their own right to influence the course of the southern struggle. For many on the SNCC staff, the Albany protests were an important training ground in which to learn the techniques of mobilizing the dormant black populace of the deep South. Perhaps of greatest importance, they became more aware of the cultural dimension of the black struggle. SNCC workers in Albany, for example, quickly recognized the value of freedom songs, often based on black spirituals, to convey the ideas of the southern movement and to sustain morale. Bernice Reagon, an Albany student leader who joined SNCC's staff, described the Albany Movement as "a singing movement." Church music, which was an integral part of the black cultural world, became in Albany a symbol of the civil rights struggle as well. Singing had special importance at mass meetings, Reagon observed: "After the song, the differences among us would not be as great. Somehow, making a song required an expression of that which was common to us all . . . This music was like an instrument, like holding a tool in your hand."[22]

Freedom songs had been a part of the protest movement for some time, but the Albany songs carried greater emotional force and were more often rooted in the Afro-American cultural heritage than was earlier the case. Reagon noted that many of the songs which had previously been used by students were altered to make them more appropriate for a "basically adult" movement.[23] The songs of the Albany Movement were used at countless mass meetings held by SNCC in the deep South. When Sherrod drew up an outline of community organizing for the SNCC general conference in the spring of 1963, the first point on his list was to teach freedom songs.[24]

Albany songs were also given national exposure by the SNCC Freedom Singers, a fund-raising group formed in 1962 and composed largely of participants in the Albany protests. Reagon, one of the original Freedom Singers, described the songs as "more powerful than spoken conversation. They became a major way of making people who were not on the scene feel the intensity of what was happening in the South."[25]

Freedom songs popularized during the Albany protests remained with the southern movement for years, and many were adopted by protest movements elsewhere in the nation and even by protest movements outside the United States.[26] One song in particular, first used during the summer of 1962, became a favorite of SNCC workers:

> Ain't gonna let nobody turn me 'round
>   turn me 'round, turn me 'round,
> Ain't gonna let nobody turn me 'round,
> I'm gonna keep on walkin', keep on a-talkin'
> Marching up to freedom land.

Other verses specifically referred to events or personalities associated with the Albany protests, such as, "Ain't gonna let Chief Pritchett turn me 'round." Another traditional song adapted by members of SNCC was "Oh Freedom":

> No segregation, no segregation,
>   no segregation over me,
> And before I'll be a slave, I'll
>   be buried in my grave
> And go home to my Lord and be free.

Although the emotional enthusiasm displayed in the Albany protests was a source of inspiration for SNCC, the protests confronted SNCC idealists with a difficult dilemma. The demonstrations that SNCC stimulated sometimes prompted outbursts of violence and often lacked the discipline so noticeable in early student-led protest movements. The reluctance of many SNCC workers to exercise leadership endeared them to local blacks who did not wish to see their movement restrained, but it also reflected the tenuousness of SNCC's role in the expanding protest movement.

Caught between the new mood of racial anger and the reticence of the Kennedy administration to exert federal authority against southern white officials, the proponents of nonviolent direct action continued to agitate, but they became increasingly aware of both the potential for racial violence in the South and the limitations of moralistic idealism when pitted against determined opposition. With a note of resignation Sherrod observed in 1963 that "nonviolence as a way of life was a long way off for most of us"; he nevertheless argued that it was still "an invincible instrument of war." The only question was whether nonviolent activists were willing to continue to suffer.[27]

Despite Sherrod's lingering doubts, the Albany protests reinforced the confidence of SNCC workers in their organizing approaches. For the first time they had mobilized large numbers of black adults for a sustained struggle. They had demonstrated that patient efforts to win the confidence of local residents and calculated acts of civil disobedience could unleash dormant feelings of racial militancy. With greater success than in McComb, SNCC had sunk roots in the fertile soil of an emerging mass movement.

# 6. SUSTAINING THE STRUGGLE

The initial venture into McComb and the rise of the Albany Movement marked the beginning of SNCC's transition from its role as a coordinator of campus protest activities to one as the vanguard of a broadly-based mass struggle in the deep South. Although many SNCC workers continued to be involved in periodic desegregation protests, most concentrated on expanding the voter registration projects. Already a singularly militant group, SNCC workers during 1962 and 1963 became increasingly effective as community organizers. While retaining the qualities of informality, openness, and impetuousness that had made the group unique, field secretaries established permanent projects in many southern communities and gained the trust and support of local black residents. They developed a new sense of commitment and social responsibility as a result of their contacts with poor and politically unsophisticated black residents. Although SNCC remained under the nominal control of student representatives on the Coordinating Committee, its policies, values, and image were shaped by the increasingly confident and knowledgeable full-time staff.

Despite the SNCC workers' generalized distrust of authority and bureaucracy, Jim Forman took the lead in building an administrative structure that could provide the needed support for field operations without stifling spontaneity and local initiative. He recruited skilled personnel for a national fund-raising network and for communications and research departments. Despite their various backgrounds, the new staff members were attracted by the uncompromising militancy and creative enthusiasm that had marked SNCC during its first two years of existence. They brought new expertise into SNCC to complement the emerging insights of the southern struggle. In short, SNCC became an important and durable civil rights organization. Its tentative institutionalization strengthened rather than weakened the willingness of its staff to challenge existing authority and disrupt the status quo.

SNCC's third general conference, held in Atlanta on the weekend of April 27–29, 1962, marked the beginning of a period of rapid growth and change. The gathering attracted over 250 persons from 22 states. Despite the general decline in black student activism since the spring of 1960, there were still a substantial number of representatives from black colleges, especially those in urban and border state areas. Delegates also came from predominantly white universities where student political involvement had been stimulated by the black student movement. About 30 percent of the delegates and observers were white students, mostly from southern schools. In addition, the conference attracted representatives from the NAACP, CORE, SCLC, SCEF, SDS, American Friends Service Committee, Southern Regional Council, and National Lawyers Guild.[1]

SNCC staff members directed the course of deliberations, speaking with authority based on their experiences as full-time activists. They stressed the need for students to inform themselves about a broad variety of political issues. Unlike earlier SNCC conferences, neither Martin Luther King nor James Lawson spoke at the 1962 meeting, and there was little discussion of the philosophy of nonviolence. Instead, the students heard sociologist Robert Johnson proclaiming the importance of the black student movement for students around the world and lawyer Len Holt discussing the legal implications of the movement. Reflecting the broadening of SNCC's concerns, Carl and Anne Braden of SCEF and Tom Hayden of SDS conducted a workshop on civil liberties and academic freedom.

The conference's most important outcome was the adoption of a constitution reorganizing SNCC. To ensure representation from the most active local protest groups, the delegates changed the criteria for membership on the Coordinating Committee to include representatives from each group rather than from each state. In addition, to increase administrative efficiency, they established an Executive Committee to carry out the policies of the organization between general conferences. The Executive Committee was composed of eight Coordinating Committee members, SNCC's chairman and executive secretary, two advisers, and three at-large student members.

Although staff members were excluded from the formal policy-making structure, they exerted great influence over student representatives, who saw the SNCC field secretaries as models of militancy and dedication. Thus, SNCC's new structure maintained the illusion that the primary function of the organization was to coordinate campus protest activities, whereas SNCC now existed mainly to support the efforts of the ex-students who had become staff members. Illustrating this trend was the fact that, within fourteen months of their election to the Executive Committee, the three at-large members—Ruby Doris Smith of the Atlanta Committee on Appeal for Human Rights, John Lewis of the Nashville Student Central Committee, and William Mahoney of NAG—had left school to become full-time staff members.

The approximately twenty members of SNCC's staff in April 1962 were a transitional group, possessing characteristics of both the black student protest movement of prior years and the mass protest movement that would engulf the South in 1963. Interviews with thirteen staff members— eleven black, two white—shortly before the 1962 conference revealed the changing orientation of SNCC. Only three of the thirteen had attended the Raleigh conference, although most dated their involvement in the movement from the spring of 1960. Six reaffirmed their belief in nonviolence as a feasible way of life, but only three felt that most SNCC workers accepted this belief. Most staff members sensed a basic change in the nature of the southern movement, especially a loss of spontaneity and an increase in white resistance. Nine staff members saw themselves as "professionals," and all but three of the group expected to stay active in the movement "as long as possible" or "the rest of their lives."[2]

A distinguishing quality of most of the early staff members was their willingness to confront segregationist forces with civil disobedience. Status in SNCC depended partly on the number of times a worker had been arrested, which by the spring of 1962 sometimes exceeded twenty arrests. Bob Zellner, for example, could not attend the SNCC conference because of his arrest in Talladega, Alabama, after leading a student protest. A few months before, Zellner, along with SNCC workers Dion Diamond and Charles McDew, had been jailed in Baton Rouge on a charge of criminal anarchy, based on their membership in "an organization [namely SNCC] known to advocate, teach, and practice the overthrow of the state of Louisiana." After the arrest Zellner displayed a mixture of bravado and sincere moral courage which was typical of SNCC workers when he asserted that, even if "some of us have to spend ten years at hard labor, we'll come out stronger—both physically and spiritually."[3] The charge, however, was later dropped.

Diane Nash Bevel, recently married to SCLC staff member James Bevel, was also unable to attend the 1962 conference because she was scheduled to appear in a Mississippi courtroom. At the hearing on April 30, she announced that, although expecting a child in the fall, she would drop her appeal of a conviction in the previous fall for contributing to the delinquency of minors by teaching nonviolent tactics to McComb teenagers. She felt that she could no longer cooperate with Mississippi's "evil and unjust" court system, adding that her decision was the best thing she could do for her unborn child, since any black child born in Mississippi was already in prison: "I believe that if I go to jail now it may help hasten that day when my child and all children will be free—not only on the day of their birth but for all of their lives." Apparently reluctant to risk unfavorable publicity, the judge ruled that she could not abandon her appeal and suspended her sentence. Nonetheless she went to jail for ten days on a contempt charge for sitting in the white section of the courtroom.[4]

Such examples of open defiance of segregationist authorities formed the basis of SNCC's distinctive reputation for militancy. The civil rights movement included many non-SNCC activists, but there was no other group of individuals who were as uniformly willing to "put their bodies on the line." Student protesters had in fact associated themselves with SNCC because they believed that it was unlike other civil rights organizations, whose more cautious leaders and entrenched bureaucracy discouraged local initiative.

SNCC moved only gradually from its role as a gathering point for leaders of localized student movements to a role as an active stimulus of mass protest in the deep South. Students who joined SNCC's staff retained their generalized distrust of existing institutions and leaders; yet by the time of the 1962 conference they acknowledged that they could not successfully attack the deep South strongholds of racism simply through sporadic, small-scale, nonviolent protests and lengthy stays in jail. They realized that SNCC would have to become a political organization with skilled, full-time, politically sophisticated personnel—albeit with a loose and flexible structure. Just before the conference, SNCC had taken a step toward stability and increased effectiveness by moving its headquarters from a one-room office to more spacious quarters on Auburn Avenue in Atlanta.

Forman played a crucial role in making SNCC a stronger, more durable organization, capable of competing with other civil rights groups to determine the future direction of the southern struggle. As executive secretary of a group that in his view had "a generalized disdain for 'leadership,' " Forman gained the respect of other staff members by assuming responsibilities which few sought but most deemed necessary. Paul Brooks, who had recruited Forman in 1961, told him—in language that would later be unthinkable in SNCC—that the organization needed "a dictator to organize and pull strings and tell us what to do." By the spring of 1962 Forman had become assured in this role, believing that certain "non-democratic powers," similar to "the war powers of Congress," were necessary during this crucial period of SNCC's development.[5] Although SNCC workers at times resented Forman's use of his authority, his tireless and selfless devotion to the organization remained unquestioned. In a typical recollection, one SNCC worker stated that she first met Forman when, upon entering a SNCC office late at night, she discovered him alone, cleaning the toilets.

Forman recognized that SNCC would not survive merely with enthusiasm and a willingness to suffer. He saw the need for specialized skills and succeeded in convincing young people to express their discontent through office work and fund-raising as well as protest activity. Late in 1961, for example, he hired Norma Collins, a black student from Baltimore, to become SNCC's first full-time secretary. The following spring he convinced Julian Bond to forgo his final semester at Morehouse College and become

SNCC's communications director. Later he hired Dotty Miller, a white Queens College graduate who had worked for the Southern Regional Council and who subsequently married Zellner, to help Bond with publicity and the *Student Voice*. Ruby Doris Smith Robinson, who, like Forman, believed that the black struggle required hard work and discipline as well as rebelliousness, became Forman's administrative assistant. During 1962 and 1963, Forman also hired Casey Hayden and Mary E. King, two white students who had worked for a southwide campus YMCA human relations project headed by Ella Baker, to help build SNCC's publicity operations, which by the mid-1960s reached hundreds of thousands of supporters.

The Atlanta office staff not only channeled resources to SNCC projects but also became the center of SNCC's nationwide fund-raising network. When SNCC initially became involved in voter registration, staff members expected that financial support would come from foundations or through Harry Belafonte's fund-raising efforts. Their hopes were only partially realized. The Voter Education Project (VEP), financed by contributions from the Taconic Foundation, Field Foundation, Stern Family Fund, and other tax-exempted organizations, was created early in 1962, but SNCC did not begin to receive money from it until June. Even then, SNCC received a much smaller share of VEP funds than did the other major civil rights organizations. Of over half a million dollars distributed by VEP during 1962 and 1963, less than $24,000 went to SNCC, despite the fact that it recruited the largest staff of full-time voter registration workers.[6] The low level of VEP contributions to SNCC was largely the result of SNCC's having chosen to work in difficult areas which were not likely to produce the large number of registered black voters needed by VEP to justify continued expenditures.

Rather than relying primarily on VEP and other institutional sources, SNCC began in June 1962 to develop its own network of financial supporters by opening its first northern offices in Chicago and Detroit. Later in 1962 SNCC opened offices in New York, Washington, Philadelphia, and Cleveland. In addition, SNCC encouraged northern supporters to form "Friends of SNCC" groups, which organized appearances by SNCC workers at fund-raising parties and rallies. To direct these northern operations, Forman hired two white activists, Constancia (Dinky) Romilly, a Sarah Lawrence graduate and daughter of writer Jessica Mitford, and Betty Garmen, a former Berkeley student and SDS leader.

SNCC's efforts to build northern support led to conflicts with SCLC leaders because, as Forman reported, SNCC workers had to "correct the illusion ... that we were an arm of SCLC and [were] being run and supported financially by them." At a 1961 meeting with SCLC leaders, SNCC representatives had pointed out that SCLC received an $11,000 contribution from a union which had earmarked one-third for the southern student movement. As Forman recalled, Baker "in her principled and very gently direct manner" questioned the propriety of SCLC keeping the funds intended for students. Soon afterward, SNCC received a check from SCLC for $1000.[7]

Even as SNCC began to garner national publicity, its financial resources remained meager in comparison to those of the NAACP or SCLC. The organization was able to expand its operations so rapidly only because of the willingness of staff members to work without pay or for token wages. The standard salary of SNCC field secretaries was $10 per week, or $9.64 after deductions. Workers with families received larger salaries, but few staff members could have survived on their salaries alone had they not lived with black residents in areas where they were organizing or in "freedom houses" rented by SNCC. SNCC's wage scale was an essential element in its uniqueness, since it made the organization less vulnerable to financial pressures than were other civil rights organizations. Forman wrote that SNCC's salaries made it "impossible for anyone to develop a vested interest in the survival of the organization."[8]

The belief among northern sympathizers that contributions to SNCC would actually reach the front lines of the struggle rather than being used for office expenses and administrative salaries increased the contributions, which enabled SNCC to become solvent despite its rapid growth. Starting with a deficit of over $10,000 on June 1, 1962, SNCC raised almost $50,000 during the remainder of the year, ending with a slight surplus. During 1963, SNCC's income increased to $309,000.[9] The rising level of support enabled SNCC by August 1963 to establish projects in more than a dozen Mississippi communities as well as in southwest Georgia; Selma, Alabama; Danville, Virginia; Pine Bluff, Arkansas; and several other places. By that time, SNCC's staff included 12 office workers, 60 field secretaries, and 121 full-time volunteers.

As SNCC increased the size of its staff, it attracted activists whose backgrounds and attitudes set them apart from the sit-in participants of 1960. The new activists were more likely to have undergone a process of radicalization even before joining SNCC. Unlike the politically conventional sit-in leaders of 1960, who joined with a large proportion of their fellow students in protesting lunch counter segregation, many of those who joined the staff during 1962 and 1963 came from a small minority of campus dissenters who were seeking major social changes. Indeed, after 1961 the act of joining SNCC itself indicated a willingness on the part of students already engaged in protest activity to take the further step of breaking previous social ties and becoming revolutionaries. Association with SNCC meant not only a willingness to be arrested but also a desire to identify with oppressed people, to abandon or postpone middle-class career plans, and to take the risk of assuming new tasks. These goals were symbolized in the SNCC workers' typical dress of blue jeans and work shirts or farmer's overalls.

Before joining SNCC's full-time staff, activists generally had participated in sustained protest movements or had acquired unconventional attitudes through involvement in campus activist organizations. Despite their resulting predisposition to see their participation in SNCC as a logical outgrowth of these previous experiences, many staff members made the decision to join the staff only after a sudden realization that they had become too deeply involved in the civil rights movement to return to normal lives. The experiences of four SNCC staff members who joined after 1961 illustrate SNCC's emerging character and the tendency for impetuous involvement in protest activity to lead to a long-term commitment to the movement.

Bill Hall, born in 1939 in Harlem, attended private school in New York and served in the marines before enrolling at Howard University in 1959 as a premedical student. Though not a participant in the sit-ins of 1960, he approved of them. His personal involvement in protests began in 1962 at the urging of a girlfriend: "If I wanted to be with her, we were going to be on the line together picketing." Hall began attending NAG meetings and was impressed with the articulateness of its leaders, particularly Bill Mahoney and Stokely Carmichael. "They were bright in a way that very few people attempted to challenge them," he recalled. With other NAG members, Hall participated in weekend forays into Maryland to aid the Cambridge SNCC affiliate headed by Gloria Richardson. As activists discovered in many communities with local movements, Hall found the civil rights struggle beginning to consume all his energies and becoming the center of his life. His grades suffered, with the result that he was not accepted to medical school. Instead, he enrolled as a graduate student in zoology while continuing his NAG activities. He intended to pursue the objective of studying medicine but also felt an increasing sense of responsibility to the Cambridge blacks who endangered their own livelihoods to join the movement. When finally admitted to medical school, Hall decided to work in Cambridge full-time until the start of medical classes. But when the new school year began, he found that he could no longer leave SNCC: "I just became so involved, so much in love with the people."[10]

John Perdew, born in 1941, grew up in a Denver neighborhood that was "middle-class, professional, all-white . . . liberal in the sense that we were Democratic, talked about the ideals of the Constitution: justice for all, equality, and so forth." The son of a college professor, Perdew was a junior at Harvard in 1963 when he heard that SNCC was recruiting white students to work in Georgia. Because he "wanted to do something adventurous and different" that summer, he drove with friends to Albany, Georgia. "I grew up with only an abstract, intellectual concept of race relations," he explained. "I had no idea at all of any kind of violence and daily oppression that millions of people went through. That's the way I went into SNCC thinking. But then I got my ass kicked." In August 1963 Perdew participated in a civil rights march, was arrested, and spent the next three weeks in jail. After his release, Perdew went to Americus, Georgia, where he was arrested again during a demonstration. Although he had known that he faced arrest in the South, he was shocked when he was charged with multiple offenses, including unlawful assembly, disorderly conduct, and insurrection. Because the insurrection charge was a capital offense, he remained in jail for three months until the Reconstruction statute was declared unconstitutional by a federal court, and he was released on bail. By that time Perdew no longer wanted to return to Harvard, and soon he joined SNCC's field staff in Sumpter County, Georgia.[11]

For Johnny Wilson, participation in the protest movement began late in 1961 when he was still a student at an all-black high school in Princess Anne, Maryland. Upon hearing that a freedom ride campaign had been launched against segregated restaurants in Maryland, he hitchhiked to Chestertown, about seventy miles from his home, to join the riders. "To show you how naive I was," he recalled, "the first policeman I saw, I asked him where were the freedom riders . . . I ended up in jail and the freedom riders were gone when I got there." After entering Maryland State College, Wilson organized the Students' Appeal for Equality, an affiliate of SNCC. He attended SNCC meetings as the college group's representative, then joined the staff as a full-time field secretary, working in Danville and Grenada, Mississippi. For Wilson, SNCC provided a setting where his discontent could be expressed. "SNCC people exemplified a sense of freedom that I think every black person wants to have," he commented. "It's a sense of saying, Fuck it. If we want to do it, we'll do it."[12]

Fannie Lou Hamer was forty-four when she first learned about SNCC at a 1962 voter registration meeting in a church in Ruleville, Mississippi. The youngest of twenty children of black sharecroppers, she had grown up in Sunflower County unaware that black people had the right to register and vote. Yet when she heard Moses, Forman, and Reginald Robinson call upon blacks at the meeting to go to the courthouse and register, she volunteered, reasoning that there was no point to be scared: "The only thing they could do to me was kill me and it seemed like they'd been trying to do that a little bit at a time ever since I could remember." Hamer was arrested while attempting to register in Indianola, and after her release on bail the owner of the plantation where she lived told her to withdraw her name from the registration roles or leave. Hamer left that night. A few days later, shots were fired into the friend's house where she was staying, forcing her to leave the county for several months. But Hamer did not give up her efforts to vote, despite repeated threats and a severe beating in the Winona, Mississippi, jail which left her permanently injured. In 1963 she became a member of the SNCC's staff, explaining that she had become "just really tired" of what she had to endure. "We just got to stand up now as Negroes for ourselves and for our freedom, and if it don't do me any good, I do know the young people it will do good."[13]

SNCC staff members brought into the organization diverse attitudes drawn from their increasingly varied backgrounds, but at the same time a growing radicalism began to emerge from their intense involvement in the southern black struggle. Day-to-day interactions with each other and with politically awakened blacks in communities with SNCC projects made staff members more willing to look to their own experiences in the struggle as a source of alternative values. Despite the fact that most had attended college, SNCC workers strongly believed that their role was to encourage blacks to participate in the direction of the local movements regardless of their level of education. Techniques for mobilizing black communities were developed by field secretaries in different areas of the South through a process of trial and error, but a distinctive common element in all these techniques was a recognition of the importance of overcoming the psychological heritage of racial oppression through patient efforts to develop local leadership and through public displays of racial militancy.

The two most important testing grounds for SNCC's community organizing approaches were southwest Georgia and Mississippi. SNCC's work in these areas in 1962–1963 reflected differences in the personalities of the two project directors, Charles Sherrod and Bob Moses. Sherrod infused his work with the religious zeal of a southern black preacher and with the idealism of SNCC's early years, whereas Moses, the northern intellectual, evinced a patient pragmatism and an overriding commitment to humanist values. Sherrod was influenced by his past success in building a mass protest movement in Albany using civil disobedience as a stimulus. Moses was influenced by his discovery in McComb that direct action was difficult if not infeasible in many areas and that desegregation protests could harm voter registration efforts.

Sherrod's approach was defined in a SNCC report of early 1962 on the subject of sending workers into the rural areas near Albany. The group intended "to engage in a battle for men's minds," Sherrod wrote. They would lift the "veil of fear from the eyes of the people and provide in its place the motivation to become responsible citizens." The basic premise of SNCC's operations was that its own workers "cannot and should not do the work themselves; it is desirable to involve local citizens and groups as much as possible."[14]

The first task faced by Sherrod and other SNCC workers in organizing in rural Georgia was to find black residents who were willing to provide assistance. As in Albany and elsewhere, a SNCC organizer's skills included the ability to identify local leaders who could provide a foothold in the black community. Sherrod described one such leader in 1961: "Because of [D. U. Pullum's] efforts to vote and encourage others to do the same, he was beaten, robbed, and his machinery burned . . . He is the personification of resistance to the powers that be in Terrell County . . . he almost begged on bended knees for students to come to Terrell to get people registered to vote . . . He has a fanatical trust in the student movement."[15]

When the first group of SNCC voter registration workers arrived in Lee County in June 1962, they were offered a place to stay by "Mama Dolly" Raines, described by Sherrod as "a gray-haired old lady of about seventy who can pick more cotton, 'slop more pigs,' plow more ground, chop more wood, and do a hundred more things better than the best farmer in the area." In nearby Terrell County, other SNCC workers lived with Mrs. Carolyn Daniels. "There is always a 'mama,'" Sherrod noted. "She is usually a militant woman in the community, outspoken, understanding and willing to catch hell, having already caught her share."[16]

As in Albany, Sherrod continued in rural Georgia to stress the symbolic importance of the actions of his staff. His recognition of the need to resist white authorities publicly was demonstrated when a voter registration meeting in Mount Olive Church in Sasser was suddenly invaded in July 1962 by the county sheriff, Z. T. Mathews, and other white men. A reporter, Pat Watters, described the scene. The congregation grew silent in fear until Sherrod began to lead them in the Lord's Prayer. Then they "began to sing, faces calmer now, voices weak at first, but gaining strength, 'We Are Climbin' Jacob's Lad-der.'" Sheriff Mathews interrupted the singing to announce that whites were "a little fed up with this registering business," adding that "Negras down here have been happy for a hundred years." While the sheriff was haranguing them, the blacks began to hum "We Shall Overcome." Soon the humming became words, at which point the whites retreated. "Sherrod prayed once more," Watters continued, "loud enough to be heard by the whites outside the door: 'As we come to the close of this meeting, we thank Thee. Hear our white brothers trying to understand themselves, explain themselves. May we be able to communicate to them what we are trying to do. Which is not to destroy, but to build a community where all can live in self-respect and human dignity.'"[17]

Sherrod's desire to free southern blacks from their fear of whites played a part in his decision to use interracial teams of civil rights workers. At first he attempted to recruit southern whites, but when no volunteers were found, he hired northern white students. Although aware of the need for local black support, he concluded that the use of white voter registration workers was necessary to "strike at the very root of segregation . . . the idea that white is superior. That idea has eaten into the minds of the people, black and white. We have to break this image. We can only do this if they see white and black working together, side by side, the white man no more and no less than his black brother, but human beings together."[18]

In the spring of 1963, Sherrod's staff of eleven included five northern white students; three of the six black staff members had also attended northern universities. Many of these staff members were students of religion or were motivated by religious beliefs. SNCC field secretaries in southwest Goergia, aware of the experimental nature of their project, were determined to demonstrate that interracial idealism could work. Peggy Dammon, a student from Boston University who arrived during the summer of 1962, remarked: "We've been singing long enough about 'Black and white together.' We have to practice it, live it, and as we do we make real a certain kind of dream."[19]

Black field secretaries apparently accepted their white counterparts, as did many black residents who opened their homes to white workers. Perdew recalled that acceptance was based on "the fact that you had gone to jail and knew what they was like." Ralph Allen, a white student from Trinity College, described his reception by black residents as the most rewarding experience of his life—"the grin of a teenage girl when I tell her how to say something in French, a little kid who ran from me when I first came and now comes up and hugs me, kids coming to bring you things when you're in jail."[20]

Yet the whites on the Georgia staff encountered special problems because of their race. Anne Braden reported in December 1962 that white students in SNCC did not have "an easy time communicating with Negroes who have known whites only as oppressors. (One says if he ever writes a book about his experiences, he'll call it 'Don't Call Me Mister.')" Perdew found that poor blacks were "frequently afraid of me as a white (sometimes they will not answer the door, other times they will agree to everything the canvasser says in order to get rid of him)." Perdew, who was probably the only white to live in the black community of Americus, recalled that he was "like a man from Mars . . . I talked with a different accent . . . a different language. I was from Harvard which was a world away . . . So there was a distance. There was definitely a barrier there, not so much hostility, as just an unfamiliarity. And I had a lot of adjustments to make even understanding people."[21]

The difficulties encountered by the small group of whites were minor in comparison to those that would arise in 1964 when large numbers of white volunteers entered black communities. Many of the whites who worked in southwest Georgia were able to overcome the problems of interracial communication. Nor did their presence prevent the development of local black leaders. A SNCC worker noticed the "increased sureness" of black leaders after SNCC had been active for several months in Lee County: "They were always impressive personalities whose bearing and eloquence . . . matched the quality of their heroism, but now they are developed and experienced leaders. Lee County is the most remarkable example I have seen of the catalytic action that SNCC's presence can have in starting a community toward using its own undeveloped potential."[22]

Given the enormous white resistance to civil rights reforms in southwest Georgia, the SNCC staff succeeded as well as could have been expected, registering a few hundred black voters during 1962 and 1963. But Sherrod's conviction that the use of white students did not detract from efforts to develop local black leadership became less convincing to other SNCC workers as the movement stimulated the growth of black racial consciousness. Sherrod's commitment to interracial and religious ideals was a clear expression of the ideas expressed in SNCC's original statement of purpose, but it contrasted with the trend in the most important SNCC effort of the first half of the 1960s, the Mississippi project.

Although no less committed to interracialism than Sherrod, Moses placed greater emphasis on the development of local black leadership in Mississippi. He had no philosophical objections to using white field secretaries, but he believed that the high degree of white resistance in Mississippi made the use of whites counterproductive. A spring 1963 SNCC report noted that it was "too dangerous for whites to participate in the project in Mississippi—too dangerous for them and too dangerous for the Negroes who would be working with them." The report cited the increased problem of "obtaining a place to meet" and of "convincing local leaders . . . to take an active stand" when white civil rights workers were involved.[23]

In addition to these pragmatic concerns about white field secretaries, Moses stressed the importance of recruiting young black Mississippians "who identified with SNCC . . . [and] with each other in terms . . . of being from Mississippi and more or less thinking that their job, and even their life's work, would be to work to make some sense out of living in Mississippi." He believed that young blacks, unlike their elders, "would not be responsible economically to any sector of the white community and . . . would be able to act as free agents."[24]

Moses began rapidly to expand his staff early in the summer of 1962. He arranged for a group of blacks to receive a week of training in voter registration techniques at the Highlander Folk School, since conducting such workshops in Mississippi was deemed too dangerous.[25] Among the first group of field secretaries to begin work were Hollis Watkins and Curtis Hayes, two McComb high school students who had been arrested in demonstrations the previous fall. Early in July, they went to Hattiesburg, about seventy miles from McComb. Soon afterward, Sam Block, a vocational college student from Cleveland, Mississippi, initiated a voter registration drive in Greenwood in the Mississippi Delta, where he was later joined by another Mississippi native, Willie Peacock, a graduate of Rust College.

By the end of the summer Charles McLaurin had opened an office in Ruleville, the home of Senator James O. Eastland, an ardent foe of civil rights legislation. By the following spring, six offices had been opened in Mississippi, with a staff of twenty black field secretaries. Only three were from outside the state—Moses, Bevel, and Charles Cobb, son of a Springfield, Massachusetts, Congregational minister and a former Howard University student.

SNCC field secretaries in Mississippi worked under the auspices of the Council of Federated Organizations (COFO), a coalition of civil rights organizations formed in 1962 partly to prevent conflict between the different groups over the distribution of VEP funds. Moses was named director of COFO's voter registration work, and David Dennis of CORE was chosen as his assistant. Aaron Henry of the NAACP was elected president. From the beginning, COFO's staff was composed largely of SNCC personnel, and SNCC provided most of the money for its operations.

Moses concentrated SNCC's work in Mississippi in the western part of the state, an area where the majority of the population was black and where there had been, he noted in 1963, "a tradition of Negro organizations." Conceding that the area was the stronghold of the White Citizens Council, a segregationist group, Moses nevertheless asserted that it would someday be possible for blacks there to elect a black man to Congress, an act "which would have tremendous symbolic and political value."[26]

Like Sherrod, Moses stressed the importance of eliminating black fears that had resulted from a history of enduring violent racial oppression. "You dig into yourself and the community to wage psychological warfare," he commented in 1963, "you combat your own fears about beatings, shootings and possible mob violence; you stymie, by your mere physical presence, anxious fear of the Negro community . . . you organize, pound by pound, small bands of people . . . you create a small striking force." Moses himself established a model of quiet courage that became a distinguishing trait of SNCC organizers. McComb resident Ernest Nobles, who saw SNCC workers return to the town in which they had received an early setback, recalled having to hide Moses many times in his dry cleaning establishment. "Poor Bob took a lot of beatings," he remembered. "I just couldn't understand what Bob Moses was. Sometimes I think he was Moses in the Bible. He pioneered the way for black people in McComb . . . He had more guts than any one man I've ever known."[27]

Mississippi staff members knew they had to overcome the concern of local blacks that SNCC workers were, in Block's words, "only going to stir up trouble . . . and then leave." Thus, when Block had his first encounter with the local sheriff soon after arriving in Greenwood, he made a public show of his willingness to stand up to white authority:[28]

> The sheriff came up to me and he asked me, he said, "Nigger, where you from?" I told him, "Well, I'm a native Mississippian." He said, "Yeh, yeh, I know that, but where you from? I don't know where you from . . . I know you ain't from here, cause I know every nigger and his mammy." I said, "Well, you know all the niggers, do you know any colored people?" He got angry. He spat in my face and walked. So he came back and turned around and told me, "I don't want to see you in town any more. The best thing you better do is pack your clothes and get out and don't never come back no more." I said, "Well, sheriff, if you don't want to see me here, I think the best thing for you to do is pack your clothes and leave, get out of town, cause I'm here to stay, I came here to do a job and this is my intention, I'm going to do this job."

Despite such displays of defiance, SNCC's work was often crippled by arrests and violent attacks. McLaurin reported in September 1962 that after three shots were fired into the home of a Ruleville resident, wounding two young women, SNCC workers "could not get a person to come to the meetings." Local blacks felt that if SNCC "had not come to Ruleville all this wouldn't have happened." Through the rest of the fall, McLaurin and other SNCC workers tried to regain the blacks' confidence by going "house to house asking them about everyday problems, we would carry them to the store downtown, help pick cotton and cut wood."[29]

Although the tenacity of SNCC workers in Mississippi became legendary and their identification with the poor ultimately won them the support of many black residents, the Mississippi voter registration effort made slow progress. Constant harassment and intimidation hampered the project. A group of armed whites attacked the voter registration office in Greenwood in August 1962, forcing SNCC workers to flee through a second-story window. After police harassed their black landlord, SNCC workers were forced to search for new quarters. For the rest of the year, SNCC conducted what Moses called "holding operations," convincing local residents that they were going to stay. According to Moses, "the deeper the fear, the deeper the problems in the community, the longer you have to stay to convince them."[30]

In October 1962, the county supervisors of Leflore, where Greenwood was located, voted to withdraw from the federal program which supplied surplus food to thousands of black residents. SNCC workers saw the action as an intimidation attempt, designed to weaken further the voter registration effort. Cobb and McLaurin noted that the surplus food was "the only way many Negroes make it from cotton season to cotton season. If this is taken away from them, they have nothing at all. The success of our voter registration program depends on the protection we can offer the individual while he is waiting for his one small vote [to] mean something. It doesn't take much to tide [over] the rural Mississippi Negro, but the commodities are vital."[31]

SNCC organized a massive food drive involving its growing number of northern affiliates. This campaign not only greatly increased awareness in the North of the problems of Mississippi blacks but also marked the beginning of a shift away from Moses' policy of relying entirely on local black leadership. On December 28 two black students from Michigan State University, Ivanhoe Donaldson and Benjamin Taylor, were arrested in Clarksdale, Mississippi, while sleeping in a truck filled with over a thousand pounds of food and medicine for Leflore County. Although they insisted that the truck was carrying nothing illegal, the students were charged with violating Mississippi's drug laws. Despite the arrests, SNCC continued to bring large quantities of food, medicine, and clothing into the county.[32]

The ability of SNCC workers to provide food for Leflore County residents aided their efforts to overcome the reticence of blacks to register. "Whenever we were able to get a little something to give to a hungry family," Moses explained, "we also talked about how they ought to register." The food was "identified in the minds of everyone as food for those who want to be free, and the minimum requirement for freedom is identified as registration to vote." Moses also commented that the food distribution helped SNCC gain "an image in the Negro community of providing direct aid, not just 'agitation.' "[33]

By February 1963 the results of the food distribution program were becoming apparent. Blacks in groups of several hundred each were attempting to register at the Greenwood courthouse. The increased activity led to incidents of intimidation. On February 20, following a threatening telephone call to the SNCC office, four nearby black businesses were burned. Two days later Greenwood police arrested Block and charged him with "making statements calculated to incite the breach of the peace." The intimidation efforts were not successful, however, and more than one hundred people went to the city hall in Greenwood on February 25 to protest Block's trial, while several more hundreds attended a mass meeting that night. The following day, black residents again stood at the county courthouse seeking to register. "This is a new dimension for a voting program in Mississippi," Moses concluded, "Negroes have been herded to the polls before by white people, but have never stood ... in protest at the seat of power in the iceberg of Mississippi politics. Negroes who couldn't read and write stood in line to tell the registrar they still wanted to vote, that they didn't have a chance to go to school when they were small and anyway Mr. John Jones can't read and write either and *he* votes."[34]

On February 28, Moses left a meeting at the Greenwood SNCC office to drive to Greenville with SNCC worker Jimmy Travis and Randolph Blackwell of VEP. Three white men trailed them until no other cars were in sight and then pulled alongside. Travis, who was driving, recalled that he thought the white men "were going to throw something at us or try to run us off the road. I felt something burn my ear and I knew what they were doing. They had opened fire on us . . . it sounded like a machine gun. I yelled out that I had been shot, as I let go of the wheel. Moses grabbed hold of the wheel and brought the car to a stop on the shoulder of the highway."[35] The group was able to drive on and get medical help for Travis, who was shot in the head and shoulder. Doctors in Jackson who removed the bullet from Travis' head reported that he would have died instantly had the bullets penetrated his body with more force.

The day after the shooting, the voter registration effort in Greenwood took a new direction. While continuing to rely on a black staff of organizers, Moses announced plans to bring civil rights workers from outside the state to the city for prolonged demonstrations. Thus, having attempted to build an indigenous movement in Mississippi, Moses now realized the need to return to the strategy developed during the freedom rides of using militant protests to attract national attention and to prod the federal government into intervening on behalf of the civil rights movement. After being arrested with Moses and other SNCC workers for leading demonstrators to the Greenwood courthouse on March 28, Forman explained that the imprisonment of the civil rights workers would "dramatize to the nation and to the world that the black man does not even have the right to *try* to be an American citizen in some parts of our so-called democracy."[36]

When SNCC held its fourth general conference on April 12–14, 1963, an important transition had been completed. SNCC's field staff, particularly in southwest Georgia and Mississippi, had encountered severe opposition but also gained the confidence of many local blacks. They had adjusted to the conditions which they found in the deep South and had begun to formulate new ideas with which to sustain their struggle.

Sherrod outlined some of these ideas for the conference when he advised organizers to "acknowledge standing leadership," even when that leadership was more conservative than the community it led. Organizers should use local churches and black newspapers to communicate with residents and should develop personal relations by working with youth groups, including gangs, and living with local families. Finances should be arranged locally: "when 'push comes to shove,' we are willing to pick cotton, scrub floors, wash cars and windows, babysit, etc. for food and lodging." In addition, Sherrod urged organizers to teach freedom songs to local residents.[37]

Moses drew more far-reaching implications than Sherrod from SNCC's work in the deep South. He expressed doubt at the conference whether

Mississippi blacks would "gain the vote rapidly enough to win electoral victories before they lost their jobs and were forced to move because of automation and the lack of educational opportunities." The black struggle would therefore have to go beyond the Kennedy administration's goal of forcing state officials to apply registration laws equally. Instead, since white illiterates often voted and blacks were denied equal education opportunities, "the country owed blacks, either the right to vote as a literate or the right to learn how to read and write *now*."[38]

Moses' speech signaled the beginning of a "one man, one vote" campaign, which was rooted in SNCC's emphasis on encouraging even poorly educated blacks to participate in the political process. SNCC's radicalism was initially defined by the willingness of its staff to suffer hardship in order to speed the pace of racial change. By the spring of 1963 SNCC was beginning to move toward a different radicalism, motivated by its efforts to mobilize poor and illiterate blacks in the deep South. Although SNCC members were not yet able to define this new radicalism precisely, they were ready to suggest some of the limitations of conventional liberal civil rights strategies.

SNCC demonstrated during 1962 and 1963 that its organizing tactics could mobilize large numbers of blacks, and this achievement gave staff members confidence to re-examine their goals. SNCC's survival, Forman wrote at the time of the 1963 conference, "was no longer in question . . . we had achieved more than a certain sense of organizational security. The meeting was permeated by an intense comradeship, born out of sacrifice and suffering and a commitment to the future, and out of knowledge that we were indeed challenging the political structure of the country, and out of a feeling that our basic strength rested in the energy, love, and warmth of the group. The band of sisters and brothers, in a circle of trust, felt complete at last."[39]

*Stokely Carmichael leaving Jackson, Mississippi, courthouse after arrest during 1961 freedom ride*

*Reginald Robinson, Bill Hansen, Ruth Harris, Charles Jones, Cordell Reagon, and Ruby Doris Robinson at SNCC workshop in Shiloh, Alabama, church, 1962*

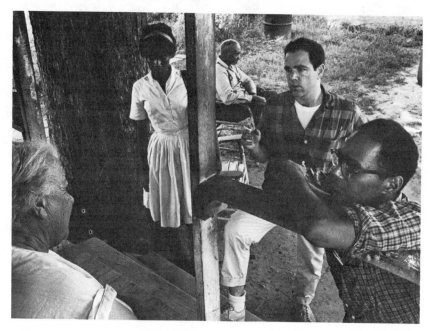

*Robert Moses (extreme right) and other SNCC workers urging black residents of Rule-
ville, Mississippi, to register, ca. 1963*

COME...TOGETHER
Let Us Build A
Non-Violent World

*Frank Smith, Robert Moses, and Willie Peacock at SNCC office in Greenwood, Missis-
sippi, the day before it was gutted by fire, 1963*

# 7. MARCH ON WASHINGTON

During 1962 and 1963 SNCC workers became increasingly critical of the Kennedy administration, charging federal officials with hypocrisy for failing to back their expressions of support for civil rights with the enormous forces at their disposal. The administration's claim that new civil rights legislation was needed to give it the authority to protect civil rights workers and prospective black voters did not convince SNCC activists, who were willing to engage in civil disobedience to demonstrate their own commitment to egalitarian ideals.

Despite the caustic nature of SNCC criticisms of the Kennedy administration, staff members still saw the federal government as a force that could be prodded to act on their behalf. The increasingly militant tone of their entreaties revealed disappointment in the government's refusal to come to their aid forthrightly and in its failure to acknowledge the priority of social justice over political expediency. Nonetheless, when SNCC's criticisms of the administration's civil rights policies came into public view during the March on Washington in August 1963, their tone was moderated by the organization's continuing desire to remain part of the dominant national civil rights coalition. A process of disillusionment with the prevailing liberal strategies of social change was already well advanced, but SNCC workers were not yet ready to offer a coherent alternative worldview distilled from their experiences in the southern struggle.

The demands of SNCC activists for federal protection of civil rights workers in the South led to a new combativeness in SNCC's relations with the administration. This change became evident early in 1962 when SNCC responded to the arrest in Baton Rouge, Louisiana, of three of its workers on criminal anarchy charges by demonstrating against the arrests in the nation's capital. On February 29, NAG members picketed the Washington home of Louisiana Senator Allen J. Ellender. Two weeks later, Charles Sherrod, Bill Hansen, Reginald Robinson, and several NAG members sat in at the office of Attorney General Robert Kennedy. Department officials, hoping to avoid an embarrassing incident, did not order the arrest of the group, although a few days later participants in a sit-in were forceably removed from the office on wheelchairs.[1]

The sit-in at the Justice Department established a pattern for later SNCC actions, which were intended to embarrass the Kennedy administration by exposing what SNCC workers considered to be federal complicity in southern racial oppression. In May 1962, for example, following the conviction of Bob Moses and Charles McDew on charges of disorderly conduct during the McComb protests, SNCC suggested that Attorney General Kennedy go to Mississippi "to witness the travesty of Justice taking place" in that state. Similarly, when students in the Jackson Nonviolent Movement were harassed by local police, SNCC field secretary Paul Brooks suggested that they demonstrate at the post office, believing that city police would not make arrests on federal property. Four students were arrested anyway, and SNCC sent a telegram to Robert Kennedy asserting that if the United States government could not guarantee the right to protest on its own property, "then you must be considered a party to these violations of constitutionally guaranteed civil rights."[2]

During July 1962, several attacks on participants in the Albany desegregation protests prompted further SNCC appeals for federal help. Following assaults on Hansen in the county jail and on Marion King as she tried to deliver packages to jailed protesters, SNCC telegraphed Robert Kennedy, "When will the federal government act to halt the Nazi-like forces operating against democracy in southwest Georgia?" Another telegram to Kennedy demanded prosecution of the policeman responsible for the attack on King, explaining, "We expect the federal government to halt the rising tide of police brutality in southwest Georgia." In December, Albany Movement leaders drove to Washington to meet with Assistant Attorney General Burke Marshall to discuss "the death of the First Amendment in Albany."[3]

SNCC's voter registration activities in rural Georgia and Mississippi brought still stronger criticisms of the federal government. Field secretaries in these states believed that they and local blacks seeking to register were entitled to federal protection, since their activities were clearly legal and supported by the Kennedy administration. Organizers in the rural South not only faced greater resistance than activists in large communities such as Albany but also lacked the safety of numbers, for few rural blacks were willing at first to risk association with civil rights workers. There was often a tone of desperation in SNCC's pleas for federal intervention in these areas. When McDew asked President Kennedy to send federal marshals to Greenwood, Mississippi, to protect voter registration workers, he warned that without such protection "there is great possibility of more Emmett Till cases"—referring to the lynching of a black youth in the Delta in 1955. In September 1962 McDew urged prominent political leaders to press for a Justice Department investigation of the killing of an unidentified black man whose body was found in Goodman, Mississippi, and to request investigations of attacks on civil rights workers in Georgia and Mississippi. "A wave of terror and Klan reactivity is sweeping over southwest Georgia and Mississippi," McDew asserted, and "we cannot protect our field secretaries and potential voters without direct intervention of federal government."[4]

SNCC workers recognized that the federal government was not likely to respond to many of their appeals for assistance, yet they also knew that their requests would dramatize the situation and that such help was within the power of the White House. As SNCC field secretary Charles McLaurin wrote to President Kennedy in September 1962 regarding the shooting of the two young black women in Ruleville: "The people of Ruleville . . . wonder why protection can be given to people 6,000 miles away and not be given to American citizens in the South."[5]

The dilemma of SNCC workers in the deep South who needed federal help but recognized that such help could not always be expected was illustrated by incidents in southwest Georgia. Sherrod, speaking to a group of blacks in a Sumpter County church in December 1962, assured them that the federal government was "as close as the telephone." But a short time later, after the deputy town marshal of Sasser, Georgia, was acquitted by an all-white jury of charges that he had chased SNCC workers out of town, Sherood reacted with a bitter indictment of the administration: "What are we to tell the people down here? Must we die before the federal government stops compromising with bigots?" SNCC workers were particularly angered during the trial by the behavior of Justice Department observers who were friendly with opposing lawyers. According to the workers, government lawyers asked that black witnesses be "Uncle Toms" and requested that Prathia Hall, a black SNCC worker, remove her hat in court so as not to offend local residents. Sherrod placed the responsibility for losing the case against the deputy marshal squarely on the Kennedy brothers, whose failure to throw their weight behind the case was a "black mark" for the administration: "If we are murdered in our attempts, our blood will be on your hands; you stand in the judgment of God and of our people."[6]

Although Moses, like Sherrod, was increasingly disturbed by the failure of the federal government to protect civil rights workers, he remained convinced that appeals for federal assistance could be successful. Moses maintained friendly relations with Assistant Attorney General John Doar and other Justice Department officials. Unlike FBI agents, young Justice Department lawyers were "sympathetic" to the movement and played "a positive role" in Mississippi, Moses believed. He argued that a distinction should be made "between the people who work for the Justice Department and the policies of the Kennedy administration," since the policies were subject to political considerations rather than "the principled issue of the right to vote." Moses was particularly critical of Kennedy's judicial appointments in the South, because "one district judge can do away with two years' work and can seriously delay the work of the Justice Department."[7]

In January 1963, Moses and six members of his staff, along with William Higgs, a white lawyer from Jackson, filed suit in the District of Columbia against Attorney General Kennedy and FBI Director J. Edgar Hoover to force them to prosecute southern officials responsible for acts of violence and intimidation against civil rights workers. The complaint, recounting the many assaults and arrests of SNCC workers during 1961 and 1962, noted that Kennedy and Hoover had "been repeatedly requested by plaintiffs and others [to] arrest, imprison, and institute prosecutions against all persons who willfully subject any inhabitant of any State to the deprivation of any rights, privileges or immunities secured or protected by the Constitution or laws of the United States."[8]

Although Moses probably was not surprised when the suit failed, the legal action demonstrated his increasing emphasis on building public support for federal intervention in Mississippi. Despite his previous desire to allow black Mississippians to solve their problems alone, the constant harassments faced by the civil rights workers convinced him that federal protection was necessary to achieve a significant breakthrough in the Mississippi voter registration effort. This was clearly evident in the aftermath of the shooting of Jimmy Travis in February 1963, when Moses participated in a series of demonstrations in Greenwood designed to bring about forceful federal intervention.

During March and April 1963, Greenwood was the scene of protests involving not only the Mississippi staff but SNCC workers from elsewhere in the South. As activists arrived, white acts of violence intensified. On March 6 a shotgun blast shattered the window of a car, parked in front of the SNCC office, containing Block, Peacock, and two others from Greenwood. Later in the month, the SNCC office was set on fire; all of the office equipment was demolished, although most of the records were saved. On March 26, shots were fired into the home of Dewey Greene, father of two SNCC workers. After leading a march to the Greenwood courthouse on March 28, Moses, Forman, and other SNCC workers were arrested and charged with disorderly conduct. Hoping to force the Justice Department to file suit against local officials to gain their release, eight SNCC workers refused bail and remained in jail for over a week.

The Justice Department responded to the situation by seeking a temporary restraining order to force the release of the jailed workers and to prevent Greenwood officials from interfering further in the voter registration campaign. On April 4, a compromise was reached in which the request for a temporary restraining order was dropped in exchange for the release of the civil rights workers. Although the Justice Department continued to seek a permanent injunction against Greenwood officials, Moses felt the compromise still left the basic issues unresolved. Doar, who directed the negotiations with Greenwood officials and who was the Justice Department official most trusted by SNCC workers, recalled that Moses "was really depressed" after his release, feeling that SNCC had "finally created a situation which if it was followed to its logical conclusion would have led to federal marshals being in Leflore County" and that the administration's response was to avoid a decisive confrontation with Mississippi officials.[9]

The SNCC workers' increasing disillusionment with the Kennedy administration's policies was made more poignant by their belief that their civil rights goals were the same as those of the administration. They were dismayed that federal officials appeared willing to attenuate their civil rights efforts in order to preserve southern political support and states' rights. Nor did White House responses to SNCC pleas reassure them. In September 1962 the President's assistant Lee White responded to a series of SNCC telegrams with a perfunctory letter referring them to a presidential statement condemning acts of violence in the South. Without indicating specific actions to be taken, White relayed the President's assurance that "every effort is being made to apprehend the guilty parties and bring them to justice." Another letter from White giving similar assurances included a phrase that went to the crux of the dispute between SNCC and the administration: the administration would "do everything that *can properly be done* to insure that those qualified citizens who wish to register are given the opportunity to do so."[10] For SNCC workers there was no doubt that the federal government's "proper" role was forthrightly to use its power to aid the struggle.

SNCC's appeals for federal intervention had little impact on the basic civil rights policies of the Kennedy administration. Although President Kennedy submitted new voting rights legislation in February 1963, the legislation contained no provisions for expanded federal protection of civil rights workers. Instead, it called for the appointment of temporary federal referees to determine the qualifications of registration applicants in counties where fewer than 15 percent of the blacks were registered. The proposed legislation also prohibited the use of different standards for black and white applicants and established a presumption of literacy for voting in federal elections for those who had completed sixth grade. Although these proposals were significant improvements on existing civil rights legislation, they did not satisfy many SNCC workers, who believed that the administration had failed to use the powers it already possessed to prevent both police brutality and the intimidation of those involved in voter registration work.

The Justice Department did make some attempt to use its legal authority to initiate civil litigation against southern officials when there was clear evidence of civil rights violations. Thus, when SNCC worker John Hardy was assaulted by a Mississippi registrar in September 1961, his prosecution on trumped-up charges was enjoined by Justice Department lawyers. And on August 28, 1962, in the case of *United States* vs. *Mississippi,* the Justice Department filed suit against six Mississippi officials who had failed to register black voters. In this case, the department sought to have various Mississippi voting laws declared unconstitutional because they discriminated against blacks.[11]

As in the freedom ride campaign, however, the Kennedy administration reacted to pressures from civil rights militants by attempting to avoid crises in order to achieve civil rights goals at its own pace and in its own way. When SNCC workers demanded a firm stand against southern segregationist officials, administration officials typically exerted pressure behind-the-scenes and only as a last resort took the politically damaging course of overt intervention. Thus, after Leflore County officials stopped distributing surplus food in 1962, the Justice Department opened an investigation, and as a result, county officials were warned that unless they resumed the food distribution, the Department of Agriculture would take over and continue the program. Early in April, county officials decided to acquiesce.[12]

Even after President Kennedy responded in the spring of 1963 to massive black demonstrations in Birmingham by expanding his civil rights proposals to include desegregation of public accommodations, the issue of federal protection continued to divide SNCC workers from the administration. Although some Justice Department officials considered such protection to be impractical, many SNCC workers believed that the President was simply unwilling to risk the loss of his southern support and lacked any deep moral commitment to the cause of civil rights. The conflict was in essence between administration officials who saw themselves as political realists and activists in SNCC who emphasized individual commitment. "We weren't a national police force," Doar later explained. "We weren't going to put policemen down there to guard every SNCC worker wherever he might go . . . We were going to enforce the law through the standard method of law enforcement, which was to bring actions against persons who interfered with citizens' rights to register and to vote, and the right of citizens to encourage, persuade and urge people to register to vote."[13]

In May 1963, Moses responded to arguments such as Doar's when he testified before a congressional subcommittee on Kennedy's civil rights proposals. Moses reported that the main problem blacks faced in rural Mississippi was fear. Many of the black residents with whom he worked were small farmers who could not easily be intimidated economically. Neither could such people be intimidated by "mobs who come out to their homes, because they are willing to protect their homes." The question was simply one of "being afraid to go down to the Courthouse because they are exposed at the Courthouse and they are subjected to violence at the Courthouse."

Moses mentioned the case of Hartman Turnbow, a voter registration leader in Holmes County who a few weeks before had fired on white attackers as they firebombed his home. The following day Turnbow was arrested—along with Moses, who had come to investigate—and charged with setting fire to his own home. Although the Justice Department had asked for a preliminary injunction to stop the prosecution, the case would go before a judge known to be a racist, Moses argued. Thus, if the judge refused the injunction, the blacks would think "the sheriff got away with it," creating "a very dangerous situation because they are not going to stand by much longer and have people shot in their homes. This is in the delta of the Mississippi and they outnumber whites two to one. If they start shooting back and organizing you are liable to have a situation on the country's hands which will be ten times worse than Birmingham."

Moses also explained why SNCC was not satisfied with the pending voting rights legislation. The Kennedy administration's proposal that a sixth grade education be accepted as proof of literacy did not go far enough. Since blacks in Mississippi had been denied an equal education, the nation had an obligation either to register them outright or to provide a massive adult education program for them. This statement of the "one man, one vote" idea became a basic part of SNCC's policies and reflected the emerging identification of SNCC workers with poor and often uneducated blacks. Moses insisted that Mississippi blacks were "now motivated to learn. They want to learn. They want to vote. They feel that for once they have a chance at bettering their conditions." He argued that a literacy program could be effective if it were administered by local blacks.[14]

SNCC's deteriorating relations with the Kennedy administration were affected not only by the lack of federal response to their pleas for protection but also by the tremendous upsurge in black protest activity in southern cities. A wave of civil rights demonstrations swept through the South, as well as through northern urban centers, during the spring and summer of 1963, re-emphasizing the role of the direct action proponents in SNCC. SNCC activists were encouraged by the popularization of protest activity among blacks. Uncertain whether the black revolt was the beginning of the nonviolent revolution for which they had waited or of a racial war, SNCC's nonviolent radicals nonetheless joined the revolt and attempted to articulate its goals.

SNCC workers were involved in many of the major civil rights protests of

1963. Although they played only minor roles in the Birmingham demonstrations, which resulted in more than 3000 arrests during April and May, SNCC militants elsewhere supported protests even when they were likely to result in violence. During May, John Lewis led a series of tumultuous demonstrations in Nashville, and Marion Barry led demonstrations against segregated theaters in Knoxville which resulted in about 150 arrests. Other SNCC workers were prominently involved in demonstrations in Pine Bluff, Gadsden (Alabama), Atlanta, Greensboro, Raleigh, Jackson, and Savannah.

In Cambridge, Maryland, after several violent clashes between police and SNCC-supported demonstrators, over four hundred National Guard troops were ordered into the city in June by the governor. On July 23, after the personal intercession of Robert Kennedy and other Justice Department officials, an agreement was signed under which black leaders agreed to end the demonstrations and white leaders promised to desegregate public schools, construct low-rent public housing for blacks, and appoint a biracial Human Relations Commission. The truce was only temporary, however, for blacks complained that most of their demands had been compromised and that desegregation of public accommodations would be submitted to a fall referendum.[15]

Demonstrations in Danville, Virginia, also led to violent clashes between blacks and whites. The Danville Christian Progressive Association began a campaign for black employment during May, for which they requested help from SNCC and other civil rights organizations. SNCC field secretaries Avon Rollins, Bob Zellner, and Ivanhoe Donaldson went to Danville in June shortly before a march by blacks to the city hall, which was broken up by police using firehoses and nightsticks. During the following days more marches were held, and on June 21 a grand jury indicted several SNCC workers and Danville black leaders on charges of "inciting the colored population to acts of violence and war against the white population." Continued protests in Danville resulted in more than three hundred arrests during the summer, while white officials continued to reject black demands.[16]

The protests of the spring and summer of 1963 exceeded in intensity and size anything that had preceded them. Southern Regional Council researchers estimated that during 1963, 930 public protest demonstrations took place in at least 115 cities in 11 southern states. Over 20,000 persons were arrested during these protests, compared to about 3600 arrests in the period of nonviolent protests prior to the fall of 1961. In 1963, ten persons died in circumstances directly related to racial protests, and at least 35 bombings occurred.[17] SNCC activists who were involved in the mass protests became aware of a militant mood among urban blacks that surpassed their own discontent and which compelled them to reassess their own views regarding nonviolent protest.

The protests during the first half of 1963 provided a new impetus to SNCC proponents of direct action, who were being eclipsed in the organization by voter registration workers. Although SNCC community organizers were not fully convinced that protest activity was useful, the President's decision to submit new civil rights legislation in the aftermath of the Birmingham protests seemed to confirm the effectiveness of direct action tactics, particularly when associated with the threat of mass violence. SNCC agitators who participated in the 1963 protests attempted to articulate the aspirations of the newly mobilized black populace, expressing the anger as well as they could while retaining their commitment to nonviolent principles. Still uncertain of the reaction of the Kennedy administration, SNCC representatives used the climate of social disorder as an opportunity to renew their pleas for federal intervention in the South and for an increased national concern for the plight of southern blacks. Their protests culminated in the March on Washington on August 28, 1963.

The idea for a march on Washington was initially suggested by A. Philip Randolph, who had planned a similar march in 1941 to prod President Franklin Roosevelt into improving employment opportunities for blacks. The earlier threat of a march had been successful, since Roosevelt established the Fair Employment Practices Committee in return for a promise to call off the demonstration. In November 1962, Randolph raised the idea again, hoping that another march, or even the threat of it, might put additional pressure on the Kennedy administration to support equal employment legislation. At first the idea failed to attract notice because of a lull in black protest activity, but during the spring of 1963, as thousands of blacks in both North and South took to the streets, the proposal gained support.

On June 22, 1963, President Kennedy met with thirty civil rights leaders—including John Lewis, who had recently replaced McDew as chairman of SNCC—to try to dissuade them from going ahead with the march, which Kennedy believed might lead to violence and thus hurt the civil rights cause. Randolph explained to the President that blacks were already in the streets and it was "very likely impossible to get them off. If they are bound to be in the streets in any case, is it not better that they be led by organizations dedicated to civil rights and disciplined by struggle rather than to leave them to other leaders who care neither about civil rights nor about non-violence?"[18] Although Kennedy remained unconvinced, he subsequently encouraged administration officials and liberal supporters to work with the planners of the march.

In the following weeks Lewis argued for continued protest, feeling that

SNCC could not and should not stop the demonstrations until there were "definite signs of progress. It would be very dangerous if we did, because it would lead to violence. Demonstrations will continue regardless, but if the Negro leaders attempted to halt them before equal rights are assured, the demonstrations would merely continue without leadership." Lewis, who had been arrested twenty-four times during his career in the civil rights movement, announced that SNCC would intensify its drive for equality because of the serious threat of race riots and violence over the summer unless black demands were met: "We do not want violence and we do not advocate it. But we will not slow down because of the possibility. Violence represents the frustration of the Negro community and the slow pace of progress in achieving real democracy; the only way to avoid this is to show tangible proof to American Negroes that his life is getting better."[19]

During this period, liberal financial backers of the civil rights movement took steps to unify black civil rights leadership and to slow the turn toward militancy. Under the direction of philanthropist Stephen Currier of the Taconic Foundation, a United Civil Rights Leadership Council was established to coordinate planning for the March on Washington. Currier raised $800,000 to be distributed among the major civil rights groups. The lure of financial support attracted SNCC into the coalition with leaders from the NAACP, Urban League, CORE, and SCLC. Although SNCC officials opposed the council's domination by moderates, Forman insisted that SNCC be included in the deliberations. The meetings of the council became increasingly acrimonious, marking the beginning of an open conflict between SNCC and the liberal establishment. SNCC representatives wanted the financial backing of liberals but refused to restrain their militancy or to discontinue their attempts to expose liberal hypocrisy. The council leaders, for their part, began to view SNCC as the *enfant terrible* of the civil rights movement. Accordingly, SNCC received only $15,000 of the initial funds.[20]

In August 1963 SNCC workers received confirmation that southern authorities were attempting to crush their work when SNCC workers Perdew, Don Harris, Ralph Allen, and Zev Aelony of CORE were charged with inciting insurrection in Americus, Georgia. This incident provided further support for the belief that SNCC was engaged in a life-or-death struggle, since the charge carried a death penalty. During the same month a federal grand jury in Macon, Georgia, indicted nine leaders of the Albany Movement who were charged by Justice Department officials with conspiracy to obstruct justice. The leaders had picketed a store owned by a member of a jury which had earlier found a sheriff innocent of charges of shooting and beating a black man. Although the demonstrators argued that their picketing was not related directly to the jury action, the Justice Department for the first time in the 1960s prosecuted persons involved in civil rights activity. For SNCC workers the federal action was a transparent attempt, by appearing to be "even-handed," to gain southern political support and to mollify the whites who believed that the movement had gone "too far."[21]

As a result, Lewis, Forman, and other SNCC representatives suggested that demonstrations at the Justice Department be included in plans for the March on Washington, but other civil rights leaders rejected the idea. The fact that Lewis was to deliver a speech at the march would nevertheless offer him the opportunity to express SNCC's criticisms of the federal government before a national audience. With the help of other SNCC leaders, Lewis drafted an address designed to bring SNCC's break with conventional liberalism into the open.

In the draft speech Lewis withheld support from the Kennedy administration's civil rights bill before Congress as being insufficient to protect blacks from police brutality. He also charged that the indictment of the nine Albany Movement leaders was "part of a conspiracy on the part of the federal government and local politicians in the interest of expediency." He asked, "I want to know, which side is the federal government on?" He then insisted, "the revolution is at hand and we must free ourselves of the chains of political and economic slavery. The nonviolent revolution is saying, 'we will not wait for the courts to act ... We will not wait for the President, the Justice Department, nor Congress, but we will take matters into our own hands and create a source of power, outside of any national structure, that could and would assure us victory.' "[22]

An advance text of the speech was given to other civil rights leaders the day before the march, and Lewis was informed that, unless he made changes in it, the Catholic archbishop of Washington would not appear on the same platform. When other civil rights leaders also objected to portions of it, Bayard Rustin arranged a meeting on August 27 to resolve the controversy. Lewis initially rejected the pleas to remove objectionable phrases, feeling "angry that someone would tell me what to say and what should be deleted."[23] Finally, however, a committee was formed to make revisions.

The committee—comprising Lewis, Forman, and Cox of SNCC as well as Rustin, Randolph, Martin Luther King, Ralph Abernathy, and Eugene Carson Blake of the National Council of Churches—met on the day of the march in a room inside the Lincoln Memorial. As Lewis recalled, Randolph pleaded with him, "John, for the sake of unity, we've come this far. For the sake of unity, change it." According to Forman, special objections were raised to the reference to "*revolution*" ("Even ... Randolph had to speak out against that argument") and to the statement that SNCC could not "wholeheartedly support" the Kennedy civil rights bill. Lewis was finally convinced to soften the text, even though any deviation from the original speech which was in the hands of the press, Forman noted "was certainly going to call further attention to it and indicate disagreement." Forman therefore rewrote parts of the speech while Lewis absented himself at the march ceremonies.[24]

The attitude of SNCC workers toward the march was ambivalent. Some SNCC activists did not bother to attend the largest civil rights demonstration of the decade, since they resented the moderation of its demands and the restrictiveness of its rules, such as allowing only prescribed picket signs. Yet many other SNCC workers were present, caught up in the excitement of the event. Among the freedom fighters introduced by Randolph to the audience of more than 200,000 were Diane Nash Bevel, Gloria Richardson, and Mrs. Herbert Lee, widow of the Mississippi voter registration worker killed in 1961, along with a large delegation from Mississippi COFO. Martin Luther King's "I Have a Dream" oration symbolized the optimistic tone of the march. A SNCC activist recalled that, despite his "disillusionment with the whole affair," the march was a "tremendous inspiration" to the poor blacks from the deep South who had been brought there by SNCC organizers. "It helped them believe that they were not alone, that there really were people in the nation who cared what happened to them."[25]

Lewis' speech did not attract the attention of King's, but even the revised version was a powerful expression of SNCC's radicalism. "We march today for jobs and freedom," Lewis told the crowd, "but we have nothing to be proud of." He cited those who could not afford to come because they were "receiving starvation wages . . . or no wages at all." He told of "sharecroppers in the Delta of Mississippi" who received "less than three dollars a day for twelve hours of work" and of "students in jail on trumped up charges." SNCC supported the proposed civil rights bill only "with great reservations" because it included nothing "to protect young children and old women from police dogs and fire hoses" or "the hundreds of people who have been arrested on phony charges." Nor would it protect the three SNCC field secretaries in Americus who faced "the death penalty for engaging in peaceful protest." Lewis especially criticized the voting rights section of the bill, since it would not help blacks who lacked the educational qualifications to vote. " 'One man, one vote' is the African cry," Lewis continued. "It is ours, too."

Lewis' criticism of the existing political system reflected the moralistic orientation of many nonviolent activists in SNCC. He charged that American politics was "dominated by politicians who build their careers on immoral compromises and ally themselves with open forms of political, economic, and social exploitation." Asserting that "the party of Kennedy is the party of Eastland" and "the party of Javits is also the party of Goldwater," Lewis inquired: "Where is our party? Where is the political party that will make it unnecessary to have Marches on Washington?" The nine activists in Albany had been indicted "not by Dixiecrats, but by the federal government." He warned those who had counseled patience that blacks "do not want to be free gradually. We want our freedom and we want it now." He urged blacks to join the "great social revolution sweeping our nation" and to "stay in the streets of every city, every village and every hamlet of this nation ... until the unfinished revolution of 1776 is complete."[26]

Lewis' speech expressed the militancy of SNCC, but its religious imagery and emphasis on nonviolent protest were out of step with SNCC's dominant orientation by the summer of 1963. Lewis was not extensively involved in the community organizing activities in the deep South that had become the main preoccupations of SNCC's staff and the principal sources of their insights. SNCC had been an organization of nonviolent activists seeking to appeal to the nation's conscience; it was becoming a cadre of organizers seeking to mobilize blacks to coerce the federal government into using its power to achieve civil rights goals. Although Lewis remained convinced that nonviolent direct action was the best tactic for the southern movement, many other SNCC workers did not believe that the economic and political changes they desired could be brought about through nonviolent protest alone.

# 8. PLANNING FOR CONFRONTATION

Despite their increasing suspicions about the motives of the Kennedy administration, most SNCC workers agreed that federal intervention was needed to overcome segregationist resistance in the deep South. Nowhere was this more evident than in Mississippi, where Bob Moses had concluded that his earlier strategy of relying mainly on local black organizers could not succeed in registering large numbers of black voters. Frustrated by their failure to achieve a decisive civil rights breakthrough in the deep South, SNCC workers initiated extended discussions of their policies and projects. Moses gave added urgency to these discussions when he proposed SNCC's most ambitious project, a massive invasion of Mississippi during the summer of 1964 by northern white student volunteers.

The Mississippi Summer Project was designed to force a confrontation between state and federal authorities and thereby to prevent the intimidation and violence that had stymied previous civil rights work in Mississippi. The plan was another expression of SNCC's increasing militancy, but it also required the organization to strengthen its ties with other groups that would provide necessary assistance during the summer. In their preparations for the crucial Mississippi confrontation, SNCC workers became more aware than ever before of the difficulties of working within a liberal civil rights coalition. As they began to explore their points of departure from conventional liberalism, they also faced internal differences regarding fundamental policy issues, such as the role of whites in SNCC, the adequacy of its economic programs, and the nature of its relations with more moderate civil rights organizations.

Before the summer of 1963, Moses had patiently attempted to build a strong black movement in Mississippi by recruiting his staff almost entirely from black residents. Although he usually explained his policy of excluding whites from the staff in terms of the dangers for whites, he believed the policy was also important for the blacks. "Some of the Negro organizers for SNCC feel that this is their movement," he later commented, "that it belongs to them . . . that it's their energy that made it, so it's theirs." Despite his awareness of the importance of stimulating local black leadership,

Moses came to realize that years of work had resulted in the registration of only about 5 percent of the black voting age population. This lack of success was finally brought home to him in November 1963 when VEP withdrew its financial support from COFO, the Mississippi umbrella civil rights organization. VEP Director Wiley Branton explained that, until the Justice Department could enjoin Mississippi officials from interfering with voter registration efforts, it would not be possible to register many people successfully.[1]

Moses' participation in the Greenwood protests in the spring of 1963 and his use that summer of white workers in the COFO headquarters in Jackson indicated his awareness of the need for new tactics. He decided that outside intervention alone would make possible a significant breakthrough in voter registration in Mississippi and that this intervention could come about only with greater national publicity regarding Mississippi civil rights activities. Moses was searching for new alternatives when in July 1963 he encountered Allard Lowenstein, one of the many white activists participating in demonstrations in Jackson after the assassination of Mississippi NAACP leader Medgar Evers in June 1963.

Lowenstein, having expected to find Mississippi "only somewhat worse" than North Carolina, where he had been active in a protest movement, found instead that it was "like South Africa, only a little bit better."[2] Recalling the days of mourning held by black South Africans to protest their disenfranchisement, Lowenstein suggested that Mississippi blacks cast protest votes. A Harvard law student working with COFO found that under Mississippi law voters claiming to have been illegally excluded from registering could cast ballots which would be set aside until they could appeal their exclusion. With Moses' approval, COFO workers mobilized about one thousand blacks, mostly in Greenwood and Jackson, to enter protest votes in the August Democratic primary.

Moses was sufficiently encouraged by the protest vote in the primary to ask SNCC's Executive Committee to give highest priority to the work in Mississippi. At a meeting in September 1963, the committee agreed to launch immediately a "one man, one vote" campaign in the sate and to use as many staff members as necessary. Moses and Lowenstein then formulated a new plan. Rather than requiring blacks to vote at regular polling places, where they would face intimidation, they proposed that a "freedom vote" campaign be organized to allow blacks to vote for their own set of candidates in their own communities. Although this arrangement would detract from the voter registration campaign, the freedom vote was seen as another way of demonstrating the desire of black Mississippians to vote. It would also allow blacks to vote for candidates who favored civil rights. At a COFO meeting in October, Aaron Henry, head of the Mississippi NAACP, and Edwin King, a white chaplain at Tougaloo College in Jackson, were selected as candidates for governor and lieutenant governor respectively. In order to ensure publicity for the vote and to aid the COFO staff, Lowenstein contacted friends at Yale, where he had been a student, and Stanford, where he had been a dean, and recruited about a hundred northern white students to work in Mississippi during the two weeks before the November general election.[3]

Over 80,000 blacks voted in the symbolic election held the first week in November. Although COFO workers had hoped for an even larger turnout, the freedom vote made its point. Its success was measured in part by the small number of incidents of violence directed against civil rights workers. SNCC worker Ivanhoe Donaldson commented that after the election there "was less fear in the Negro community about taking part in civil rights activities." According to two other SNCC workers, Lawrence Guyot and Mike Thelwell, the most significant result of the campaign was that for the first time it took the movement "beyond activities affecting a single town, county, municipality or electoral district, and placed us in the area of state-wide organization."[4]

Soon after the election, Moses and Lowenstein thought of bringing even more white students, perhaps over a thousand, to Mississippi during the summer of 1964. They assumed that Mississippi officials could not crush such a massive force of civil rights workers and that national sentiment would not tolerate assaults against white students, especially those from leading colleges and prominent families. The experiences of SNCC workers in the South had shown Moses that the only hope for blacks lay in creating a crisis that would force a confrontation between federal and state authority. Since there was little possibility that southern whites would voluntarily make changes in the status of blacks, Moses felt that SNCC's job was to "bring about just such a confrontation ... to change the power structure." He described SNCC's plan as an "annealing process. Only when metal has been brought to white heat, can it be shaped and molded. This is what we intend to do to the South and the country, bring them to white heat and then remold them."[5]

The COFO staff discussed the proposal at a meeting on November 14, 1963, attended by seven white and about thirty-five black field secretaries, mostly affiliated with SNCC. Several black SNCC workers complained about the tendency of white civil rights workers to take over leadership roles and suggested that the role of white volunteers should be restricted. Black members also felt that the presence of white students reinforced traditional patterns of racial dependence. As recalled by SNCC adviser Howard Zinn, "One man noted that in Africa the new nations were training black Africans to take over all important government positions. Another told of meeting a Black Muslim in Atlanta who warned him that whites were taking over the movement." But other black members, including Guyot, joined Moses in defending the use of white volunteers. Fannie Lou Hamer insisted, "If we're trying to break down this barrier of segregation, we can't segregate ourselves." Moses argued that the only way to break down the false idea that blacks could change things all by themselves "is to have white people working along side of you, so then it changes the whole complexion of what you're doing, so it isn't any longer Negro fighting white, it's a question of rational people against irrational people." To the assertion that blacks needed to lead at least something in American society, Moses responded, "I always thought that the one thing we can do for the country that no one else can do is to be above the race issue."[6] Although only a small minority of the COFO staff objected strongly to the use of whites, most other staff members refused to take an outright stand in support of Moses' plan. After further heated discussion in December, the COFO staff decided to recruit only one hundred white students for the Mississippi Summer Project.

Despite the resistance in the COFO staff, Lowenstein and others went ahead with their own preparations to bring in a much larger force of white students to the state. During a visit to New York in late fall Moses discovered that many Yale students were planning to participate in the Mississippi Summer Project at their own expense and that the National Council of Churches was organizing summer projects of its own. Growing support was indicated by John Lewis' assertion in December that SNCC planned to create a crisis of such magnitude that "the Federal Government will have to take over the state." Conceding that the planned invasion by civil rights workers might result in violence, he insisted that "out of this conflict, this division and chaos, will come something positive."[7]

When the Mississippi Summer Project was finally discussed by SNCC's Executive Committee on December 30, Moses assumed a cautious role, repeating the reasons that led him to support the plan while also attempting fairly to represent the views of those on his staff who opposed it. He presented Lowenstein's plan to bring "thousands" of students to Mississippi to force a showdown between state and federal officials along with several more modest proposals. Charles Cobb, a member of the Mississippi staff, attacked the more ambitious plan, asserting that SNCC could not handle a large number of volunteers and that, when the students left at the end of the summer, the project would be disrupted. Sherrod expressed concern over the effect of the effort on SNCC's other projects— "are we willing to risk disintegration of our total operation in such a confrontation?"

Support for the Summer Project came mainly from SNCC veterans, such as Lewis and Marion Barry, who believed that SNCC should take advantage of the opportunity to exert pressure on the federal government during an election year. Forman too felt that the northern students would bring with them "channels of publicity and communication" and that SNCC could train people to lead the volunteers. Moses reaffirmed his view that a confrontation would be "an opening wedge for further pressure" and might force concessions and negotiations that could lead to social change. However, he also admitted the possibility that the federal government was "simply not prepared to make the kind of commitment we will be demanding from them." SNCC must consider whether it could mount sufficient pressure "to make them be prepared" and whether the plan would initiate "the threatened bloodbath and have violent consequences we cannot handle." The Executive Committee adopted a motion offered by Barry that committed SNCC "to obtain the right for all citizens of Mississippi to vote, using as many people as necessary to obtain that end."[8]

Although the motion was imprecise, its adoption indicated acceptance of the idea that large numbers of white students would go to Mississippi during the summer, since a negative decision would have been necessary to restrain the recruitment efforts of Lowenstein and others. Recognizing the probability that Mississippi staff members would continue to object, the committee agreed to send other SNCC leaders along with Moses to discuss the matter with the COFO staff. This strategem apparently worked, because COFO gave its consent in January 1964.[9]

Even before the adoption of the Summer Project, black SNCC workers had raised questions concerning the entrance during 1963 and 1964 of increasing numbers of white activists into SNCC. SNCC had always been a black-led organization with a staff overwhelmingly composed of blacks, but northern whites in particular often entered SNCC with skills that allowed them to dominate discussions. That SNCC had become a magnet for northern white students was apparent by the spring of 1963 when they comprised one-third of the participants at SNCC's annual conference. One black student expressed fear at the time that whites would "take over the movement."[10] By the fall of 1963, about 20 percent of SNCC's staff were white. SNCC's Executive Committee had attempted to deal with this problem by hiring campus travelers to recruit students from black colleges, but their efforts had little impact on recruitment patterns.

Most SNCC veterans remained committed to the ideal of building an interracial community inside the southern struggle. In the spring of 1964, Zinn optimistically referred to the "magical social effect that comes from people living, working, sacrificing together. Friendships, and love affairs, have crossed race lines in SNCC." Zinn asserted that "recent calls by Malcolm X and others for Negroes to use self-defense, and even retaliation, against acts of violence by whites, have not found approval by the SNCC organization," even though "individual SNCC members have sometimes expressed sympathy for this position." But Zinn's belief that SNCC's work "pointed the way to a race-less society" contrasted with the suspicion among many SNCC veterans that the opposite trend was occurring.[11]

In February 1964, Moses questioned whether the "humanitarian values" that had been part of SNCC's character could be maintained in the face of deep-rooted southern economic and political problems. Racial outbursts had occurred at staff meetings, he explained, because it was "very hard for some of the students who had been brought up in Mississippi and are victims of this kind of race hatred not to begin to let all of that out on the white staff." One "tirade" by a black member against white members consisting of a "whole series of really racial statements of hatred" lasted about fifteen minutes while other staff members "just sat there." The white workers were criticized for their tendency "to gravitate to command posts" because of their skills and training. Moses acknowledged the growth of racial militancy but believed that blacks in the civil rights movement could "find a broader identification, identification with individuals that are going through the same kind of struggle, so that the struggle doesn't remain just a question of racial struggle."[12]

Lewis, a firm advocate of nonviolent principles, noticed an increasing degree of racial consciousness among southern blacks. "Something is happening to people in the Southern Negro community," he remarked in the spring of 1964. "They're identifying with people because of color . . . They're conscious of things that happen in Cuba, in Latin America, and in Africa. Even in SNCC, we talk about integration, about the beloved community, but there have been great changes going on. There's been a radical change in our people since 1960; the way they dress, the music they listen to, their natural hairdos—all of them want to go to Africa . . . I think people are searching for a sense of identity, and they're finding it."[13]

The general issue of the use of white organizers was raised in December 1963 when the Executive Committee discussed Sherrod's southwest Georgia project, the only SNCC project that had recruited white students to work in black communities. Forman defended the project's use of white students as an experiment and observed that the effectiveness of white workers in Georgia had "opened the doors to the use of white people in other areas." He argued that the real conflict was between political and religious or philosophical goals, a conflict that existed in other SNCC projects. Courtland Cox observed that the stagnation in Georgia resulted from Sherrod's emphasis on freeing the minds of black people, which was too nebulous to serve as a basis for organizing. Sherrod, though promising to "broaden" his program, still maintained that in the beginning "all we had were minds and bodies" and he had to use these resources "to try to get across a concept of freedom, which, in a very practical sense, is the necessary first step for all other activity."[14]

SNCC's white staff members, aware of the new currents of racial consciousness in SNCC, struggled to come to terms with their implications. For Sam Shirah, a southern white student who had replaced Bob Zellner as a field secretary under the SCEF grant during 1963, the issue assumed new urgency after Bayard Rustin, at a November 1963 SNCC conference, challenged young whites to "go into the white communities, work as hard as any black SNCC worker to convince white people to support" the civil rights movement. Shirah, who grew up in Alabama and northern Florida, had taken part in the Danville demonstrations. After listening to Rustin, he decided that protest was not enough and that "something had to be done to reach the great number of white people in the South who have felt that this movement is their enemy. It's not their enemy. It might be their salvation."[15]

In the December 1963 SNCC discussion of the southwest Georgia project, Shirah commented that the concept of "freedom of the mind" applied to whites as well as blacks. He noted that many whites in the movement were "crippled by guilt," and this guilt forced them to embrace "blackness." Although such identification might be a first step toward "true integration," it was necessary to "move on to a white nationalism"; that is, whites must learn to accept themselves and free their own minds. White activists should therefore create programs for white communities and recruit white students to work on these programs.[16]

During the spring of 1964 Shirah and other white students took steps toward the creation of a southern white student counterpart to SNCC. They succeeded in attracting forty-five white student activists to a meeting in early April in Nashville, at which a new organization, the Southern Students Organizing Committee (SSOC), was founded. One of SSOC's purposes was to involve more southern white students in the civil rights movement, but its leaders were uncertain of their relationship with SNCC. Anne Braden, who was in close contact with the new leaders, opposed establishing a separate organization for white students, raising "the specter of segregated student organizations in the South." She suggested that SSOC become an autonomous "affiliate" or "associate" of SNCC. She also urged that SSOC work to resolve "the tensions created by centuries of separation . . . and not pass them on untouched to the next generation. I think that your job is to *challenge* the moderate white student."[17]

Encouraged by Braden to believe that they would be supported by SNCC, an SSOC delegation, including Shirah, Ed Hamlett, and Sue Thrasher, appeared before SNCC's Executive Committee on April 19, 1964, to propose that SNCC provide financial support for a "white student project," which would involve organizing in white communities. Shirah asked SNCC to consider the project "as important as any other project" and to hire and provide equipment for teams of organizers. The response was favorable, some SNCC members even arguing against Braden's suggestion that SSOC become autonomous. Cox, for example, insisted that blacks in SNCC be made to see the similarities between the problems of blacks and whites, through the example of whites confronting the same dangers as blacks. Moses suggested that SSOC become part of SNCC and be given representation on the Executive Committee, because one of the reasons for "black-white tensions" was the desire of whites always to work in black communities. Without dissent, the committee agreed to provide $900 to help finance another conference of white students in May and to establish a committee to discuss future relations betweeen SNCC and SSOC.[18]

Although most of SSOC's initial leaders had been active in SNCC, relations between the two groups remained in flux during the spring and summer of 1964. Hamlett, who was Shirah's successor under the SCEF grant to SNCC, directed a white community project as part of COFO's Summer Project of 1964, but subsequent SSOC projects were generally independent of SNCC. Although contacts between the two groups continued, SSOC moved closer to SDS than to SNCC, and Hamlett became a member of the SDS National Council in 1965. In that year a scholar who was close to both groups observed that SSOC was "attracting the same kinds of students who joined SNCC efforts in 1960—but SNCC [had] become too radical, too professional, too full-time revolutionary to recruit large numbers of idealistic college students."[19]

The issue of the role of whites in SNCC was one aspect of a broader set of concerns regarding SNCC's efforts to organize southern blacks. Although some SNCC workers concluded that whites could not be effective organizers in black communities, a larger number felt that the organizer's race was less important than the kind of program offered. Prior to 1964 most discussion within SNCC concerned matters of tactics, while the organization's objectives were assumed to be limited to civil rights reforms. Early in 1964, a few SNCC workers began to ask whether such goals warranted the expenditure of so much energy or whether they truly met the needs of southern blacks. Many felt that just as the desegregation of lunch counters was not a major concern for blacks who lacked the money to eat at them, so too voter registration was of little concern for blacks who had pressing economic problems. As a SNCC worker in Cambridge, Maryland, put it, the goals of the movement had "shifted from hamburgers to bread," from desegregation to unemployment and "how to put bread in people's stomachs."[20]

Although Moses, Forman, and other veteran SNCC leaders recognized the importance of economic programs, SNCC's move in this direction was initiated by NAG. NAG members had engaged in a conscious process of political education during 1962, when they founded Project Awareness at Howard University to inform students about social issues. The project's first activity was a debate between Malcolm X and Bayard Rustin. Other speakers included Norman Thomas of the Socialist party and Communist historian Herbert Aptheker. The intellectual atmosphere within NAG was vibrant and intense. Cleveland Sellers recalled that at Carmichael's apartment, which was NAG's unofficial headquarters, members spent hours "arguing politics and movement strategy. When it was time to eat and a good argument was in progress, we would pass a hat and send out for cold cuts."[21]

By 1964 many NAG members had adopted socialistic views. For example, Carmichael wanted to have the government take over big corporations, "see more than one hundred people control over sixty percent of the industry," and "see all these plantations divided up until everybody who was on the plantation had his plot of land."[22]

In September 1963, Bill Mahoney, NAG's representative on SNCC's Executive Committee, urged SNCC to develop economic programs. SNCC approved Mahoney's plan to establish a Washington office, of which he became director, and to develop employment or other economic programs in areas where SNCC was active. Mahoney also played a major role in organizing a leadership conference at Howard University in November 1963 to bring together SNCC representatives with leaders of labor and democratic socialist organizations. Although the results of the conference, financed largely by contributions from labor unions, did not fulfill Mahoney's expectations—he later criticized SNCC leaders for not showing up for a meeting with officials of the Industrial Union Department of the AFL-CIO—most subsequent SNCC meetings addressed economic problems.[23]

At a December 1963 Executive Committee meeting, Mahoney and Courtland Cox led an attack on Sherrod and Moses for failing to develop economic programs for their projects. Mahoney criticized SNCC for not engaging in union organizing and for not having any long-range programs to achieve full employment. Frank Smith, a former Morehouse College student from LaGrange, Georgia, who was working in Mississippi, asserted that rather than promoting "stopgap measures which buy off revolution," SNCC might "take all the Negroes from the rural areas into the cities and force the revolution." Others suggested that SNCC workers consider tactics such as marching on grain storage bins and staging a "general strike." But Barry was among the veteran activists who counselled against such drastic measures, insisting that SNCC needed "stopgap" measures in order to gain time to "work out the long-range programs." And Moses argued that SNCC workers did not know the meaning of revolution or how to "revamp the economy" and thus should take "time out from action" to study the problems confronting southern blacks. The alternatives need not be simply those offered by the United States and the Soviet Union: "It may be that no one knows the answers to the technological revolution in which we are caught."[24] Moses' remarks apparently convinced other SNCC workers who soon afterward took a cautious step toward creating a staff education program by approving a work study program at the Institute for Policy Studies in Washington.

The discussions of economics indicated a change in SNCC's conception of its own work. Administrative secretary Ruby Doris Robinson concluded in the spring of 1964 that civil rights was a dead issue, since it no longer meant anything to blacks concerned "with the basic necessities of life." Asserting that there had been a serious neglect of overall strategy, she suggested that SNCC discuss "new and creative tactics, and how our work is affecting basic changes in the power structure." SNCC should "define its ideology," "establish specific goals," and explain "in very definite terms how it will project itself in the mass media." Smith also recommended that SNCC operations cease after the summer so that the staff could rest and re-evaluate their work.[25]

Yet as the Summer Project approached, SNCC was too involved in planning its immediate future to spend much time developing long-term programs. The intellectual ferment simply complicated SNCC's efforts to plan its most ambitious project and was a source of tension in SNCC's relations with other groups. There had always been differences of tactics and style separating SNCC from other civil rights and reform organizations, but by the spring of 1964 the gulf separating it was based increasingly on matters of policy.

The most important cause of the mounting tension between SNCC and its liberal allies was SNCC's failure explicitly to exclude communists from its activities. Since the late 1940s, nearly every major reform organization in the United States had adopted such a policy, but SNCC had not. During the summer of 1963, some SNCC workers criticized Martin Luther King for capitulating to government pressure and firing one of his associates, Jack O'Dell, after O'Dell's past association with the Communist party had been revealed by the FBI.[26] Carmichael, for example, argued that participants in the civil rights movement should "stop taking a defensive stand on communism," for when blacks tried to defend themselves against the charge of being communists, it took "the whole emphasis off the civil rights issue and [put] it on the issue of Americanism vs. anti-Americanism."[27]

SNCC had never taken a formal stand on the issue of communist exclusion, since it rarely took formal stands on any issue, but its implicit policy was to accept help from anyone sincerely and actively willing to support the civil rights cause. Since the incident in 1961 when SNCC had allowed outside forces to bar Rustin from a conference, SNCC had never excluded anyone from its staff or broken relations with anyone simply because of political affiliation. The long-standing relationship between SNCC and SCEF had been maintained despite considerable negative comment in southern newspapers regarding SCEF's reputed communist ties. Yet SNCC had not been confronted with the question of whether it would fire a known communist or would openly accept help from the Communist party, and thus its informal policy of "freedom of association" was simply an aspect of its general openness to new people and ideas and its common practice of establishing policy through impulsive action.

Only after the March on Washington, when SNCC established both its importance and its militancy, did civil rights supporters outside the South begin to raise questions regarding the possibility of communist influences inside SNCC. The publication of an article by Theodore H. White in *Life* in November 1963 was the first time a major national publication expressed clearly negative attitudes toward SNCC. White referred to the "serious penetration by unidentified elements" in SNCC and charged that SNCC "agents" had tried during the spring demonstrations in Jackson and Birmingham "to convert a peaceful march into a violent *Putsch* on government offices." White mentioned a SNCC "battle plan," which had been "rejected by Negro leaders" but which called for "nonviolent battle groups ... to cut Montgomery off from all communication with the outside world—presumably to provoke 'nonviolent' combat between Alabama and the U.S."[28]

SNCC leaders were greatly disturbed by these unsupported charges, but the focal point of their concern was the possibility that SNCC workers would be called before the House Un-American Activities Committee (HUAC) to answer questions regarding communist influences. Although they privately opposed HUAC, and in December 1963 John Lewis spoke on behalf of the National Committee to Abolish HUAC, they were uncertain whether SNCC should take a public position on the matter. Carmichael insisted at an Executive Committee meeting in late 1963 that, because HUAC's actual purpose was not to find communists but to render the organizations under investigation ineffective, SNCC should simply declare that it was doing what was "right" and refuse to defend itself. Some members agreed that SNCC should take a "principled stand" against establishing political criteria for hiring, but others favored a more pragmatic stance. Bernard Lafayette argued that SNCC should choose the issues for which it wanted to fight and "not try to fight everywhere at once." Moses similarly urged that SNCC should avoid contacts which would damage the movement, except that, in the case of a regular staff member who was "known and trusted," SNCC should stand "in total solidarity" with that person. Moses felt that the real disagreement was "between a principled position that political association is never relevant even when it causes turmoil, and a pragmatic one that it would have occasional relevance." What SNCC needed was "a criterion of flexibility without a flat statement one way or the other." Moses' approach apparently prevailed, for the general consensus at the meeting "seemed to indicate a position of non-alignment, of no political test for members. There was no position on whether to declare this openly, however."[29]

During the spring of 1964, SNCC was forced to return to the issue of freedom of association when Jack Greenberg, head of the NAACP Legal Defense and Education Fund, threatened to cancel plans to provide legal assistance for the Summer Project rather than work with members of the National Lawyers Guild, a leftist group which did not bar communists. SNCC's Executive Committee reaffirmed its opposition to any attempt to force SNCC to alter its "open door" policy. After Greenberg modified his stand and offered to give volunteers for the project the choice of retaining a guild or fund lawyer, SNCC insisted that Greenberg not be allowed to use the orientation of volunteers as a forum to attack the guild. According to Zinn, the principle at stake was that SNCC should not allow the "legal establishment" to decide the groups with whom it could associate.

Shortly afterward Lewis publicly expressed the evolving attitudes of SNCC on the issue of communist involvement. Responding to a charge by FBI Director J. Edgar Hoover that communists had infiltrated the civil rights movement, Lewis asserted that such charges merely aided the segregationist opponents of civil rights. Hoover's agents "could more wisely spend their time finding the bombers, midnight assassins, and brutal racists who daily make a mockery of the United States Constitution."[30]

Although SNCC may have alienated a few liberal allies by its decision to accept the aid of the National Lawyers Guild, the main thrust of SNCC's activities during the first half of 1964 was to build support among northern liberals for the Summer Project. Despite its increasing radicalism, SNCC was by this time a regular participant in meetings involving major civil rights organizations, particularly those of the United Civil Rights Leadership Council. SNCC was determined to share in the funds contributed by foundations and wealthy individuals to support southern civil rights activities, since such support was vital to sustain SNCC's large-scale project in Mississippi without abandoning its work elsewhere in the South. SNCC leaders sometimes derided the motives of others at the Leadership Council meetings, but they attended nonetheless. "Looking around at the setting, the way people were dressed and talked, I knew I would have to stay on my toes not to be swallowed up by this slick band of competitors and circle of distrust," Forman commented about one such meeting. "There I sat, representing an organization whose workers rarely had more than fifty cents in their pockets, hustled hamburgers to keep going, and wore overalls as a matter of course."[31]

Every national civil rights organization and many liberal reform groups were involved in the Mississippi Summer Project. Indeed, a SNCC leader warned that SNCC must do more to "project" its own "image or else we'll be continually overidden."[32] Although SNCC continued to provide the bulk of the financial support for COFO, which allowed it to dominate that group, the NAACP, SCLC, and CORE also made substantial contributions to the Summer Project. The National Council of Churches, through its Commission on Religion and Race, contributed to the project by underwriting the orientation program for the student volunteers and by sending to Mississippi its own staff of ministers and lawyers under the auspices of its Delta Ministry. In addition, the Medical Committee for Human Rights was established to aid the project.

SNCC greatly expanded its northern operations during the spring in order to develop its alliances with liberal leaders and to raise the funds needed for the summer. Comedian Dick Gregory went on a tour to raise money for SNCC, and Friends of SNCC in the North arranged fund-raising engagements for southern workers. SNCC raised $97,000 during the first three months of 1964, but since its needs had also expanded enormously, staff members missed at least three paychecks during that spring.[33]

In Mississippi, despite the differences within the COFO staff, there was enthusiasm for the Summer Project among local blacks. This became apparent at the Hattiesburg Freedom Day on January 22, 1964, when more than fifty northern white clergymen under the auspices of the National Council of Churches stood by as more than 150 blacks tried to register. Although Moses was arrested for obstructing a sidewalk and another SNCC worker was beaten in jail, integrated groups were able to picket in front of the Hattiesburg Courthouse without being arrested. Despite continued obstinacy on the part of white officials, the demonstrations revealed the willingness of a sizable number of blacks to attempt to register when southern policeman were restrained by the presence of northern whites. During the following month, more than five hundred blacks tried to register to vote. Afterward, blacks in other Mississippi communities organized freedom days of their own.[34]

In the beginning of February, SNCC workers decided to launch a campaign to register blacks through a separate "freedom registration" process while continuing efforts to register in the official Democratic party. Moses explained at the COFO convention on February 9 that the objective of the new campaign was to create separate registration requirements so that all black residents would be able to demonstrate their desire to participate in the political process. Another objective was to create a political organization that could successfully claim recognition as the legitimate Democratic party organization in Mississippi. This new party, soon called the Mississippi Freedom Democratic party (MFDP), was designed as a vehicle to challenge the regular party at the national Democratic Convention, to be held in August in Atlantic City, New Jersey.[35]

Northern support developed quickly for the MFDP challenge of the regular Mississippi Deomcratic party. In February the California Democratic Council offered its backing, and soon other northern liberal groups followed suit. During March, Moses and Ella Baker met with Joseph Rauh, vice-president of the Americans for Democratic Action (ADA), general counsel of the United Automobile Workers, and a powerful figure in Democratic party affairs. Rauh offered to help the MFDP and later agreed to become its counsel for the challenge.[36]

The MFDP was officially founded on April 26, 1964, at a rally in Jackson attended by only two hundred persons. According to black attorney Len Holt, the meeting was pervaded by a sense of "impertinence and irrelevance: these few dare to dream of challenging the traditional Mississippi Democrats ... It was ridiculous by any standard other than that of SNCC." A twelve-member executive committee was temporarily elected to decide the policies of the party until a permanent committee could be formed. In the weeks that followed, MFDP supporters tried to attend precinct and county meetings of the regular party, and when these attempts failed, they held MFDP precinct and county meetings to establish their party's legitimacy. Four MFDP candidates qualified for the Democratic primary on June 2. Victoria Gray, a Hattiesburg civil rights worker, was chosen to oppose Senator John Stennis, and SNCC worker Fannie Lou Hamer was selected as a congressional candidate.[37]

Plans were also developed for a "freedom school" program, an idea that had been conceived by SNCC worker Charles Cobb in the fall of 1963. Cobb recognized the inadequacy of the public education system in Mississippi, because of its "complete absence of academic freedom" and its repression of "intellectual curiosity and different thinking." He suggested that schools be established to "fill an intellectual and creative vacuum" in the lives of young black Mississippians and to "get them to articulate their own desires, demands and questions." Cobb proposed that the teachers be the hundreds of northern college students who would be arriving in Mississippi during the summer: "These are some of the best young minds in the country, and their academic value ought to be recognized, and taken advantage of."[38]

The curriculum for the freedom schools was developed in March 1964 at a meeting of educators, clergymen, and SNCC workers in New York. The course included normal academic subjects, contemporary issues, cultural expression, and leadership development, the last course covering the history of the black liberation movement and the study of political skills. Staughton Lynd, a white professor teaching at Spelman College in Atlanta, became director of the freedom school program.[39]

In May, recruitment of teachers began. Thoe who applied were told that their work would be closely related to COFO political programs and that the purpose of the freedom schools was "to provide an educational experience for students which will make it possible for them to challenge the myths of our society, to perceive more clearly its realities, and to find alternatives, and ultimately, new directions for action." As Cobb noted, blacks in Mississippi would have to overcome the accommodationist tradition that was a product of white oppression. "Here, an idea of your own is a subversion that must be squelched; for each bit of intellectual initiative represents the threat of a probe into the why of denial. Learning here means only learning to stay in your place. Your place is to be satisfied—a 'good nigger.' "[40]

The plans for the Summer Project reflected both SNCC's past development as a protest group and its emergence as a cadre of radical community organizers. SNCC prepared for a decisive test of its integrationist orientation by seeking to mobilize white liberal support outside the South. The complex mixture of idealism and realism that guided preparations for the summer was evident in a prospectus for the project written during the spring. "A large number of students from the North making the necessary sacrifices to go South would make abundantly clear to the government and the public that this is not a situation which can be ignored any longer, and would project an image of cooperation between Northern and white people and Southern Negro people to the nation which will reduce fears of an impending race war." The goal of the project would be to force either Mississippi officials to change their policies or "the federal government to intervene on behalf of the constitutional rights of its citizens." As indicated by Forman at the beginning of the summer, the Summer Project had another goal besides showing "the rest of the United States what really goes on in Mississippi." The project also aimed "to develop and strengthen a homegrown freedom movement that will survive after the 1,000 visitors leave."[41] Most SNCC leaders assumed that these two goals were compatible. But their residual belief in the efficacy of the strategy of appealing to powerful institutions through individual commitment and sacrifice was combined with a growing awareness that new black-controlled institutions were necessary both in Mississippi and in the nation.

# 9. MISSISSIPPI CHALLENGE

In a dramatic effort to overcome racial oppression, SNCC concentrated its resources in Mississippi during the summer of 1964. Combining both the idealistic fervor and the organizing skills that had made possible its emergence as an important civil rights group, SNCC simultaneously launched new institutions and mounted a powerful challenge to the national Democratic party leadership. In the process, earlier internal differences regarding SNCC's purpose and direction were temporarily pushed into the background, although the issues themselves affected the success of the project.

SNCC staff members became increasingly aware of the tension between their efforts to bring about federal intervention and their desire to develop self-sufficient local black movements. Believing they could utilize the skills and contacts of the summer volunteers, they found that although the presence of the volunteers helped create a more favorable climate for change, white workers could unwittingly hamper the efforts of local black leaders to create enduring black-controlled institutions, such as the MFDP. The difficulty of retaining elements of SNCC's former protest strategy for achieving civil rights goals while developing a radical alternative to that strategy became apparent during a summer of continued violence and finally frustration.

On June 13, 1964, the first group of summer volunteers began training at Western College for Women in Oxford, Ohio. Almost three hundred college students participated in a week of orientation to prepare them to work in COFO voter registration projects. The following week another group of volunteers attended orientation sessions to teach in freedom schools.

Both groups had been screened by psychiatrists and civil rights workers to eliminate persons who were deemed "dangerous to the movement." A COFO memorandum cautioned against anyone who was "wrapped up in himself" and thus could not "reach out and help those we are dealing with." It also recommended avoiding those who were "limited in their perspectives," such as only being willing to teach in a freedom school. Another poor candidate was the "well-meaning idealist who wants to secure equality and brotherly love for all, and is solidly anti-politics," since COFO was "totally involved in politics." Finally, the memorandum warned against the "bright college student" who had "all the answers" and knew "what's being done wrong" and "how to do it right." On the contrary, COFO sought people who were "realistic," "responsible," "flexible," and "understanding." They must be willing to listen and also to accept other people for what they were without trying to change them—"We are *not* trying to make the Mississippi farmer just like us."[1]

The racial and class backgrounds of those selected for the Summer Project reflected COFO's strategy of seeking outside intervention in Mississippi. "These students bring the rest of the country with them," Moses remarked. "They're from good schools and their parents are influential. The interest of the country is awakened, and when that happens, the Government responds to that interest."[2] Most of the volunteers were white students who had participated in civil rights activities in the North. Their middle-class backgrounds and experiences set them apart from most COFO staff members with whom they would work. The fact that the volunteers were expected to forgo summer jobs, to pay for their own transportation, and to provide their own bond money in the event of arrest ensured that affluent students predominated. There had been no effort to increase the number of blacks by providing financial aid. "Feeling outnumbered and misunderstood, most of the black students withdrew," a participant recalled.[3]

The teachers for the volunteers were SNCC field secretaries, native Mississippi movement workers, and a few outside experts. Although the black civil rights workers generally accepted the idea of the Summer Project, many were ambivalent about working with white volunteers. A few days after arriving in Oxford, a white volunteer noted that the black staff members, especially those from Mississippi, were "very much an in-group, because of what they have gone through together. They tend to be suspicious of us, because we are white, northern, urban, rich, inexperienced. We are somewhat in awe of them, and conscious of our own inferiority."[4]

The COFO staff members were uncertain in their new roles as teachers and leaders and doubtful of the consequences of the large-scale use of northern whites. Never before had so many persons entered the southern struggle at once. Some staff members simply resented the white volunteers for threatening to overwhelm the veteran staff with their superior numbers and academic skills. A few found it difficult to alter long-established racial attitudes. "I grew up hating all white folks," SNCC worker Frank Smith was quoted as saying. "It wasn't till a couple of years ago that I learned that there could be good whites—and even now I sometimes wonder." Muriel Tillinghast, COFO's project director in Greenville for the summer, recalled that the volunteers undermined the close personal ties which held the staff together. A "hierarchy developed," according to her, as soon as staff members were compelled to provide leadership for the "absolute novice."[5]

Resentments came into the open on June 16 when the staff and the volunteers were watching a television report on voter registration work in Mississippi. According to Bill Hodes, a white volunteer, the students began to laugh at the "idiotic registrar" and the "incredible double-talk of the rabid lawyer" who had prevented blacks from registering to vote. Six black staff members stood up and walked out of the room. Afterward an older staff member declared, through tears, "Maybe you won't laugh when you meet these guys and hear them talk, and know that they are doing it every day with or without the Feds." His remark gave the volunteers "a sharp realization that the whole affair was no picnic."

Later, Hodes recalled, as the white volunteers talked about the incident among themselves, some criticized the staff workers as "distant" or uncommunicative, while others defended them as having "a lot on their minds." After joining the discussion, staff members displayed the complex interplay of resentment and compassion that was to affect their relationships with white volunteers throughout the summer. One worker, citing the shooting of Travis and the beating of another staff member, told the volunteers that, if they were not scared, they should "get the hell out of here because we don't need any favors of people who don't know what they are doing here in the first place." Another worker explained, "We cried over you in the staff meeting, because we love you and are afraid for you." He assured the volunteers that although staff members had walked out during their laughter, no one would walk out when they confronted white violence: "When you get beaten up, I am going to be right behind you."[6]

Sally Belfrage, another white volunteer, described the responses of volunteers to being told by black staff members that they were "victims of the very prejudice we fought." The volunteers were forced to look for their own unconscious prejudices, and "those who exonerated themselves could see no contradiction in their innocence and their parallel desire for gratitude." The volunteers, aware that they had come without having to—"We could have stayed home and gone to the beach, or earned the money . . . for next semester at old Northern White"—felt that they deserved some recognition, even praise: *"I want to be your friend, you black idiot,* was the contradiction evident everywhere." Belfrage concluded that the basic source of tension was the feeling of racial pride that had developed among blacks in the southern struggle. "SNCC is not populated with Toms who would wish to be white. They are not the ones who fill closets with bleaches and straighteners, who lead compromise existences between reality and illusion." Instead, SNCC workers were engaged in working out their racial destiny. "To bend to us was to corrupt the purity of their goal. To understand us meant to become like us."

As director of the Summer Project, Moses understood the extent of racial tensions, since he had had to respond to the objections of black staff members who opposed the project. In dealing with the problems of the volunteers, he told them of the discussions "about race hatred" that had taken place at COFO meetings and then drew an analogy from Camus's *The Plague,* stating that the "country isn't willing yet to admit it has the plague, but it pervades the whole society." The problem, however, had to be discussed "openly and honestly, even with the danger that we get too analytical and tangled up. If we ignore it, it's going to blow up in our faces."[7]

The ambivalence of black staff members working with white volunteers was complicated by the staff's awareness that only further violence—against the volunteers rather than against black Mississippians—would prompt forceful federal intervention. SNCC's research department had already recorded over 150 incidents of intimidation and violence directed against civil rights workers and black residents in the years since SNCC began its work in the state, but none had attracted a vigorous federal response.[8] There was therefore an element of cynicism in the summer plan, although the COFO staff were prepared to share in any hardships to be suffered by the volunteers. Throughout the orientation, staff members repeatedly stressed the dangers that awaited the volunteers, who were told to shave their beards and to avoid speeding, traveling alone or in integrated groups, and going anywhere at night. Even before the orientation ended, the volunteers had learned that the danger of serious violence in Mississippi was real.

On June 21 SNCC workers were informed that three civil rights workers had not returned after leaving Meridian, Mississippi, to investigate the burning of a black church. The three workers were James Chaney, a black Mississippian on the staff of CORE; Michael Schwerner, a white CORE worker from New York who had been in Mississippi since January; and Andrew Goodman, a white Queens College student who was in the first group of volunteers at Oxford. The workers had disappeared after being arrested in Philadelphia, Mississippi, and then released at night without being allowed to telephone anyone. The Justice Department was immediately informed of the disappearance, but the FBI did not enter the case for more than a day.[9]

After the three had been missing for several days, Moses told the volunteers at Oxford what SNCC veterans had felt all along: "the kids are dead." He warned of the possibility of more deaths, since killings of blacks by whites were already common in Mississippi. But as Moses explained, "No privileged group in history has ever given up anything without some kind of blood sacrifice." Acknowledging that the project had been characterized by some observers as "an attempt to get some people killed so the federal government will move into Mississippi," he asserted that COFO workers were in fact willing to assume "tremendous risks" to combat the evil of racism.[10]

Although the disappearance of the three civil rights workers immediately focused national attention on the Summer Project, the incident did not result in a basic change in federal policy regarding protection of civil rights workers. Instead, the federal government reacted by focusing its resources solely on the Philadelphia incident. President Johnson authorized the use of 200 navy men in the search for the missing workers, and at least 150 FBI agents—more than ten times the normal number—were assigned to Mississippi during the summer. Former CIA Director Allan Dulles and FBI Director J. Edgar Hoover visited the state to coordinate the new federal involvement. Although these actions probably reduced the level of violence that would otherwise have occurred, SNCC workers were dubious and unsatisfied. "It is a shame that national concern is aroused only after two white boys are missing," John Lewis commented, adding that if the federal government did "not provide protection for civil rights advocates in the state, then their blood will be on [the government's] hands." Late in June, Moses called for "immediate and strong action" by the federal government to protect those involved in the Summer Project, requesting specifically "that Federal Marshals be stationed throughout the state." He pledged in exchange that no desegregation demonstrations would be conducted and that volunteers would limit their work to areas near project centers.[11]

On August 4 the bodies of the three murdered civil rights workers were found in an earthfill dam near Philadelphia. Several months later, twenty white men, including the sheriff of Nashoba County and one of his deputies, were arrested by federal authorities. Since the murder of the three workers did not constitute a federal crime and successful state prosecution was unlikely, those arrested were charged with conspiracy to deprive the dead men of their civil rights. In 1967, seven white men were convicted and sentenced to prison terms.[12]

Although the possibility of being killed was an ever-present concern of the volunteers in Mississippi, their immediate task was to gain the trust and support of black residents. The volunteers hoped to attract national attention and build new institutions, but they were also aware of the need to avoid subverting local black leadership and thereby maintaining patterns of racial and class dependence. They would face many dilemmas during the summer in their efforts to create a climate in which black Mississippians could carry on the struggle without further need for outside assistance.

As invited guests, the volunteers found their freedom of action greatly limited when they arrived at their assigned projects. They were given strict

rules of behavior. "Everyone is to be on his job by eight-thirty each morning," proclaimed Holly Springs project director Ivanhoe Donaldson. "No
one is to make any trip into the city or county without leaving his time of
departure and expected return ... local whites and the police are to be
avoided and never unnecessarily provoked." Donaldson warned the volunteers against "affairs between blacks and whites," because "even if the
whites don't find out about them, the people will, and we won't be able to
do anything afterwards to convince them that our primary interest here is
political." He summed up: "Our entire effort will be negated if we lose the
support and respect of the people. I don't intend for that to happen. Anyone who violates any of these rules will have to pack his bag and get his ass
out of town. We're here to work. The time for bullshitting is past."[13]

In areas where there had already been civil rights activity, the volunteers
were generally accepted by black Mississippians. Many lived with black
families. "Negro people here are happy that we're here," a volunteer reported. "They feed us, take care of us, protect us." Another volunteer remarked, "We are constantly on display when we're at the house; neighbors
file in and out to have a look at us."[14] Other summer workers commented
on the courage of blacks who willingly housed and shared their few possessions with volunteers at the risk of losing their jobs or suffering attacks on
their homes.

Belfrage's experiences in Greenwood illustrated the pattern of friendliness combined with fear and reticence. Upon the arrival of her group, some
people "greeted us with smiles and waves," while others were "polite but
withdrawn, sitting on their porches as though bonded to them, rocking in
apathy." Belfrage, who was staying at the home of a black family, the
Amoses, for several weeks attempted unsuccessfully to talk to Mr. Amos,
who had never sat at a table with a white woman. Finally, Belfrage realized
that "in some extraordinary paradox he would never think of us as equal
until I ordered him to. I begged him to sit down; he wouldn't; I *told* him to
sit down. He did, in great confusion. Somehow or other, everything was all
right after that. Later Mrs. Amos reported to me that he had been amazed
to find we could be friends."[15]

There is no way of accurately assessing how most black Mississippians
felt about the volunteers. Certainly the Summer Project could not have
taken place without their assistance, yet there was an ambivalence among
some black Mississippians who supported the volunteers but remained
skeptical of the project and disturbed by the lifestyles of the newcomers.
Journalist Paul Good recalled that the local blacks "who each day brought
marvelously cooked" meals to the McComb Freedom House were probably
"scandalized" by the slovenly conditions they encountered and also "must
have questioned the sleeping arrangements which generally put boys in one
house and girls in the other, but admitted exception existed." The anti-

white feelings that later confronted white organizers in black communities were as yet hardly visible during the summer's unprecedented experiment in race relations. "Some of these kids were so innocent," a black woman recalled. "We were too! We all honestly believed that just one year a trouble, just gettin' everybody registered and then everything is going to be changed. These kids thought people was people and they could just talk to [whites] and they would straighten out . . . These kids had faith in people. We had faith in *them*."[16]

When volunteers ventured from the homes of black supporters or freedom houses to try to get black residents politically involved, they soon recognized the slow pace of progress in the deep South. Not only did they have difficulty in convincing blacks to go to local courthouses and attempt to register in the regular Democratic party, but even the less formidable registration process of the MFDP was a difficult step for economically vulnerable blacks. An experience of volunteer Len Edwards, the son of a California congressman, demonstrated the problems of working in communities in which there had been little previous civil rights activity. Edwards, followed by a police car, was canvassing a black neighborhood in Drew when he stopped at one house:[17]

> The men on the porch were just in from the fields. Some of the women were wearing maid's uniforms. No one stood up to shake hands with Len. No one said hello. No one even looked directly at him.
> "We're on a voter-registration drive, and we'd like to have you join us," said Len. Still no one looked at him, but it was not wise to ignore a white man. "Well," someone finally said, "I don't know about that." That was the end of the conversation.

The volunteers tried valiantly to overcome the fears of residents while recognizing that black reticence was often based on realistic doubts about the chances for progress. A summer's effort could not undo the psychological consequences of generations of racial oppression. The Summer Project was only the first step in a long process of political development for Mississippi blacks. Although about 17,000 blacks were convinced to fill out registration forms at Mississippi courthouses over the summer, only 1600 were allowed to register. In addition, more than 80,000 blacks registered as members of the MFDP.

These modest measures of success were ultimately less significant than the enormous amount of national press coverage given the Summer Project, in part as a result of the skillful use of the press by SNCC's Communications Department. This publicity created a climate in which future black gains could take place. "Quite literally," one study concluded, the project's "triumph may be measured in column inches of newsprint and running feet of video tape. Easily the most spectacular and sustained single event in recent civil rights history, it provided summer-long, nationwide exposure of the iniquities of white supremacy in the deepest of the Deep South states."[18]

SNCC's experiment in white community organizing, called the White Folk's Project, had the same pioneering importance as SNCC's work in McComb during the fall of 1961. Yet like the McComb effort, the White Folk's Project ended with little tangible evidence of success. Those involved in the project were initially uncertain regarding their tactics and were forced to learn through experience. At first many of the students involved in the project concentrated on building support for COFO among white liberals. By the end of the summer, however, most workers had come to believe that their primary goal should be to attract support among working-class whites by emphasizing economic issues. "This movement isn't getting white poor folks to fight for themselves," noted Bruce Maxwell, one of the workers. "The less the movement does for them, the more they will be threatened by us, and the more they will be violent toward us. These are the reasons why the movement must work with white poor folks."[19]

The most significant aspect of the White Folk's Project was the attempt by eighteen members of the project's twenty-five person staff to establish a beachhead for the movement among whites in Biloxi. The staff members arrived in Biloxi early in July, after training at Oxford and the Highlander Center in Tennessee. Most of the group were newcomers to the southern movement; none had previously organized in white communities.

The group was soon torn by disagreements over tactics. These internal differences were intensified by the fact that at first all of the workers lived together in a hotel. "We spent more time attempting to resolve the problems of our in-group than we did learning the problems of the community," Maxwell recalled. The volunteers argued about matters of dress or the possession of leftist literature. Within a month, six of the volunteers had left the project in frustration. Maxwell concluded that future groups of community organizers should number no more than three or four members and preferably less. "The smaller the number of people the less time they will spend relating to each other and the more they will be forced by their isolation to relate to the people in the community." The volunteers who remained in Biloxi were mainly those who favored organizing poor and working-class whites. They had found, according to Maxwell, that the middle-class liberals and moderates "were just as paralyzed in fear of retaliation from the rest of the community as the white poor folks were."[20]

Some of the organizers moved to Point Cadet, a Biloxi suburb populated mainly by fishermen, where they continued to encounter resistance from local whites. As Ed Hamlett analyzed the opposition, many local whites "who realize what needs to be done fear to act; others are angry with outside agitators; others have been duped by the power structure." Nonetheless, the Biloxi organizers succeeded in registering a few whites in the MFDP and made contact with one white fisherman, Bob Williams, who became a SNCC supporter and an MFDP delegate to the Democratic National Convention.[21]

Early in August, the Point Cadet organizers received a fatal setback when rumors circulated that the local SNCC office was to be used to help get jobs for blacks rather than whites. "These rumors would not have gotten started had we been skilled community organizers," Maxwell observed. "For one thing, a skilled organizer would not let his identity be known until he had the backing of the key potential leaders in the community. For another, he would quickly inform the community about the nature of his program and not sit idly by to have rumors kill it before it gets started. He certainly wouldn't have put a SNCC sign in the office window or attempted to have a precinct meeting of the Freedom Democratic Party to get people curious enough about him to call the owner and make bomb threats."[22]

The white organizers were evicted from their office and forced to leave Point Cadet, but the lessons they learned proved invaluable in subsequent attempts, especially by the Southern Students Organizing Committee (SSOC), to establish projects in southern white communities. By the end of the summer, Maxwell and others were preparing to recruit more white volunteers to work with poor whites. "Right now it is only a dream," Maxwell admitted, "but I feel it is a dream which can catch fire in the minds of a lot of people."[23]

The response of Mississippi blacks to the freedom schools was an encouraging aspect of the Summer Project, but the innovative educational program only partially removed the barriers of distrust and fear that separated white teachers from black residents. Although SNCC had previously conducted educational programs to prepare black residents for Mississippi's voter registration test, and in 1963 Maria Varela of SNCC had established an adult literacy project in Alabama, the freedom schools were the first comprehensive educational program for a large number of black youngsters. The schools were not as closely linked to COFO's political effort as many SNCC workers desired, but they were an important experiment in the creation of parallel institutions to foster SNCC's ideology.

A statewide enrollment of about a thousand students had been expected for the freedom schools, but over twice that number attended classes in forty-one schools. Response was greatest in areas where there had already been civil rights activities. In Hattiesburg, for example, over six hundred students enrolled. Participation was much lower in plantation areas. As a teacher in Shaw explained, black youngsters in that community attended public schools during the summer so as to be available to pick cotton in the fall. Thus, after leaving public school in the afternoon, many of the youngsters preferred to sleep rather than going to the freedom school to study "in the blazing heat of the Mississippi sun and dust."[24]

The freedom school teachers eliminated traditional classroom rules and developed innovative teaching techniques designed to encourage the free expression of ideas. A curriculum guide developed for boycotting students in Boston was adapted for use in the freedom schools. As part of leadership training, for example, the students discussed the role of freedom schools and the need for blacks to preserve their own culture rather than uncritically adopting white cultural values.[25] In addition, students were offered courses in creative writing, drama, art, journalism and foreign languages. In some schools, there were evening classes in literacy, health, and typing. Many students also attended performances of the Free Southern Theater, a touring company organized as part of the freedom schools by John O'Neal at Tougaloo College. It performed *In White America*, a play written by historian Martin Duberman, depicting the history of American race relations from the era of slavery to the killing of the three civil rights workers at the beginning of the summer.

Most freedom school teachers were both encouraged and frustrated by their experiences during the summer. The students "hardly trust whites," a volunteer in Indianola wrote, "and there is a lot of 'Yes Ma'am' and constant agreement with what you say." Overcoming the students' reticence was the schools' major accomplishment. Another teacher described her gratification when students discovered they could "translate ideas into concrete written words. After two weeks a child finally looks me in the eye, unafraid, acknowledging a bond of trust which 300 years of Mississippians said should never, could never exist."[26]

Freedom school activities sometimes had a direct impact on the success of COFO political work. In communities such as McComb, where the civil rights movement had made little headway, the freedom school served, according to Staughton Lynd, "to loosen the hard knot of fear and to organize the Negro community." Ralph Featherstone, director of the McComb freedom school, asserted that "old people are looking to the young people and the [young people's] courage is rubbing off."[27]

Although freedom schools varied in effectiveness, many youngsters were deeply and permanently affected by the unique educational experience. When freedom school students from across the state gathered for a convention early in August, their increased confidence and political awareness were manifest in their approval of resolutions asking for enforcement of the Civil Rights Act of 1964, slum clearance, low-cost federal housing, free medical care, economic sanctions against South Africa, federal public workers jobs programs, equal employment opportunities, abolition of HUAC, elimination of the poll tax, and many other reforms.[28]

The freedom schools, which survived the summer, represented one of the first attempts by SNCC to replace existing institutions with alternative ones. As Zinn noted, they were a challenge to American education, embodying "the provocative suggestion that an entire school system can be created in any community outside the official order, and critical of its suppositions." For Zinn, the freedom schools raised questions regarding the future of American education. Could teachers and students get together "not through the artificial sieve of certification and examination but on the basis of their common attraction to an exciting social goal?" Could teachers instill values "while avoiding a blanket imposition of the teacher's ideas?" And would it be possible for teachers "to declare boldly that the aim of the schools is to find solutions for poverty, for injustice, for race and national hatred, and to turn all educational efforts into a national striving for those solutions?"[29] Although few SNCC workers were subsequently involved directly in the operations of the freedom schools, the schools continued to be characterized by SNCC's antiauthoritarianism. They were models and testing grounds for later alternative schools and tutorial projects throughout the nation.

The success of the freedom schools was important to the Summer Project, but the crucial test of COFO's strategy for the summer was whether it could provoke a decisive confrontation between segregationist Mississippi leaders and the federal government. No such confrontation took place, although in response to the murders the federal presence in Mississippi was dramatically strengthened. Analyzing the civil rights work of the FBI in Mississippi, John Doar and Dorothy Landsberg noted that the "magnificent change" in its performance after the disappearance of the three civil rights workers was mostly in the area of trying to infiltrate the Ku Klux Klan to find the murderers rather than providing protection for voter registration workers.[30]

The federal response reinforced the belief of many COFO workers that the government would become involved only when white violence was widely publicized or involved white volunteers. When FBI agents arrested three whites responsible for threatening two newly arrived volunteers, COFO Congressional District Director Stokely Carmichael reassured a group of volunteers that the FBI wasn't "going to let anything happen to them. They let the murderers of Negroes off, but already men have been arrested in Itta Bena just for *threatening* white lives." Belfrage sarcastically remarked that when Martin Luther King arrived for a visit in July accompanied by four cars of FBI men, their function was unclear, "Since they

were not, of course, a police force and could not, of course, protect anyone."[31]

To a degree, underlying the criticisms of SNCC workers was their dismay at the dispassion of FBI agents, who were sometimes seen taking notes
during attacks on blacks or acting in a cordial manner toward local police
officials known to be racists. The criticisms were also based on the fact that
harassment of civil rights workers peaked during the summer, though in
some communities antiblack violence declined from the presummer levels.
A summary of incidents compiled by SNCC's communications staff for the
first two months of summer recorded over three hundred arrests of civil
rights workers, usually on misdemeanor charges, over twenty-five bombings of homes and churches in black communities, and dozens of other incidents in which civil rights workers were beaten, shot, or threatened by
whites. Violence was most evident in McComb, where seventeen bombings
occurred during the period from June through September.[32]

The relative paucity of violence in some communities was attributed by
SNCC workers not to the federal presence but to the willingness of blacks
to arm themselves. Even prior to the summer, according to Zinn, there was
agreement among those in SNCC "that they would not stop a Negro
farmer in Mississippi from arming himself to defend his home against attack." Many Mississippi blacks kept weapons in their homes and were willing to use them to fight off attacks. Tillinghast, for example, recalled that
after whites began shooting at the home of Silas McGhee in apparent retaliation for the family's civil rights activities, "Mrs. McGhee called the sheriff
and told him . . . she knew exactly who was out there shooting at her and
that the sheriff should come and tell these here boys to go home, because
they were going to be picking up bodies the next time that she called." In
the rural community of Harmony local blacks stood armed guard around a
community center that was being constructed with the help of volunteers.
A volunteer in Gulfport told of a "man, and some of his friends, who took it
upon himself to protect us from the white men who visited us yesterday. He
came over at night with his friends and brought along a machine gun and
ammunition. And he told us not to worry. But he finally got ticked off at
us, because we got ticked off at him. That machine gun made us edgy."[33]

In the aftermath of the discovery in August of the murdered workers'
bodies, COFO staff members in Greenwood were torn between their responsibility to uphold SNCC's policy of nonviolence and their personal inclination to support local demonstrations that were likely to end in violence. Carmichael felt that he could not prevent blacks from carrying guns,
since the practice was legal in Mississippi. As Belfrage recalled a COFO
staff discussion of the planned protests, when a question was raised as to the
aim of the Greenwood protesters, a worker answered, "The first thing they
want is to kill white people." Among the other black members "there was

an instant, uncommunicated electric current running from one to the other. It was suddenly understood by all the whites how little they had ever understood." The situation cooled only after Carmichael left to telephone COFO headquarters in Jackson for Moses' opinion and returned "a different man. As calm and thoughtful as Moses himself, Stokely said, 'What I think we ought to do is work harder on freedom registration forms.' "[34]

Although the incidents of violence contributed to the radicalization of those involved, COFO veterans also recognized that the Mississippi Summer Project had resulted in a new social climate in which blacks in most areas of the state could concentrate on achieving long-range goals rather than on solving immediate problems of personal security. "Now," Moses commented in August, "except for some rural areas and the southwest, there is less harassment of workers by police and very little by local people. We interpret that as meaning that police put out the word to the local citizens."[35]

Although they failed in their attempt to bring about massive federal intervention, SNCC leaders still hoped to unseat the regular Mississippi delegation at the Democratic National Convention. By early August, when eight hundred delegates attended the MFDP state convention in Jackson, COFO had built a powerful, though fragile, liberal coalition to support the challenge. The sixty-eight MFDP delegates, including four whites, chosen to go to Atlantic City manifested the continued belief among Mississippi civil rights workers that their appeals to the outside world would be answered.[36] SNCC leaders, though probably less sanguine than most of the delegates, mobilized nearly all of SNCC's resources for the challenge, drawing personnel from its Mississippi projects as well as from projects elsewhere in the South. The delegation included SNCC workers Charles McLaurin, Larry Guyot, Fannie Lou Hamer, E. W. Steptoe, Annie Devine, and Hartman Turnbow.

The hopes of the MFDP delegation were based on the belief that they, rather than the regular, all-white delegation, represented the expressed principles of the national Democratic party. The white Democratic organization in Mississippi had systematically excluded blacks from participation and opposed much of President Johnson's domestic program. Indeed, many Democratic leaders in Mississippi publicly supported the candidacy of Republican Senator Barry Goldwater. In contrast, the MFDP was open to all Mississippi residents, had followed Mississippi rules regarding political party operations, and was committed to the election of Johnson.

During the months prior to the convention, SNCC veterans such as Ella Baker, Reginald Robinson, and Marion Barry mobilized northern support on behalf of the challenge. Although many SNCC workers later claimed that they had always been skeptical about the challenge's chances for success, it is more likely that, as the MFDP received additional commitments of support from liberal Democrats outside the South, few SNCC workers remained totally pessimistic. According to one source, by the beginning of August nine Democratic state delegations and twenty-five Democratic congressmen had expressed support for the challenge.[37]

President Johnson nevertheless remained determined to avoid any action that would weaken his southern white support. On August 12, Mississippi Governor Paul B. Johnson told the regular delegates that he had been personally assured by the President that the MFDP would not be seated.[38] When Johnson invited Lewis and other civil rights leaders to meet with him at the White House on August 19, he bluntly told them that he would not discuss his views regarding the convention challenge. Even before the meeting, Johnson had asked the FBI to establish surveillance of the pro-MFDP forces at the convention. Hoover agreed to send a squad to the convention to advise the White House concerning the MFDP plans. Phones in SNCC's Atlantic City offices were bugged as part of this surveillance.[39]

By early August, Joseph Rauh, MFDP's counsel and its link to Democratic leaders, learned that the vice-presidential candidacy of his friend and political ally, Senator Hubert Humphrey, would be harmed by his role in MFDP. Although Rauh insisted that Humphrey himself never tried to influence him, Humphrey's staff "was not as kindly and generous." Searching for an acceptable compromise at an August 13 meeting with Democratic National Chairman John Bailey and Credential Committee Chairman David Lawrence, Rauh proposed the seating of both delegations. The two party leaders reacted positively, but the White House did not. Rauh concluded that at best he could hope only that the President would take a position of "benevolent neutrality."[40]

By the start of the convention, most MFDP delegates and supporters knew that the challenge would not receive majority support in the Credentials Committee. Nonetheless, they hoped that their supporters on the committee would be able to bring a minority report to the floor of the convention, where presumably they would receive extensive backing from liberal delegates forced to state their positions openly. Even if they did not achieve their goal of unseating the regular delegation, they expected that a compromise could be arranged to seat both delegations. Rauh's brief filed in support of the challenge suggested many historical precedents for such a compromise.[41]

Recognizing that the challenge would be won or lost on political as well as legal grounds, MFDP supporters lobbied day and night among the delegates. When Jim Forman arrived at the convention, he was surprised to see Ivanhoe Donaldson and Charles Cobb, "the blue jeans twins of Mississippi . . . all dressed up now in Ivy League outfits." Meetings were arranged with state delegations, and massive amounts of material were reproduced and distributed with the help of SNCC.[42]

On August 22, the MFDP presented its case to the Credentials Committee. Rauh, King, and Aaron Henry, among others, spoke on behalf of the delegation, but the highlight of the day's testimony was the appearance of Hamer. By then an experienced SNCC organizer, Hamer gave an emotional account of being fired from her job and then beaten in jail by black prisoners on orders from state highway patrolmen:[43]

> The first Negro began to beat, and I was beat until I was exhausted . . . After the first Negro . . . was exhausted, the State Highway Patrolman ordered the second Negro to take the blackjack. The second Negro began to beat . . . I began to scream, and one white man got up and began to beat me on my head and tell me to "hush."
> One white man—my dress had worked up high—he walked over and pulled my dress down and he pulled my dress back, back up . . . All of this is on account we want to register, to become first-class citizens, and if the Freedom Democratic Party is not seated now, I question America.

Although the television networks cut away from Hamer's testimony before the end to cover a hastily called press conference by President Johnson, her remarks had an immediate impact on the television audience and soon on the delegates, who received numerous telegrams urging support for the MFDP. As a result, the Johnson forces tried to arrange a compromise. On August 23, Rauh was told that the Johnson backers were prepared to offer the MFDP delegates the right to participate vocally in the convention proceedings but not to vote. All major MFDP backers rejected this compromise.

MFDP's support within the Credentials Committee began to slip, however, as pressure was exerted by supporters of Johnson and Humphrey. According to Rauh, a black California supporter was told "that her husband wouldn't get a judgeship if she didn't leave us, and the Secretary of the Army told the guy from the Canal Zone that he would lose his job if he didn't leave us."[44] Several committee members shifted their support from the MFDP to a new compromise backed by Johnson, which would give Aaron Henry and Edwin King at-large seats at the convention while the other delegates would be accepted as "guests" of the convention. In addition, the convention in 1968 would bar any state delegation that discriminated against blacks.

On the evening of August 23 a caucus of black delegates was held at which the administration's new compromise was discussed. As Charles Sherrod recalled, when Congressman Charles Dawson and other black politicians argued that blacks must support President Johnson, MFDP delegate Annie Devine responded passionately, her voice quivering: "We have been treated like beasts in Mississippi. They shot us down like animals. We risk our lives coming up here . . . politics must be corrupt if it don't care none about people down there . . . these politicians sit in positions and forget the people put them there." The meeting was adjourned without reaching a decision.[45]

In the meantime SNCC leaders were subjected to intense pressure to support the administration's compromise. Bayard Rustin and Martin Luther King, who favored it, arranged a meeting at which Humphrey tried unsuccessfully to persuade Moses to accept the plan. On August 25, the MFDP delegation, recognizing at last that they had little hope of displacing the regular delegation, threw their support to a proposal by Congresswoman Edith Green of Oregon to seat every member of both delegations who signed a loyalty pledge and then divide Mississippi's votes proportionately among the delegates seated. But Rauh, under intense pressure from Walter Reuther, who had hired him as counsel for the United Automobile Workers, announced that he and MFDP's remaining supporters on the Credentials Committee would back the administration's compromise.

On August 26, the MFDP delegates met to make a final decision on the compromise. "You could cut through the tension," Sherrod recalled. "People were touchy and on edge. It had been a long fight." Rauh, King, Rustin, and other liberal leaders spoke in favor of the compromise. Moses stated that, although the COFO staff still did not support the compromise, the delegates should make their own decisions. Forman urged rejection, as did Hamer, who said, "We didn't come all this way for no two seats!"[46] After hours of discussion, the compromise was overwhelmingly rejected.

Although the MFDP was defeated in its attempt to unseat the regular delegation and the convention accepted the administration's compromise, demonstrations in support of the MFDP continued. MFDP delegates and their supporters gained access to the convention floor, using passes obtained from sympathetic delegates. After the regular Mississippi delegation left the convention in protest, a few MFDP delegates occupied their seats until forcibly ejected. Apparently the controversy over the MFDP challenge had little effect on President Johnson, who failed to mention it in his memoir, which described the convention as "a place of happy, surging crowds and thundering cheers" and a welcome "display of unity."[47]

The compromise proposal was intended as a symbolic gesture of support for the MFDP by the liberal Democratic leadership and sympathetic delegates. The rejection of the offer by MFDP delegates was just as symbolic a gesture of their unwillingness to accept a proposal that did not acknowledge their right to represent Mississippi and to choose their own representatives. Although the delegates had risked their lives to attend the convention and had gained sufficient support on the Credentials Committee to bring the matter to the floor, where they felt assured of being seated in a roll call vote, they were prevented from achieving their goal, according to an MFDP report, by "the most massive pressure from the White House, through the mediation of Hubert Humphrey." Although the MFDP would have accepted "any honorable compromise," the Democratic leaders did not meet the test. "This kind of dictation is what Negroes in Mississippi face and have always faced, and it is precisely this that they are learning to stand up against."[48]

The MFDP nevertheless supported Johnson and his running mate, Humphrey, in the general election in November. They were among the minority of Mississippians to do so, as Goldwater easily carried the state. Although for some MFDP members the experiences at Atlantic City led to their disillusionment with national liberal leaders and contributed to their radicalization, most MFDP leaders believed that, despite the disappointment, they should continue to seek entry into the national Democratic party.

SNCC workers were even more embittered by the Atlantic City experience than were the MFDP delegates. Feelings of disappointment were most intense among veterans who saw the challenge as a test of their strategy of appealing to the federal government. For Lewis, the lesson of Atlantic City was that, "when you play the game and go by the rules, you still can lose, if you don't have the resources, if you're going to disrupt the natural order of things." He admitted that "in a sense we were naive to go on believing that somehow the Democratic Party in 1964 would have unseated the Mississippi regular Democrats." Donaldson remarked that if the MFDP delegates had accepted the compromise, it would have negated everything they had struggled for—"whether people should have to sit down with racists to discuss their humanity."[49]

Sherrod, proud of the fact that the delegation had not "bowed to the 'massa,' " claimed that "the masters of political power" were still not willing to trust blacks with "real power." Although Sherrod had been at odds with black SNCC workers because of his faith in religious radicalism and his policy of using white field secretaries, after the convention he voiced the new mood of militancy within SNCC. "We are not only demanding meat and bread and a job," he declared, "but we are also demanding power, a share in the power!" The question for blacks in America was whether to share power "in reconciliation" or, out of frustration, to seize power "in rioting and blood." Sherrod blamed the MFDP defeat on the fact that there were no blacks at the convention with the power to oppose the Johnson forces. "We want much more than 'token' positions. We want power for our people." Castigating those who argued that the Mississippi delegation should have been "responsible" and not engaged in acts that would benefit

Goldwater, Sherrod countered: "Who runs our society? . . . Who makes the laws? Who interprets the law? Who holds the power? Let them be responsible!" Although the delegation could have accepted the compromise to satisfy the liberals, such a course would have had damaging consequences: "It would have said to blacks across the nation and the world that we share the power, and that is a lie! The 'liberals' would have felt great relief for a job well done. The Democrats would have laughed again at the segregationist Republicans and smiled that their own 'Negroes' were satisfied. That is a lie! We are a country of racists with a racist heritage, a racist economy, a racist language, a racist religion, a racist philosophy of living, and we need a naked confrontation with ourselves."[50]

Like Sherrod, Carmichael believed that the defeat of the MFDP challenge indicated the need for racial power. The experience showed "not merely that the national conscience was generally unreliable but that, very specifically, black people in Mississippi and throughout this country could not rely on their so-called allies. Many labor, liberal, and civil rights leaders deserted the MFDP because of closer ties to the national Democratic party." MFDP chairman Guyot and Mike Thelwell, a SNCC worker who directed the MFDP's Washington office, compared the situation to SNCC's strategy in the Mississippi Summer Project, which was similarly based on a "confidence in the ultimate morality in national political institutions and practices—'They *really* couldn't know, and once we bring the facts about Mississippi to national attention, justice must surely be swift and irrevocable'—which was a simplistic faith somewhat akin to that of the Russian peasants under the Czars. Caught in the direst kind of oppression and deprivation, the peasants would moan, 'If the Czar only knew how we suffer. He is good and would give us justice. If only he knew.' The fact was that he knew only too well."[51]

The defeat of the challenge was perhaps most painful for Moses. After the convention he drifted away from the MFDP, believing that there was no longer any point to working within the Democratic party. The compromise offered at the convention had been meaningless because it required the regular party to open future meetings to blacks but did not guarantee that blacks would be allowed to register. Thus, the regular Democrats could allow token black participation in 1968 and claim to have complied with the new rules. Rather than continuing to see the MFDP as a means of opening the Democratic party to black participation, Moses suggested a more radical course: "Why can't we set up our own [state] government? So that in 1967, if we get organized enough between now and then, we can . . . declare the other one no good. And say the federal government should recognize us."[52]

Moses' remarks hinted at the course he and other SNCC workers would shortly follow. Having demonstrated their ability to mobilize large numbers of blacks, they began to search for radical political alternatives. Their search was complicated, however, by the responsibilities that had been thrust on them as a result of the Summer Project. SNCC had helped to create institutions, such as the MFDP and the freedom schools, which required continued attention and guidance. The Summer Project had also strengthened SNCC's ties with the growing white student left.

The summer volunteers, who returned home greatly influenced by their experiences in Mississippi, would bring a measure of SNCC's radicalism into the student rights and antiwar movements. "Last summer I went to Mississippi to join the struggle there for civil rights," explained Berkeley Free Speech Movement leader Mario Savio. "This fall I am engaged in another phase of the same struggle, this time in Berkeley . . . In Mississippi an autocratic and powerful minority rules, through organized violence, to suppress the vast, virtually powerless majority. In California, the privileged minority manipulates the university bureaucracy to suppress the students' political expression."[53]

SNCC had previously focused its energies on the task of breaking new ground—garnering popular support for militancy and staging continuous but small-scale assaults on the segregationist social order. The character of SNCC had been forged during a period when idealists could accomplish important social goals through a willingness to engage in protest and thereby create a crisis that required outside intervention. The new leadership responsibilities of SNCC required additional talents that would test the abilities and dedication of its still young staff. SNCC's period of rapid and uncontrolled growth had come to an end; its most significant period of intellectual ferment was about to begin.

# PART TWO
# LOOKING INWARD

# 10. WAVELAND RETREAT

During the months after the Mississippi Summer Project, SNCC's staff began to confront the difficult task of critically examining their past work and formulating a future strategy. They had accomplished much since coming together in McComb three years before. They had roused thousands of southern blacks to political action and had launched new black-controlled institutions, most notably the MFDP and the freedom schools. They had created a strong base of northern financial support, prodded the federal government to act with increasing firmness on behalf of black civil rights, and brought together a coalition of liberal forces in support of the MFDP challenge. They had done this by developing distinctive and effective techniques of community organizing that relied on local leadership and on the use of militancy as a catalyst for mass mobilization.

Yet many SNCC workers had begun to doubt the value of their work, and their uneasiness grew after the summer of 1964. The Summer Project was one of the last major interracial civil rights efforts of the 1960s, although elements of a national civil rights coalition would again join forces during the Selma, Alabama, voting rights campaign of 1965. SNCC's youthful, impulsive activism, its moralistic sense of purpose, and its openness to new ideas and people had made it the most dynamic of all civil rights organizations, but staff members wondered whether the attitudes and values of its years of growth were still appropriate. They questioned whether reliance on leadership without specialized skills and uninstitutionalized insurgency were adequate means of moving beyond the civil rights gains of the first half of the decade. Some staff members urged that SNCC consolidate previous gains by following the life cycle of other social movement organizations and becoming more formalized and bureaucratized. SNCC's anti-authoritarian orientation, however, guaranteed strong resistance to such a course.

Retaining a common belief in sustained, militant mass struggle as the major agent of social change, staff members nevertheless differed in their proposals for increasing SNCC's effectiveness and broadening its range. The bonds that held the staff together in confrontations with southern racists also began to weaken as SNCC came into increasing conflict with for-

mer liberal supporters. Like the rest of American society, SNCC was entering a period of divisive conflict, with staff members becoming more aware
of the varied and sometimes subtle dimensions of social oppression. The internal debates that began with the position papers written for the retreat in
November 1964 at Waveland, Mississippi, were largely ignored by those
outside SNCC, but they foreshadowed important trends in American political life.

Spurred by the defeat of the MFDP challenge, SNCC workers began to
look beyond their own experiences for ideological insights. An unexpected
turn in this search for new ideas came in the fall of 1964 when SNCC accepted the invitation of Harry Belafonte to send a delegation to Africa. Belafonte, a long-time SNCC supporter, arranged for the trip through his
contacts with the government of Guinea. Although Jim Forman later concluded that it was "a serious mistake" to approve the trip before resolving
questions about SNCC's direction at home, the chance to tour Africa was
irresistible.[1] SNCC workers welcomed the opportunity for a break from the
pressures of their work. Moreover, they had been inspired by the example
of young black leaders of newly independent African nations. On many
occasions they had rhetorically linked their struggle with the African nationalist movements and had appealed to Africans for support of civil
rights efforts. In December 1963 a group of staff members had met with
Oginga Odinga, the Kenyan leader, on his brief stop in Atlanta.

The African tour, which began on September 11, 1964, had a profound
impact on the SNCC delegation, composed of Forman, John Lewis, Bob
and Dona Moses, Prathia Hall, Julian Bond, Ruby Doris Robinson, Bill
Hansen, Donald Harris, Matthew Jones, and Fannie Lou Hamer. As guests
of the government of Guinea, a former French colony that had determined
to remain politically independent of the West, they were able to see
American society from a new perspective. Guinean President Sekou Touré,
a proponent of African socialism and of nonalignment in the Cold War,
encouraged them to take a broad view of the goals of their struggle, stating
that there was a close relationship between what SNCC did in the United
States and what happened in Africa.[2] The delegates were impressed not
only by their warm reception from government officials but also by their
observations of daily life in a nation dominated by blacks. "I saw black
men flying the airplanes, driving buses, sitting behind big desks in the bank
and just doing everything that I was used to seeing white people do," Hamer
recalled.[3]

The SNCC representatives, in becoming aware of how their own struggle
was perceived by Africans, discovered that the United States government
had far more control than they over the image of the American civil rights
movement in the minds of Africans. Bond expressed dismay about the mis-

leading information provided by American information offices in Africa. "There were all these pictures of Negroes doing things, Negro judges, Negro policemen, and if you didn't know anything about America, like Africans would not, you would think these were really commonplace things. That's the worst kind of deceit."[4]

After the rest of the delegation returned to the United States on October 4, Lewis and Harris continued on a month-long tour of Liberia, Ghana, Zambia, Kenya, Ethiopia, and Egypt. Their meetings with African student leaders and Afro-American expatriates convinced them that SNCC should establish permanent ties with Africans. While in Zambia for that nation's independence ceremonies, they talked with African revolutionaries who, according to their subsequent report, also "knew the insides of many jails and the loneliness of being separated from family and friends." The revolutionaries told delegates that they wanted closer contacts with SNCC: "As one brother said, 'Let's join hands so we can all be free together.' "[5]

Perhaps the most significant episode of their stay in Africa was an unexpected encounter in Nairobi with Malcolm X, the Afro-American leader who had recently broken with the narrowly religious focus of Elijah Muhammad's Nation of Islam. Even before the meeting, Lewis and Harris had learned of Malcolm's considerable influence on the African continent, for Africans occasionally greeted them with "skepticism and distrust" because, as one explained, "if you are to the right of Malcolm, you might as well start packing right now 'cause no one'll listen to you." Malcolm, however, had resolved to abet the radical tendencies in the civil rights movement, and was eager to meet with representatives of SNCC, his favorite civil rights organization. At the meeting he criticized American civil rights groups for neglecting African affairs, despite the fact that African leaders and citizenry themselves supported the Afro-American struggle. Although Malcolm felt that Africans would not endorse particular groups or factions, he hoped that his recently formed Organization of Afro-American Unity (OAU) would bring together American blacks who were interested in closer ties with Africa.[6]

The Nairobi meeting was followed by a series of attempts by Malcolm to forge links with SNCC. Malcolm's Pan-African perspective and his awareness of the need for black self-defense and racial pride converged with ideas gaining acceptance in SNCC. He spoke at an MFDP rally in Harlem and invited Hamer and the SNCC Freedom Singers to appear at a meeting of the OAU. While hosting a group of Mississippi teenagers in New York under the sponsorship of SNCC, Malcolm identified the greatest accomplishment of the 1964 struggles as "the successful linking together of our problem with the African problem, or making our problem a world problem." In February 1965 during the voting rights campaign in Selma, Malcolm addressed black demonstrators at the invitation of SNCC activists.

Then on February 21, the developing ties between SNCC and Malcolm were severed by the nationalist leader's assassination in New York. Afterward Lewis commented that Malcolm, "more than any other single personality," had been "able to articulate the aspirations, bitterness, and frustrations of the Negro people," forming "a living link between Africa and the civil rights movement in this country."[7]

The African tour contributed to SNCC's increasing awareness of the international implications of its struggle, but pressing internal problems prevented the organization from following up at once on its contacts in Africa. Although columnists Rowland Evans and Robert Novak warned in December 1964 that SNCC, whose delegation had failed even to report to government officials upon their return, would "put into practice the revolutionary techniques" of the emerging African countries, not until visits in subsequent years by Moses, Forman, and other staff members did SNCC finally establish an office of international affairs. Despite the tour's lack of tangible results, it strengthened the emotional bonds that SNCC workers had long felt toward Africa. Most agreed with Lewis that the destiny of Afro-Americans was "inseparable from that of our black brothers in Africa. It matters not whether it is in Angola, Mozambique, Southwest Africa, or Mississippi, Alabama, Georgia, and Harlem, U.S.A. The struggle is . . . the same . . . It is a struggle against a vicious and evil system that is controlled and kept in order for and by a few white men throughout the world."[8]

Enthusiasm for African revolutionary ideas was soon tempered by a realization of the enormous difficulties to be faced at home. Not only were SNCC workers exhausted after the summer ordeal, but many were uncertain of their future roles in the changing southern struggle. In addition they were coming under attack from liberals who were beginning to doubt whether SNCC militants would continue to play useful roles as the shock troops of the civil rights movement or would instead become the spearhead of a new assault against conventional liberalism.

Charges that SNCC was a subversive organization or was communist-controlled, which had previously been discounted by northern liberals, gained increasing support after SNCC's display of radicalism during the March on Washington and again at the 1964 Democratic convention. The fact that the Summer Project volunteers were, in a few cases, children of communists and that communist literature was available in certain freedom houses and community centers led to further adverse comment in the North. Moses acknowledged during the summer of 1964 that SNCC was "open and totally exposed" to such criticism "because we make no attempt to screen people for their political affiliation." Moses himself was denounced by Evans and Novak as "dangerously oblivious to the Communist menace to the rights movement and so militant in his championship of

Negro rights that at times he approaches black nationalism."[9] No evidence was presented to support charges of communist influence, but the changing stance of northern reporters toward SNCC contributed to the erosion of its previous sources of support.

SNCC's deteriorating relations with more moderate civil rights organizations became evident at a meeting of the different groups in New York on September 18 to discuss future strategy in Mississippi. Gloster Current of the NAACP attacked SNCC's continuing relationship with the National Lawyers Guild, and Joseph Rauh agreed that it was "immoral" to accept help from such groups deemed to be communist-dominated. In addition to its associations, SNCC was criticized for failing to cooperate with the other national civil rights groups in supporting a compromise at the Democratic convention and for controlling the MFDP. Program Director Courtland Cox, representing SNCC while the other officers were in Africa, defended the group by insisting that the MFDP delegates, not the COFO staff, had rejected the seating compromise. He suggested that differences among the civil rights organizations should be resolved through a "low-level meeting" involving local black leaders from Mississippi. Although Andrew Young of SCLC supported this suggestion, others argued that policy issues should be resolved by leaders at the national level. Allard Lowenstein argued for "structured democracy" rather than SNCC's "amorphous democracy." Current, who had "been listening to people from Mississippi cry for seventeen years," felt that a high-level meeting was needed "so we can cut away the underbrush." The gathering ended without a resolution of the differences and with increased suspicion among the SNCC representatives and civil rights moderates regarding each others' motives.[10]

The breakdown in SNCC's relations with moderate civil rights groups resulted not only from SNCC's militancy, which had been apparent for some time, but also from its emergence as a serious competitor to the NAACP and SCLC for dominance within the civil rights movement. By initiating and leading the Summer Project, SNCC had demonstrated its increasing effectiveness. The Summer Project also revealed the problems inherent in SNCC's attempting to mobilize black communities under indigenous leadership while also relying on northern white support.

These contradictions could no longer be ignored when at the end of summer more than eighty volunteers who had stayed on to work in Mississippi asked to become permanent members of SNCC's staff. Recognizing that the addition of this large, predominantly white group would significantly alter the racial and class composition of SNCC and probably result in increased racial tensions within the staff, Cox called a general staff meeting for October 10 in Atlanta. Those who attended were prepared to discuss not only SNCC's racial composition but also its decision-making structure and future direction.

Although SNCC had tried to resist the development of leadership roles within its organization, the views of two participants in the meeting were of crucial importance. Forman and Moses had not only earned the respect of other staff members but also come to symbolize competing tendencies within the group. Both accepted the need for a new orientation in SNCC, but Forman was prepared to abandon a large measure of SNCC's freewheeling style in order to achieve political power, whereas Moses believed that SNCC should encourage individuals to break free of all centralized structures of power rather than build new ones.

Several weeks prior to the October meeting, Forman and Moses apparently found common ground when they came together to formulate the Black Belt Program, a plan to expand SNCC's work throughout the deep South during the following summer. This proposal did not require SNCC to change the tactics used in the Summer Project but rather to broaden the use of those tactics by establishing new projects staffed by black student volunteers. The idea of using black rather than white volunteers reflected Moses' concern about both the breakdown in effectiveness of some Mississippi projects because of racial conflict and the inability of local black leaders to gain confidence in their abilities as long as large numbers of white volunteers remained on the scene.[11]

Yet the possibility that SNCC might agree on this program was lessened by the unsettled and weakened state of the organization. Rational discussion of the options available required energy, resolve, and foresight not possessed by the staff after the grueling events of the summer. "For the first time in my life, I understood how soldiers feel when they return from wars and have to grope unwillingly for answers to the terribly innocent 'How was it?' questions of family and friends," Cleveland Sellers recalled. Many people who had participated in the Summer Project used the phrase "battle fatigue" to describe the condition afflicting civil rights workers. "Fixed anger and suspicion plague them," reported psychiatrist Robert Coles, who worked closely with Mississippi civil rights workers during 1964. "They lose not only perspective and humor, but they begin to distrust the intentions and aspirations of others, so that fewer and fewer people, even among their own co-workers, can be trusted." Although staff members at other periods had gone to meetings, according to Forman, "with a tremendous amount of accumulated tension, anxiety, frustrations," the added emotional strains of the summer contributed to the conflicts that would soon divide the staff.[12]

Such strains were immediately evident at the October meeting when the Black Belt Program was introduced for discussion. Frank Smith charged that staff members had not been adequately involved in developing the proposal, whereupon the meeting took "a disastrous turn," according to Forman. "A few people were raising the cry, 'Who made that decision?' as if somebody had tried to sneak something over on them." MFDP leader Lawrence Guyot opposed the plan because it would divert SNCC's resources from Mississippi to elsewhere in the South. Even Moses did not speak up for the proposal, despite his role in preparing it.[13]

With some justification, Forman interpreted the resulting failure of the staff to accept his plan as a personal defeat. In an organization that often resented assertive leadership, there were some members who saw the ambitious proposal as an attempt by Forman to increase his authority. Forman indeed confirmed that his goal during this period was to transform SNCC into "a strong, centralized organization expanding its power and moving toward becoming a mass organization," rather than allowing it to remain "a limited cadre of organizers who moved around instigating protests, and who might catalyze the emergence of [a mass] organization—but never themselves grow to become it."

Forman's objectives were shaped by his reading of revolutionary thought, particularly that of African leader Kwame Nkrumah, but at the time he did not clearly set forth the rationale for his actions. The Black Belt Plan gave few hints of a new conception of SNCC's role. Although Forman later disparaged middle-class protesters in SNCC who fostered individualistic values, during the fall of 1964 he commended SNCC for being comprised of "action oriented intellectuals" and "agitators, rabble-rousers who were always forcing the issue." He described himself as a leader of the "field machine," the southern black field secretaries, but he was at least partially responsible for the fact that whites and northern blacks rather than "local people" dominated SNCC's headquarters. His explanation for displacing Lewis as SNCC's representative in meetings with other civil rights groups revealed his ambivalence regarding the notion that blacks from the deep South should lead SNCC. Describing Lewis as "young, inexperienced, from a small southern town," Forman found in him "fine qualities as a symbol of black resistance, but he was lost among these overpowering tricky infighters."[14]

Moses was the nominal leader of an anti-Forman faction, but unlike Forman, he became increasingly uneasy with the influence he had acquired in SNCC. His failure to support the Black Belt Plan reflected his philosophical opposition to the use of intellectual skills to control others and his recognition of the need to allow less articulate civil rights workers to develop their own leadership abilities. Rather than viewing SNCC as a permanent political organization, as did Forman, Moses wanted it to remain an informal community of organizers whose task was first to identify local leadership, foster its development, and then step aside, allowing that leadership to determine its own direction. Ironically, his unwillingness to manipulate others and his selfless devotion to the struggle caused him to gain an unwanted personal following, particularly among white student activists, who saw in him the archetype of the intellectual activist. Recognizing that others in SNCC and COFO had grown dependent on his leadership, Moses became more and more reluctant to express his views, but this attitude merely strengthened his appeal among those who opposed Forman's assertiveness.

Throughout the fall of 1964 Moses and Forman drew further apart. Seeking to retain the momentum of the Summer Project, Forman became increasingly insistent on the need for planning, staff discipline, and organizational structure. He attributed Moses' failure to exert leadership to "the pressure on him of that liberalism which said, beware of your own leadership, your own power." Forman encouraged Moses to become more involved in SNCC policy discussions but found that Moses "was disturbed by an almost Jesus-like aura that he and his name had acquired. 'Nobody would ever call me a mother fucker,' he once said, or words to that effect, meaning that he was receiving a kind of respect which he considered false."[15] Moses, for his part, followed the example of his ideological mentor, Camus, in giving higher standing to his humanistic values than to the goal of political power. Although he attempted to lessen SNCC's internal conflicts by meeting with Forman and agreeing to discuss SNCC's problems in staff meetings, Moses would never again play a major role in SNCC policy decisions. Those who looked to him for guidance nevertheless continued to invoke his name in support of their opposition to centralized authority in the organization.

After the October meeting, Forman and others planned a staff retreat for early November to prevent the further deterioration of SNCC's effectiveness. Rather than focusing on day-to-day problems, they hoped to address issues of long-range strategy and goals and to begin a program of internal education. The site chosen was the Gulfside Methodist Church in Waveland, Mississipppi, a small community in the southeast corner of the state.

According to a notice sent to the approximately 160 staff members, the purpose of the retreat was to confront a broad range of questions: "where ... how ... why do we organize? Who should be on the Executive Committee? ... Where is the civil rights movement now and what does that mean? ... What should SNCC do about the civil rights bill?"[16] The planners knew that one meeting would not be sufficient for such an ambitious, wide-ranging agenda, but they hoped that for a week the staff could overcome their previous tendency to emphasize action rather than deliberation. Staff members were asked to write position papers in advance of the retreat so that ideas could be expressed more coherently than through SNCC's typically rambling discussions.

The thirty-seven papers written for the retreat revealed a pervasive concern about SNCC's loss of a common sense of purpose and its resulting failure to act decisively and effectively after the summer. Although providing no solutions to SNCC's dilemmas, the papers suggested the general outlines of the subsequent development of American radicalism in the 1960s. As had been the case with the nineteenth century abolitionist movement, the debates and conflicts within the southern movement provided a seedbed for the resurgence of the moribund American traditions of Afro-American separatism, feminism, and participatory democracy. They would also influence later techniques used by community organizers in the poverty program, Peace Corps, and Vista.

Veteran staff members remarked on the need to assess SNCC's previous work before moving ahead. They recognized, however, the difficulty of pausing during an intense social movement to undertake a process of self-criticism and systematic self-education. Moses was probably the author of an unsigned paper describing SNCC's situation as that of "a boat in the middle of the ocean. It has to be rebuilt in order to stay afloat. It also has to stay afloat in order to be rebuilt. Our problem is like that. Since we are out on the ocean we have to do it ourselves." The paper urged a flexible approach to making decisions: "Important problems at the center of our work need longer exposure and a wide forum. Every-day problems on the edge can be decided immediately by the person responsible in forum with himself or whoever."[17]

Sherrod noted in his paper a new stage in the movement. SNCC, which had once appealed effectively to "the white man's guilt," now faced "a 'backlash' of the white man's conscience." Conservative forces were gaining in the nation, and SNCC needed to organize its own bases of power. It also needed to produce an ideology and to "organize along more rigid lines." Sherrod warned that staff members were "grasshoppers fighting the sleeping giant. When the giant awakens and puts on a unified armor, we're going to have hell to pay. We were kids; now we're grown-up—almost. We still have a little time before the giant awakes."[18]

Sherrod's warning was reiterated by an anonymous writer who asserted that SNCC could not "afford the luxury of rambling and inconclusive discussion which will leave us all spiritually purged but still in organizational chaos." The writer advised against allowing internal dissension to create a situation in which SNCC was "able to survive outside pressures—beatings, killings, terrorism—and choke and strangle on its own size and affluence."[19]

SNCC was at a turning point, and the militancy of SNCC's early years would have to be supplemented by new strategies. A consensus about the need for civil rights reforms had held SNCC together during its years of growth, but the staff's unity of purpose could not be maintained in the face of questions as to whether voting rights or desegregation were sufficient to improve conditions of life for southern blacks. The Summer Project had

been a crucial test of the prevailing postwar civil rights strategy, which relied on efforts to publicize the worst aspects of the Jim Crow system and on
the use of civil disobedience and mass demonstrations to coerce the federal
government into action. The Civil Rights Act of 1964 marked an important victory for this strategy, but by the time of its enactment SNCC workers saw themselves as part of a struggle for more fundamental social
changes.

Several of the Waveland papers touched on the issue of whether SNCC
could continue to play a crucial role in future black struggles. Howard
Zinn argued that SNCC was "best suited to be a relatively small, mobile,
striking force, guerilla fighters in the field of social change, who will get into
the heart of where problems are deepest, awaken people . . . and create
pockets of power all over the nation which remain outside the official
channels of power but bombard these channels with demonstrations of
what is wrong in the nation." Yet this kind of protest activity which had
established SNCC's militant reputation might not be appropriate for confronting the deeply rooted problems of poverty and powerlessness of blacks
in the deep South. A staff member pointed out that those in SNCC had
never decided whether they wanted to be agitators or demonstrators or organizers— "and we can't fool ourselves into believing that we can be all
three because we can't do it effectively."[20]

Despite their growing doubts about SNCC's future role, staff members
remained convinced of the validity of SNCC's distinctive values even as the
goals of the black struggle changed. While questioning former assumptions
about the direction of change, they affirmed even more strongly their belief
that all people, regardless of educational background and class status,
should have meaningful roles in the political process. The notion that local
black leaders rather than SNCC workers should determine the tactics and
goals of the southern movement had been a central tenet of SNCC projects
and formed the basis of what was called participatory democracy. But the
loss of momentum after the summer of 1964 led to the conclusion that
SNCC had not entirely succeeded in conveying to local leaders the skills
and confidence necessary to sustain the struggle.

Several Waveland papers suggested that college backgrounds of SNCC
workers hindered their efforts to develop self-confident leadership among
poorly educated blacks. Sherrod, who had known poverty as a youth, remarked that a person may be too "ignorant to make a pair of shoes, but not
so ignorant that he doesn't know when a pair of shoes pinches him or that
the roof leaks or that white folks have power over that his belly is empty."
Sherrod urged SNCC to strive for a new society "based on the wisdom of
the pinched toe and the empty belly." Maria Varela, head of SNCC's liter-

acy project, commented on the need for organizers to abandon "the habits that come from a system of values almost all of us have had—that is that educated, better-off people naturally dominate under-educated, less well off people." Another staff member urged SNCC workers to "respect the way [local people] think and work and not impose an organizing pattern that is foreign to them."[21]

These ideas, though restatements of assumptions that had been implicit in SNCC's most successful projects, received impetus from the growing demands of community oganizers for greater influence within the organization. SNCC's most pressing problem, according to an anonymous paper, was the differences in background of SNCC's college-educated central office staff and its black field staff in local offices. The field workers were "closer in backgrounds" to the local people, "while those making broad policy decisions [were] further removed physically, if not also in terms of backgrounds and experiences from the people out in local communities." One way to show office workers "that they exist to service the field" would be to have them "work out in the field among the people" so that they would not "push grand intellectual schemes about what we will do with the local people." Such statements were motivated by the frustrations of field workers who had begun to see themselves as local leaders rather than as outside organizers. "I don't think Executive Committee should make decision for SNCC," noted James Pittman, a Mississippi field secretary. "I think all people can make decision no matter what kind of people they are and I think we should think in these terms."[22]

Another spokesman for the Mississippi field staff, Frank Smith, caustically attacked SNCC workers who resisted giving power to community organizers without college training or believed "that what we really need was a few sober-headed, intelligent, educated people to sit down and make decisions because the whole staff is just not capable." He accused them of giving lip service to the idea of one man, one vote, but in their own affairs being "scared to give every man a voice and a vote." The staff had "the right to make decisions about what programs it wants to run and how it wants them organized," and this could be accomplished only by organizers electing their own administrators.[23]

SNCC faced the enduring dilemma of those who seek to improve the lot of the less privileged without creating a lasting dependency. Because SNCC workers were so determined to act consistently with their ideals, they devoted an enormous amount of intellectual energy to this difficult issue, which was generally ignored by other contemporary civil rights or social reform organizations. In their efforts to find a satisfactory solution to the problem of eliminating oppression without becoming a new source of oppression, SNCC workers directed each other's attention to the subtle injustices and inequities that existed inside the organization as well as in the surrounding society. In the process they gained valuable new insights and exposed tensions and resentments that had previously been suppressed.

Among the sources of tension within SNCC was the biracial character of the organization. Racial hostilities underlay many of the criticisms of black organizers against their white counterparts. The steady increase in the proportion of whites on the staff during 1963 and 1964 concerned many who doubted whether local black leadership could develop in the presence of large numbers of whites. Many black organizers feared that white volunteers would push aside indigenous black leaders and inadvertently reinforce traditional patterns of racial deference and dependence. Moreover, years of protest and collective struggle had wakened feelings of racial solidarity and anti-white anger among southern blacks.

During and after the summer of 1964, there were numerous instances in which white civil rights workers became targets for black frustrations. A white COFO worker remarked on "race riots" at the Jackson headquarters during the fall and mentioned that whites were "often subject to severe racial abuse and even violence from Negro workers." Freedom school director Liz Fusco recalled that "all the white workers in Mississippi were intimidated by black staff and increasingly by local people."[24] Moses noted that certain blacks considered white activists to be "other people." He described the racial tensions as "the kind of things that don't seem to be exhaustible." They were "welling out like poison and they spew out over everybody."[25]

SNCC workers had been reluctant to question the interracial character of the organization, but as the situation worsened, the unwillingness to discuss the future role of white organizers lessened. In a Waveland paper SNCC's Alabama State Director Silas Norman doubted whether he was "willing to work in an integrated project simply to prove a point." Although whites brought "wider publicity and thus wider support," integrated groups in segregated areas were "spotlights," and white women with black men were a "declaration of war." These concerns were similar to Moses' reasons for barring the use of white field secretaries in Mississippi before the summer of 1963, but Norman also foreshadowed a new racial consciousness that would pervade the black struggle in the last half of the decade when he referred to the "ethnic relationship" between black staff members and the black community. "I do not feel that this relationship can be entered into by whites."[26]

Defenders of SNCC's interracialism were compelled to argue for what had once been assumed. Sherrod, the first SNCC leader to integrate a project as a matter of policy, remarked in his Waveland paper that there was "no place for race hatred" in SNCC; blacks must recognize that the needs of whites "are not so different from our own as regards recognition, fulfillment, status in our group and so forth." Another black staff member expressed dismay at hearing black workers "ridicule our white brothers due to our own petty prejudices." Still another argued that the idea of limiting the number of whites on SNCC's staff would not solve its problems: "We might kick 'them' out of SNCC, but we cannot kick them out of the movement. Because the movement is more than SNCC." Whites did not want to "take over" but only wanted "to do a job." The question was whether the blacks wanted "to do the same job. If not, then tell the whites and let them go their merry way." Mike Miller, a white activist in charge of SNCC's San Francisco office, cautioned that "if we are building in our own movement that beloved community, then race cannot be used to automatically disqualify the argument of a white field secretary when policy matters are being discussed."[27] But he begged the question of whether in fact most SNCC workers still accepted the notion that SNCC could become an ideal community within an injust and increasingly hostile world. SNCC had been a community in which black and white activists could rid themselves of many of the racial prejudices that infected American society, yet most of its staff resisted the tendency to become a utopian sect seeking to separate itself from social evils rather than to eliminate them.

The papers written for the Waveland retreat represented an initial step toward identifying the central issues of subsequent American social movements, but they suggested an agenda far too extensive for a single week of discussion by weary staff members. They created expectations that could not be fulfilled. Staff members who read the papers were made aware of the extent to which SNCC had become divided on basic issues, but at best they could respond only by developing procedures for resolving internal differences, and even this proved difficult in an organization that had traditionally made decisions through consensus and which lacked definite lines of authority. The retreat that began on November 5 thus proved anticlimatic—a letdown from the feverish activity of the summer and the pioneering intellectual ferment of the early fall.

In opening the meeting, Forman stressed the need to change SNCC's decision-making structure. Although the staff had gradually gained a greater role in determining SNCC's policies, nominal control of the organization remained in the hands of the Coordinating and Executive Committees, which were composed mainly of student representatives. Forman proposed that those at the retreat take over the functions of the Coordinating Committee, placing control directly in the hands of the full-time staff. This recommendation, which reflected a change that was already underway, acknowledged that the group was no longer a coordinating body for campus-based organizations but instead a group of professional organizers.

Forman did not, however, suggest how SNCC should approach its work once the new structure was created. He simply proposed that the staff "begin to study more diligently the political and economic forces operating in this country, to continue to criticize those forces and to continue to construct new alternatives for the people and for ourselves." He also alluded to the moral qualities which had defined SNCC and might still provide a means to achieve radical social change: "We must continue, not necessarily to work for the redemptive society, but to work toward a new spirit of brotherhood, a spirit that transcends both blacks and white . . . a spirit that sees all of us simply as men and women, struggling for a sense of dignity."

Forman recognized the difficulty of charting a course for the southern struggle. His own exhaustion as a result of the previous summer's work had weakened his health, necessitating his taking a leave from his duties as executive secretary for three months in order to rest and reflect. However, Forman rejected the notion that SNCC workers should withdraw from their roles as the vanguard of struggle in the mistaken belief that projects could continue on their own. Southern blacks were depending on the staff to "continue the work we started. People do see us as a band of brothers. We must decide if the circle will be unbroken. If we remain a band of brothers, a circle of trust, We Shall Overcome!"[28]

Despite Forman's guarded optimism, there were many signs at the retreat that the emotional bonds which held the staff together had already been broken. As the southern struggle moved beyond civil rights goals to issues of economics and politics and as northern liberal support became more problematical, SNCC workers questioned whether to accept every applicant or even every existing member of the staff. Before the retreat, anyone with a measure of persistence could still join SNCC and no one had yet been fired, but SNCC workers, having grown increasingly skeptical about liberal allies and liberal values, were now also increasingly skeptical of each other's motives. After a few days many staff members walked out of the retreat, disgusted over the extended and inconclusive discussions. According to a summary of the proceedings, "It was mentioned that we must realize we are not a band of brothers—we all come from different backgrounds." A suggestion that the staff divide into workshops groups according to seniority was rejected because "older members of the organization operated in entirely different spheres than most of us do now."[29] Although no one at Waveland offered a coherent statement of SNCC's future goals, the increasingly restive black organizers on the staff were convinced that SNCC would require more in the future than a willingness to sacrifice oneself on behalf of humanistic ideals.

Despite the staff's inability to resolve the many issues raised at Waveland, the retreat was an important step in SNCC's transformation from being simply a militant civil rights organization to becoming a major source of radical ideas and strategies. The retreat was a valiant attempt to begin a difficult process to self-criticism and self-education in the midst of social struggle. "It was a very productive conference," Cleveland Sellers recalled. "We returned to our various outposts afterward with a better sense of who we were and what we were trying to accomplish. We didn't answer all the questions, it was impossible to do that."[30]

While the staff at Waveland unsuccessfully attempted to resolve old dilemmas and repair widening internal rifts, they were confronted with new tensions from an unexpected source, the emerging feminist consciousness. Just as the origins of the nineteenth century women's rights movement can be traced to the involvement of women in the abolitionist struggle, so the modern movement received an important impetus from SNCC and the civil rights struggle of the 1960s. In both cases, women gained from the struggles of black people an increased sense of their own potential political significance and a heightened sensitivity to the restrictions placed upon them because of their sex. SNCC, as the twentieth century counterpart of the radical abolitionists, suggested ways in which individual discontent could become the basis for large-scale political activism, and women were only one of the many segments of the American populace to learn from SNCC's efforts.

A workshop on the role of women was held at Waveland, and from this worshop came a demand that SNCC confront the issue of sexual discrimination within the organization. A paper was written by a group of female staff members, including some of the most influential white members. Casey Hayden of SNCC's Jackson office and Mary King of the communications department were the principal authors, although at the time they insisted that anonymity was needed in order to avoid retaliation—"nothing so final as being fired or outright exclusion, but the kinds of things which are killing to the insides—insinuations, ridicule, over-exaggerated compensations." The paper charged that women were routinely asked to perform mundane office chores and rarely asked to chair meetings or take important roles in policy making. Although these and other grievances might "seem strange to some, petty to others, laughable to most," much talent and experience were wasted when women in SNCC were "not given jobs commensurate with their abilities."

The paper compared the status of women to that of blacks. Just as whites found it difficult to understand why blacks resented being called "boy" or being considered "musical" or "athletic," so the average SNCC worker found it difficult to understand the resentment of women. "Assumptions of male superiority are as widespread and deep rooted and every much as crippling to the woman as the assumptions of white supremacy are to the Negro." Not only did male staff members feel "too threatened" to face the subject, but many female members were "as unaware and insensitive as men, just as there are many Negroes who don't understand they are not free or who want to be part of white America." SNCC should "force the rest of the movement to stop the discrimination and start the slow process of changing values and ideas so that all of us gradually come to understand that this is no more a man's world than it is a white world."[31]

Male SNCC workers at Waveland derided the complaints of the female staff members by arguing that sexual discrimination was a minor matter when compared with other issues. Although Forman acknowledged that "both within and without SNCC subtle blatant forms of discrimination against women exist," the feminist position paper had little impact on most of the staff. SNCC, like other civil rights organizations, had not developed an egalitarian ethic regarding sexual relations similar to racial egalitarianism. Furthermore, the decreasing sense of trust that had resulted from the traumatic experiences of the previous year made staff members less willing to confront the unexpected new issue thrust upon them.

Stokely Carmichael was one of those who regarded the charges of sexual discrimination as a bothersome intrusion on SNCC's efforts at Waveland. To a question about the proper position of women in SNCC, Carmichael jokingly responded, "prone." The comment, which was widely circulated in feminist circles and became a source of embarrassment for Carmichael, merely reflected the lack of serious attention given to feminist concerns by most people at the time. In addition, the fact that the principal backers of the paper were white led many black staff members to discount its significance. Muriel Tillinghast, one of several blacks whom Carmichael had appointed to head Mississippi offices, and who initially reacted with anger to Carmichael's comment, was nevertheless unaware of sexual discrimination in SNCC at the time. Cynthia Washington, another black project director appointed by Carmichael, thought that her "relative autonomy" as an administrator denied the validity of Carmichael's statement. She and other black women in SNCC "were proof that what he said wasn't true— or so we thought. In fact, I'm certain that our single-minded focus on the issues of racial discrimination and the black struggle for equality blinded us to other issues."[32]

Although the paper on women effected no noticeable changes in SNCC's policies, it was an opening salvo of the feminist movement of the 1960s. A year later Hayden and King would raise similar concerns for a wider audience in a manifesto addressed to "other women in the peace and freedom movement."[33] They and other women brought many of the values and tactics of the civil rights struggle into the nascent women's liberation movement.

Despite its long-term historical importance, the feminist issue was ignored by staff members, who were absorbed in problems that seemed more immediate. During the weeks after the Waveland retreat SNCC's effectiveness was threatened by irresponsible behavior that resulted from the staff's declining morale, lack of direction, and opposition to authority. Some of those involved in the Summer Project abandoned their responsibilities, citing fatigue and a desire to allow local back residents to assume greater control over civil rights activities in their communities. Freedom schools and community centers in Mississippi were closed, owing to the absence of dependable personnel. "People were wandering in and out of the organization," Marion Barry recalled. "Some worked, some didn't work."[34] There was a noticeable increase in marijuana usage, which contributed to the discipline problems. Since there were few tangible rewards to withhold from misbehaving staff members, SNCC officers and project directors could do little to compel staff members to carry out their responsibilities. It was difficult during the fall even to define who belonged to the staff, since many members had not committed themselves to remain at their posts after the summer and were undecided about their future plans. Like previous expressions of American radicalism fueled by middle-class idealism, the southern civil rights struggle faced the dilemma of reconciling individualistic values with political effectiveness.

The breakdown in the effectiveness of SNCC projects in Mississippi was particularly troublesome because the state had always been the center of SNCC's operations. Because SNCC offered no new programs to attract the continued support of politically awakened black Mississippians, the MFDP did little during the fall. That was "the crucial time," Lawrence Guyot noted regretfully. "We had jolted the country. The state of Mississippi was on the defensive."[35] Another freedom vote was held in November, in which blacks expressed support for an MFDP slate of candidates, but there was little enthusiasm regarding this return to the tactic of holding a separate election.

Mississippi residents who had been attracted to SNCC began to loosen their ties with the organization. Charles Evers and other NAACP leaders who had long been disturbed by SNCC's radicalism reasserted their claim to dominance of the Mississippi civil rights movement. The state conference of the NAACP in November withdrew its tenuous support of COFO, condemning SNCC's domination of the federation.[36] Many COFO members, who still considered themselves to be SNCC workers and were dependent on SNCC for financial support, nonetheless moved toward greater independence as they became more aware of SNCC's limitations.

MFDP leaders began to assert independence from both COFO and SNCC, seeking to transform the party from a social movement organization into a permanent political institution. Whereas the MFDP was criticized by outsiders as unduly influenced by SNCC, the party was taken to task by SNCC workers for its increasing caution and its support of Lyndon Johnson in the November presidential election. SNCC continued to offer financial support to the party, and some MFDP leaders retained their status as SNCC staff members, but the MFDP followed a middle course during the fall between SNCC and the liberal forces. Among the actions taken by the party's leadership was to fire Joseph Rauh as counsel in order to express their dissatisfaction with his actions in Atlantic City. They also announced plans for a challenge in 1965 of Mississippi's newly elected congressional delegation. To direct this effort to unseat the white congressmen, they hired three radical lawyers—Arthur Kinoy, William Kunstler, and Benjamin Smith.[37]

The increasing isolation of SNCC from its former bases of support led the Mississippi staff to press more vigorously for changes in the organization. Their dissatisfaction became apparent at a COFO meeting in early December 1964 at Hattiesburg. Of the more than 350 people—COFO staff members, volunteers, and Mississippi residents—who attended, many complained about the loss of momentum in Mississippi and the lack of new programs to sustain community interest. A major complaint was the inefficiency of COFO headquarters in Jackson, which had been closed by disgruntled staff members in order to force its reorganization. Sellers, newly named project director in Holly Springs, complained that since August his project had received nothing from the Jackson office: "the only way that we have been able to get food and clothing is to make appeals to the North for it to be sent directly to us." He threatened to suspend his project unless he received greater support from either COFO or SNCC. Expressing displeasure with the attention devoted to reforming SNCC's decision-making structure, Sellers argued that "the structure doesn't matter; the service the structure renders is what counts. And until some people become responsible, the structure, regardless of what it might be, will not render service."[38]

The problems of disorganization and lack of resources plaguing the COFO staff were even more apparent in SNCC projects elsewhere in the South. Those projects had already suffered because of the commitment in 1964 of most of SNCC's resources and attention to Mississippi. They had also been less successful in building local black-controlled institutions. Their lack of stability was indicated by the fact that none of the people who had initiated the projects during 1962 and 1963 were still at their posts in the fall of 1964. Bernard Lafayette had resigned as director of the central Alabama project in September 1963; Sherrod had left southwest Georgia after the summer of 1964 to attend Union Theological Seminary; and Hansen had stepped down as head of the Arkansas project, citing the need for black leadership. Those who replaced the SNCC veterans in these states were typically southern-born blacks, willing to join with the Mississippi organizers to demand greater staff discipline and more effective administration.

Forman and Lewis sympathized with the efforts of the field staff to make

SNCC's headquarters more responsive, but both were seen as too closely tied to the Atlanta office staff to understand fully the problems of the field. Although Forman later asserted that he tried to pull the field staff together for a takeover of SNCC, the impetus for change came from the staff. Slowed by poor health—apparently an ulcer made worse by the pressures of work—Forman, like other SNCC veterans, responded to the demands of field organizers by attempting to articulate their ideological implications.[39]

When the SNCC staff met on February 12, 1965, in Atlanta, Lewis reiterated the view of organizers that SNCC's "primary concern must be the liberation of black people." Conceding that white people were also exploited, Lewis argued that blacks were "not only economically exploited and politically denied but . . . also dehumanized by the vicious system of segregation and racial discrimination." In the future, therefore, SNCC should not count on the support of "white liberals and the so-called affluent Negro leader . . . They will sell us down the river for the hundredth time in order to protect themselves." White staff members "must recognize the fact that we are caught up with a sense of destiny with the vast majority of colored people all over the world who are becoming conscious of their power and the role they must play in the world. If the movement and SNCC are going to be effective in attempting to liberate the black masses, the civil rights movement must be black-controlled, dominated, and led."[40]

The field staff achieved their major objectives at the meeting. Impatient with extended arguments, they brought discussions to a close with demands for formal votes, which they easily won. The staff voted to make themselves members of the Coordinating Committee, in effect becoming SNCC's official policy-making body. Although the proposal of Mississippi field secretary Jesse Morris that membership on the Executive Committee be limited to black southerners who had not gone to college was not adopted, several of those elected to the Executive Committee met his requirements. Of the twenty committee members, thirteen had worked with COFO, and most of these were natives of Mississippi. They ranged in age from Silas McGhee, a nineteen-year-old Greenwood resident, to forty-six-year-old Hamer. In addition, Sellers left his post as a project director in Mississippi to become SNCC's new program secretary and a member, along with Lewis and Forman, of its newly formed secretariat, which was given authority to make decisions between Executive Committee meetings.

The SNCC field workers who had gained control of the Executive Committee offered few definite plans at the meeting for SNCC's future. They could agree on only two items: to reaffirm their support of MFDP, including its plan to bring student activists to Washington to lobby for the unseating of the Mississippi Delegation, and to hold "people's conferences" under SNCC's auspices in the deep South to allow residents to develop their own local programs. Rather than offering innovative ideas, most of the field workers were content to do what local residents asked. They also rededicated themselves to struggle in behalf of poor blacks, "for despite the gains that the student movement has assisted in making, people are still poor, voteless, without jobs, suffering from police brutality, inadequate housing and denial of dignity."[41]

Although the February meeting was a victory for the black community organizers, the ideological implications of that victory did not immediately become apparent. Having lost much of their faith in the federal government and the liberal conscience and increasingly cut off from most social ties outside the movement, SNCC workers began to move in different directions that reflected differences in class and racial background. The Waveland papers suggested some of these differences, but they merely provided hints of the extent to which some staff members were prepared to break with the past and develop new strategies to deal with deeply rooted economic and political problems. Criticism of SNCC's previous efforts and recognition of internal differences were combined with a willingness on the part of some staff members during 1965 to launch innovative projects that could become the basis for renewed commitment and struggle.

*by Doris Robinson, 1965*

*Stokely Carmichael during voter registration drive in Lowndes County, Alabama, 1965*

*Julian Bond, ca. 1967*

*Fannie Lou Hamer testifying for the Mississippi Freedom Democratic Party at the Democratic National Convention, Atlantic City, 1964*

# 11. BREAKING NEW GROUND

The crucial series of civil rights demonstrations that began early in 1965 in Selma, Alabama, set the stage for several pioneering SNCC ventures; they also stimulated increasingly bitter internal debates that revealed SNCC's importance as a source of innovative ideas and its weaknesses as a political institution. Buoyed by their success in challenging SCLC's more cautious leadership over the protests associated with the Selma to Montgomery march, SNCC organizers entered the rural area between the two cities and helped black residents create the Lowndes County Freedom Organization (LCFO), soon known as the Black Panther party. They also entered complex and volatile urban black ghettos where they would encounter their most difficult challenges.

These and other new projects might have signaled the beginning of SNCC's reinvigoration, but many staff members were enervated by dissension within projects and confusion about SNCC's future direction. In deep South communities where SNCC had once attracted black support through idealism and militancy, more pragmatic and parochial black leaders were assuming control of local movements. Some SNCC workers, particularly northern activists, responded to their displacement by leaving SNCC or by "floating" from project to project searching for more meaningful roles and in the process acquiring the appellation of being "high on freedom." Other staff members, determined to play a role in the changing southern struggle, accepted the need for local black leadership but still saw themselves as necessary catalysts of the black struggle. This group included a faction of "hardliners" who wished to impose on other staff members an unprecedented degree of organizational discipline and structure. Between the extremes of floaters and hardliners was a large group of staff members, including most of SNCC's leaders. This intermediate group was aware of the extent to which irresponsible staff actions and the lack of effective programs hampered SNCC's work, but was unwilling to abandon the unstructured militancy and decentralized decision-making process that had made possible SNCC's previous success. This group struggled to preserve SNCC's ties to its past while maintaining its role in the vanguard of black struggles that were no longer focused on civil rights or concentrated in the South.

153

\*   \*   \*

Although staff members disagreed about the extent to which SNCC would have to change, the internal debates in the wake of the Waveland retreat clarified the nature of SNCC's distinctive radicalism. Occasional overstatements of SNCC's generalized opposition to authority did not obscure the staff's continued belief that institutions and leaders should not restrain mass struggles but instead should emerge from them.

Insistence on local leadership had been a basic element of SNCC's efforts to mobilize southern black communities. Thus, Stokely Carmichael argued that "the only radical thing" that was happening in the United States was that people were beginning to question how things got done and how people could participate in making political decisions. "It's not radical if SNCC people get political offices, or if M. L. King becomes President, if decisions are still made from the top down," he wrote. "If decisions get made from the bottom up, then that's radical."[1]

Many SNCC organizers shunned leadership roles because of the increasing assertiveness of local black leaders and because they opposed all forms of authority, even those that emerged in the course of struggle. Often referring to the need to free people's minds from the restraints of established order, SNCC workers had unparalleled success in breaking through the socialized inhibitions of blacks in the rural South by undermining the legitimacy of existing white-dominated institutions. For workers who had spent years protesting established authority, living in an unstructured community of activists, and building confidence in their own ability to live their ideals, the southern struggle became an assault on all barriers to individual freedom. To veteran Mississippi field secretary Charles Cobb, the perception of one's "daily oppression" and questioning of authority were the first steps toward overcoming injustice. "This is the latent threat of the 'Negro movement' in the South, for 'keeping the niggers in their place' is just an extreme of keeping *people* in their place, all of which is keeping everybody from dealing with what is relevant in their lives."[2]

These broader implications of the southern struggle were the basic motive for many who had associated with SNCC. SNCC's appeal was based not on its political effectiveness and certainly not on its material rewards, but on its identity as a morally consistent activist community. During the summer of 1965, a volunteer in Laurel, Mississippi, described the spirit of "joy" that had once sustained workers. This spirit was based on the hope that the United States and then the world could be changed "by nonviolence and real honesty, and letting everybody say things, and not even have to do such things as vote or have leaders or officers." A lessening in this moral purity of the movement was shown by the widening gulf between the volunteers and black residents. The volunteers were willing to devote all their time and energy "to do something that they see has a good chance of succeeding or even something that turns out to be a gesture," but local blacks had more pragmatic concerns, "something concrete, something they can touch," such as "better jobs and paved streets."[3]

Rather than using their skills to aid local residents, however, some college-educated workers idealized oppressed blacks. Freedom School Director Liz Fusco described workers who withdrew into shells of guilt and meek deference to those who were poorer and less educated, "apologizing for Harvard and Smith and Berkeley. Apologizing for knowing how to spell." Jane Stembridge, SNCC's first executive secretary, saw black Mississippians as freer than activists like herself, because poor blacks had not been socialized to repress their emotions. She wrote that she had been made to feel shame and guilt by the institutions of her childhood, and she feared that SNCC was being destroyed by those who wished to make it into an "institution" with a "party line." These people, she wrote, were "afraid to be free" and preferred "revolution" to "freedom." In contrast, rural blacks possessed "a closeness with the earth . . . a closeness with each other in the sense of community developed out of dependence . . . the strength of being poor."[4]

Stembridge's fear that SNCC was being transformed into an institution sharply contrasted with the concerns of SNCC workers who stressed the instrumental functions of the southern struggle. During 1965 SNCC was torn by a dispute between staff members who resisted tendencies toward centralization and bureaucratization, believing that this would inhibit the development of local leadership, and those who believed that radical social change required restraints on individual freedom in order to achieve collective goals.

In the latter group was Cleveland Sellers, who became SNCC's program director at the February 1965 staff meeting. Like most self-described hardliners, Sellers was a southern-born black organizer whose political education had taken place largely within SNCC. Displaying little interest in the philosophical issues that absorbed his opponents, he described SNCC's "most flamboyant faction" as "stars," also using the epithets "philosophers, existentialists, anarchists, floaters and freedom-high niggers." Most floaters were well educated, he asserted, and blacks as well as whites exhibited the characteristics he derided: "They were integrationists who strongly believed that every individual had the right and responsibility to follow the dictates of his conscience, no matter what." Sellers' antipathy toward floaters was based on his awareness of the damage they did to SNCC projects. He was also disturbed by the tendency of floaters to dominate discussions at meetings "they saw fit to attend," thereby further widening the gulf between SNCC and the often poorly educated blacks it sought to organize. "They loved to bring meetings to a screeching halt with open-ended, theoretical questions," he wrote. "In the midst of a crucial strategy session on the problems of community leaders in rural areas, one of them might get the floor and begin to hold forth on the true meaning of the word *leader*."[5]

Sellers' exaggerated characterization of the floaters reflected the personal animosity that developed because of his sometimes ruthless use of authority against recalcitrant staff members, a group that included for a time his friend Carmichael. "Stokely thought I was more concerned with [SNCC's] cars, money and equipment than with people. He was convinced that I had become a bureaucrat." Sellers conceded that his opponents were "closer to SNCC's free-wheeling, anarchistic origins" than the hardliners, but he attributed the growing strength of his faction to the feeble state of SNCC projects. "The only thing that kept us Hardliners in the running was our 'guarantee' that we could move SNCC beyond the morass in which it was stuck."[6]

The hardliners convinced many veteran SNCC leaders that their complaints about undisciplined workers were valid. Forman, for example, later commented on the negative consequences of the withdrawal of some staff members from active roles in Mississippi projects, sardonically referring to "an ailment known as local-people-itis—the romanticization of poor Mississippians. This carried with it the idea that local people could do no wrong; that no one, especially somebody from outside the community, should initiate any kind of action or assume any form of leadership."[7]

Forman backed Sellers' efforts to exercise greater control over staff activities, but his belief that SNCC should become a centralized political organization set him apart from many organizers, including some hardliners, who wanted the Atlanta headquarters to concentrate on fund-raising and resource distribution while not interfering with local autonomy. Forman also engendered criticism by neglecting his administrative duties to take part in protests on several occasions during 1965. Like many who joined SNCC in the early 1960s, Forman had difficulty restraining his desire to express his discontent publicly even after he had concluded that disciplined political action was needed to affect those in power.

Moses was less willing than Forman to accept the idea that political expediency should ever take precedence over moral consistency, and this led many floaters to look to him for ideological leadership. Yet Moses never resolved to his own satisfaction Camus' dilemma of maintaining a balance between moral purity and political effectiveness. He resigned as COFO director late in 1964, explaining that his position in Mississippi had become "too strong, too central, so that people who did not need to, began to lean on me, to use me as a crutch."[8]

In an obvious attempt to escape from leadership burdens, Moses announced at a staff meeting in early 1965 that he was changing his surname to Parris (his middle name). At the same gathering his wife announced that she would return to her maiden name, Dona Richards. Although the two broke their contacts with other staff members, Moses, followed by his reputation, remained a highly respected figure in SNCC.

The impact of Moses' withdrawal was graphically illustrated when Sellers interrupted a rump meeting of floaters in the spring of 1965. Sellers recalled that he and several other staff members, including Carmichael, Ivanhoe Donaldson, and H. Rap Brown, dominated an informal debate with Casey Hayden and others identified as floaters. Sellers knew that Moses could have prevailed against the argument that SNCC should become a strong institution. "He was smart enough to tie . . . us into philosophical knots," Sellers wrote. "He didn't do it because he realized that he would have had to become what he abhorred, a manipulator, in order to do so."[9]

Hardliners, who were generally politically inexperienced, could not fill the leadership vacuum created by Moses' withdrawal, and, despite their apparent victory at the February 1965 staff meeting, older veterans of the early-1960s protests continued to dominate the organization, resisting the rapid imposition of organizational constraints. Avoiding the extremes of the two factions, Cobb recognized the dilemma facing SNCC idealists when he wrote that living with others implied "some sacrifice of personal freedom and some conscious feeling of responsibility to other people as well as to yourself." The decision to join SNCC, he concluded, indicated an acceptance of "a responsibility to the many people operating within the organizational framework" and an awareness of "the needs of other people even when they conflict with what we believe."[10] That Cobb and other SNCC veterans would find it difficult to reconcile their need to freely express their discontent with their desire to increase organizational effectiveness became apparent when many of them unexpectedly became involved in a series of demonstrations in Selma, Alabama.

At the beginning of 1965 few SNCC workers would have surmised that Alabama would become the focus of their activities. Compared to projects in Mississippi and Georgia, SNCC activities in Alabama had garnered little publicity. In the fall of 1964 there were only three full-time workers in SNCC's headquarters in Selma. Former Nashville student protest leader and freedom rider Bernard Lafayette and his wife, Colia, a Tougaloo student activist, had launched the project in February 1963. After the Lafayettes left to return to college, the project continued under the direction of Worth Long, John Love, and finally, in the spring of 1965, Silas Norman, a graduate of Paine College in Augusta, Georgia.

Martin Luther King's announcement of a major voting rights campaign in Selma early in 1965 was met with ambivalence among SNCC's Alabama staff. They knew that King's effort would aid their own voter registration

work by attracting national publicity and perhaps prompting federal intervention against white Alabama authorities. With the exception of Mississippi, Alabama had the lowest proportion of blacks on the registration
rolls. Only two percent of eligible black residents had been registered in
Dallas County, the site of SNCC's headquarters, and even fewer in the surrounding rural areas. Yet staff members feared that King's presence would
undermine their long-standing efforts to develop black leadership. They
agreed not to hamper SCLC's campaign and even offered the use of their
equipment and facilities to SCLC representatives, but expected to remain
on the sidelines, hoping that local blacks would recognize the deficiencies of
SCLC's leader-centered approach to organizing.

Many SNCC staff members outside the state, however, could not resist
the temptation to become involved, expecially after violent clashes between
police and local residents. The jailing of King during a February 1 demonstration at the Selma courthouse sparked marches that led to the arrest of
more than one thousand protesters, including hundreds of black school
children. The escalating protests prompted President Johnson to announce
to the nation that he intended to see that the right to vote was "secured for
all of our citizens."

The first fatality of the campaign occured in Marion, a town near Selma.
Jimmy Lee Jackson, a twenty-six-year-old black protester, was killed by a
state policeman as he attempted to aid his mother, who had been clubbed
by police. Jackson's death stimulated renewed mass protests, and early in
March SCLC leaders announced plans for a march from Selma to the Alabama capitol in Montgomery to dramatize the plight of Alabama blacks.
Still faced with the difficult choice regarding official involvement in the
civil rights campaign, SNCC representatives met with SCLC leaders on
March 5, two days before the planned march, to discuss their differences.
Despite their opposition to the march, the Alabama SNCC staff agreed
that, in view of their personal commitment to local residents, they should
continue to provide promised assistance. Meeting in Atlanta later that day
and the next, some members of SNCC's Executive Committee argued that
SNCC should join the march in order to counteract SCLC influence. The
meeting ended with the decision that SNCC remain officially uncommit-
ted. Recognizing, however, that a few SNCC workers, including John
Lewis, were already involved, the Executive Committee voted to allow
SNCC workers to participate as individuals. The Committee also agreed to
draft a letter to King describing SNCC's position and requesting a meeting
with SCLC leaders.[11]

To the surprise of SNCC workers, King did not join the two thousand
marchers who began their trek from Selma to Montgomery on the afternoon of Sunday, March 7, but returned to Atlanta to deliver a sermon instead. His absence left leadership of the march in the hands of Hosea Wil-

liams of SCLC and John Lewis and Robert Mants of SNCC. At Pettus Bridge on the outskirts of Selma, the marchers encountered a combined force of deputies and state troopers commanded by Sheriff Jim Clark and Major John Cloud. Cloud ordered them to disperse within two minutes, and when the marchers refused they were attacked by police using billy clubs. "We passed the word back for everybody to bow down in a prayerful manner," Lewis recalled. "Then the troopers came back at us again, this time with tear gas as well." Lewis' skull was fractured in one of the attacks, but he managed to regroup the marchers and lead them back to a church. Before leaving for a hospital, he angrily remarked, "I don't see how President Johnson can send troops to Vietnam [and] the Congo . . . and can't send troops to Selma, Alabama. Next time we march, we may have to keep going when we get to Montgomery. We may have to go on to Washington."[12]

The brutal assault on marchers at Pettus Bridge dispelled the previous reservations of many SNCC workers. Four carloads of Mississippi staff members suddenly left a COFO meeting in Jackson in cars assigned to the Mississippi projects to drive to Selma. Another group attending the Executive Committee meeting in Atlanta decided to charter a plane rather than make the five-hour drive to Selma. This response revealed the deeply engrained desire for militant action even among hardliners who believed that protests were counterproductive. "We were angry," Sellers recalled. "And we wanted to show Governor [George] Wallace, the Alabama State Highway Patrol, Sheriff Clark, Selma's whites, the federal government and poor southern blacks in other Selmas that we didn't intend to take any more shit. We would ram the march down the throat of anyone who tried to stop us."[13] Concern for those who had been attacked and an understanding of the value of protest activity as a training ground for those who would sustain the struggle prompted the SNCC workers' reaction, but it also indicated an absence of staff discipline and the tendency of SNCC's decision-making process to break down in a crisis.

Once in Selma, SNCC workers openly criticized SCLC tactics. Forman and other SNCC militants condemned federal judge Frank Johnson's request for postponement of the march as a condition of hearing SCLC's demand for an injunction against state officials. King initially agreed to march despite federal warnings but decided against a confrontation with police after discussions with Attorney General Nicholas Katzenbach and other government officials. King did not inform SNCC workers of his intentions, however, when on March 10 he joined a group of more than one thousand protesters confronting a police barricade outside Selma. The SCLC leader led the group in prayer and then told the marchers to turn around and go back. King's action angered many SNCC workers and local residents. The open road to Montgomery, an obvious police challenge,

heightened the marchers' anger. "With an irony that must have graven itself into the minds of the SNCC students," wrote King biographer David
Lewis, "the three thousand demonstrators headed back to the church,
many of them singing 'Ain't Gonna Let Nobody Turn Me 'Round.' "[14]

Shortly after the abortive march, local whites attacked three white ministers who had joined the demonstrations. One of the ministers, the Reverend James Reeb, died a few days later. In sharp contrast to the earlier
death of Jimmy Lee Jackson, the killing of Reeb brought an immediate
national response. Civil rights supporters from across the nation arrived in
Selma for a memorial service. Thousands of demonstrators demanded federal intervention during sympathy protests in many northern cities. On
March 15 President Johnson, who had sent a plane to transport Reeb's
widow back to her home in Boston, used the Selma crisis as an opportunity
for a nationally televised address proposing new voting rights legislation.

Many SNCC workers heard Johnson's speech while leading demonstrations near the Alabama Capitol in Montgomery. Conceding SCLC's dominance in Selma, SNCC organizers had mobilized black students at Tuskegee Institute and at colleges in the Montgomery area in order to keep
pressure on state officials.

Although Jim Forman would later be criticized for unilaterally spending
about five thousand dollars of SNCC's scarce funds to support the Alabama demonstrations, he could not resist the opportunity to "radicalize the
students" and the Montgomery demonstrations of mid-March succeeded
beyond his expectations. Along with Bill Hall, Bill Ware, and Willie Ricks,
Forman encouraged the students to continue their demonstrations near the
Capitol and tried to counteract the influence of moderate black ministers
and SCLC officials. "I saw the demonstrations as a vital learning experience and as a basis for commitment," he later wrote. "The only way to get
the students involved, it seemed to me, was to get them in motion, try to
make them militant, explain—for example—what the ministers were
doing." On Monday, March 15, violent clashes took place between demonstrators and police, and the following night about six hundred marchers,
including Forman, clashed with mounted police with billy clubs and electric prods. Moderate black leaders and administration officials tried to restrain the student protesters, but SNCC workers retained the support of a
hard core of several hundred students. At a rally called on March 16 by
SCLC officials hoping to assert their control over the demonstrations, Forman revealed the escalating verbal militancy that accompanied the protests when he told an audience that included many newsmen and ministers,
"If we can't sit at the table of democracy, then we'll knock the fucking legs
off." Although he immediately regretted using such strong language, he
later wrote that "the charge by the posse earlier that day . . . was still in my
mind. It was difficult not to speak out in anger."[15]

When the march from Selma to Montgomery finally occurred it was anticlimactic in contrast to the tumultuous demonstrations of previous weeks. About 25,000 people marched peacefully to the state capital, where a mass rally was held on March 25. King delivered a rousing address while the subdued Governor George Wallace sat in his nearby office. Southern white resistance remained fierce, however. After the rally, Mrs. Viola Liuzzo, a white housewife from Detroit, was shot to death while driving back to Montgomery after transporting protesters to Selma.

In retrospect, the Selma campaign was a victory for King's protest strategy. If his presence interfered with SNCC's long-range efforts to develop self-sufficient local black leadership, it also provided the spark for a crucial confrontation between Alabama blacks and obstinate state officials which in turn contributed to a favorable climate of public opinion outside the South and to subsequent passage of Johnson's voting rights proposals. Despite this decisive victory, the Alabama campaign contributed to the further disillusionment of SNCC workers. Even activists who still believed in the power of nonviolent direct action had begun to doubt whether the resulting reforms were worth the sacrifices. "We're only flesh," remarked Lewis. "I could understand people not wanting to be beaten anymore ... Black capacity to believe [that a white person] would really open his heart, open his life to nonviolent appeal was running out."[16]

Other SNCC workers who had long since decided that appeals to the national conscience were useless saw the Selma and Montgomery protests as a confirmation of their attitudes. The bitterness verging on spite felt by many staff members was expressed in Carmichael's complaint that the march to Montgomery, which began as a protest of the death of a black man, Jimmy Lee Jackson, attracted major national attention only after the death of Reverend Reeb. "Now, I'm not saying we shouldn't pay tribute to Rev. Reeb," Carmichael explained. "What I'm saying is that if we're going to pay tribute to one, we should also pay tribute to the other. And I think we have to analyze why [ Johnson] sent flowers to Mrs. Reeb, and not to Mrs. Jackson."[17]

The Alabama demonstrations illustrated the SNCC workers' ambivalence toward the use of protest tactics. Staff members were torn between their desire to encourage mass militancy among southern blacks and their conflicting desire to avoid actions that would disrupt ongoing projects and interfere with the development of long-range programs. While the Alabama campaign provided an unexpected opportunity for SNCC proponents of nonviolent protest to regain a central role in the organization, it strengthened the hand of hardliners who wanted greater staff discipline and more definite lines of authority. In April, for example, Alabama project director Silas Norman pointed out that SNCC workers from other states had not consulted him before arriving in Alabama for the protests.

He added that former Mississippi project director Ivanhoe Donaldson became marshal of the march "even though he was against it." As for SNCC's chairman, Norman sarcastically remarked, "John, being a chief executive of SNCC, can do as he pleases." Disgruntled workers who remained in Mississippi while SNCC activists left to join the march complained that initially they had been told that SNCC was opposed to the demonstration. They had later learned, however, that SNCC, "with Forman in the lead, seems to be leading demonstrations day and night and fighting with SCLC ostensibly because they are opposing demonstrations. What the hell is going on?"[18]

Despite the exacerbation of SNCC's internal conflicts, few staff members could ignore the resurgence of mass activism, particularly among students, which breathed new life into the organization. Even staff members who opposed SNCC's involvement in the voting rights campaign exploited the opportunity to recruit a sizeable group of young blacks from Alabama colleges—the first significant body of black students to enter SNCC since the arrival of a group of NAG members in the spring of 1964.


The Alabama demonstrations which stimulated black militancy nationwide, also led to the launching of the Black Panther Party in the rural black belt county of Lowndes, situated between Selma and Montgomery. Like the Mississippi communities where SNCC workers had previously broken new ground, the black residents of Lowndes County were typically poor, landless, and economically dependent upon a small elite of white plantation owners. Even though the black residents greatly outnumbered whites, they had not been able to register to vote, and few even dared to express support for civil rights reforms. It was in this county that Viola Liuzzo was murdered. The day after her death, Carmichael was driven to the county and dropped off with a sleeping bag, a few dollars in his pocket, and the name of a resident with whom he could stay.

Carmichael was already a veteran of political activism, beginning with his association with young white leftists while in high school. Born in the West Indies, he moved with his family to New York as a child and later was admitted to the selective Bronx High School of Science. Through his friendship with Gene Dennis, whose father was national secretary of the Communist Party, Carmichael met veteran black Party leaders, including Benjamin Davis, who had served on the New York City Council during the 1940s. During his high school years, Carmichael maintained informal ties with several Marxist student organizations and participated in demonstrations sponsored by socialist youth groups and the Fair Play for Cuba Committee.

Initially Carmichael was unimpressed with the politically unsophisticated southern black student activists. "I remember . . . throwing the paper down and saying, Niggers'd do anything to get their names in the paper." He told friends that the southern students were not going to get far because they were "going about it wrong." His attitude changed when he met NAG members at a demonstration against HUAC in Washington and later, in the summer of 1960, he joined NAG demonstrations in Maryland.

In part because of these contacts, Carmichael enrolled at Howard University in the fall of 1960. He soon became one of NAG's leaders, representing them at SNCC meetings. Reflecting the influence of democratic socialists, such as Bayard Rustin, and Tom Kahn, a white classmate who became head of the League for Industrial Democracy, SDS's parent organization, Carmichael argued for greater emphasis on economic issues.

Carmichael became a full-time SNCC worker after college graduation in 1964 and was named to direct the COFO office in Mississippi's second congressional district. He later described his participation in the Mississippi Summer Project as an attempt to implement black nationalism, but Carmichael's attitudes more accurately stemmed from a growing awareness of the problems caused by white participation in the civil rights struggle.[19] He recruited an all-black staff for his district, but maintained friendly relations with the many white volunteers with whom he came into contact at COFO headquarters in Greenwood (Carmichael often received gifts from an informal group of northern supporters called the Friends and Admirers of Stokely Carmichael).[20]

Carmichael, like other veterans, was not allied with either of the extreme SNCC factions. His resignation as district director suggested, however, that he shared SNCC's prevailing distrust of institutions. While a strong proponent of poor, even uneducated, blacks making their own political decisions, Carmichael did not take the extreme view that former college students should play no leadership role in the southern struggle; instead, he urged organizers to make their skills and information available to southern rural blacks.[21]

Carmichael's talents as an organizer were soon demonstrated, given the opportunity to initiate a black political movement in a county like Lowndes. He combined astute political awareness with an ability to communicate with less-educated people on their own terms. Along with other SNCC workers, including Bob Mants, Scott B. Smith, Willie Vaugn and Judy Richardson, Carmichael gained the confidence of a few local black leaders who then directed the course of the Lowndes County movement.

Rather than impose his views on Lowndes County blacks, Carmichael avoided discussing the differences between SNCC and SCLC. He knew that civil rights workers were not separated into groups by local residents; they were just "civil rights workers" or "freedom fighters." Carmichael dis-

agreed with Forman's belief that SNCC should challenge King's leadership, asserting instead that SNCC should exploit the enthusiasm created by
King's presence:[22]

> People loved King . . . I've seen people in the South climb over each
> other just to say, "I touched him! I touched him! . . . I'm even talking
> about the young. The old people had more love and respect. They
> even saw him like a God. These were the people we were working with
> and I had to follow in his footsteps when I went in there. The people
> didn't know what was SNCC. They just said, "You one of Dr. King's
> men?" "Yes, Ma'am, I am."

Although SNCC workers had few tangible results during their initial
months in Lowndes County, they did succeed in uniting a group of militant and self-reliant local black residents who sustained the movement in
Lowndes County. Like the rural areas of Mississippi, black farmers in
Lowndes County owned weapons and were willing to defend themselves
when attacked. Black rallies in the county were often protected by armed
guards, sometimes affiliated with the Louisiana-based Deacons for Defense
and Justice. During the summer of 1965 Carmichael told a reporter for a
national magazine that he was actually a restraining influence on local
blacks. He could not convince a local leader, R. L. Strickland, who unsuccessfully tried to register in 1958, of the virtues of nonviolence and the reporter quoted Strickland as telling Carmichael, "You turn the other cheek,
and you'll get handed half of what you're sitting on."[23]

That the attitudes of the SNCC workers were affected by daily contacts
with militant black farmers was vividly demonstrated by their response to
the arrest in southwest Georgia of a SNCC worker for possession of three
pistols. Roy Shields, project director for the region, was forced to respond
to criticisms by John Lewis, Marion Barry, and other proponents of nonviolence who maintained that he should have discouraged his staff from
carrying weapons. Members of the Alabama staff, vigorously defended
Shields. "We are not King or SCLC," Carmichael exclaimed, "They don't
do the kind of work we do nor do they live in the areas we live in. They
don't ride the highways at night." He asserted that for King nonviolence
was "everything" but for SNCC it had always been simply a tactic. When
Bill Hansen asked why workers did not get permits for their guns, Carmichael protested: "Be reasonable. Can you imagine us going to the local
communities for a permit?" Another Alabama staff member, Fay Bellamy,
commented that if the SNCC leadership could "spend six thousand dollars
in Montgomery [they] should be able to get this man out of jail and hire a
lawyer." Carmichael recalled that the discussion ended when he asked
those carrying weapons to place them on the table. Nearly all of the black
organizers working in the deep South were armed.[24]

Despite the increasing militancy of the SNCC workers and local black leaders in Lowndes County, only about 250 blacks were registered by the beginning of August. The voter registration effort received a boost on August 10, however, when a federal registrar arrived in the county under the provisions of the recently enacted Voting Rights Act. Afterward black residents were able to register without taking a literacy test.

The upsurge in black registration brought intensified white resistance. In Fort Deposit, police arrested a group of black picketers and two white civil rights workers. When the demonstrators were released on August 20 after a week in the county jail in Hayneville, a white part-time deputy sheriff fired shots into the group, killing one of the civil rights workers, Jonathan Daniels, a ministerial student and Carmichael's friend. The other white civil rights worker, the Reverend Richard Morrisroe, was wounded in the incident, for which the deputy sheriff was later acquitted by an all-white jury.

Rather than halting registration efforts the shooting strengthened the resolve of black residents. Two days after the killing of Daniels, Carmichael bitterly expressed the defiant mood of blacks in the county when he told an audience at an evening rally, "We're going to tear this county up. Then we're going to build it back, brick by brick, until it's a fit place for human beings."[25]

Since voter registration in Lowndes County was so threatening to white leaders, SNCC workers began to question whether they should continue to encourage blacks to register as Democrats or to form an independent party. Late in the summer Carmichael telephoned SNCC's research director, Jack Minnis, to ask about the procedures for creating such a party. After a few days of research Minnis discovered an unusual provision in Alabama law that allowed for the formation of a political party at the county level. Residents of a county could nominate independent candidates simply by holding a nominating convention. If these candidates received twenty percent of the votes cast in county elections, their party would gain official recognition. SNCC workers decided to build an independent party, to which the black residents enthusiastically responded. Many felt it futile to seek entry to a party led by segregationist George Wallace which used the words "White Supremacy" in its slogan. As one resident recalled, "SNCC mentioned about the third party and we decided we would do it, because it didn't make sense for us to go join the Democratic party, when they were the people who had done the killing in the county and had beat our heads."[26]

The new political organization was called the Lowndes County Freedom Organization (LCFO), and John Hulett was chosen as its chairman. Hulett, a 37-year-old father of seven, was politically active in the county prior to SNCC's arrival. He founded the Lowndes County Christian Movement for Human Rights with other local leaders after discussions with Andrew Young and James Bevel of SCLC. When SCLC failed to send a full-time organizer to the county, Hulett decided to work with SNCC staff with whom he had established contact during the Montgomery march.

The LCFO was established as an independent political party rather than a racial separatist group, yet the emblem chosen for the new organization—a snarling black panther—was unmistakably significant. "The black panther is an animal that when it is pressured it moves back until it is cornered," explained Hulett, "then it comes out fighting for life or death. We felt we had been pushed back long enough and that it was time for Negroes to come out and take over."[27]

An all-black party was initially unintended—there were simply no whites who wanted to join it. Carmichael recalled that some of the local black residents at first resisted the idea of an exclusively black organization. "Local people would not touch something all black because they think it's bad," he commented a few months later. He overcame resistance by telling residents that "this is a party, it's like the Democratic party and the Republican party. We want power, that's all we want. After we get power we can talk about whether we want all black or not."[28]

Rhetorical appeals for racial separatism were rarely used by SNCC workers in Lowndes County during 1965. Later that year Courtland Cox's written assessment downplayed the separatist implications of SNCC's effort. "The major emphasis is to bring political power at the county level to the poor and excluded—the color of skin is incidental," he wrote. "The extent to which blackness is seen as a 'problem' is one of the manifestations of a segregated and racist society."[29]

The Lowndes County project was an important aspect of SNCC's transformation, yet so were its efforts to apply in urban black communities the ideas culled from its work in the rural deep South. SNCC was afforded an unexpected opportunity to mobilize a political force of urban blacks when a Supreme Court decision required the reapportionment of Georgia's legislature. This resulted in the creation of a predominantly black district near SNCC's Atlanta headquarters. Ivanhoe Donaldson urged Julian Bond, SNCC's communications director, to run for the new seat in the House of Representatives.

Bond, the son of noted scholar Horace Mann Bond, was an atypical SNCC worker, although he had been associated with SNCC since the founding conference in Raleigh. He had not participated in protest activity since 1960, and his position in the Atlanta headquarters, coupled with the responsibility of providing for a wife and children, had isolated him from SNCC's field operations. Nonetheless, he was greatly respected within the organization for his dedication and intelligence. Donaldson doubtless believed that the slightly-built, softspoken writer-activist was the staff member most likely to attract moderate black support. Although Bond disliked making public appearances, he had long urged SNCC to establish a project in Atlanta and recognized that a political campaign would stimulate SNCC's organizing efforts in the city.

Rather than run as an independent candidate, Bond entered the Democratic primary. But his campaign was a demonstration of SNCC's distinctive approach to electoral politics. Deciding that poor black voters in the district could not be reached through traditional candidates' rallies, Bond emphasized personal contacts. "We would go around to people, knock on their doors, and ask them what they wanted their state representative to do," he recalled. "And it was at first confusing for a great many people, because they had never had a real state representative. . . . We had to try to explain to people what it was that a state representative did, and after we explained it, people began to tell us their problems were largely economic." Based on these conversations, Bond drew up a platform that called for a two dollar minimum wage, improved urban renewal programs, repeal of the right to work law, and an end to the literacy test for voters.[30]

Entry into conventional politics prompted criticism from SNCC workers who objected to working within the Democratic party and believed that SNCC should not "play the political game." Cobb, who became Bond's campaign manager, was told by other SNCC workers that those in the campaign must have "sold out," since many were wearing ironed shirts, ties, and slacks instead of overalls. Defending the campaign workers, Cobb argued that their conformity to this middle-class standard avoided "the irrelevant question of dress" and allowed them to focus on the important issues. Cobb admitted that he "approached the campaign with some misgivings and ambivalence." He seriously questioned whether one could "function effectively in the state legislature without the support of the 'establishment.' " Nonetheless, he defended the campaign as an attempt "to explore American politics and the ways it can be shaped (if it can at all) to meet our needs." He hoped that the campaign could "mesh and hook up with the radical forms of our own (like FDP)." Although a few members objected, a majority of SNCC's Executive Committee agreed to loan Bond the money to pay his qualifying fees and to provide funds to establish a campaign headquarters.[31]

Black residents were enthusiastic about the Bond campaign. Cobb noted that many were impressed by the willingness of Bond to come into their homes and listen to them. "I think that literally 100% of the people I canvassed had never had anyone come to their house, sit down and seriously talk to them about their community." Bond easily won the primary election in May, defeating a black minister, and received eighty-two percent of the vote in the June election, running against a black Republican who was dean of men at Atlanta University.

Unaware of the obstacles that still awaited Bond in his attempt to represent the blacks in his district, the campaign encouraged SNCC workers
who were intent on mobilizing blacks to achieve political power. "Imagine,
ten SNCC guys in the Georgia House committed to . . . using the seats in
the House to meet community needs defined by the community," Cobb
wrote. Fascinated with the idea of using traditional political forms on
behalf of "people whose needs are not being and probably will not be met
by these forms anyway," Cobb concluded that organizing in the urban
areas was the same as rural organizing. "What people need—all over!—is
something they can grab hold to, to build; that is their own."[32]

Bond's successful campaign encouraged several veteran SNCC workers
who had grown up in the cities to launch organizing efforts in other urban
communities. Donaldson left the Bond campaign to begin work in Columbus, Ohio; Bill Hall went to Harlem; Marion Barry moved to Washington, D.C. Within a year SNCC had also established footholds in Newark,
Philadelphia, Chicago, and Los Angeles.

These urban efforts strained SNCC's capabilities and made the staff
painfully aware of their meager resources and lack of long-range programs
to confront urban problems. For some staff members, organizing among
urban blacks was a way of escaping the responsibilities they had faced in
the deep South or, in some northern cities, of abandoning fund-raising ob-
ligations. Most of the urban offices floundered during 1965, although Donaldson had some success in helping to establish a "community foundation"
in Columbus that made small grants for local projects approved by a dem-
ocratically-elected community board.

Once they began working in cities, SNCC organizers found that their
rural experiences had not prepared them to deal with the problems of
urban black residents who were more varied than rural blacks in their class
and educational backgrounds, institutional ties, and political experiences.
There were no black institutions in cities comparable to the rural black
church which served as a cohesive force in the deep South capable of
reaching large segments of the black populace. Urban organizers were
forced to discover new issues around which to mobilize blacks, since many
of the civil rights reforms of the rural South were available to urban blacks.
They found that the poorest urban blacks, who were the focus of their efforts, were more alienated, anti-social, and angrier than their counterparts
in the rural South. Lacking the sharply defined target of southern racism,
SNCC workers in urban areas began the formidable task of building a social movement among blacks filled with undirected hostility and generalized distrust. They soon realized that their previous victories in the deep
South had exaggerated their sense of power to confront the entrenched, re-
silient institutions responsible for the social problems of urban, industrial
society.

\* \* \*

SNCC organizers' attempts to expand the scope of their work demonstrated both their unyielding enthusiasm and their limitations as a political force. After five years of existence SNCC retained much of its earlier dynamism, but programmatic uncertainty and organizational disarray were dissipating its resources. Staff members were initiating new projects while neglecting old ones, breaking ties with former white allies before consolidating their southern black support. Despite the increased representation on the Executive Committee gained by the hardliners at the February staff meeting, SNCC members were reluctant to accept the constraints of institutional roles and political pragmatism. Recognizing that their objective now was to challenge liberal power rather than prod that power into action on behalf of southern blacks, SNCC leaders hoped to eliminate the most debilitating manifestation of its anti-authoritarianism without completely abandoning SNCC's unique style of individualistic, rebellious activism.

In April 1965 Forman identified a source of SNCC's weaknesses when he noted that the staff was "oriented to breaking ground, mobilizing people, and getting them to think they should move on issues." He argued that these activities were part of a passing phase of the civil rights movement in Georgia and Mississippi. He suggested that the new phase of the southern struggle would require different skills but that SNCC workers had not yet begun to discuss emerging issues such as the Johnson administration's recently launched "War on Poverty" or proposed voting rights legislation.[33]

The setting for Forman's remarks was a crucial meeting of the Executive Committee in Holly Springs, Mississippi at which SNCC's leaders tried to reverse the deterioration occurring in projects by imposing a measure of control over staff activities. They recognized the seriousness of SNCC's problems, but the desultory quality of their comments reflected their uncertainty about the extent to which SNCC would have to change to remain in the vanguard of the black struggle.

When SNCC's administrative secretary Ruby Doris Robinson opened the Holly Springs meeting by reporting that some staff members "just float and don't do any work," other committee members joined in an attack against those they considered to be irresponsible. Dispensing with the civility that had previously softened staff members' criticism, executive committee members resolved to take firm action against the floaters. Ben Grinnage, head of the Arkansas project, warned that if the committee evaluated each staff member's work it might be necessary to fire most of them. Alabama staff member Fay Bellamy asked rhetorically, "Where on earth did the idea come from of being able to hire but not fire?" Bill Hansen added that SNCC workers could "stay around any town they want to forever, but they don't have to be financed by SNCC." John Lewis agreed, stating that he was "strongly for people shaping up or shipping out."[34]

Thus began a person-by-person evaluation, lasting almost two days, of the activities of over one hundred staff members. Without procedures for supervision or rules governing staff assignments and behavior, the assessments were often arbitrary or inconsistent and sometimes based merely on reputations. A committee member tried to cut off a discussion of Donaldson with the comment, "We all know Ivanhoe works, so there is no need for further discussion."[35]

Good reputations did not spare other staff members, however, particularly if they had become identified with the floaters. Hardliners on the Alabama staff were particularly disturbed by the failure of Moses and his wife, Dona Richards, to work under Project Director Norman after their arrival in Birmingham. Although Moses's record of accomplishment had previously shielded him from personal criticisms, Norman insisted that he and Richards be treated like other staff members. "I will not look for them; they must contact me," he stated. Others agreed. "Someone should find out what they are doing," Robinson advised. "They can't say their work is irrelevant to SNCC." Casey Hayden was similarly attacked for leaving her position in Mississippi without authorization. "Some people want to do what they want and go where they want," Lewis commented. "They want to experiment with personal freedom." A Mississippi resident, Lee Bankhead, derided all staff members who "talk of personal freedom and what they will and won't do. How can these confused staff people work in the communities?"[36]

Although Lewis and Forman agreed with the need for greater discipline, their actions in Selma and Montgomery and their long absences from Atlanta while on northern speaking tours left them open to criticisms. Like the criticisms of Moses, those directed against the two SNCC officials were indicative of the weakening of the bonds of respect and friendship that had once made SNCC "a band of brothers, a circle of trust."

Few concrete suggestions were offered to resolve SNCC's problems. Carmichael spoke for other staff members when he stated that the Executive Committee was only dealing "with symptoms rather than the cause," since SNCC needed to develop radical programs to sustain the interest of activists. He complained that staff members continued to rely on protest tactics, although these tactics were no longer appropriate. "When people ask us how to get their streets paved, we say, 'Go down to the courthouse.' "[37]

At a gathering of the Alabama staff shortly after the Holly Springs meeting, Moses defended the notion that SNCC organizers should not exert leadership in local movements and instead expressed support for People's Conferences, from which would emerge new programs. As explained in a leaflet distributed during April, these conferences would "bring together people from across each state to share movement experiences and hold workshops on their problems.[38] Moses assumed that, freed of outside domination and allowed time to develop, local movements would gradually recognize their common problems and would conclude that people everywhere should join in creating a society in which everyone participated in political decison making. De-emphasizing the need for expertise in the political process, he argued that SNCC workers should not impose their ideas on local residents. "Organizers raise certain questions, people develop answers," he told the staff.

A few Alabama staff members challenged Moses' proposals, suggesting that organizers would have to be more assertive in working with local residents to solve complex problems. Carmichael asserted that SNCC needed a program beyond "just talking to people" and Hall pointed out that some workers were frustrated by the lack of a "structured program in Alabama." Norman agreed, adding that he needed programs to evaluate staff performance.[39]

The discussions at the Alabama staff meeting clearly indicated that many staff members were disturbed by the tendency of others to equate a belief in local leadership with a generalized rejection of all authority and institutions. They believed that SNCC's organizing techniques would continue to produce important gains in counties such as Lowndes, where blacks were only beginning to acquire the confidence to exercise their rights, but not in Mississippi, where the black struggle had reached a new stage requiring some measure of institutionalization and specialized skills.

Some SNCC workers who agreed that SNCC would have to alter its techniques and structure nonetheless had difficulty making the transition to new roles. Mississippi workers who once played a unique role in challenging the state's white establishment, were often ambivalent about their continued involvement in institutions such as the MFDP and the freedom schools. Illustrating the low morale was the need of COFO staff members at a May meeting to applaud their own success in concentrating on organizing concerns instead of "personal and personnel problems," as at earlier meetings. Yet, despite three days of candid and often insightful discussion, their meeting made little progress in reversing COFO's decline.

Staff members at the meeting debated whether COFO was prepared to confront a new phase of struggle. Johnnie Mae Walker, asserting that COFO had failed to organize "these uneducated people—that guy in the pool hall, drinking that wine," led the discussion back to the festering issue of whether white workers inhibited the development of local black leadership. "Some things have to be said by blacks to blacks," a worker stated. Others recalled the difference in the civil rights movement before the arrival of white volunteers. "Now I sit back because I don't understand what's going on," a staff member said. Criticism was directed not only at whites but at college-educated blacks whose academic training intimidated many local activists. "Although I have finished high school some of them big words they say, man, I just don't know the meaning of them," a worker complained. Another agreed: "It is true ain't nobody like to be made like a fool when he come to contribute something."[40]

Although eager to avoid the resentments of local blacks, many college-educated SNCC workers saw that their distrust and avoidance of institutionalized leadership roles had contributed to a lack of concrete programs in Mississippi. Some workers took cautious steps toward involvement in black-controlled institutions during 1965, while others pleaded with MFDP leaders not to compromise their principles and " 'take on' bad values" of the established political system as they sought to change it.[41] Jessie Morris helped found the Poor People's Corporation, becoming its executive secretary, and through this institution provided financial assistance for economic projects determined by residents of black communities. Similarly, two COFO workers mobilized black farm laborers in the Mississippi Delta region into the Mississippi Freedom Labor Union (MFLU). Within a few months the MFLU attracted over a thousand members in several counties through its demands for a $1.25 an hour minimum wage, free medical care, social security, accident insurance, and equality for blacks in wages, employment opportunities, and working conditions. Using SNCC fund-raising contacts, the union survived an unsuccessful strike by its members in the spring of 1965, and by the fall had developed its own sources of financial support and was no longer dependent on SNCC.[42]

Rather than regretting the fact that such institutions became independent, many COFO workers saw the weaning process as inevitable and took pride in their reluctance to assume permanent institutional roles. They sneered at professional reformers who worked regular hours and submitted to organizational restraints. "A good organization brings people together," Dona Richards commented at the Alabama staff meeting, "a bad one makes everything neat and compartmentalized." Even those who saw the necessity of working within other reform organizations often had difficulty adjusting to their new roles. This was demonstrated in the case of SNCC-COFO workers employed during 1965 by the Mississippi Child Development Group (MCDG), a federally-funded pre-school education program conceived by Tom Levin, a New York psychologist who had worked in the Freedom Schools. The workers' ambivalence about their participation in the "poverty program" led to many conflicts with MCDG leaders, and none of the workers—nor Levin, who had hired them—remained on the staff for more than a few months. The qualities that made it difficult and at the same time necessary for SNCC workers to assume institutional roles were indicated in a MCDG staff member's assessment of Frank Smith:[43]

Frank was a very insubordinate staff member. He wouldn't cooperate with anybody about anything . . . But he mobilized many hundreds of poor people into feeling themselves as a force. He attacked the educators on the staff endlessly. But I never saw poor people so feverishly interested in education, as Frank stirred them to be . . . I discovered that there are some things more important than orderly procedure and controlled staff.

SNCC workers would bring distinctive and beneficial qualities into the reform movements of the late 1960s, but these qualities sometimes led to tensions even between SNCC and organizations it had helped to create, most notably the MFDP. Thus, some of the most pragmatic organizers in Mississippi decided to leave behind the frustrations of working within COFO and join the staff of MFDP or other organizations. In November 1965 SNCC disbanded COFO and gave SNCC workers in the state the option of either working under the direction of MFDP or taking part in the few remaining effective SNCC programs in the state. Although SNCC assumed responsibility for paying the salaries of staff members working for the MFDP, and offered to pay for office expenses in the MFDP headquarters, this commitment was as much a hope as an expectation.[44]

The problems that afflicted COFO affected other SNCC operations, including its fund-raising network. SNCC no longer received substantial contributions from the institutional sources—churches, labor unions, and foundations—that had made possible the summer project. Instead it depended almost entirely on personal contributions, which had declined during 1965, in part due to SNCC's floundering northern offices. The only substantial sources of northern support came from the New York office and from areas such as San Francisco, where there were strong support groups. At the end of the year SNCC was forced to secure a short-term loan of $10,-000 to maintain its operations.[45]

The decline in SNCC's income was of course partly the result of liberal opposition to its activities as well as the inefficiency and irresponsibility of some staff members, but these factors were not unrelated. Although SNCC found a receptive audience outside the South for its distinctive radical activism, the organization suffered because it failed to create dependable—that is, institutionalized—bases of support, either in the South or the North. With the exceptions of Lowndes County and Atlanta, where SNCC workers were initiating new efforts, SNCC projects in the deep South deteriorated through the failure of staff members to balance their desire for mass participation with the need to create durable and powerful black-controlled institutions to deliver tangible benefits to black people. The individualistic forms of rebelliousness that hampered the process of building southern bases of support had great appeal outside the South, but northern support activities on behalf of SNCC were largely superseded during 1965 by movements focusing on other isues, particularly the war in Vietnam. The staff meetings of the spring of 1965 indicated that many SNCC workers were aware of the problems of extreme individualism, but they and the many young activists for whom SNCC was a model were only beginning to recognize the many forms these problems could assume.

# 12. THE NEW LEFT

By 1965 SNCC had become, in the eyes of supporters and critics, not simply a civil rights organization but a part of the New Left: an amorphous body of young activists seeking new ideological alternatives to conventional liberalism. Some observers attributed SNCC's radicalism to the presence of white leftists in the southern struggle; yet SNCC is more accurately seen as a source of insights and inspiration for the New Left. Just as its unique style of unstructured, rebellious activism broke through the ingrained patterns of southern black accommodation, SNCC undermined the pervasive patterns of political and cultural conformity embraced by white college students in Cold War America. SNCC inspired the small band of activists who launched the student rights and anti-war movements of the mid-1960s. Although lacking a developed ideology of its own, the implicit assumptions underlying SNCC's work attracted activists who were unaware of or unconvinced by the strategies of the Old Left.

SNCC's example was particularly important for SDS, whose emergence as the largest New Left organization coincided with the rise of SNCC. A number of SNCC workers—including Casey Hayden, Betty Garman, Jim Monsonis, Bob Zellner, and Maria Varela—played significant roles in SDS. Through these and other SDS members, many of the values and organizing techniques developed inside the southern struggle were absorbed by SDS and combined with ideas drawn from a growing body of non-Marxian, radical literature, including the writings of Albert Camus, Allen Ginsberg, C. Wright Mills, and Paul Goodman. At an annual convention in 1962, SDS delegates drafted the Port Huron Statement, a manifesto describing the many sources of their alienation and acknowledging that the southern struggle had "compelled" them to move "from silence to activism."[1] In 1964, SDS launched its Economic Research and Action Project (ERAP), an attempt to apply many of SNCC's techniques developed in the deep South to the problems of the urban poor.

Despite important differences, a convergence in the ideological evolution of SNCC and predominantly-white New Left groups allowed them to share, for a time, a common radical vocabulary and anti-imperialistic perspective. While the radicalism in SNCC grew from different cultural and ideological sources, nearly all SNCC workers were willing to support the major New Left effort: the resistance to United States involvement in the Vietnam War. Only gradually did the black leaders who dominated SNCC during the mid-1960s develop a racial perspective that threatened the New Left dream of an interracial radical movement.

Tom Hayden's meetings with SNCC workers in McComb, Mississippi, in 1961 established the tone of subsequent relations between SNCC and SDS. Openly displaying his envy, Hayden suggested that white activists recognize the change that had occurred among militant black students: "In our future dealings we should be aware that they have changed down there, and we should speak their revolutionary language without mocking it, for it is not lip service, nor is it the ego fulfillment of a rising Negro class." Hayden advised northern radicals to support the southern struggle without hesitation. "There is no reason for us to fear that the civil rights movement is degenerate," he wrote, apparently commenting on the reluctance of some northern leftists to associate with a movement emphasizing mass civil disobedience rather than intellectual analysis. He added that the southern civil rights movement had "turned itself into the revolution we hoped for, and we didn't have much to do with its turning at all." Black students were "miles ahead of us, looking back, chuckling knowingly about the sterility of liberals . . . In the rural South, in the 'token integration' areas, in the cities, they will be shouting from the bottom of their guts for justice or else. We had better be there."[2]

Hayden combined an infatuation with SNCC's revolutionary élan with a belief that all activists should move beyond civil rights reforms and join in a movement for broad social change. Shortly after his trip to McComb, Hayden helped draft the SDS Port Huron Statement, which applauded the new political emphasis of the southern struggle, noting that previously "the moral clarity of the civil rights movement" had not always "been accompanied by precise political vision, and sometimes not even by a real political consciousness." The statement was addressed to middle-class white students rather than to poor southern blacks, but it nonetheless suggested some of the future lines of intellectual development both SNCC and SDS would follow. Echoing some of SNCC's guiding assumptions, the statement proposed a social system based on "individual participation, governed by two central aims: that the individual share in those social decisions determining the quality and direction of his life; that society be organized to encourage independence in men and provide the media for their common participation."[3]

After the creation of ERAP early in 1964, SDS leaders intensified their efforts to strengthen ties with SNCC. They encouraged the shift in the focus of SNCC's activities from civil rights to economic issues. SDS officers were especially interested in SNCC's initial ventures into white community organizing and they established contact with Sam Shirah and other future members of SSOC. In addition to sending literature to SNCC projects in the deep South, SDS attempted to recruit ERAP workers from among the Mississippi Summer Project volunteers. By the end of 1964 ERAP head Rennie Davis had proposed exchanges of personnel between SNCC and SDS projects, and Todd Gitlin of SDS's Peace Research and Education Project had sought SNCC's participation in a sit-in protesting American investments in South Africa.[4]

Although SDS's overtures to SNCC did not result in joint endeavors, relations between the two groups were cordial and supportive at a time when both were becoming increasingly isolated from former allies. A transformation of consciousness similar to that which occurred within SNCC also occurred within the fledgling ERAP ventures in poor areas of northern cities. Mostly white and college-educated, SDS organizers' self-conscious awareness of their class and racial advantages fostered attitudes similar to those found among members of SNCC's freedom-high faction. Thus, some SDS members idealized the virtues of poor and uneducated black people and were determined to avoid the institutionalized leadership roles that normally accrued to persons from affluent backgrounds or possessing academic credentials. Like SNCC militants, SDS organizers helped develop the leadership abilities of local residents, but sometimes took their own anti-authoritarian orientation to extremes. An account of an ERAP meeting early in 1965 noted that SNCC organizers attending the gathering "managed to impress ERAP with the image of an organizer who never organized, who by his simple presence was the mystical medium for the spontaneous expression of the 'people.' " The report added that the "staff meeting ended in exhaustion, with a faith that the spirit would decide, that an invisible hand would enable all to be resolved if honesty prevailed."[5]

By the time of this meeting some of the SNCC field secretaries who served as role models for many SDS organizers were also questioning their own attitudes and organizing techniques. Northern radicals with close ties to SNCC only gradually became aware that it was divided over basic issues. Thus, many sympathetic observers retained a view of SNCC that only partially described its ever-changing reality.

Activist historian Staughton Lynd noted the "fascinating intellectual ferment" taking place within SNCC at the end of 1964. Former director of Mississippi's freedom schools and closely associated with both SNCC and SDS, Lynd was one of many white supporters of the southern struggle who feared that SNCC's internal debates might result in an anti-white orientation if staff members gave in to the feeling "that so deeply prejudiced a society as ours can never create a permeating atmosphere of equality." He nonetheless suggested that SNCC must abandon its "mystique of action" which had interrupted attempts to plan for the future and had prevented SNCC from making "contact with groups who might be partners in a more broadly-conceived movement."

The kind of radicalism that Lynd and other white radicals hoped would emerge from SNCC's ferment was indicated in an essay Lynd wrote in response to Bayard Rustin's advocacy of electoral politics as a new direction for the civil rights movement. Lynd dismissed "the Social Democratic vision of electing more and more radical legislators until power passes peacefully to the Left." He proposed instead a "scenario" attributed to Moses, in which blacks of Nashoba County, Mississippi recognized only the authority of their own "Freedom Sheriff" rather than that of the white sheriff responsible for the murders of three civil rights workers in 1964. Moses wondered, "What if the Freedom Sheriff impaneled a Freedom Grand Jury which indicted Sheriff Rainey for murder?" For Lynd, these ideas showed that revolution was not "a monolithic, unitary event" but instead began "as the decision of individuals to say, No, and take a first step." Lynd linked Moses' scenario to a plan suggested by Tom Hayden to convene a new "continental congress" for people who felt that the existing national government did not represent them.[6]

Like many other activists who had become radicalized during the early 1960s, Lynd believed that fundamental social change could be achieved through a broadening of the challenge to existing authority initiated by SNCC. Courageous black SNCC workers inspired white activists who had begun to question not only Cold War political orthodoxes but also the cultural assumptions of white, middle-class American society. Journalist Jack Newfield asserted that within the New Left SNCC was the one word which, "above all others, [had] the magic to inspire blind loyalty and epic myth." He quoted Carl Oglesby, a leader of SDS, who identified SNCC's concern as the elimination of that which interfered with love: "the inequity that coordinates with injustice to create plain suffering and to make custom of distrust. Poverty. Racism. The assembly line universities of this Pepsi Generation. The ulcerating drive for affluence. And the ideology of anti-communism, too, because it smothers my curiosity and bribes my compassion."[7]

For many young radicals who did not wish to conform with prevailing American values, SNCC appeared to offer an outlet for discontent without the compromise of individual ideals. Few outsiders were aware of the problems caused by SNCC's unwillingness to accept the need for discipline and structure. Moreover, observers failed to recognize that SNCC's success in the early 1960s was aided by the threat of federal intervention against a vulnerable southern political system.

Howard Zinn's sympathetic history of SNCC—a new edition of which appeared in 1965—contributed to the popularization of SNCC's romantic image. Zinn described one of SNCC's most important qualities as the "re-nunciation, without the pretense of martyrdom, of the fraud and glitter of a distorted prosperity. It is also a recapturing from some time and place long forgotten of an emotional approach to life, aiming, beyond politics and economics, simply to remove the barriers that prevent human beings from making contact with one another." In an approving review of Zinn's book, SDS leader Tom Hayden claimed that the source of SNCC's "special character" was "its origins in the experience of Negro oppression." Black organizers in SNCC derived their strength from southern blacks in places remote from "urban industrial society," who had learned to endure suffering. "The honesty, insight and leadership of rural Negroes demonstrate to the students that their upbringing has been based on a framework of lies," wrote Hayden. "The movement takes root in places which testify tragically to the flaws of American morality and promise."[8]

White activists' view of SNCC was sometimes distorted by racial romanticism, but it nonetheless had seminal importance in the development of the New Left. SDS leader Norm Fruchter revealed a common view of SNCC in an essay written after a week of meeting with Mississippi workers. "SNCC's cardinal assumption is that an individual is free only when he can effectively control, and carry out, all the decisions affecting the way he lives his life," Fruchter wrote. Fruchter was untroubled by the organizational problems within SNCC. While failing in some respects, SNCC had fulfilled its more important purpose in raising "the question of just how well all the organizations operating on bureaucratic assumptions within the majority society have served human freedom." Fruchter asserted that SNCC should be judged "by the numbers of local people it has involved, the qualities of relationships within the local organizations, and the new forms and institutions local people evolve to meet their own needs."[9]

Fruchter was one of a group of young activists on the editorial board of the New Left journal, *Studies on the Left*, who saw civil rights as the pivotal issue in American politics. This group, which included Tom Hayden and Alan Cheuse, argued that civil rights organizations such as SNCC required new kinds of radical allies who had abandoned the notion of "fixed leaders, who inevitably develop interests in maintaining the organization (or themselves) and lose touch with the immediate aspirations of the rank and file." They pleaded for radicals to recognize that they had "failed so far to discover the relationships and forms that [would] free individuals to think and work as radicals, and build a movement where 'everybody is a leader.'"

Identification with SNCC's anti-authoritarian values separated the New Left from older leftists on the journal's editorial board who asserted that SNCC's radicalism was effective only to the extent that SNCC was allied with moderate civil rights forces, since it had not developed an independent base of support. Similarly, Victor Rabinowitz, whose daughter was once a SNCC staff member, argued that Fruchter described only one of the opposing trends in SNCC while ignoring aspects that place SNCC closer to traditional leftist groups. Rabinowitz asserted that at its February 1965 staff meeting SNCC had established a bureaucratic structure by creating a secretariat to make policy decisions and had set forth "orthodox political demands."[10]

Although they often failed to note the conflicting tendencies inside SNCC, the younger leftists came closer than the older ones to understanding SNCC's distinctive attributes. As the New Left grew more anti-authoritarian, its estrangement from traditional Marxists increased. SDS became increasingly unstructured during 1965 as its national leaders lost their ability or willingness to shape organizational policies. SDS severed ties with its moderate parent organization, the League for Industrial Democracy when it decided to remove bars to Communist participation. Ironically the League then was led by Tom Kahn, a former member of NAG. By the end of 1965 SDS was isolated from most traditional leftist groups much as SNCC was isolated from the traditional civil rights movement.

The complexities and ironies of SNCC's relations with white leftist radicals were not evident in the national press during 1965. Publications formerly friendly to SNCC began to comment critically on its increasingly radical bent, focusing on the leftist orientation of its rhetoric while largely ignoring the stronger element of racial separatism that was beginning to pervade the group. As observers sympathetic to the New Left tended to see in SNCC what they wanted to see, so also did hostile observers stress SNCC's links to the subversive ideas of the Old or New Left. These intimations ignored the fact that publicly identified New-Left affiliated SNCC members were often whites or northern blacks who were not involved in SNCC projects and sometimes were not even active members of the staff. Concern about their increasing vulnerability did not lead SNCC to purge its ranks, however, and, though it made some efforts during 1965 to prevent unauthorized statements by staff members, SNCC reaffirmed its long-standing policy against Communist exclusion.

SNCC was willing to accept help from all who were willing to "put their bodies on the line," but control of the organization remained in the hands of blacks whose attitudes were shaped by their experiences in the southern struggle rather than by revolutionary doctrines emerging from previous movements. SNCC was too decentralized and too unstructured to be dominated by any outside group. Its militancy, however, made SNCC prey to the widespread belief of Americans that reform groups refusing to exclude and renounce Communists were inevitably controlled by them. Although southern whites had often charged that SNCC was a subversive organization, such charges were not a serious concern for SNCC workers until 1965, when northern liberals joined southerners in "red-baiting" them.

SNCC staff members worried that they would be called to testify before congressional committees such as HUAC regarding Communist involvement in the civil rights movement. SNCC recognized that congressional hearings would emphasize their informal ties to the Left, thereby further weakening their liberal support. In February 1965 Senator James Eastland of Mississippi, long a critic of SNCC, provided more ammunition by charging that many MFDP supporters, including several SNCC staff members, had subversive backgrounds.

Eastland noted that Moses sought exemption from the draft as a conscientious objector, that Jim Forman was involved in the Robert Williams affair in 1961, that Jack Minnis (SNCC's research director) once gave a speech critical of the FBI, and that Joni Rabinowitz (a former member of the southwest Georgia staff) was the daughter of a man whose law firm had represented the Cuban government.[11]

Eastland's attempt to undermine SNCC through innuendo and guilt by association would have been ineffective were it not for a weakening of SNCC's liberal congressional support by a growing northern white backlash against black militancy. Forman's highly publicized statements and the involvement of other SNCC staff members in a White House sit-in during the Selma and Montgomery demonstrations led many former supporters to view SNCC as a liability for the civil rights movement. SNCC's criticisms of the voting rights legislation and its sponsorship of the independent political movement in Lowndes County triggered further withdrawal of liberal support. Forman and Lewis continued to meet with leaders of other civil rights organizations, but SNCC's relations with the NAACP and SCLC were greatly strained by the rapid pace of SNCC's radicalization.

SNCC was indeed becoming more radical, but many critics erroneously attributed this shift to its policy of open association. *Newsweek* magazine quickly discounted charges of Communist involvement in other civil rights organizations, but noted that "anxiety about SNCC [was] less easy to dismiss." Calling SNCC's leaders "romantic, idealistic, perhaps dangerously innocent," *Newsweek* editors conceded that SNCC workers were "openly contemptuous of stuffy Marxist-Leninism or, for that matter, any organized ideology," preferring instead "a jazzy, free-form individualism." Nonetheless, they warned, "for all their hip enthusiasm, the bleak history of Communist efforts to subvert good causes is against them. Time and again, liberal movements have had to banish Communists from their midst or take the bitter consequences."[12]

This self-fulfilling prediction was repeated by SNCC's long-standing critics, columnists Rowland Evans and Robert Novak, whose attacks on SNCC were often reprinted in the *Congressional Record*. In March, Evans and Novak bluntly charged that SNCC was "substantially infiltrated by beatnik left-wing revolutionaries, and—worst of all—by Communists." They offered no evidence to support these charges, referring only to SNCC's criticisms of moderate civil rights leaders. Afterward they tried to support their claims by mentioning that SNCC received assistance from the National Lawyers Guild, that the leftist publication *National Guardian* was "standard equipment at Snick field offices," that SNCC founder Ella Baker served as a liaison between SNCC and SCEF, and that Reginald Robinson from SNCC had attended the Moscow World Youth Forum the previous year. They concluded that although "only an infinitesimal fraction of Snick workers have Communist ties," even these few "can be quite influential." Lewis, they said, "seems to be no Communist. But he is repeating the error of so many liberals of the past who believed that they could use the Communists rather than be used." Evans and Novak advised that unless SNCC expelled "the ultra-Leftists, it should be isolated for the sake of Negro rights."[13]

Lewis reacted to these and similar charges by stating that they were "part of a conspiracy . . . to discredit [the] work of SNCC in the civil rights movement." He conceded that there might be Communists in SNCC, but insisted that the organization would "accept anybody who [was] willing to go into the Mississippi Delta or the Black Belt to work for freedom." While supporting SNCC's long-standing policy of non-exclusion, some staff members believed that SNCC would be less vulnerable with fewer undisciplined staff members. They believed that SNCC should not specifically exclude Communists but that it should make pragmatic judgments about the negative consequences of any hiring decision. Lewis's strong public advocacy of a policy of non-exclusion contrasted with his remark during an April Executive Committee meeting that "sometimes we leave ourselves too open by the company we keep." At that meeting the Executive Committee urged more restraint in the staff's public statements. SNCC worker Jimmy Garrett, for example, was criticized for allegedly telling a *Newsweek* reporter that SNCC was actually "subverting" Communists—"We're more revolutionary than the Communists." Although insisting that he had been misquoted, Garrett's alleged boast came closer to the truth than the claims that SNCC was dominated by Communists.[14]

Knowledgeable observers who continued to defend SNCC had different views of its radicalism, but accurately insisted that it had little to do with traditional leftist doctrines. "SNCC is part of the 'new radicalism,' or the 'student left,' and is closer to Mario Savio than to Marx," wrote Andrew Kopkind in the *New Republic. Ebony* editor Lerone Bennett Jr. found SNCC "tough, abrasive, and avowedly revolutionary (in a nonviolent way)" but also "an organization in revolt against organization, a formless form." He concluded that "SNCC is not now, nor has it ever been, an un-American organization. But its refusal to impose a loyalty oath on staff members has given critics a weapon which they have been using with increasing effectiveness." Historian C. Vann Woodward identified SNCC with the "Spontaneous Left," which included activists whose hearts were "in Mississippi or Harlem, not in Moscow or Peking, but [who] often profess a profound alienation from American society, refuse to ally themselves with labor, liberals, and church groups, reject established civil-rights leaders and despair of established institutions." Although liberal journalist Pat Watters hoped that SNCC would abandon its dogmatic "anti-anti-Communism," he applauded the development of a "redefinition of what is respectable on the American left—with SNCC and the campus radicals setting the limits and beyond, and forcing America back to some of its pre-McCarthy intellectual freedom."[15]

These defenses did not counteract the negative public opinion that resulted from SNCC's militant activities. In a Gallup poll conducted in November 1965, forty-eight percent of Americans sampled believed that there was "a lot" of Communist involvement in the civil rights protest movement and twenty-seven percent believed that there was "some" degree of Communist involvement.[16] Encouraging such beliefs was the fact that American attention in 1965 was increasingly directed to the war against communists in Vietnam. Groups seeking social change, including SNCC, could not avoid taking public stands on the war issue. Ironically this issue obscured a growing gulf between white New Leftists and black SNCC workers.

Most SNCC workers opposed U.S. involvement in Vietnam as soon as they became aware of it. The current of pacifism that still existed within SNCC, combined with SNCC workers' generalized distrust of the motives of the federal government and their sympathy for Third World struggles against white domination, made this opposition inevitable. Moreover, SNCC workers resented the military draft for it threatened to deprive the organization of many of its male personnel. SNCC workers generally lacked the deferments available to college students, and they could expect little sympathy from their draft boards, most of which were in the South. For varied reasons, an overwhelming majority of SNCC's staff chose to express their festering resentment of the national liberal establishment by taking an anti-war stand that would unmistakably indicate their commitment to radical ideals.

While SNCC's position on the war was never in doubt, its official statement was formulated only after extended discussions that indicated the imcompleteness of SNCC's ideological development. Some staff members were eager to become involved in the anti-war movement. Staff members who were involved in organizing southern black communities approached the war issue with caution, however, because they did not see the relation of anti-war activity to their organizing efforts. SNCC's difficulty was not in determining the essence of its position on the war but in presenting its stand in terms that could unify the staff and appeal to SNCC's poor black constituency.

Before 1965 several SNCC leaders, including Forman and Moses, had publicly criticized American involvement in Vietnam at a time when the federal government was unwilling to intervene on behalf of southern civil rights workers. These criticisms did not represent organizational policy; they were instead another manifestation of SNCC workers' willingness to state their opinions regardless of the consequences. SNCC staff members regarded the war as simply one of many indications of the hypocrisy of the nation's liberal leaders, who proclaimed their support of democracy while tolerating undemocratic practices in the South. Until 1965, Forman recalled, most SNCC workers, including himself, "had considered the war not irrelevant, but simply remote."[17]

The war became less remote during 1965 as the nation poured more and more of its human and material resources into the struggle. Early in the spring a small band of campus New Leftists launched the anti-war protest movement with a teach-in at the University of Michigan which was followed by teach-ins and protests across the nation. When SDS announced plans for an anti-war protest scheduled for April 17 in Washington, D.C., SNCC's Executive Committee decided, with little discussion and no dissent, to support the plan. Moses was one of the speakers who addressed the crowd of between fifteen and twenty-five thousand at the Washington Monument on April 17 in the first massive demonstration against the war.

Moses remained active in the nascent anti-war movement, invariably linking his opposition to the war to his experiences in the southern struggle. He told ten thousand people at a teach-in on the Berkeley campus that he spoke "as a member of the Third World." He mentioned the different public reactions to the deaths of Jimmy Jackson and the Reverend James Reeb and suggested that, if those in the audience began to understand the reasons for that difference, they could "begin to understand this country in relation to Vietnam and the Third World, the Congo, and Santo Domingo." Recalling his reaction to a newspaper photograph of an American Marine capturing an enemy soldier—"a little colored boy standing against a wire fence with a big huge white Marine with a gun in his back"—he told his listeners that, if they recognized that part of the Third World was in the United States, they would be able to understand the significance of the southern struggle. "The South has got to be a looking glass, not a lightning rod. You've got to learn from the South if you're going to do anything about this country in relation to Vietnam." He compared Vietnam with southern towns where murderers of civil rights workers and Negroes were not convicted of their crimes. "You can learn when it is that a society gets together and plans and executes and allows its members to murder and then go free. And if you learn something about that, then maybe you'll learn something about this country and how it plans and executes murders elsewhere in the world."[18]

Although Moses' speech at Berkeley expressed sentiments that were common among blacks in SNCC, he was more involved in anti-war activities than most other black staff members. At a time when staff members agreed that their energies should be devoted to black community organizing, Moses stressed the need to broaden the goals of the black struggle. Although he took a leave of absence from SNCC to avoid criticisms from hardliners who were disturbed by the diffusion of the staff, Moses defended his activities by claiming that civil rights groups "must maintain the right of people who are part of it to function as individuals." He also challenged the argument that civil rights workers should not risk previous black gains through involvement in the anti-war movement. "Certainly one of the most basic rights we have been seeking is the right to participate fully in the life of this country. Now if by participating—that is, taking part in the discussions of the great issues that face the country—we threaten the right to participate, we have to begin to wonder whether the right is real."[19]

Moses' activities in Washington resulted in more demands for a congressional investigation of SNCC. Although few SNCC staff members joined Moses in his efforts to bring together an Assembly of Unrepresented People, Representative Joe Waggoner of Louisiana charged that "the Communist-backed" SNCC was planning to "seize" the House chambers during August. He also asserted that SNCC was "a mob," which contained no students, "only radical, Communist-infiltrated gangs of agitators" who were "dedicated to violence for the sake of the party line." Evans and Novak reported ominously that Moses, though no longer a SNCC staff member, used SNCC's Washington office as his base of operations. "Unhappily, with the civil rights movement in the doldrums in the Deep South," they announced, "the main target for Bob Moses and his civil rights militants is Lyndon Johnson's foreign policy."[20] Actually, the summer's major demonstration, which occurred on August 9 and resulted in about two hundred arrests, included only a handful of southern civil rights workers.

For SNCC workers, the most important protest activity planned for the summer was that in support of the MFDP's challenge to the seating of the Mississippi congressional delegation. Though not as controversial as the anti-war protests, the challenge had an equally small chance of success. Interestingly, support for the congressional challenge was itself undermined by the publication late in July of an MFDP newsletter containing an anti-war text circulated in McComb. The leaflet, written following the death in Vietnam of a McComb resident who had been involved in the 1961 demonstrations led by SNCC, argued that Mississippi blacks should not "fight in Vietnam for the white man's freedom, until all the Negro people are free in Mississippi." The authors of the leaflet added that "no one has a right to ask us to risk our lives and kill other colored people in Santo Domingo and Vietnam, so that the white Americans can get richer. We will be looked upon as traitors by all the Colored people of the world if the Negro people continue to fight and die without a cause." Although MFDP leaders quickly disavowed responsibility for it, the leaflet increased opposition to the congressional challenge, which was voted down in September.[21]

SNCC never again attempted to revive the national civil rights coalition that had made possible the black gains of the first half of the decade. Nonetheless, staff members recognized that they had not yet created alternative bases of power in black communities and were reluctant to destroy the remaining links between themselves and their former allies. SNCC representatives continued to attend meetings of the Council on United Civil Rights Leadership, hoping to share in the decreasing bounty of contributions distributed through that umbrella organization. Although SNCC could not hope to bridge the gulf between it and the two most moderate civil rights organizations—the Urban League and NAACP—relations with CORE were not significantly damaged by SNCC's radicalization and relations with SCLC actually improved after reaching a low point during the Alabama demonstrations in the early months of 1965.

CORE was itself undergoing an ideologial transformation similar to that occurring inside SNCC. Although less often identified with the New Left than SNCC, CORE contained a large proportion of young white leftists in its membership and drew much of its support from the same northern campuses as SDS. CORE's leaders were older than those of SNCC, but the most active local chapters were coming under the control of activists who had been radicalized by their experiences in northern protest activities and occasionally by their involvement in the southern struggle. At their annual convention, held in July 1965, CORE's leaders barely fought back an attempt to put the organization on record against the Vietnam War. In addition, as the organization launched projects in urban black ghettoes, CORE, like SNCC, experienced a growing trend toward racial separatism. In the South, black organizers associated with CORE joined with their counterparts in SNCC as advocates of grass-roots strategy of leadership.[22]

SCLC also experienced a process of radicalization, although it was much less pronounced than that taking place inside SNCC or CORE. King's staff was comprised of both militants such as James Bevel, who had been active in the southern struggle since the early 1960s, and more cautious leaders such as Andrew Young. Resentment of King by SNCC workers receded somewhat as their emphasis changed from protest activity, which almost always led to competition with King or his lieutenants, to political organizing, which could benefit from King's ability to mobilize the black masses.

SNCC's Alabama staff, for example, worked amicably with the large force of northern volunteers brought in by the SCLC for its 1965 Summer Community Organization and Political Education (SCOPE) project. Moreover, at a time when SNCC workers were debating whether to assume the risks of formally opposing the Vietnam War, King's occasional statements against the war probably increased his stature among SNCC workers, even as they prompted criticism from within SCLC ranks.[23]

Of all the civil rights organizations, SNCC was the group least willing to temper its criticisms in the interest of expediency, but the slowness with which they arrived at their anti-war position indicates that SNCC leaders continued to avoid a complete rupture of relations with the administration. During the fall, Lewis, along with Marion Barry, worked with planners of the White House Conference on Civil Rights, scheduled for June 1966, urging planners to give poor blacks and community organizers a meaningful role at the conference. By the end of fall, however, SNCC's failure to publicly break with the Johnson administration on the war issue had become a source of embarrassment for a few staff members. Julian Bond recalled that SNCC activists grew tired of "disassociating themselves from their organization" when they opposed the war. Zinn wrote that SNCC could not expect to receive support from the rapidly expanding anti-war movement if it refused to take a firm stand on the war. Undoubtedly, SNCC stood to lose more financial support as a result of an anti-war statement than it would gain, but Zinn's appeal to the moral sensibilities of SNCC workers probably swayed a few undecided staff members. He asked what SNCC workers would think if members of a peace organization refused to take a stand on the Mississippi challenge, because they did not want to commit themselves on issues peripheral to their primary concerns. "I think Movement people would be indignant, and rightly so. They would ask: 'Isn't ALL human suffering our concern?' "[24]

Dona Richards replied to Zinn that dissent on the war issue would lead to more "red-baiting" of SNCC and further damage the organization's ability to raise funds. She wrote that, although SNCC had a chance to build a significant black political force, leftist opposition to the war would not "have any impact on curent policy decisions in Vietnam, and the help of all the civil rights organizations can't change that . . . While we care a great deal about both Vietnam and civil rights, we can't do anything to help the Vietnam situation, and we can hurt ourselves by trying."[25]

At the November staff meeting many staff members agreed with Richards and urged that the Vietnam issue not be discussed. Only on the final day of discussions did the staff decide to discuss the matter. Some staff members objected to the war on moral grounds, but a larger number made clear that their opposition to the war was not based on a commitment to nonviolence. One staff member announced that he was willing to fight on behalf of the "Viet Cong" in the United States. Many felt that SNCC should direct its attack against the military, since this was the aspect of the war that had a direct impact on black people in the South and on SNCC's staff. After much discussion the staff concluded that although their reasons differed for opposing the war they should authorize the Executive Committee to draft an anti-war statement that would be acceptable to all factions of the staff.[26]

Preparation of such a statement proceeded slowly until January 3, 1966, when an unexpected event provided the emotional impetus for SNCC's leaders to reveal their stand. Sammy Younge, one of the black students from Tuskegee Institute who was recruited by SNCC during the Montgomery demonstrations of the previous spring, was shot to death as he attempted to use the "white" restroom at a filling station in Tuskegee. On the day of his death, Younge had been threatened with a knife by a registrar in the Macon County Courthouse as he took forty blacks to register.[27] The death of the twenty-one-year-old Navy veteran who had worked on SNCC projects in Mississippi and Alabama symbolized for the staff the racism and hypocrisy that infected the nation.

Three days after Younge's death the Executive Committee announced that SNCC had "a right and a responsibility to dissent with the United States foreign policy on any issue" and charged that "the United States government [had] been deceptive in its claims of concern for the freedom of the Vietnamese people, just as the government has been deceptive in claiming concern for the freedom of colored people in such countries as the Dominican Republic, the Congo, South Africa, Rhodesia, and in the United States itself." SNCC's statement compared the murder of Younge with the murder of Vietnamese, stating that "Younge was murdered because United States law is not being enforced" and "Vietnamese are murdered because the United States is pursuing an aggressive policy in violation of international law. The United States is no respector of persons or law when such persons or laws run counter to its needs and desires." Denouncing the hypocrisy of the nation's desire to "preserve freedom in the world," SNCC leaders announced their sympathy and support for draft resisters.[28]

> We believe that work in the civil rights movement and with other human relations organizations is a valid alternative to the draft. We urge all Americans to seek this alternative, knowing full well that it may cost them their lives—as painfully as in Vietnam.

SNCC's statement unleashed a flood of criticism and left the organization more isolated than ever from the Johnson administration and the mainstream of the civil rights movement. Administration officials reacted by urging moderate black leaders to disassociate themselves from SNCC's position. Johnson advisor Louis Martin talked with NAACP leader Roy Wilkins about the SNCC statement, and soon afterwards Wilkins condemned SNCC in his nationally syndicated newspaper column. Clifford Alexander, another Johnson aide, privately advised the President that a possible course of action would be to "have the six Negro Congressmen issue a statement expressing the wholehearted support of the Negro people for our actions in Vietnam." Alexander indicated that his main concern was the response of Martin Luther King, and he informed the President that he was going to talk with King aide Andrew Young "to impress upon him the seriousness of the [SNCC] statement and the over-all negative consequences of it for the civil rights movement."[29]

Most major civil rights leaders needed little urging to intensify their efforts to isolate SNCC. After meeting in January with Wilkins and Clarence Mitchell of the NAACP and Whitney Young of the Urban League, Vice-President Humphrey reported that they were concerned that the administration appeared to treat "leaders of civil rights groups with a sort of benevolent equality." The black leaders, according to Humphrey, were disturbed by the even-handed treatment of SNCC and Lewis, despite the fact that SNCC engaged "in the most outrageous attacks on the President and the Administration."[30]

Having already publicly stated his personal feelings against the war, King did not join the new attacks on SNCC. He refused to engage in the public debate regarding SNCC's statement, although the following summer he did support the decision of the SCLC convention to issue a statement critical of the war effort. King did, however, come to the defense of Julian Bond after the SNCC leader was denied his seat in the Georgia legislature because he had backed SNCC's anti-war stand.[31]

Bond had been on leave from SNCC since his campaign during 1965 and had not participated in the drafting of SNCC's statement, yet his strong pacifistic inclinations ensured that he would give the statement his support. When Bond appeared on January 10 at the Georgia statehouse to take his oath of office, denunciations of him had already appeared in most Georgia newspapers. A letter in the *Atlanta Constitution* by Lillian Smith, a southern white author who had once supported SNCC and had spoken at its meetings, hinted that SNCC was now dominated by Communists. She wrote that "Bond (whose parents are wonderful people, one of the finest Negro families in Georgia) is, I fear, pulled this way and that."[32] Bond's fate was sealed even before he was asked to stand aside while other legislators took their oath.

Bond's long fight to gain his seat in the legislature occupied most of the following year, but, by the time he won his case in the United States Supreme Court, he was no longer a member of SNCC. SNCC itself changed dramatically during 1966, in part because of a new project that was launched in Bond's district in Atlanta soon after he was barred from the legislature. Although he and other SNCC staff members remained publicly linked with the New Left because of their anti-war activities, SNCC radicals were developing their own contentious and far-reaching critique of American society. While white New Leftists attempted to undermine the Cold War political consensus that had made possible American intervention in Vietnam, SNCC workers assumed the more fundamental task of challenging the cultural assumptions that underlay white racist attitudes and black feelings of inferiority and powerlessness.

# 13. RACIAL SEPARATISM

While SNCC staff members opposed U.S. involvement in Vietnam and generally agreed with the New Left critique of American liberalism, many were losing faith in the New Left dream of an interracial movement of the poor. Believing that they should not only stimulate black militancy but also create black-controlled institutions to secure lasting social gains, SNCC workers gradually abandoned strategies based on assistance from the federal government or the emerging New Left. A group of SNCC activists began to see racial separatism as an ideal that would awaken the consciousness of black people and begin a new phase of the black struggle.

Members of SNCC's newly formed Atlanta Project promoted black separatism with singular fervor. Unlike SNCC workers in Lowndes County, Alabama, who had generally avoided explicit racial appeals, the Atlanta Project staff used racial separatism as their basis for appealing for black support. Despite their limited accomplishments as community organizers, the Atlanta separatists spearheaded a major shift in SNCC's leadership and policies by voicing the unspoken beliefs of many staff members.

Though desiring to break with SNCC's past, the Atlanta separatists retained some aspects of the distinctive radicalism born in the struggles of the early 1960s. Like most earlier SNCC activists, they believed that militancy should not be restrained by political expediency. Thus, their insistence that black people, especially those in SNCC, adopt an ideal of "blackness" became the basis for an individualistic radicalism based on the notion, rooted in SNCC's past, that uncompromising commitment to ideals would bring about major social change. They demonstrated that they were as willing as those once identified as floaters to sacrifice political effectiveness in order to pursue their ideals. They also foreshadowed a trend toward ideological dogmatism that would become more pronounced during SNCC's final years.

The staff members who assumed control of SNCC during the spring of 1966 shared many of the views of the Atlanta separatists, but were unprepared to adopt a comprehensive separatist ideology. SNCC's new leaders, like its old, remained eclectic and tentative as they progressed beyond the

prevailing civil rights strategy, but their departure from the liberal mainstream initiated the most controversial period of SNCC's history.

Southern blacks took pride in their own efforts to initiate and direct the
course of their local movements even while accepting outside assistance.
After 1964 this racial pride grew stronger as they began to exercise newly
won civil rights and became more confident of their leadership abilities.
SNCC workers recognized the growth in black consciousness, but had only
begun to articulate the significance of the emerging sense of racial potency
and pride. The primary contribution of the Atlanta Project staff was in ex-
plicating the relationship between black separatist principles and the
southern black struggle. Drawing ideas from Malcolm X and Franz
Fanon's *The Wretched of the Earth,* they analyzed the previous failures of the
civil rights movement and suggested what SNCC workers must do to revive
and expand the scope of projects in black communities. Their brash self-as-
surance, based on their sense of rectitude rather than political accomplishments, promoted their influence among staff members who were searching
for a coherent view of their changing world.

The Atlanta separatists unhesitatingly rejected many of SNCC's prevailing values. Most joined SNCC after it had turned from desegregation protest toward organizing efforts focused on political and economic goals.
Thus, they were less likely than SNCC veterans from the earlier period to
have been exposed to Christian and Gandhian doctrines of nonviolent
struggle and less likely to have developed close relationships with white activists. Approximately half of the Atlanta staff members were from the
North; prior to joining SNCC several had been involved in urban-based
black nationalist organizations, such as the Nation of Islam. Most had attended college and generally were more politically sophisticated than
SNCC's southern black recruits. Perhaps because they were not associated
with SNCC's early years, the Atlanta separatists soon became sufficiently
confident to challenge SNCC's leadership. The seriousness of this challenge
was not immediately apparent, however, when the Atlanta Project was
founded under the direction of Bill Ware.

Ware was traveling through Atlanta to a civil rights workshop in South
Carolina when he saw a headline mentioning the Georgia legislature's vote
to exclude Julian Bond. Ware, who had worked for SNCC in Mississippi
and Alabama, later explained that he saw little point in continuing his civil
rights work in Mississippi if a black elected official such as Bond could not
freely express his opinions. He and a handful of other staff members proposed to Forman that SNCC respond to the legislature's action by working
in Bond's district to build support for the embattled representative. Forman approved the proposal and Ware was chosen to head a new project in
Atlanta's Vine City area.

Born and raised in rural Mississippi, Ware attended college in Minnesota. In 1962 he joined the Peace Corps and worked for a year in Ghana. Influenced by black scholar St. Clair Drake, who helped train the Peace Corps volunteers, Ware adopted a Pan-Africanist perspective that stressed the need to unite black people worldwide. A participant in protests in Mississippi during the summer following the assassination of Medgar Evers, Ware recalled that his preference for African clothing, his Pan-Africanist views, and his decision late in the summer to grow a beard set him apart from most blacks then in the movement. After a brief SNCC fund-raising stay in Minnesota, Ware returned to the South in 1964 to become a full-time SNCC worker. He stood aside from the factional disputes of 1965 and soon gained the respect of other staff members for his diligence and militancy. Although he was one of the SNCC workers who went to Alabama and attempted to "radicalize" black students in Montgomery during the spring of 1965, he argued within SNCC for cooperation with the SCLC. He later spoke of the racial significance of his involvement in a "black Christmas" boycott campaign during the fall of 1965 in Natchez, Mississippi, but he did little to push his racial views.[1]

Once involved in the Atlanta Project, Ware's experiences reinforced his belief in the need to stress racial appeals. He and other members of the Atlanta staff saw themselves as conscious innovators participating in a unique experiment in urban organizing. Vine City was an area afflicted with all the classic problems of urban slums: unemployment, poor housing, inadequate schools and public services, all of which led to feelings of powerlessness and political apathy. Atlanta was reputed to be the most progressive southern city, yet the SNCC staff believed that the city's liberal white establishment and their moderate black allies neglected the problems faced by blacks in the city. The Atlanta staff strove to increase black "control over the public decisions which affect" the lives of black people. They warned that without such control southern blacks would "succumb to the fate of most of the Northern ghettoes: a welfare and patronage system will be established and the new voting power of Negroes will work to the benefit of a small few." This process was already at work in Atlanta, according to the SNCC staff, where "the small established Negro leadership is working rapidly to solidify still further its political control." They urged SNCC to develop programs to take advantage of the demographic process that they referred to as the "Blackening" of urban areas. "We shouldn't have to say too much about the potential Black power that this represents," staff members wrote.[2]

The Atlanta staff initially worked inobtrusively with local black leaders. With the aid of an unofficial local group called the Vine City Council, they arranged warm meals and housing for poor residents who were suffering during the cold winter. While Bond appealed to city, state, and federal officials, staff members investigated local conditions and organized community protests. Early in February three SNCC workers, including Ware, were arrested trying to prevent the eviction of a black family. "There must be unity among black people," Ware told a crowd of blacks before his arrest. "The only way we can stop evictions is for the people to come together."[3]

The Atlanta staff departed from SNCC's previous organizing strategies after the initial weeks of operation of the project, becoming increasingly concerned with the racial dimension of the black struggle. SNCC workers had always recognized the need for pride and self-reliance, but the Atlanta separatists concluded that a drastic transformation of the black community's racial consciousness was necessary. This could not be achieved simply through participation in militant struggle—a crucial tenet of SNCC's previous ideology—instead, racial values distinct from those dominant in the surrounding society must be adopted in black communities, and in SNCC itself. The Atlanta separatists urged SNCC to emphasize racial identity to eliminate racial inferiority and political impotence that limited the potential of Afro-Americans.

A central element of the Atlanta staff's efforts to stimulate racial pride was its community newspaper, the *Nitty Gritty*. The name was chosen to reach alienated urban blacks—"the cat who's wearing that stockingcap around his head and has got his hair slick, on the corner drinking wine." According to Ware, the words "nitty gritty" reflected the desire of blacks to "tell it like it is." To gain SNCC's financial backing, staff members wrote of the need to alter the basic attitudes of "the frustrated, despondent masses of Black Americans. We can see no meaningful, long range social changes coming about for these masses, until we can change each individual's belief in himself," they continued. "We can see no long standing structures created by Blacks who are emotionally, socially, politically and economically dependent upon those individuals who are non-black." The staff hoped to awaken in blacks "a sense of pride in their beauty, strength and resourcefulness; and also a meaningful sense of self-respect that they can only gain when they see Black people working together accomplishing worthwhile programs—without the guidance and/or direction and control of non-Blacks." Without this, they concluded, "Black people in this country will know no freedom, but only more subtle forms of slavery."[4]

What separated the Atlanta organizers from other SNCC staff members was their willingness to embrace racial separatist doctrines. Not simply arguing for black institutions to achieve common goals, the Atlanta separatists were demanding the exclusion of whites from SNCC in order to achieve their ideal of "blackness." The distinctive orientation of the Atlanta staff became evident when they rejected several applications by white workers who wanted to join the project. Those rejected included Mendy Samstein, a capable activist who had worked with SNCC since the summer of 1963 and had helped draft the original prospectus for the Atlanta Project.

Atlanta staff members, many of whom had only recently joined the civil rights struggle, began to construct a general critique of it. "The TRUTH is that the civil rights movement is not and never was our movement," Atlanta staff member John Churchville argued in a paper on the "death" of the movement. He insisted that the civil rights movement had simply maintained the divisions within black communities that had been present since the slavery era. "This means that the civil rights struggle since slavery (except for the *revolts* during slavery and the *riots* now) has been one of advancing our position as slaves, but not abolishing slavery." He argued that "all white people are racists; that is, no white person (when you really get down to the nitty-gritty) can stand to deal with black people as humans, as men, as equals, not to mention superiors. They can't stand the thought of black people ruling over them or ruling independently of them." He concluded by asking rhetorically, "What would have happened if the field nigger had revolted and confiscated the master's land? What will happen when we (whether we be in the house, yard, or field) begin to assert ourselves as non-niggers and non-slaves? The Bible refers to that day as Armageddon. Let's work toward making that biblical day come true."[5]

The Atlanta Project began with the assumption that urban organizing required a different set of principles than those SNCC organizers had developed while working in the rural areas and small towns of the deep South. Rather than following SNCC's long-established pattern of allowing ideas to emerge from struggle, the Atlanta Project staff sought to formulate a plan for their activities by drawing ideas from sources outside SNCC. Their statements, written in a burst of enthusiasm during the winter and spring of 1966, set forth many of the basic themes that would dominate black politics during the late 1960s. The Atlanta separatists ignored many of the valid lessons of SNCC's past, however, and thus offered only partial answers to the dilemmas SNCC faced. In their uncompromising effort to impose their ideas on other SNCC workers, they further undermined the trust, mutual respect, and interdependence without which SNCC could not survive.

The first indication of the Atlanta separatists' dogmatism came after the project received a three thousand dollar contribution that was intended to finance SNCC's effort to build black support for Julian Bond. Recognizing that the funds could be used to support their propaganda activities in Vine City, project staff members debated whether to keep the contribution or turn it over to SNCC's leaders. Ware realized that the former course would be a "declaration of independence" from SNCC, yet he did not argue against the idea, merely urging the staff to consider the consequences of whatever they decided to do. Staff members voted to place the money in an escrow account at a bank. As they expected, Forman and other SNCC leaders learned of their action and demanded that the money be turned over to SNCC. The Atlanta staff responded by asking that they be given an opportunity to explain their actions and their criticisms of SNCC's policies at the March staff meeting.

Once given a place on the agenda of the meeting, the Atlanta Project staff began to develop a position paper that ignored the insubordination issue and instead sought to place SNCC's leaders on the defensive by attacking the presence of whites in the organization. They did not expect their blatant challenge to the authority of SNCC's leaders to be well received, but they were eager to express their views even in a hostile setting. In part, the position paper described the programs planned for Vine City, but its most important aspects were its arguments for a new racial consciousness among blacks as a first step toward revoluntionary struggle. The notion that the black struggle should be led by blacks and that whites should begin to organize poor whites had been accepted for some time by nearly all SNCC workers, but the position paper transformed what had been a pragmatic judgment into an absolute principle. Although the paper was put forward as a call for racial unity around the ideal of blackness, it was actually the initial volley in a struggle among blacks over the control of SNCC and the future direction of black struggles.

Since the paper was a group effort, it contained numerous inconsistencies in style and content, yet its basic separatist ideas were expressed with clarity and force. The crucial section on ideology was written by Ware, Donald Stone, a former graduate student at Atlanta University, and Roland Snellings, a former member of the Revolutionary Action Movement, formed in 1964 by followers of Robert F. Williams.[6] The position paper, which was designed largely to defend the Atlanta staff from expected charged of racism, probably understated their racial sentiments. It was, nonetheless, the strongest statement against white participation in the civil rights movement that had yet been presented. Although most SNCC workers rejected the notion that SNCC should become an all-black organization, they found many of the Atlanta separatists' ideas convincing. Some of these arguments had been offered by Silas Norman at the Waveland retreat in November 1964; now they were buttressed with historical examples and the authors' conception of the effects of white participation on SNCC's ability to eliminate feelings of racial inferiority among blacks.

The major thesis of the position paper was "that the form of white participation, as practiced in the past, is now obsolete." On a pragmatic level, the authors asserted that many blacks were "intimidated by the presence of whites, because of their knowledge of the power that whites have over their lives." A single white person who participated in a meeting of black people could change the tone of that meeting: "People would immediately start talking about 'brotherhood,' 'love,' etc.; race would not be discussed." A climate had to be created, they argued, in which black people could freely express themselves. SNCC, they wrote, had isolated itself from blacks because of the presence of whites. Referring to the organization as "a closed society," they insisted that blacks could not "relate to SNCC, because of its unrealistic no racial atmosphere, denying their experiences of America as a racist society." On a deeper level, the Atlanta separatists argued that white people were inherently incapable of understanding the black experience. Despite this, whites had shaped blacks' views of themselves. "Too long have we allowed white people to interpret the importance and meaning of the cultural aspects of our society."

The authors of the position paper conceded that some white radicals wanted to eliminate racial supremacy, but these whites could not admit that they were "part of the collective white America." The Atlanta staff's portrait of America was categorical: "When we view the masses of white people we view the over-all reality of America, we view the racism, the bigotry, and the distortion of personality, we view man's inhumanity to man; we view in reality 180 million racists." They charged that most white radicals had "sought to escape the horrible reality of America by going into the black community and attempting to organize black people while neglecting the organization of their own people's racist communities. How can one clean up someone else's yard when one's own yard is untidy?" They declared that whites should try to raise themselves to the "humanistic level" of blacks. "We are not, after all, the ones who are responsible for a genocidal war in Vietnam; we are not the ones who are responsible for neo-colonialism in Africa and Latin America; we are not the ones who held a people in animalistic bondage over 400 years."

The authors stated that SNCC would have to rid itself of the influence of white activists in order to become the type of organization they envisioned. "We can contract work out to them, but in no way can they participate on a policy-making level," they wrote. Although whites might "insist on remaining because of their longevity or because they have feelings that we are indebted to them," they continued, "whites who are sensitive to our problems will realize that we must determine our own destiny." They insisted that white people should not come in contact with the black masses since they were "not equipped to dispel the myths of western superiority. White people only serve to perpetuate these myths." Instead, organizing must be done by "Black people who are able to see the beauty of themselves, are able to see the important cultural contributions of Afro-Americans, are able to see that this country was built upon the blood and backs of our Black ancestors."

For the Atlanta separatists, the expulsion of whites from SNCC was seen as an essential step toward confronting the crucial issue of racial identity. Black leadership of the black struggle was put forward not only as necessary to assure mass support but as a vital element in the creation of a new African cultural consciousness. Blacks should reject white participation and begin to eliminate many of the cultural values of white society. "The systematic destruction of our links to Africa . . . are not situations that conscious Black people in this country are willing to accept," the Atlanta separatists wrote. "Black people are not willing to align themselves with a western culture that daily emasculates our beauty, our pride and our manhood."

Reflecting the influence of Franz Fanon, the Atlanta Project position paper described the cultural subordination of Afro-Americans as analogous to the situation of colonized people in the Third World. White civil rights workers were compared to "the white civil servants and missionaries in the colonial countries who have worked with the colonial people for a long period of time and have developed a paternalistic attitude toward them." Apparently not recognizing the complexities of the answer, the authors asked, "What part did the white colonizers play in the liberation of independent African nations; who were the agitators for African independence? Answers to these questions compel us to believe that our struggle for liberation and self-determination can only be carried out effectively by Black people."

The paper called for the creation of "a mystique" of black leadership that would allow blacks to identify with "the movement." The authors proposed that SNCC be "black staffed, black-controlled and black-financed" to demonstrate to black people that such an organization could succeed. Furthermore, they called for a general turn toward black separatism. "If we are to proceed toward true liberation, we must cut ourselves off from white people. We must form our own institutions, credit unions, co-ops, political parties, write our own histories."

The ideas and even many of the phrases of the position paper would reappear later in the 1960s in countless speeches by militant blacks, and the paper itself would be reprinted. Yet, its importance lay in bringing to the surface ideas dormant in SNCC's past. By the spring of 1966 only a few dozen whites remained on SNCC's staff since many whites had left to participate in anti-war activities or returned to college. White staff members had little voice in determining SNCC's policies, and most had concluded that their proper roles were as support personnel or as white community organizers. Yet for the Atlanta separatists, the remaining whites were a contaminating element preventing SNCC's ideological development from reaching its logical conclusion. By pressing for their removal, the separatists incurred the opposition of most of SNCC's leaders and provoked an intellectual debate that would change the course of SNCC's development.

When the Atlanta separatists presented their position paper at the March staff meeting, their intention was more to embarrass SNCC's leaders than to convert them. They had already obscured their ideological concerns through their insubordination. Expecting strong opposition, the separatists tried unsucccessfully at the beginning of the meeting to have the proceedings taped, implying that they would later expose the hypocrisy of supposed black militants who argued against the demand that whites be expelled from SNCC. The Atlanta staff expected to garner support from other black organizers who also believed that whites should not attempt to work in black community projects and who had adopted militant racial rhetoric. Julius Lester, a Fisk graduate who would soon afterward join SNCC's staff, visited the Atlanta headquarters during March and reported that conversations were dotted with such words as "whitey," and "black consciousness" and staff members addressed other blacks as "brother." Nonetheless the separatists had seriously overestimated their strength. Even many anti-white staff members objected to the disruptive tactics of the Atlanta Project staff and refused to accede to their demands for the expulsion of whites. Willie Ricks, one of the most outspoken militants on the staff, was unconvinced by the position paper: "We would always say, 'Mr. Say aint' the man, Mr. Do is the man.' They talked about nationalism and that kind of thing on the inside of SNCC, but they did not have an organization in the community."[7]

Stokely Carmichael joined in opposing the Atlanta separatists. Although criticized in the press as a separatist because of his work in Lowndes County, he refused to accept the extreme formulations of separatism implicit in the demand for white expulsion. Carmichael agreed with many of the views presented in the position paper, and ironically became their principal popularizer. Nonetheless, he had maintained close relations with white staff members and with northern white New Leftists. He was also aware of SNCC's dependence on northern white support. Like other staff members, he objected to the separatists' disregard of SNCC's leadership. "It was done in a most divisive way," he remembered. He saw the Atlanta group as "opportunists" attempting to use the issue of white participation to gain control of SNCC by appearing as "Blacker than thou."[8]

Although Carmichael joined with a majority of the staff in rejecting the separatists' demands at the March meeting, he was greatly affected by the ideas expressed in the position paper. He recognized that it had forced to the surface the feelings of many staff members. Sensing the increasing support for a shift in SNCC's direction toward the kind of organizing approach he had developed in Lowndes County, Carmichael announced soon after the meeting that he would break with tradition and actively campaign for SNCC's chair, then held by John Lewis, the SNCC officer most irrevocably tied to its past.

Prior to 1966 the annual election of SNCC's officers had been an uneventful formality, as there had rarely been open competition for any leadership position. Despite considerable changes in the composition of the staff and in SNCC's policies, Forman had served as executive secretary since 1961 and Lewis as chairman since 1963. Of the elected officers only Cleveland Sellers, chosen the previous year as program secretary, was among the group of younger black militants who had joined the staff during 1964 and 1965. The rapid changes that had taken place in the southern struggle since 1964, however, severely tested the adaptability of Lewis and Forman. Lewis, in particular, had difficulty reconciling his soft-spoken commitment to nonviolent militancy with the increasingly abrasive radicalism of other staff members. During the spring of 1966 staff members openly criticized Lewis for his continuing involvement in the planning sessions for the White House Conference on Civil Rights, and for his decision to go on a European fund-raising tour, sponsored by the Norwegian Student Association.

While criticisms of Lewis' associations and tactics increased, the success of the Lowndes County Freedom Organization boosted Carmichael's candidacy. At a time of declining support in many southern black communities, Carmichael built a strong, militant political movement that became a model for "Freedom Organizations" throughout the black belt of Alabama. Carmichael's ample self-confidence was further heightened when he pressured Justice Department officials to intervene on behalf of the LCFO by suggesting that local blacks would use arms to prevent white interference with their convention on May 3. SNCC workers in Lowndes garnered support from local blacks despite verbal attacks from SCLC officials and moderate Alabama Democrats who condemned SNCC for urging blacks to support the Black Panther Party rather than voting in the Democratic primary. Carmichael succeeded in convincing residents that it was impossible for blacks to participate in both the LCFO and the Democratic Party, adding that it was "as ludicrous for Negroes to join [the Democratic Party] as it would have been for Jews to join the Nazi Party in the 1930s."[9]

SNCC staff members were encouraged by Carmichael's success in Lowndes County but were not prepared to replace Lewis when they arrived on May 8 at the Kingston Springs retreat near Nashville. Despite grumblings about his leadership, staff members felt a sense of loyalty to Lewis, who had been arrested over forty times in his movement career. Even disgruntled workers respected his courage and dedication. Most also believed that leadership roles were not important enough to fight over. In addition, nearly all Atlanta Project staff members who were most critical of SNCC's veteran leaders did not attend the crucial staff meeting.

Rather than face another confrontation, most Atlanta separatists attended an Afro-American Festival held in New Orleans. Bill Ware later charged that project staff members were physically threatened by other SNCC workers in the weeks after presentation of the separatist position paper and were told that their opponents would be carrying weapons at the May meeting, but Forman insisted that the Atlanta group was invited to again present their views to the staff.[10] It is possible that Ware and Forman were both correct. In any case, Atlanta Project staff members were attracted to New Orleans by the prospect of presenting their ideas to a receptive audience. Bob Moses organized the New Orleans meeting to discuss the "decolonization" of black people after announcing that he was breaking off all relationships with whites.[11]

The absence of separatists allowed staff members at the Kingston Springs meeting to separate policy considerations from their feelings toward the Atlanta group. Donald Stone later admitted that separatists' efforts to "organize SNCC" may have been too abrasive and thus counterproductive. He was probably right in his guess that if they had been present at the May meeting, other SNCC staff members would have been less willing to move in the direction suggested by the Atlanta Project.[12]

Unrestrained by fear that they would be associated with the Atlanta Project, black staff members at Kingston Springs were more willing to argue for reorientation of SNCC's policies. Ivanhoe Donaldson, a veteran organizer, told the staff that the "vague concepts" that were the focus of SNCC's previous activities—"the development of an interracial democracy in this country, of the right of the people to participate in decisions that affect their lives, the development of an interracial democracy in this country, of the right of the people to participate in decisions that affect their lives, the development of black leadership, pockets of power"—were no longer the kinds of issues that could mobilize black people. He argued that SNCC would have to begin acting on three levels. First of all, SNCC workers would have to recognize that "nationalism helps [to] organize in the black community." Secondly, they would have to begin building community-wide political movements, such as the Bond campaign and the Black Panther Party. White organizers, he asserted, should begin "to organize the white community around black needs, around black history, the relative important of blackness in the world today." Finally, SNCC workers should develop ties with the Third World by protesting against the Vietnam War, supporting black resistance in South Africa, and developing international alliances. Donaldson urged SNCC "to build a resistance movement" in the United States.[13]

Donaldson's speech was part of an extensive and critical examination by

SNCC staff members of the assumptions that had previously governed their work. The notes of the week of discussions reveal a sometimes painful effort by veteran SNCC workers to evaluate the consequences of their own former idealism. Many concluded that they had been too naive, that they had believed "that poor people were good and could do no wrong," that "such things as leadership, money, power, etc. were by definition wrong and were things that SNCC people should avoid," and that they could forget history because they were different, that since they were "pure" then that which they organized "would be equally good, pure, incorruptible and durable," and could survive by itself. SNCC workers questioned their own position as the vanguard of the black struggle, noting that blacks in northern cities had surpassed them. John Lewis added that SNCC workers had assumed that they had "a monopoly on truth" and were the best organizers.[14]

After recounting their previous assumptions, staff members proceeded to put forward some new goals. Nearly all staff members agreed with the general policies outlined in Donaldson's address. John Lewis called for the establishment of a Bureau of International Affairs to forge Third World alliances. SNCC founder Ella Baker suggested that the organization establish a seminar in "revolutionary ethics" led by revolutionaries from Third World nations. Stanley Wise proposed that SNCC only accept speaking engagements in black communities, that news releases only be sent to black community publications, and that SNCC staff members strengthen their psychological ties with their African heritage. Cleveland Sellers and others argued for a greater emphasis on building SNCC's support on black college campuses.[15]

The stream of criticisms and proposals functioned as an emotional release for the staff and provided a backdrop for the election of SNCC's new chairperson. When the nominations for offices commenced, most staff members favored the retention of incumbent leaders, including Lewis, although Forman had already indicated that he wished to relinquish the position of executive secretary. Lewis's support had declined since 1964, but, when the first vote was held on the last evening of the staff meeting, Lewis handily defeated Carmichael, while Sellers was again chosen as program secretary and Robinson was elected to replace Forman.[16]

Immediately after the vote was taken, however, Worth Long, a former SNCC staff member, challenged the election. Long had no valid basis for his challenge and was himself only allowed to participate in the meeting because of his previous extensive involvement in SNCC. He succeeded, nonetheless, in reopening the discussion of the chair. Staff members quickly shifted the focus of their comments from the legitimacy of the election to the issue of whether Lewis represented the dominant ideological orientation of SNCC.

Long himself had ambivalent feelings about Lewis. Like most staff members, he admired and respected the veteran activist. "John was the most courageous person that I have ever worked with in the movement," he later commented. "John would not just follow you into the lion's den, he would lead you into it." Long said that his motive in challenging Lewis's election was to keep SNCC on "the cutting edge of the civil rights movement" by electing a chairperson who was prepared to reflect the increasingly militant mood of the staff.[17]

As the discussion continued into the early morning hours, the fragility of Lewis' support became apparent. Many of his strongest supporters left the meeting after the first vote, exhausted by the extended discussions of SNCC's past and its future. Lewis's position was also severely weakened by Forman's suggestion that both he and Lewis resign "to give some of the young staff members a chance to acquire the experience we had acquired."[18] Forman and other staff members also criticized Lewis's continuing relationship with SCLC, on whose governing board he served, and his involvement in the planning of the White House Conference on Civil Rights, scheduled for the following month.

Sensing his vulnerability, Lewis's opponents held strategy sessions to determine how to replace him. Several staff members urged Forman to take the chair, but he refused, leaving the field open for Carmichael. Although some staff members were less than enthusiastic about Carmichael, resenting his close ties with white staff members, they felt he was clearly preferable to Lewis. Remarkably, considering the separatist trend in SNCC, Jack Minnis, a white leftist who headed SNCC's research department played a major role in mobilizing support for Carmichael. Minnis was convinced that Lewis's religious orientation was not "what the times required."[19] With other Carmichael supporters, Minnis convinced Sellers and Robinson to resign their positions to force another election. Initially, Lewis refused to go along with the maneuver and resign his own position, but his obstinacy strengthened his opponents' determination. He finally accepted the inevitable defeat and resigned, allowing the exausted remnants of the staff to elect Carmichael overwhelmingly.

Lewis was bitter about his defeat, blaming it on the machinations of Forman. He described Carmichael, with whom he was on friendly terms, as a pawn of others. "I think certain forces and a certain faction within the staff used Stokely," he later concluded. Years later, he remembered the event painfully as "not a good night—not the election itself, but the discussion and some of the hard feelings, animosities that were created."[20]

With the election of Carmichael and the subsequent re-election of Robinson and Sellers, the staff clarified their desire to embark on a new course. Although the three leaders qualified as veterans, they had in the past been consistent voices for greater militancy. Carmichael at twenty-four was the oldest of the three. Robinson, twenty-three, had been active in the black struggle since spring 1960. She was a tireless woman who had managed to obtain a degree and maintain a family life while becoming one of SNCC's most effective and respected leaders. Sellers was only twenty-one when he was re-elected to his post, but he had already spent two years as a full-time SNCC worker and had firmly established himself as one of the strongest advocates of the hardliner position within SNCC.

After the election of the new officers, staff members established a ten-member Central Committee to replace the unwieldy Executive Committee. Seeking to repair the internal rift created by the election of Carmichael, they named Lewis to the Central Committee and to the post of director of a new internal education program. Five of the new committee members—Forman, Cox, Donaldson, Ralph Featherstone, and Jack Minnis—had worked in the Atlanta headquarters and were aware of the administrative problems caused by irresponsible staff members. Carmichael, Bob Smith and Fred Meely of the Mississippi staff and Bob Mants of the Lowndes County staff were the remaining committee members.

As was customary, reporters were barred from the staff meeting at Kingston Springs, but immediately after Carmichael's election journalists proclaimed it a victory for black nationalism. An article in the *Atlanta Constitution* predicted that SNCC, under Carmichael's leadership, would "become more oriented toward the philosophy of black nationalism." Jack Nelson of the *Los Angeles Times* referred to Carmichael as "one of the more radical leaders of SNCC," pointing to his role in forming an all-black party in Lowndes County. Carmichael was quoted in the *New York Times* as saying that SNCC would not fire its white organizers, "but if they want to organize, they can organize white people. Negroes will organize the Negroes."[21]

SNCC's new leaders tried to play down the significance of the leadership change, insisting that there had been no serious internal schism. Lewis said that the new officers had his "support and cooperation in implementing the programs of SNCC to rid society of racism and build a world community at peace with itself." Despite such assurances, the contrast between Lewis' moderation and Carmichael's outspoken militancy was obvious to observers. Moreover, when the Central Committee announced on May 23 that the organization was withdrawing from the White House Conference on Civil Rights, Lewis, although present at the press conference, attracted attention by his silence. Lewis nonetheless signed the withdrawal statement, which charged that the conference was an attempt "to shift responsibility for the degrading position in which blacks now find themselves away from the oppressors to the oppressed."[22] (This was a reference to a speech by President Johnson suggesting that the problems of blacks resulted largely from the deterioration of the black family structure.)

SNCC's withdrawal from the White House conference prompted further press criticisms. Evans and Novak wrote that SNCC had "disengaged" itself from the civil rights movement. "For responsible Negro leaders who long have viewed SNICK's extremism as self-defeating, such disengagement would be too good to be true," the columnists commented. "It would constitute SNICK doing to itself what the rest of the civil rights movement had not dared to do." *Time* editors similarly conceded that Carmichael's plea for an all-black party was "an emotional and possibly persuasive argument to many Negroes—yet it could only lead to even greater isolation and bitterness for the Negro in the South."[23]

In the weeks after the Kingston Springs meeting Carmichael made a few attempts to reassure former white allies that SNCC's new policies were not "racism in reverse" or a call for black violence. He told a reporter for the radical weekly *National Guardian* that whites could still play an important role in aiding the black struggle by going "into the white communities and . . . developing those moderate bases that people talk about that do not now exist." Insisting that there was "nothing wrong with anything all black," he said that columnists such as Evans and Novak, who had once "red-baited" SNCC, had now begun to "black-bait" the organization. He advised SNCC's former supporters that they had to understand that the Negro wanted "to build something of his own, something that he builds with his own hands. And that is *not* anti-white. When you build your own house, it doesn't mean you tear down the house across the street."[24]

Sounding many of the same themes, SNCC's New York office issued a statement to correct the "vastly distorted reports and outright lies" concerning SNCC that had appeared in the press. Conceding that SNCC had changed its course, the statement insisted that the election of Carmichael did not represent a "take-over" by "anti-white extremists" but instead represented SNCC workers' awareness that they must "seek to overcome the Negro's sense of shame about such things as 'Negroid' physical characteristics, and to encourage the sense of dignity which enables a people to free themselves internally and externally." The statement compared the building of black consciousness to the way in which "other ethnic groups [had] developed and sustained cultural awareness, pride, particularly in times of struggle." SNCC's northern supporters were told that "what attracted Negro students to SNCC in the first place was that nowhere else in the society could they participate in something which had social significance and was not dominated by whites." Supporters were assured that SNCC's "emphasis on the need for power co-exists with the basic, humanist spirit for which SNCC has long been known."[25]

Iconoclast I. F. Stone and long-time SNCC supporter Anne Braden were among the few white journalists to be reassured by SNCC. Stone wrote in his self-published weekly that "a certain amount of black nationalism is inevitable among Negroes; they cannot reach equality without the restoration of pride in themselves as Negroes." He added that such pride could not be achieved unless blacks learned "to fight for themselves, not just as wards of white men, no matter how sympathetic." Braden, who in 1961 had recruited SNCC's first white field secretary, saw SNCC's new direction as a confirmation of her belief that "the job of white people who believe in freedom is to confront white America." She wrote that SNCC was "not rejecting white people." By sending white workers into their own communities where so much work was needed, SNCC "may be providing this generation with the last chance white people may ever have to overcome the racism and white supremacy by which western man has come close to destroying this planet."[26]

Such sympathetic coverage of SNCC by leftist journalists with few readers did little to reverse the continued deterioration of SNCC's public image. Carmichael's confident description about SNCC's future programs helped to reassure supporters, but many of his public statements were calculated to demonstrate that SNCC's militancy would not be restrained by public relations considerations. For many SNCC workers racial separatism met psychological needs that were not as easily satisfied through patient efforts to mobilize black communities to achieve concrete goals. Carmichael was faced with the choice of building political institutions such as he had created in Lowndes County or following the example of the Atlanta Project and becoming preoccupied with rhetorical appeals for the unification of black people on the basis of separatist ideals. His expressed preference was to move in the former direction, but events that occurred soon after his election drew him toward the latter.

Although community organizers supported Carmichael, thinking that he would be sympathetic to their needs, they could not have predicted how Carmichael, or any other staff member, would react to the demands placed on prominent black leaders during 1966. Early in June SNCC's New York office announced that Carmichael would be "devoting most of his time this year to traveling around our southern projects, strengthening the staff." The expectation that SNCC would solve its problems through effective organizing remained an alluring dream. This was particularly true of radicals such as Carmichael who had a far-reaching view of SNCC's purpose. Carmichael undoubtedly wanted to devote his time to strengthening SNCC's southern projects, but he believed that the consciousness of blacks would have to be changed before the conditions of life of the race could be substantially improved. The Alabama protests of 1965 had demonstrated that SNCC workers still were eager to publicly display their radicalism. They insisted that their involvement in nonviolent civil rights marches was necessary to convince others of the need for greater militancy. Thus, even before SNCC could begin to reorganize itself and strengthen its projects, its leaders became involved in a series of protests in Mississippi that would profoundly affect the future of SNCC and of the black struggle.[27]

The Mississippi protests began after the shooting of James Meredith, who had begun a walk across Mississippi on June 5 to prove that black residents could exercise their rights without fear. Meredith, a black activist whose enrollment at the University of Mississippi in 1962 was met by extensive mob violence, was wounded by three shotgun blasts and taken to a hospital in Memphis. At the time of the shooting, Carmichael, Sellers, and Wise were in Arkansas as part of their effort to reinvigorate SNCC's projects. Impulsively, the three leaders drove to Memphis in support of Meredith, planning to return the following day. After visiting him, however, they decided to stay and meet with other civil rights leaders who were also in Memphis. With Martin Luther King and CORE leader Floyd McKissick, they gathered at the church of Rev. James Lawson, the author of SNCC's original statement of purpose, and developed plans to continue Meredith's march. The SNCC representatives proposed that the march aid local voter registration efforts by bringing marchers and reporters to Mississippi towns where most blacks were still unregistered. They also insisted that marchers commit themselves to use civil disobedience in communities where they encountered resistance. According to Wise this idea greatly upset Roy Wilkins, who had joined the meeting, and the NAACP leader refused to support the march. "We used that opportunity to say to Roy Wilkins what people in our organization had been wanting to say for so long—that is, to retire, to teach in a college and write a book about his earlier days," Wise remembered. Determined to renew the march, Carmichael, Sellers, and Wise returned to Atlanta to seek approval from SNCC's Central Committee.[28]

Remembering the problems that resulted from SNCC's involvement in the 1965 Alabama protests, several Central Committee members strongly opposed participation in the Mississippi march. Cox argued that SNCC did not need a march "to do the real work of organizing." He stated that the march was only taking place because Meredith was a nationally known figure. Carmichael responded that the march would be going through communities that still supported SNCC and would publicize the fact that existing laws were not being enforced. His arguments convinced a majority of the Central Committee that SNCC should use the march to promote the idea of building independent black community organizations. Sellers recalled that advocates of the march "got a very, very reluctant okay . . . I thought several times about the Committee's words to us: 'We don't want to hear anything more about this march. Don't call us for help!' "[29]

Carmichael and Sellers returned to Memphis and met with other civil rights leaders. They angered moderates by arguing that white participation should be deemphasized and that the Deacons for Defense be allowed to provide armed protection for the marchers. Hoping to maintain at least the appearance of unity among civil rights groups, King and McKissick agreed to the participation of the Deacons. Although whites were allowed to participate, their presence was less noticeable than at any other major civil rights demonstration of the 1960s. Without time for many advance preparations, only a few hundred marchers were on hand to start the trek along the Mississippi highway where Meredith had been shot.

Newsmen covering the march were eager to report disagreements involving SNCC, SCLC, and CORE, and march leaders made little effort to keep their differences from public view. The nightly rallies in Mississippi communities became contests in which the three leaders competed for the support of black residents. Carmichael and McKissick stressed the need for greater militancy and condemned the federal government for lack of strong action on behalf of southern blacks. King was on the defensive but made effective pleas for the continued use of nonviolent tactics.

During the first days of the march King was clearly the dominant participant. SNCC workers recognized that he was still by far the most popular civil rights leader. Differences in the viewpoints of King and Carmichael were not immediately apparent to black people who idolized King and trusted his leadership. King, for his part, was aware of the growing militancy of young blacks, and his speeches during the march were attempts to reflect the new racial mood without abandoning the ideal of nonviolence. Despite their differences, some SNCC workers established friendly relationships with King during the march. "He turned out to be easygoing, with a delightful sense of humor," Sellers recalled. "His mind was open and we were surprised to find that he was much less conservative than we initially believed."[30]

Regardless of their respect for King, SNCC workers sought opportunities to dispute his positions thereby expressing the black anger, discontent, and disillusionment that could not be conveyed through King's more moderate rhetoric. While they were unable to do this through detailed descriptions of SNCC's programs, SNCC workers did discover a new means of tapping the suppressed emotions of blacks from one of the veteran SNCC workers who came to Mississippi to participate in the march. Even before Willie Ricks joined an advance group of SNCC workers to mobilize black support in small communities in the path of the march, his ability to arouse black audiences was well known. He had joined the southern struggle as a high school student in Chattanooga, Tennessee during the early 1960s. His militancy was strengthened when a close friend was killed during a demonstration. His often abrasive style lacked the studied rhetoric of SNCC workers who had attended college and dominated staff policy discussions. He avoided SNCC's factional battles, describing himself as a black nationalist, which implied acceptance of the notion of armed self-defense by blacks and a generalized antipathy toward whites.

Ricks provided Carmichael with a new weapon in his ideological struggle with King when he demonstrated the enormous appeal of the slogan "Black Power"—a shortened version of "black power for black people," a phrase used by SNCC workers in Alabama. The two words had been combined by other blacks long before Ricks used them in Mississippi. Richard Wright used them as a title for his book on African politics written in the early 1950s; black activist Paul Robeson spoke of black power during the 1950s and Harlem political leaders Jesse Gray and Congressman Adam Clayton Powell were among those who previously had used the phrase. By the time of the Mississippi march, SNCC workers had begun to speak of the need for black power. On June 10 Carmichael told Central Committee members that one of the reasons he favored SNCC's participation in the march was to gain support for "the concept of black power."[31] Undoubtedly, SNCC workers would have begun to use black power as a political slogan even if the Mississippi march had not occurred, but Ricks was the first to sense the impact that could be achieved by publicly combining a racial term that previously held negative connotations with a goal that always had been beyond the reach of black people as a group.

SNCC leaders did not believe Ricks' initial reports on his rally speeches. "Stokely tried to get me thrown off the march for exaggerating," Ricks recounted. He told SNCC leaders of the overwhelmingly positive response of the crowds. "I left the people hollering 'black power,' and they're still screaming." Although initially incredulous, Carmichael and other SNCC leaders were convinced after hearing Ricks speak at a black church.[32]

Carmichael's opportunity to use the black power slogan came as the march entered Leflore County, the site of previous SNCC voter registration efforts. During the initial stages of the march civil rights workers had met little resistance from state officials and had succeeded in registering many black residents of communities along highway 51. A small body of marchers entered Greenwood on June 16 and, following the practice established in other communities, began erecting tents on the grounds of a local black school. Told by local police that the tents could not be erected without the school board's permission, Carmichael intervened. He was arrested for attempting to defy the police order. Carmichael and two others were held in jail for six hours before being released on one hundred dollar bond. That night Carmichael was the last speaker at a rally, following McKissick, King, and Ricks. Still angered by his arrest, he told an audience of six hundred persons, "This is the twenty-seventh time I have been arrested. I ain't going to jail no more." He announced that blacks had been demanding freedom for six years and had gotten nothing. "What we gonna start saying now is 'black power.' " He shouted the slogan repeatedly; each time the audience shouted back, "black power!" Willie Ricks leaped to the platform and asked, "What do you want?" Again and again the audience shouted in unison the slogan that had suddenly galvanized their emotions.[33]

Carmichael's use of the black power slogan immediately became the central controversy of the march. Newsmen quickly focused public attention on the phrase. King, who saw the slogan as "an unfortunate choice of words" that would weaken public support for the civil rights movement, called together staff members of SNCC, CORE, and SCLC for a meeting in Yazoo City, Mississippi. At the meeting Floyd McKissick of CORE voiced support for the black power slogan. King, realizing that black audiences had lost some of their enthusiasm for his nonviolent approach, tried to convince Carmichael and others that they should not use a slogan "that would confuse our allies, isolate the Negro community and give many prejudiced whites, who might otherwise be ashamed of their anti-Negro feeling, a ready excuse for self-justification." Carmichael and McKissick responded that the black struggle needed a new rallying cry and that there was nothing wrong with the concept of black power since it was the same kind of group power that had been sought by other ethnic groups. After five hours of debate, the representatives agreed to avoid competing for the support of black audiences through the use of slogans such as black power and freedom now.[34]

While newspapers across the nation condemned the black power slogan, white resistance to the march increased in Mississippi. On June 22, when marchers arrived in Philadelphia, Mississippi to commemorate the three civil rights workers murdered near there two years before, King spoke at the county courthouse while being heckled by a crowd of whites that included Deputy Sheriff Cecil Price and others who were later convicted of conspiracy in the murders. As the marchers began walking back toward the black community they were attacked by whites. Police refused to intervene until blacks began fighting back. Later in the evening there were battles between armed blacks and whites.[35]

Two days later, when marchers attempted to erect a tent at an all-black school in Canton, they were attacked by police using tear gas and clubs. Journalist Paul Good recalled that after the Canton attack even King had begun to doubt whether his nonviolent tactics would succeed. "The government has got to give me some victories if I'm gonna keep people nonviolent." King said, "I know I'm gonna stay nonviolent no matter what happens. But a lot of people are getting hurt and bitter, and they can't see it that way any more."[36]

The march ended June 26 with a massive rally at the state capitol in Jackson. Carmichael told the approximately 15,000 persons in the audience that blacks should "build a power base . . . so strong that we will bring [whites] to their knees every time they mess with us."[37]

SNCC workers' participation in the Mississippi march was the culmination of an introspective transitional period during which their assumptions and organization were critically examined. Since the summer of 1964 they had engaged in an exhausting search for a set of goals to replace those that previously had guided the civil rights movement. Concluding that they could not depend on support from the federal government or from northern white liberals, staff members debated whether they could build independent black political organizations without imposing greater discipline on the staff and moderating the anti-authoritarian ethic that permeated the organization. During 1965 SNCC organizers had launched innovative efforts to build bases of power in black communities to replace the liberal civil rights alliance, but they had not resolved the conflict between the goal of political effectiveness and ideological purity. Thus, the emergence of a consensus within SNCC regarding the need for black power was an incomplete response to the changing context of Afro-American politics. Stokely Carmichael's election was an expression of the hope of SNCC staff members that SNCC could awaken Afro-American political consciousness as an initial step toward building a new social order. Still unresolved was the question of whether SNCC workers could build durable and powerful alternative institutions on the basis of values acquired during years of rebellion against existing authority and constant criticism of established power. The black power slogan was both a means of appealing to discontented black individuals and a suggestion of their still only partially formulated future goals. They would soon discover that their task was unexpectedly complex and their opposition more resourceful than any previously faced.

*Floyd McKissick, Martin Luther King, and Stokely Carmichael leading march into Jackson, Mississippi, 1966*

*Stokely Carmichael (on floor), Andrew Young and Martin Luther King (either side of couch), and Lawrence Guyot (extreme right) planning Mississippi march, 1966*

*Cleveland Sellers speaking to newsmen outside Atlanta induction center after refusing the draft (Carmichael behind him), 1967*

# PART THREE
# FALLING APART

# 14. BLACK POWER

Stokely Carmichael's popularization of the black power slogan began a new stage in the transformation of Afro-American political consciousness. Shattering the fragile alliance of civil rights forces, the black power upsurge challenged the assumptions underlying previous interracial efforts to achieve national civil rights reforms. The black struggles of the 1960s had awakened dormant traditions of black radicalism and racial separatism by fostering among black people a greater sense of pride, confidence, and racial identity. Through their increasingly positive response to the concept of black power, Afro-Americans in every section of the nation indicated their determination to use hard-won human rights to improve their lives in ways befitting their own cultural values.

Like the four Greensboro students who ignited the lunch counter protest movement, Carmichael was not an exceptional prophetic figure. He became a symbol of black militancy because he sensed a widespread preparedness among blacks to reject previous habits of accommodation. His attitudes, shaped by experiences in the southern struggle, coincided with the unarticulated feelings of many other blacks, especially in northern urban centers, whose hopes were raised but not fulfilled by the civil rights movement. Like his Greensboro precursors, Carmichael was an innovator who could not control nor fully understand the social forces he had set in motion, and he could only begin the difficult task of formulating a comprehensive political strategy for the post civil rights era. Nonetheless he set forth the broad outlines of subsequent black political development. Carmichael joined a line of audacious black leaders—Martin Delany, Marcus Garvey, Malcolm X—whose historical role was to arouse large segments of the black populace by reflecting their repressed anger and candidly describing previously obscured aspects of their racial oppression.

Only after Carmichael attracted national attention as an advocate of black power did he begin to construct an intellectual rationale for what initially was an inchoate statement of conclusions drawn from SNCC's work. He attempted to demonstrate that black power was a logical outgrowth of the southern struggle and a reasonable response to the conditions facing Afro-Americans. While he did clarify many misconceptions of his views, he could not eliminate confusion caused by biased press reports and SNCC workers' own uncertainty about future programs. Moreover, his writings and public statements were not only vague formulations of strategy but were also emotional responses to the frustrations of SNCC staff members and rebellious urban blacks. Disillusioned by their previous attempts to achieve change through nonviolent tactics and interracial alliances, Carmichael and other outspoken militants in SNCC were no longer restrained by concern for the sensibilities of white people. By forthrightly expressing previously suppressed anger, Carmichael and others experienced a sense of "release" similar to that felt by black activists during the early days of the lunch counter sit-in movement.

SNCC workers' satisfaction with the black power slogan was based largely on the extent to which it aroused blacks and disturbed whites. By using an ambiguous phrase that would stir racial emotions, they demonstrated their continued willingness to take risks on behalf of their ideals. While Carmichael felt the need to explain his ideas to whites, he wavered ambivalently between efforts to address his critics and repeated refusals to soften his rhetoric to allay white fears. "I have to address myself to black people, not to the press or the white bourgeoisie," he told journalist Paul Good. On several occasions he proposed that the civil rights movement abandon its role "as a buffer zone between the black community and the white community" and begin "to express the feeling of the black community in the tone of the black community."[1]

Carmichael still attempted to persuade whites who were willing to listen to his arguments. During the summer of 1966, he published two essays: "What We Want," in the *New York Review of Books*, and "Toward Black Liberation," in the *Massachusetts Review*.[2] In these often reprinted essays, Carmichael explained the reasons for SNCC's change in direction in terms that white liberals and radicals would understand, if not accept.

Carmichael argued for the cultural and political autonomy of black communities. He defended the black power concept as a response by black people to the need "to reclaim our history and our identity from the cultural terrorism and depredation of self-justifying white guilt." He argued that black people would "have to struggle for the right to create our own terms to define ourselves and our relationship to the society, and to have these terms recognized."[3]

In his call for racial self-determination, Carmichael repeated many of the arguments of the Atlanta Project position paper written the previous spring. Although he still resisted the Atlanta separatists' demand for the expulsion of whites from SNCC, he now conveyed to a national audience many of their ideas regarding the psychological implications of the black struggle. While the Atlanta separatists used the issue of white participation in SNCC to increase their influence in the organization, Carmichael used the broader issue of white political hegemony to challenge the moderate leadership of competing civil rights organizations. "We want to decide who is our friend, and we will not accept someone who comes to us and says: 'If you do X, Y, and Z, then I'll help you.' " He insisted, "We cannot have the oppressors telling the oppressed how to rid themselves of the oppressor."[4]

Carmichael did not preclude the possibility of interracial alliances. He rejected the criticism that the black power concept represented "a withdrawal into black nationalism and isolationism." Instead, he suggested that SNCC's policies could have the opposite effect: "When the Negro community is able to control local offices, and negotiate with other groups from a position of organized strength, the possibility of meaningful political alliances on specific issues will be increased." This was possible, however, only if white activists recognized their responsibility to organize white communities. "They admonish blacks to be nonviolent," he wrote. "Let them preach nonviolence in the white community."[5]

Since 1964 Carmichael had urged white radicals to assume the task of organizing poor whites, but he warned that poor whites were "becoming more hostile—not less—partly because they see the nation's attention focused on black poverty and nobody coming to them." During a talk in Atlanta he commented sardonically that "the reality of it is that poor whites are very racist, because the country is racist, and that to go into a poor white community in Mississippi or Alabama and talk about integration is to invite suicide upon one's self."[6] Aware of the enormous obstacles organizers would face in white communities, he nonetheless repeatedly complained about white activists who preferred to go to black communities— "where the action is"—rather than seeking to mobilize whites to achieve progressive social change.

Carmichael did little to encourage blacks to accept alliances on the basis of class. "The only reason [whites] suppress us is because we are black," he told an audience in the Watts section of Los Angeles. Though he identified himself with the interests of poor blacks, he did not attempt to mobilize blacks by stressing their common class interests. Sensing that they would not respond as readily to class appeals as to racial appeals, Carmichael moved ever closer to an ideology of black separatism. Carmichael probably recognized that his analytical statements were oversimplified, but support of discontented blacks rather than understanding from skeptical whites was his primary goal. In his speeches he gave little attention to the economic problems of blacks presenting instead ideas that would appeal to blacks of all classes. "The most important thing that black people have to do is to begin to come together, and to be able to do that we must stop being ashamed of being black," he said. "We are black and beautiful."[7]

Carmichael provided little advice to his black listeners regarding the political direction they should take once they had come together under black leadership. Not yet prepared to adopt completely the notion that Afro-Americans were or should become a separate cultural or political entity, he concentrated on undermining support for the existing social order rather than describing a new one. In his few explicit references to the future of the black struggle, he invoked a group uplift model based on popular conceptions of the historical experiences of European ethnic groups. "Traditionally, for each new ethnic group, the route to social and political integration in America's pluralistic society has been through the organization of their own institutions with which to represent their communal needs within the larger society," he wrote. When he appeared on "Face the Nation," Carmichael mentioned the Irish and Jews as examples of groups that had gained local political control through the electoral process. He said that his conception of black power involved the organization of blacks as an independent force that could become a "strong block" within existing political parties to force politicians "to speak to [black] needs."[8]

An element of dissimulation undoubtedly lay in Carmichael's defense of the black power concept. He was not prepared to state whether his call for black power was simply an extension of SNCC's previous militancy in pursuit of reformist goals or a fundamental redirection of that militancy toward radical or revolutionary objectives. That Carmichael presented his arguments to white liberals and radicals suggests that he retained some hope of building an interracial democracy founded on racial equality. Despite his vacillation between hope and despair, between pluralist and separatist models of social reality, Carmichael was nonetheless identified as a symbol of racial hostility and violence. During the months following the Mississippi march his effort to clarify his ideas was obscured by a controversy over the black power slogan that was more a clash of emotions than of ideas.

Carmichael stimulated a crucial debate regarding the future of Afro-American politics, but he was only one of many contending voices in the contest for political dominance in black communities. In the heated controversy over black power Carmichael and various SNCC workers competed with other black political leaders to provide a definitive statement of black power as a goal and political strategy. Indeed, even before Carmichael had published his initial essays on black power, slanted press accounts of his speeches shaped popular attitudes regarding him and his ideas.

Carmichael consistently denied that he was anti-white or that his speeches incited anti-white violence; yet these connotations were an unmistakable part of the appeal of the black power rhetoric for many discontented blacks. Carmichael's purposeful ambiguity allowed his followers and his opponents to attribute their own meanings to the black power phrase. Although a victim of the misconceptions, Carmichael contributed to them through his vague implications of future racial retribution. He usually avoided clear incitements to violence, offering instead implicit support for such activities even while explicitly suggesting more moderate courses of action. Like the black power slogan itself, his most controversial statements regarding violence were ambiguous—as when he suggested during the Mississippi march that every courthouse in the state should be burnt down "so that we can get rid of the dirt." In more restrained moods, he indicated that his goal was to achieve change through a political strategy that would make violence unnecessary.

Carmichael blamed civil rights leaders, including himself, for the racial rioting in the northern communities. They had failed to provide an outlet for the accumulated frustrations of urban blacks. "Each time the people in those cities saw Martin Luther King get slapped, they became angry; when they saw four little black girls bombed to death, they were angrier; and when nothing happened, they were steaming," he wrote. "We had nothing to offer that they could see, except to go out and be beaten again." He announced that the significance of the black power slogan was that it showed that, "for once, black people are going to use the words they want to use— not just the words whites want to hear."[9]

Asserting that "the only power that Negro leaders have is the power to condemn black people," he commented in Watts that if black leaders were "afraid to condemn white people, they ought to keep their mouths shut when they talk to black people." He compared his own candidness with the guardedness of civil rights leaders of the early 1960s who were placed on the defensive by the charge that they were seeking miscegenation. "Negro leaders, even before they would begin to move, they were apologizing," he insisted. "Now I never get embarrassed when they ask me that question. I tell them: 'Your mother, your daughter, your sister is not the queen of the world; she's not the Virgin Mary. She can be made. Let's move on.' "[10]

Rather than recognizing and promoting those elements of Carmichael's ideas that were consistent with their programs, several major black leaders focused on the connotations of anti-white violence that had been attached to the black power slogan. In their attacks on Carmichael they hoped to reassure white supporters by distinguishing SNCC from the rest of the civil rights movement. Roy Wilkins of the NAACP was the first major black leader who vigorously denounced SNCC and the black power slogan. "No matter how endlessly they try to explain it, the term 'black power' means anti-white power," Wilkins told delegates to the annual NAACP convention held in July 1966. Equating the slogan with black separatism, Wilkins conceded that it offered many blacks "a solace, a tremendous psychological lift," but he warned that "the quick, uncritical and highly emotional adoption of the slogan [by] some segments of a beleaguered people can mean in the end only black death."[11]

Wilkins's remarks set the tone for subsequent critical comments by other civil rights and liberal leaders. Hoping to stem the continued deterioration of white support for the civil rights movement, these leaders ascribed to Carmichael extreme positions, making their own more moderate positions more attractive to the white public. The day after Wilkins's speech, Vice President Hubert Humphrey addressed the NAACP convention and declared, "We must reject calls for racism whether they come from a throat that is white or one that is black." President Lyndon Johnson also denounced black power—calling for "American democratic power"—as did Senator Robert F. Kennedy, who warned that "black power could be damaging not only to the civil-rights movement but to the country." Whitney Young of the Urban League announced that his organization would repudiate any group that had "formally adopted black power as a program, or which [tied] in domestic civil rights with the Vietnam conflict."[12]

Bayard Rustin, who had once advised Carmichael and other NAG members, published one of the first extended critiques of the black power concept. Writing in *Commentary*, Rustin noted that the passions in the black power debate had "their roots in the psychological and political frustrations of the Negro community," but he contended that the black power idea not only lacked "any real value for the civil rights movement" but that it was "positively harmful." He argued that "SNCC's Black Panther perspective [was] simultaneously utopian and reactionary—the former for the by now obvious reason that one-tenth of the population cannot accomplish much by itself, the latter because such a party would remove Negroes from the main area of political struggle, [the Democratic Party] . . . and would give priority to the issue of race precisely at a time when the fundamental questions facing the Negro and American society alike are economic and social."[13]

The rupture of relations between SNCC and moderate civil rights leaders was apparent when SNCC announced plans to demonstrate against the Vietnam war at the August 6 wedding of the president's daughter. Wilkins, Young, King, and A. Phillip Randolph sent a telegram to Carmichael asking SNCC to call off the protest so that it would not "implant the erroneous idea in millions of Americans that this demonstration represents an action by the civil rights movement." SNCC's Central Committee approved a bitter reply drafted by Courtland Cox:[14]

> You have displayed more backbone in defending [the president's daughter and her fiance] than you have shown for our black brothers engaged in acts of rebellion in our cities. As far as we are concerned

you messengers can tell your boss that his day of jubilation is also the day that his country murdered many in Hiroshima.

A more serious breach between SNCC and civil rights moderates occurred when SNCC refused to support Johnson's civil rights legislation submitted to Congress during the spring. SNCC called the legislation unnecessary and argued that the administration should vigorously enforce existing legislation.

During August SNCC workers became even more adamant in their opposition to the proposed civil rights legislation when the House of Representatives overwhelmingly amended the bill to make it a federal crime to cross state lines to incite or carry out a riot or other violent civil disturbance.[15] Carmichael and other militants were held responsible for outbreaks of urban violence. Congressmen cited a particularly intemperate speech delivered by Carmichael in Cleveland shortly after a racial rebellion, in which he reportedly stated that blacks everywhere would react if a black man anywhere was "messed with." He continued: "When you talk about black power, you talk about bringing this country to its knees. When you talk of black power, you talk of building a movement that will smash everything Western civilization has created."[16]

Few journalists were able to separate Carmichael's more thoughtful criticisms of American liberalism and the civil rights movement from his sometimes bombastic public pronouncements. They often offered gratuitous advice that in itself revealed that they had missed one of the points of the black power rhetoric. A common theme was that the call for black power was synonymous with black separatism. *Time* magazine referred to black power as "a racist philosophy" advocated by "young demagogues" whose ideas were "inching dangerously toward a philosophy of black separatism." *Newsweek* provided more balanced coverage but still embellished its reports with a reference to "SNCC's hot-eyed theoreticians." Editors of the *Saturday Evening Post* offered blunt criticisms of the black power concept, warning black militants that in 1943 whites had staged an anti-black riot in Detroit "that would have made the Watts rioting seem like a musical-comedy hoedown." Unmindful of their black readers, they asserted:[17]

> We are all, let us face it, Mississippians. We all fervently wish that the Negro problem did not exist or that . . . it could be ignored. Confronted with the howling need for decent schools, jobs, housing, and all the other minimum rights of the American system, we will do our best, in a half-hearted way, to correct old wrongs. The hand may be extended grudgingly and patronizingly, but anyone who rejects that hand rejects his own best interests.

Apart from leftist journalists, only a few reporters and columnists in major newspapers departed from the general pattern of condemnation.

One of these was *New York Times* columnist Tom Wicker, a white south-erner, who concluded that "white moderates can no more remake them-selves and their instincts than slum Negroes; and it does little good for either to preach at the other in a language he cannot understand about values he finds irrelevant or unworthy." After other columnists and editors had reassessed their initial reactions to the black power idea, a few newspa-pers such as the *Christian Science Monitor* and the *Boston Herald* suggested that the negative reaction of the press may have been unwarranted. "Like any rebel with a cause, Carmichael overstates the case," an article in *Newsweek* concluded early in August. "But there is little doubt that many U.S. news-papers, perplexed by a slogan that was ambiguous and undefined, failed to examine it closely and put it in perspective."[18]

Carmichael's essays on black power contributed to a gradual softening of white criticisms, but Carmichael and other SNCC workers were far more concerned about the response of black people to the concept. They soon recognized that a large and growing proportion of blacks were attracted to the black power slogan, though they interpreted it in many different ways.

Contributing to the positive black response were favorable articles on Carmichael in black publications. *Ebony* editor Lerone Bennett, Jr. pro-claimed Carmichael the "architect of Black Power" and noted that the phrase "did not spring full-blown from" Carmichael's head. "It was in the air; it was in the heads and hearts of long-suffering men who had paid an enormous price for minuscule gains," he wrote, adding that "it was the ge-nius of Stokely Carmichael to sense the mood gestating in the depths of the black psyche and to give tongue to it." A Louis Harris poll conducted in mid-summer showed substantial black acceptance of the idea of black power. More than half of a sample of "Negro community leaders" stated that they favored black power.[19] The polls probably understated the extent of support, since many blacks doubtlessly were reluctant to publicly express support for controversial ideas which were conveyed to them mainly through hostile newspaper accounts.

Carmichael initially asserted that blacks would define the phrase for themselves, although he became increasingly aware that proponents and critics could also offer their own definitions. During the summer of 1966, for example, former COFO worker Joyce Ladner noticed a basic split in the ranks of black power advocates in Mississippi and offered a perceptive analysis of the perceived meanings of black power. On one side of Ladner's dichotomy were "locals," generally life-long residents of Mississippi who saw the black power slogan as an appealing, alternative method of obtain-ing long-standing economic and political objectives. On the other side were "cosmopolitans," typically young, well-educated activists often from the North with "wide associations with white people," who maintained "that black people in American society must redefine the term 'black' and all that it symbolizes, and that black pride and dignity must be implanted in all Negro Americans." SNCC's ranks included both locals and cosmopolitans in 1966, but, while the localist orientation clearly predominated in Mississippi, the cosmopolitan orientation was on the ascent in SNCC.[20]

Martin Luther King was caught in the split between the moderates and the growing numbers of blacks whose allegiance was shifting toward Carmichael. King criticized the black power slogan on grounds that it connoted anti-white feelings, but when other black leaders issued a statement repudiating black power, King resisted pressures to sign it. He stated that he agreed with the statement but did not want to associate himself with an effort to "excommunicate" black power advocates. King understood and sympathized with SNCC's militancy, though he believed that he had been used by SNCC workers who publicized their views at his expense during the Mississippi march. A year later, in his final published work, King retained some of his scepticism regarding the slogan but nonetheless wrote one of the most moving statements of the period regarding its necessity, citing the need to build a greater sense of racial pride and potency among blacks.[21]

Among major civil rights organizations only CORE supported SNCC in its call for black power. With predominantly northern membership, CORE was even less able than SNCC to ignore the upsurge in urban black militancy during the previous two years and had stimulated that militancy through its northern protest activities. Carmichael addressed delegates to CORE's annual convention in July and found most of them receptive to his message. The delegates endorsed black power as their theme and joined SNCC in accepting the right of armed self-defense by blacks and in officially opposing the Vietnam War.[22]

Late in July SNCC workers were surprised to learn that an informal group of forty-eight black clergy had published a full-page statement in the *New York Times* backing the black power concept. The group proclaimed that black power was a reaction to the "assumption that white people are justified in getting what they want through the use of power, but that Negro Americans must, either by nature or by circumstances, make their appeal only through conscience." The clergymen stated that blacks were "oppressed as a group, not as individuals."[23]

More predictable was the support offered by Congressman Adam Clayton Powell, since the black politician from Harlem considered himself the originator of the black power phrase. After meeting with Carmichael and other SNCC representatives, Powell announced plans for a national conference on Labor Day weekend to discuss the achievement of black power. Yet, while SNCC workers were pleased by such support from a black elected official, they were able to offer little consistent leadership for those who came aboard the black power bandwagon. In October, for example, when Powell held his conference, the Central Committee decided against sending SNCC representatives, feeling that SNCC could not successfully counter the efforts of Powell and other established black leaders to reinterpret the black power concept. "Powell is talking about stopping the throwing of molotov cocktails and not about stopping the causes that bring about the throwing of the cocktails," Carmichael complained privately during a discussion of the conference. He added that Powell had "never talked about independent politics" but instead was "trying to get people together under the Democratic party." Forman later proposed that SNCC call its own national conference on the seventh anniversary of the initial Greensboro sit-in, but he did not vigorously push the idea. He explained that SNCC "did not have its own ideological position together" and that it would have been "a tremendous mistake for us to call a conference on Black Power and fail to give it ideological direction."[24]

Powell's meeting signaled the beginning of a decline in SNCC's influence among blacks, since it was merely the first of many efforts by moderate black leaders to shape the new black political consciousness. After attending the meeting, a group headed by Dr. Nathan Wright, executive director of the Department of Urban Work of the Episcopal Diocese of Newark, announced plans for a large-scale conference of black leaders, to be held in July 1967. Significantly, SNCC representatives played only minor roles in organizing this major gathering, which helped shape popular conceptions of the black power movement.

As SNCC workers succeeded in popularizing the black power slogan, they began to lose their ability to stimulate lasting feelings of racial potency such as those nurtured by the southern black struggle. From his position as Program Secretary, Sellers observed the sharp contrast between Carmichael's confident assertion of the need for a new direction in Afro-American politics and SNCC's increasingly obvious limitations as a political organization. He had supported Carmichael at the Kingston Springs staff meeting and generally approved of his activities as chairman, yet he had conflicting feelings about the black power controversy. Referring to the "nightmare" caused by "hysteria-ridden responses" to black power, he nonetheless expressed pride that SNCC was in "the forefront of the struggle for black liberation," that SNCC workers were being "hailed as heroes" in black ghettoes, and that "journalists, intellectuals, politicians, students . . . were all responding to our radical cadence." Commenting on the contradiction between SNCC's image and its reality, he wrote, "while Establishment leaders denounced our spiraling influence, we were doing everything possible to keep the organization from collapsing."[25]

As Sellers and other staff members saw their own organization weakening, their opposition grew more determined. During the summer southern congressmen won approval for "anti-riot" amendments to the Johnson Administration's civil rights proposals. Only the defeat of the entire bill slowed the congressional drive to enact new legislation restricting black militancy. Local authorities, responding to white fears of black militancy and racial violence, attempted to disable SNCC projects in several cities by arresting and harassing SNCC workers, who sometimes played into their hands by brash and unauthorized activities.

A police raid in August 1966 on SNCC's Philadelphia office by a heavily-armed, eighty-strong strike force illustrated the type of repression SNCC and other urban-based black militant groups would face in subsequent years. The resulting headlines suggested that police found dynamite in the office and had arrested many SNCC workers. Actually dynamite was found at an apartment used by the Young Militants, a black group associated with the NAACP, and, of the four persons arrested, only one, Barry Dawson, was a SNCC staff member. Yet, since newspaper accounts of Carmichael's recent speeches had prepared Philadelphia whites to believe the worst about SNCC, Project Director Fred Meely and members of his staff who were not arrested decided to go into hiding. To justify the raid, Chief of Police Frank Rizzo and Mayor John Tate tried to link SNCC with a plot to initiate urban guerrilla warfare and suggested that Carmichael be barred from speaking in northern cities.[26]

Forman and other SNCC officers kept the Philadelphia office open and secured legal defense for Dawson. They attracted several thousand people to a support rally late in August but were unable to correct erroneous press reports regarding the incident. After Dawson confessed to bringing sticks of dynamite obtained from a friend to the SNCC office while Meely was out of town, police issued warrants for the arrest of Meely and two other SNCC workers. In November, after the situation became calmer, the three at-large SNCC workers turned themselves in and charges against them as well as Dawson were eventually dropped.[27] The Philadelphia project never completely recovered from the raid.

Soon afterward, Carmichael became involved in a confrontation with police in the Summerhill section of Atlanta. He came to the black neighborhood after hearing reports that a black man attempting to escape arrest had been wounded by police. Arriving on the scene of the shooting, Carmichael found an angry crowd already planning a rally to protest the shooting. He promised to attend the rally, and, according to police reports, stated that he would return to "tear this place up" (Carmichael denied saying this). Staff members at SNCC headquarters persuaded him to allow Bill Ware and Bobby Walton of the Atlanta Project to speak in his place. Ware agreed, hoping to repair his relations with Carmichael and other SNCC leaders. He brought a loudspeaker to the rally to allow residents to give their version of the shooting. Despite their effort to avoid making inciting statements, Ware and Walton were arrested when they refused to comply with policy requests to turn off the speaker.[28]

Their arrests further angered the crowd, which began throwing rocks and bottles at police. Mayor Ivan Allen arrived with police reinforcements and tried to speak to the assemblage from atop a car, but residents heckled him and demanded that black leaders be allowed to speak and that the policeman responsible for the shooting be fired. One account stated that after Allen was knocked from the car, he ordered police to disperse the crowd and tear down the houses of blacks if necessary. Marion Barry recalled: "Black women were clubbed to the ground. Cops fired tear gas indiscriminately into [homes]. Little kids came out gasping for air. Cops went onto Black people's porches to beat and arrest them."[29]

Although Carmichael, Ware, and other SNCC workers had left Summerhill when the major battles between blacks and police occurred, white city officials blamed SNCC for the violence. Soon afterward, Mayor Allen attended a meeting of the Atlanta Summit Leadership Conference, composed of prominent blacks, urging them to adopt a statement condemning SNCC. The Conference refrained from attacking SNCC by name but called upon blacks "not to allow any individual to use them as pawns in any evil plot they may have to injure the city." Police Chief Herbert Jenkins also blamed SNCC for the violence, calling it "the nonstudent violent committee." *Atlanta Constitution* editor Ralph McGill asserted that SNCC had been "taken over by what amounts to a secret klan-type group which openly states its racial hatreds and its objective to foment disorder and chaos in order to destroy Western civilization."[30]

Carmichael walked from door to door in Summerhill after the violence, explaining that he had not sought to cause the conflict, while Atlanta officials continued their efforts to link SNCC to the outbreak. They obtained warrants for Carmichael's arrest on charges of inciting to riot and disorderly conduct. Soon afterward, police invaded SNCC's headquarters and arrested Carmichael, who was later convicted of the charges, although his conviction and those of other SNCC workers on rioting charges were overturned on appeal.[31]

Carmichael's initial attempts to provide an intellectually defensible basis for the black power slogan soon gave way to a willingness on the part of many SNCC workers to allow black people to define the slogan through their militancy. SNCC's staff did not determine how militant racial consciousness could be used to achieve tangible gains, and they allowed more moderate leaders to take the lead in exploiting the black power rhetoric for their own purposes. As the ambiguous black power slogan became linked with programs ranging from the election of black politicians and the development of black capitalism to the creation of a new black value system and the fostering of a black revolution, SNCC workers' failure to resolve the basic conflict between class and racial strategies became more evident. They succeeded in stimulating a seminal intellectual debate while losing the opportunity to play a major role in it.

SNCC workers resented attempts by moderate black leaders to use the black power rhetoric, but Carmichael's most developed statement on black power failed to provide a coherent and radical set of ideas for future black struggles. Co-authored by political scientist Charles V. Hamilton, *Black Power: The Politics of Liberation in America* (1967) eclectically drew ideas from Third World nationalist movements and Western scholarly studies of those movements. Carmichael and Hamilton proposed that Afro-Americans could escape their "colonized" status in American society by undergoing a process of "political modernization," of which the awakening of racial consciousness was the first stage. The book, which they described as "a political framework and ideology which represents the last reasonable opportunity for this society to work out its racial problems short of prolonged destructive guerrilla warfare," contained only vague references regarding the need for blacks to reject existing political rules and to adopt "new political forms." Concluding by suggesting that black consciousness would itself provide a new framework for radical social change, the authors implicitly conceded that SNCC would not lead the way by calling for new ideological contributions from black college students and intellectuals.[32]

Carmichael's political views, like those of other SNCC workers, were changing during 1967. He retained, at least in his writings during 1966 and 1967, a fleeting belief in interracial coalitions and conventional types of political activity. This belief was not shared by other SNCC workers who were convinced that all links to white people had to be broken and that racial ideals were themselves the major goal of their struggle. Although usually conceding that black oppression had a class as well as racial dimension, Carmichael and other staff members were moving toward a perspective that emphasized race rather than class and Third World alliances rather than coalitions with poor whites. They knew that alienated black people who were prepared to strike out in violence were more receptive to arguments reflecting the overwhelming psychological importance of racial identity in American society. The gradual suppression of class concerns that had previously been a central part of SNCC's work soon would destroy SNCC's remaining links with the white Left and complicate its relations with Third World socialist governments and revolutionary movements.

Black social critic Harold Cruse, who was basically sympathetic to the racial consciousness emphasis of SNCC's rhetoric, warned in the midst of the black power controversy that "black-skin chauvinism" would be politically unproductive in the United States. He charged that "the Black Power theorists" evaded the issue of "which class is going to wield this power."

Cruse believed that one of the weaknesses of previous interracial movements for social change had been their failure to give proper emphasis to cultural matters, but he nonetheless derided the fact that contemporary black militants proposed "to change, not the white world outside, but the black world inside, by reforming it into something else politically and economically."[33]

Similarly, Robert Allen's *Black Awakening in Capitalist America* perceptively described the process through which black militancy was being subverted by the American corporate order. Allen, a black journalist who covered SNCC and other groups for the *National Guardian*, noted that Carmichael "never moved beyond ambiguity," sometimes speaking as "a reformer, who only wanted to adjust the social system and make it work better" and sometimes as a revolutionary. "On other occasions, he managed to give the remarkable impression of being at once a reformer and a revolutionary."[34]

The debate over the meaning of black power would continue after 1966, but neither Carmichael nor SNCC would be able to determine its outcome. By bravely injecting the black power slogan into an explosive context of racial conflict, SNCC workers launched a new era of black political discussion and as a result paid the price of increased notoriety. SNCC worker Ethel Minor recalled that the attention SNCC received during this period contributed to a feeling of accomplishment. "I really felt that we were among the most important people in the world, and we were definitely accomplishing world-shaking tasks," she remembered.[35] Yet there were also a considerable number of staff members who questioned whether SNCC could achieve its goals while the staff was preoccupied with a controversy over the black power slogan. Even staff members who agreed that SNCC should seek to provide ideological guidance for black people disputed Carmichael's ability to speak for them. The Atlanta separatists were foremost among those within SNCC who were determined to set forth their own views on the proper racial consciousness for blacks, and their bitter struggle for control of SNCC foreshadowed disputes that would divide blacks outside SNCC as they pursued the illusive goal of black unity.

# 15. INTERNAL CONFLICTS

Carmichael and other SNCC workers roused the racial feelings of blacks through verbal attacks on the existing leadership and prevailing strategies of the civil rights movement, but their own organization was weakened in the process. Staff members expected the external attacks and undoubtedly some believed that such attacks confirmed the correctness of their actions. Yet to many SNCC workers, the organization's vulnerability was somewhat unnecessary, because it resulted from an emphasis on militant rhetoric rather than on the development of workable programs to consolidate southern civil rights gains. As Carmichael became a nationally-known figure, SNCC shifted the focus of its activities from the deep South to urban centers, prompting some staff members to question whether tangible political gains could be realized as a result of the personal following Carmichael attracted.

That the invocation of racial ideals did not always unite black communities and could even intensify conflicts among blacks became apparent within SNCC when black separatists in the Atlanta Project persisted in their demands for the expulsion of the remaining whites on the SNCC staff. The issue of white participation became a weapon in a struggle over SNCC's future direction between the separatists and other black staff members who ultimately rejected the separatists' extremism but failed to challenge their overriding belief that adherence to racial ideals should take precedence over the issues of SNCC's effectiveness and even its continued existence. Such idealism had once been an asset in SNCC's struggle to mobilize civil rights forces; it became a liability as SNCC sought to create its own bases of power in order to achieve new goals against powerful and determined opposition.

When Carmichael's involvement in the Atlanta racial violence resulted in his arrest in September 1966, a few staff members began openly to express doubts about his public activities. Executive Secretary Ruby Doris Robinson wrote that SNCC's staff had not decided, as had Carmichael, to advocate "the destruction of Western civilization." Referring to Carmichael's public image as the "architect of Black Power," she asked other staff members, "How could one individual make such a tremendous impression on so many people in such a short period of time . . . so much so that to some people SNCC is only the organization that Carmichael has at his disposal to do what he wants to get done?" Answering her own question, she asserted that Carmichael had been "the only consistent spokesman for the organization, and he has had the press not only available but seeking him out for whatever ammunition could be found—FOR OUR DESTRUCTION." She conceded that "at his best, he has said what [the masses of black people] wanted to hear," but added that "cliche after cliche has filled his orations."[1]

A few weeks after Robinson's blast against Carmichael, similar concerns of other staff members were strengthened when a group of nine black men, carrying rifles and hand grenades, appeared at the Atlanta office claiming to be Carmichael's followers. "We had no idea they were coming down and this was the first time they had been to the Atlanta office," Fay Bellamy recalled. "Not knowing us, they were quick to let us know what equipment they had brought with them."[2]

To an extent, the criticisms of Carmichael were based on a mixture of envy, jealousy, and understandable resentment by veteran staff members who disliked being thought of as Carmichael's followers or aides. Muriel Tillinghast recalled that SNCC had previously resisted allowing the chair to become dominant but that after Carmichael's election, "the chairman began to determine policy autonomously and the rest of us had to make a decision as to whether we were going to go with the chair or not."[3] The staff's inability to control Carmichael's activities indicated that they had not yet found a means of reconciling their desire for discipline and democratic control.

Carmichael was aware of the need for discipline and even acknowledged his own shortcomings after they were repeatedly brought to his attention. At the October central committee meeting, he admitted that "rhetorically, there have been a lot of mistakes made." Reacting to suggestions of Robinson, Bellamy, Ralph Featherstone, and other strong figures in the Atlanta office, he agreed to stop making speaking engagements after December 10 and to spend his time "developing programs and working on internal structure."[4]

Carmichael was probably sincere in his promise to restrict his speechmaking, but the limelight was difficult to resist. A few months later the Central Committee forbade his appearance on a television show and decided that he should always be accompanied by another staff member at his engagements. Carmichael was undoubtedly annoyed by these restrictions, since he and other staff members realized that his speeches had dramatically increased SNCC's visibility, if not its effectiveness, and were an important source of income for the financially hard-pressed organization.

*   *   *

SNCC's initial goals had been radical in the context of southern society, and it had once faced more fierce and immediate opposition than it confronted in 1966, but the black power controversy weakened SNCC's southern bases by discouraging many veteran organizers and prompting a movement of SNCC's personnel from long-established projects in the deep South to urban areas. SNCC was not, as some critics asserted, taken over by black militants without ties to the civil rights movement. Approximately two-thirds of the one hundred staff members in October 1966 had been on the staff at least two years. In addition, some of those who had joined the staff during 1965 and 1966 had participated in earlier civil rights efforts, though not as SNCC staff members. Nonetheless, SNCC had changed in several significant ways. The most dramatic change was the movement of personnel to urban areas. During the period from 1961 to 1966 all but a small proportion of staff members were assigned to projects in Arkansas, Mississippi, Alabama, or southwest Georgia. By October 1966 only a third of the staff were in these areas; the other two thirds were gathered near SNCC's Atlanta headquarters or scattered in cities outside the South.[5]

A comparison of SNCC's staff in the fall of 1966 with the period prior to 1965 reveals that few of SNCC's officers and project directors in the fall of 1964 remained in SNCC. SNCC's new officers had hoped to keep Lewis in the organization to retain the appearance of continuity, but the bitterness resulting from the Kingston Springs meeting could not be overcome. Lewis initially offered his resignation on June 11, but the Central Committee refused to accept it. He became even more convinced he should resign, however, after hearing that a few SNCC workers on the Mississippi march tried to trick SCLC officials into being arrested. Although he felt no personal antagonism toward Carmichael, he was disturbed by the actions of SNCC workers who were openly hostile toward whites. When he finally announced his resignation late in June 1966, Lewis explained that he was not prepared to give up his "personal commitment to nonviolence." Consistently refusing to publicly criticize the black power concept, he later indicated that SNCC failed to provide "on-going" programs to meet the needs of blacks. "To have a program is one thing, to have a sort of speech-making public relations thing is another," he remarked.[6]

Julian Bond, one of SNCC's founders, resigned later in the summer, shortly after the outbreak of racial violence in Atlanta. Having been re-elected in February and once again barred by the Georgia legislature from taking his seat, Bond was in the midst of his third campaign when he decided that his ties to SNCC had become too much of a liability. He explained to reporters that he did not disagree with SNCC's policies and that his resignation was in part motivated by the inadequacy of his pay ($85 a week) to support his family. Privately he was disturbed that SNCC had lost

much of its effectiveness and was overly concerned with ideological matters. He later commented that SNCC did not "have a program to match its
rhetoric." Unlike Lewis, however, Bond evinced little bitterness in his
break with SNCC, and he continued to have close relations with SNCC
workers, many of whom participated in his successful re-election campaign.[7]

Even more damaging to SNCC's southern effectiveness than the resignations of Lewis and Bond was the deterioration of its field operations.
SNCC's ability to rebuild its southern projects was hampered by the departure of its most experienced organizers. In 1966, Charles Sherrod,
SNCC's first field secretary, ended his ties with SNCC when the Central
Committee unanimously rejected his plan to bring northern white students
to work in southwest Georgia. After resigning from SNCC, Sherrod established the Southwest Georgia Independent Voters Project, which remained
active after SNCC's efforts in the area had ceased.[8]

Several staff members in Arkansas also resigned rather than adjust to
SNCC's new ideological thrust. Most Arkansas staff members ultimately
accepted the validity of the black power concept, but one of them resigned
after reading a particularly inflammatory field report written by a SNCC
worker in New Jersey. Sellers wrote that the Arkansas worker was willing to
defend SNCC's actions against liberal criticisms but was not willing to "go
to war with some liberal shithead over some words." Bill Hansen finally left
the project, in part due to dismay over SNCC's inability to control Carmichael's public statements, as did his successor as project director, Ben Grinnage, who resigned to join the Arkansas Human Relations Council.[9]

Other projects were also weakened by resignations and declining morale
among organizers. In Mississippi serious challenges from moderate black
leaders who wished to create an alternative to the MFDP exacerbated
long-standing tensions between SNCC and pragmatic MFDP leader
Lawrence Guyot. Although staff members were disturbed by Guyot's increasingly independent course, they were unable to refute his criticism that
SNCC provided little support for the party. Sellers visited several Mississippi communities during the summer and found few SNCC staff members
carrying out their responsibilities. He was particularly disturbed by the situation in Holly Springs, where he had once been project director, believing
that the current director, Sid Walker, did not have the support of local
blacks in his decision to retain white staff members. When Sellers sum-
marily closed the office and recommended that most of the staff be fired,
Walker defended himself by arguing that the use of white volunteers was
necessary since SNCC was not able to provide funds to hire full-time black
workers. Although Walker was unable to reverse Sellers' decision, this
drastic action taken against allegedly nonproductive Mississippi staff members did not stem the decline in SNCC's effort in the state. In October Rob-

inson reported that the remaining Mississippi staff members were out of touch with the Atlanta headquarters and did not feel that SNCC adequately supported their work.[10]

Even in Lowndes County, Alabama, where SNCC leaders expected to demonstrate the potential of the black power strategy, the results of SNCC's efforts were disappointing. Carmichael's departure was followed by the gradual drifting away of other staff members, forcing the Central Committee to send Ralph Featherstone to the county in a belated attempt to revive the project. In October, however, Carmichael reported that only one of the Alabama workers, Rap Brown, planned to remain as a full-time worker after the November election. SNCC tried to remedy the situation by drawing workers from other projects in the days before the election, and this temporary influx brought the LCFO tantalizingly close to victory. Carmichael returned on election eve to address an enthusiastic gathering of black residents, telling them to remember the oppression they had endured. "We remember all the dust we ate," he cried. "We say to those who don't remember: 'You better remember, because if you don't move on over, we are going to move on over you!' " Despite this last-minute effort, LCFO workers were unable to counter the efforts of whites to transport plantation workers to the polls with instructions to vote for white candidates. Without these black votes, LCFO candidates were defeated, receiving from forty-one to forty-six percent of the vote.[11] More importantly, after the temporary additions to the staff had left, SNCC no longer could aid black residents in continuing their struggle.

SNCC organizers outside the South had little difficulty adjusting to the rhetoric of black power, but they failed to transform black support for the concept into actual political power. Los Angeles SNCC worker Cliff Vaughs announced plans during the summer of 1966 for incorporating predominantly black sections of Los Angeles into a "Freedom City," but this project never got off the ground. Early in 1967 the Central Committee concluded that Vaughs was no longer effective and asked him to hand in his resignation. Soon afterward, the Los Angeles office was closed.[12]

SNCC workers in Washington had somewhat greater success in establishing the Free D.C. Movement (FDCM), a pioneering effort to achieve self-government for the district. These efforts were eventually successful but office director Marion Barry complained during August that SNCC was losing good organizers to the federal poverty program because it could not pay sufficient wages. Sellers reported that "there was general hostility in some [black neighborhoods] because of lack of program." Other Central Committee members criticized Barry's comparatively moderate political orientation and did not object when he quietly resigned his post in SNCC to work as an independent organizer. He soon became head of an anti-poverty organization called Pride, Inc.[13]

Bill Hall's organizing effort in Harlem was intertwined in a bitter struggle by black residents to gain control over predominantly-black schools, and he became skeptical of SNCC's ability to deal with black urban problems. Hall recalled that many people who joined SNCC after 1965 did not recognize the need for technical skills. Determined to acquire such skills, he left New York and SNCC to return to college. After his departure, SNCC's activities in New York were largely limited to fund-raising.[14]

SNCC's Chicago office was raided by police late in 1966, and several months later its head, Monroe Sharpe, went into exile in Tanaznia to escape police and FBI harassment. In 1967 Joyce Brown and then Bob Brown tried unsuccessfully to revive SNCC's activities in the city.

SNCC's officers were overwhelmed as they tried to reinvigorate these waning projects. Sellers complained at one point that it was "a joke" to believe that he could "do an effective job when in fact everyone on the staff is an individual and has a parochial attitude." On another occasion he noted that SNCC could not accomplish its goals and implement programs "until we can discipline ourselves," mentioning specifically "the need to use resources wisely and to their full capacity." In a similar vein, Robinson reported that she had decided against describing the activities of all staff members, since that would be "in bad taste."[16]

SNCC's declining effectiveness not only hampered its projects but also contributed to the loss of northern financial backing. Individuals who might have backed SNCC's drive for black power were unwilling to support an organization that had few promising projects. SNCC began to rely almost totally on speechmaking and its New York office, manned by professional fund-raisers and veteran staff members, to provide funds for payroll expenses. When these sources proved insufficient, staff members were forced to skip paychecks, prompting some to leave the organization in order to support themselves and their families.[17]

SNCC's problems were by no means solely caused by its own militancy and lack of discipline. SCLC and CORE also had difficulty in adjusting to a new political context in which their previous tactics and strategies were often inappropriate. One of SNCC's strengths had always been its ability to change and to attract new personnel with new ideas. The black power controversy simply represented another example of SNCC's ability to remain in the forefront of social struggle. Yet, SNCC's problems in 1966 were more serious than ever before, because it no longer served as a catalyst for sustained local struggles. Rather than encouraging local leaders to develop their own ideas, SNCC was becoming merely one of many organizations seeking to speak on behalf of black communities. Instead of immersing themselves in protest activity and deriving their insights from an ongoing mass struggle, SNCC workers in 1966 stressed the need to inculcate among urban blacks a new racial consciousness as a foundation for future struggles. Those who joined SNCC's staff during 1966 generally were urban blacks attracted more by SNCC's militant image than by its rural southern projects. Most were dedicated activists, willing to take risks to achieve their ideals, but few wanted to engage in the difficult work of gaining the trust and support of southern black people who were older than themselves and less aware of the new currents of black nationalist thought. SNCC's rhetoric reflected the angry mood of many urban blacks, but its projects were unable to transform racial anger into local movements that could be sustained.

Although SNCC's remaining veterans recognized the need for a staff educational program to train organizers, they were no more successful than before in establishing such a program. During the hectic summer of 1966, Sellers brought together Carmichael, Donaldson, Rap Brown, George Ware, Stanley Wise, Ella Baker, and Charles Hamilton to discuss educational programs and scholarships for staff members. "We are in critical need of an educational program because of the complexity of the jobs we must do and the seeming lack of interest of the staff to fulfill this duty," Sellers commented. The group met with little success, however, and, after attending a meeting called to discuss educational programs, Jack Minnis noted that many SNCC staff members were unprepared to "sit down and listen to a lecture" and others could not read. He proposed that "people who do not read Camus and Fanon learn about them through conversation with those who have read."[18]

Despite these meetings and Bill Hall's attempt to establish an SNCC "ideological institute," little was accomplished. Forman, in a 1967 essay entitled "Rock Bottom," deplored the absence of "a systematic attempt to educate ourselves; to train new members; to instill a sense of history in the organization . . . ; to discuss and analyze many events occurring in the world." He blamed himself for this failure, considering it foolhardy "always to give in to the demands of the moment and not insist in a more active manner that we create and implement a program for the intellectual and political development of our staff." Forman argued that SNCC had played a significant role in attacking racism and segregation and in registering black voters in the deep South but staff members should have recognized that the passage of the 1965 Civil Rights Bill changed SNCC's "entire character." If SNCC did not change its "style of operation," he warned, it would continue to decline in effectiveness "through a lack of direction, lack of confidence in the future, a sense of failure, fatigue, despair, frustration, and bad health."

Unprepared to offer his own ideological formulations, Forman suggested

that the black power slogan was not an adequate guide for the future. He
asked the staff to confront broader questions regarding the significance of
racial consciousness in the black struggle:[19]

> Are the problems we face only ones of color? . . . What is upper, lower,
> middle class? Do they exist among blacks? Why is there a black banker
> in one town and a starving Negro in the same? . . . Do the problems of
> a black welfare mother arise only from her blackness? If not, then what
> are the other causes?

Forman was aware that SNCC's ability to confront these issues was limited not only by the external repression that occupied the staff's attention
but also by the internal tensions and conflicts that destroyed the mutual
respect and trust that once existed within SNCC. Implicit in his call for systematic self-criticism was his concern that SNCC staff members had mistak-
enly assumed that their verbal assaults against liberalism and white society
constituted a basis for effective political action. Although staff members
agreed on the necessity of a basic shift in SNCC's ideological orientation,
they were only gradually becoming aware of the perplexing questions of
tactics and strategy that remained to be resolved inside SNCC and within
Afro-American communities. SNCC could not evaluate its activities without first resolving these questions.

The issue of white participation superseded all others as an illustration of
SNCC's inability to resolve internal differences over policy on the basis of
coherent political principles rather than emotions and fervent adherence to
racial ideals. This issue, a source of internal conflict since 1964, was considered resolved for most staff members when SNCC decided to discourage
the use of whites as organizers in black communities and made explicit the
notion that black people should determine the direction of their struggle.
By fall 1966 only a handful of white activists remained on SNCC's staff,
and of these only Jack Minnis still exercised much influence in the organization. Nonetheless, SNCC was unable to leave behind the issue of white
involvement, because the presence of whites brought to the surface differences among black staff members. For a significant number of black separatists, this issue symbolized SNCC's general inability to break with its
past. Members of the Atlanta Project had indicated in their position paper
that black people required all-black organizations to develop the racial
confidence and militancy needed for future struggles. The separatists failed
in their initial challenge to SNCC's leadership, but after Carmichael's
election they continued to use the issue of white participation as a means of
undermining SNCC's leadership. In the process, they demonstrated how
the rhetoric of black power could be used as a weapon in the black leader-

ship battles that would take place in SNCC and in black communities during the late 1960s.

The Atlanta Project separatists reflected and contributed to a mood of racial bitterness that was perceptively analyzed by black psychiatrist Alvin Poussiant, who worked closely with SNCC during the mid-1960s. Poussiant suggested that the southern struggle was an outlet for the resentments of black activists but many felt restrained by their friendly relations with white civil rights workers and by their desire to retain northern white support. Poissiant may have exaggerated somewhat when he wrote that many of the civil rights workers who shouted the black power slogan loudest after June 1966 had once been "exemplars of nonviolent, loving passive resistance in their struggle against white supremacy." But he was on firmer grounds in arguing that the advocates of black power "appeared to be seeking a sense of psychological emancipation from racism through self assertion and release of aggressive angry feelings."[20]

Such feelings were released through public black power speeches that hinted of racial violence, and through verbal and sometimes physical attacks on other SNCC workers. Forman's description of SNCC as "a band of brothers, a circle of trust" became only a memory as the staff argued about the means of achieving black power. Ironically the bonds that held the staff together loosened while SNCC became more racially homogeneous. Eager to achieve more radical goals, SNCC workers sometimes deprecated SNCC's earlier accomplishments and lost sight of the organizing techniques responsible for those accomplishments.

Julius Lester, who joined SNCC's staff shortly after Carmichael's election, expressed the changing mood inside SNCC in an essay on "the angry children of Malcolm X." Naive and idealistic SNCC workers of the early 1960s—who had "honestly believed that once white people knew what segregation did, it would be abolished"—had given way to a new generation who believed that nonviolence did not work.[21]

> Now it is over. The days of singing freedom songs and the days of combating bullets and billy clubs with Love . . . Love is fragile and gentle and seeks a like response. They used to sing "I Love Everybody" as they ducked bricks and bottles. Now they sing
>> Too much love,
>> Too much love,
>> Nothing kills a nigger like
>> Too much love.

In his popular tract *Look Out, Whitey! Black Power's Gon' Get Your Mama!* Lester went further, suggesting that a race war might be on the horizon. "You can't do what has been done to blacks and not expect retribution. The very act of retribution is liberating." Rejecting the kind of moralistic struggle once waged by Sherrod, Lewis, Moses, and other SNCC workers, he asserted, "It is clearly written that the victim must become the executioner." SNCC workers in Chicago expressed a similar thought even more bluntly: "We must fill ourselves with hate for all white things."[22]

Lester's essays reflected the anti-white animus of some SNCC workers, but also hinted at a strong current of anti-black feeling that would become increasingly noticeable among black militants who wanted to separate themselves from all reminders of a less militant past. Black SNCC workers who had white friends or who were too light-skinned or too imbued with "white" cultural values became targets for criticism from other blacks. Militancy was no longer exhibited through the civil rights struggle but through advocacy of black ideals. Even those who did not equate black power with anti-white attitudes were reluctant to say anything that would lead others to question their racial loyalty. "Politically, Black Power meant black political, economic and cultural control of black communities," Lester later reflected, "but in the SNCC office, on the streets and in the bars of Atlanta, I heard a growing litany of hatred." Lester, who had left his white wife to join SNCC, was one of those who had difficulty conforming to the black militant image he helped to create. Although he had "reservations" about black power rhetoric, he did not voice them, "for if I had, I would have had to ask why I had enlisted. I was so determined to be a revolutionary that I refused to look at anything within me which might contradict who I wanted to be."[23]

Less subject to feelings of racial ambivalence and eager to question the racial loyalties of others, the Atlanta Project separatists placed other SNCC staff members on the defensive during the summer and fall of 1966. They achieved only modest success in organizing blacks in the Vine City ghetto, in part because they failed to acquire the support of strong, indigenous, adult leaders who had traditionally provided entree for SNCC field secretaries, but they diverted attention from their failures by blaming them on the continued presence of whites in SNCC. Bill Ware believed that SNCC's refusal to cut the "umbilical cord" that tied it to white financial support prevented it from instilling a sense of self-sufficiency in the minds of blacks. Ware and other Atlanta staff members were willing to risk SNCC's destruction to achieve their racial goals: "I said, 'My loyalty is to the black people and not to SNCC necessarily. It's to SNCC only in proportion as I determine its loyalty to black people.' "[24]

The separatist orientation of the Atlanta Project came to public attention during the summer of 1966 when staff members clashed with Hector Black, a white Harvard graduate who had received a federal anti-poverty grant to work in Vine City. "What we saw was that he was a perpetuation of the missionary mentality, of the so-called good white men that had us looking toward them for our solution rather than looking toward ourselves," Ware recalled. The fact that Black had considerable support in the community and was a member of the Vine City Council, an unofficial community forum, simply strengthened the separatists' resentments. Early in the summer Black received an overwhelming vote of confidence from the council after SNCC workers drove through the community with a loudspeaker asking residents, "What has your White Jesus done for you today?"[25]

The Atlanta Project's militancy attracted some youthful supporters, but their organizing efforts were interrupted in August when ten staff members were arrested at a military induction center while protesting the drafting of SNCC worker Michael Simmons. The protesters were found guilty of misdemeanors a few days later and sentenced to thirty days in jail. Staff member Johnny Wilson was also charged with insurrection as a result of the incident.[26]

Ware and other staff members not arrested had difficulty rallying black support to raise bail money for the jailed workers. After black as well as white leaders condemned SNCC's role in the September racial violence in Atlanta, local residents assaulted project staff members and burned a leaflet stand belonging to the project. In a letter to Vine City Council members, Ware condemned "Judas Negroes" who he charged had been paid to attack SNCC, calling them "traitors" who were "betraying their own people." He added that the "good people of Vine City" had not "come forward to build back what the traitors destroyed."[27] Interestingly, the attacks against the Atlanta Project prompted a few previously critical council members to come to SNCC's defense.

The embattled stance of the Atlanta staff members prompted them to insist even more strongly that SNCC abandon its white ties despite the firm opposition of SNCC's leaders. Freddie Greene, a Dillard University graduate working in the Atlanta office, recalled that Robinson "maintained a strong nationalist line" but insisted that staff members demonstrate a willingness to work rather than "sit around talking about white people."[28] Separatists hoped for a final resolution of the "white" question as the staff gathered on December 1 for a meeting held on the New York estate of black entertainer "Peg Leg" Bates.

SNCC's officers had planned the meeting at the secluded resort to allow the staff to confront the problems caused by the black power controversy. Discussion of the role of whites was placed on the agenda but was expected to occupy only part of the first day of the meeting. During succeeding days planners hoped that discussions in a relaxed atmosphere might reverse the decline in SNCC's effectiveness. Although they reflected the desire of most staff members to solve SNCC's many problems, they seriously underestimated the emotional force of the arguments that the Atlanta separatists and their allies would present.

The majority of the approximately one hundred staff members at the meeting initially believed that it was unnecessary to expel whites, preferring instead to encourage them to organize white communities. Carmichael stated this view in his talk at the outset of the meeting, arguing that SNCC needed white financial support and a "buffer zone" of white liberals to forestall repression. Carmichael and other blacks criticized the Atlanta separatists for refusing to allow the staff to address other important issues until whites were expelled. Yet, though nearly all of SNCC's veteran leaders agreed with this view, the separatist forces were determined to press the issue and repeatedly interrupted the meeting demanding "whites had to go."[29]

Ware opened his prepared statement by asserting that he was "convinced that Black People and [SNCC] do not understand the concept of Black Power," because if they did, "there would be no white people in the organization at this time." He explained that if SNCC's staff "understood that the cats on the corner do not dig having white people in the organization then of course they'd have to get . . . white people out." He repeated with greater force the arguments from the Atlanta project's Spring position paper, claiming that white participation was "the biggest obstacle" in the path of "Black folks getting liberation." He added that SNCC's taking time to debate the issue was in itself an argument for the expulsion of whites, since "sensitive white people" would recognize the problems caused by their presence and leave voluntarily. "Those who don't understand that ought to be expelled."[30]

To the dismay of most SNCC officers, this debate continued for several days. The discussions were intensely emotional, particularly for the seven remaining white staff members. At one point Forman became so upset over the seemingly endless proceedings that he made a proposal to disband SNCC and send its remaining funds to the African liberation movements. He was particularly disturbed when a few black separatists ridiculed veteran staff member Fannie Lou Hamer, who opposed the expulsion of whites, by claiming that she was "no longer relevant" or not at their "level of development." The small group of white staff members at the meeting said little during the days of rancorous debate, and when Cordel Reagan finally moved the question, most did not participate in the vote. The staff passed a resolution excluding whites by a vote of nineteen for, eighteen against, with twenty-four abstaining. The remainder of the staff had either left the meeting or had gone to bed before the vote, which took place at about 2 A.M. Although only nineteen staff members voted against white participation, the separatist victory was made possible by the unwillingness of most staff members to resist an outcome that seemed inevitable. Jack Minnis recalled that he considered voting on the issue, but afterwards was relieved that he and other whites had abstained rather than providing the deciding votes against their own expulsion.[31] Immediately after the vote white staff members walked out of the meeting. Some blacks who remained felt a mixture of relief and regret about the expulsion of white activists who had dedictated much of their adult lives to SNCC. Communications worker Ethel Minor supported the decision to expel whites, but recalled feeling guilty after the vote. Referring to Bob Zellner she said, "Here was someone who had been on the front lines long before I came into the organization. No one wanted to look at Bob afterwards."[32]

Through their singleminded determination, the Atlanta Project staff dominated the December staff meeting, but ironically their effort to expel whites was followed soon afterward by their own expulsion. During subsequent months they continued to challenge the racial loyalty of SNCC's leaders and sought to undermine their authority. SNCC's officers finally took decisive action against the project when staff members refused to return a car belonging to SNCC. After repeated requests for the return of the car, Sellers and Carmichael reported the car to the police as missing. An enraged Ware wrote a telegram to Forman protesting the action. "Your hand-picked Chairman, the alleged hope of Black America, has descended to the level of calling a racist henchman cop of the white master Allen of Atlanta to settle an internal dispute between the supposedly black people of SNCC." Ware also menacingly alluded to Forman's marriage to a white ex-SNCC worker and added that he might release information damaging to Forman to the press.[33]

When Carmichael heard from Forman about Ware's telegram, he acted immediately to end the insubordination by firing or suspending all members of the Atlanta Project staff. Because the Atlanta Project staff had considerable support within SNCC, Carmichael and Sellers wrote a letter listing the reasons for their action.

Most of the Atlanta separatists remained in the city after they had been expelled, hoping that they could garner enough backing to reverse the decision at the next general staff meeting. Ware accepted the finality of the decision, however, recalling that he dissuaded other project staff members from taking weapons to a central committee meeting at which the firing of all staff members except Donald Stone was ratified.[34]

Even after the dismissal of the Atlanta separatists, SNCC was troubled by internal arguments. Indeed, the issue of white participation was not finally resolved until May 1967. Hoping that SNCC's staff would narrow the scope of the December decision on white participation, Zellner and his wife Dottie asked the Central Committee to approve their plan to organize whites in New Orleans and to be given full voting rights in SNCC. The Zellners' carefully worded statement argued that the committee should grant the request "not on the basis of our deep feelings about the years we have spent in SNCC, our length of service, what we feel to have been our contributions, and our emotional and personal ties." Instead they argued that SNCC should support the plan because a future coalition could not be achieved if white and black organizers were completely isolated from each other.[35]

Forman, along with a few other SNCC veterans, initially argued for the proposal, but he feared that an attempt to overturn the December decision might prompt some staff members to question the motives of SNCC's officers in firing the Atlanta Project staff. Sellers recalled that he and other SNCC veterans were ambivalent about the Zellners' request, since Bob "was one of the few whites who commanded the unqualified respect of everyone in the organization," and that he was, like Moses, "a special SNCC person." Yet, despite these feelings, Sellers did not want to reopen the debate over the role of whites, The Central Committee unanimously denied the request, although it agreed to provide materials to aid the Zellners' work. The decision was an important one for SNCC, but Sellers recalled that the staff members were "so harried . . . that most of us hardly had time to do more than shake our heads and wish that things had turned out differently."[36]

The internal conflicts and the continuous decline in SNCC's effectiveness did not prevent the organization from greatly influencing Afro-American political attitudes. Indeed, it was during the year of Carmichael's chairmanship that SNCC acquired unprecedented importance as a source of new political ideas. SNCC did not by itself change the direction of black politics, but it did reflect a decisive shift in the focus of black struggles from the rural South to the urban North and from civil rights reforms to complex, interrelated problems of poverty, powerlessness, and cultural subordination. Like the thousands of black students who were ready to join the sit-ins of 1960 even before the initial Greensboro protest, millions of black people were prepared to adopt the rhetoric of black power in order to express their accumulated anger and to assume new, more satisfying racial identities.

Nonetheless, SNCC's efforts to transform black discontent into programs for achieving black power were hampered by the controversy that Carmichael stimulated and by the increasingly obvious political and personal differences that existed within SNCC. As the organization entered a period in which racial violence would reach new levels of intensity, SNCC endured external attacks that exacerbated its internal conflicts. SNCC sought new sources of support both within the United States and abroad, but as it became more isolated from former white allies and more openly identified with uncontrollable urban black militancy, it encountered ruthless government repression. As staff members continued to build upon the insights contained in the 1966 black power rhetoric, the deadly attacks they faced in subsequent years ensured that their message would reach an ever-decreasing number of blacks.

# 16. WHITE REPRESSION

SNCC staff members welcomed the popularity of their controversial ideas among blacks. While not the cause of urban racial rebellions, Stokely Carmichael and other SNCC militants did formulate a political vocabulary that expressed the previously unarticulated anger of many blacks, particularly the young and urban poor. Carmichael's arguments for militant racial consciousness strongly appealed to blacks who wished to assume new racial identities reflecting their distinctive cultural heritage and their separateness from the dominant white society.

The growing popularity of the black power rhetoric was both an asset and a source of concern for the organization. On the one hand, SNCC organizers quickly gained support, especially among black students. Carmichael's speeches also dramatically increased SNCC's visibility in northern urban areas and opened new possibilities for political and financial support. On the other hand, SNCC's following among college students and ghetto residents was tenuous and ephemeral. The willingness of many blacks to express racial resentments through violence made SNCC workers targets for police repression. In a context of black urban rebellion and anti-war resistance, government officials used SNCC's brash public statements to justify extraordinary police surveillance and arbitrary arrests of staff members. The publicity given to these statements also further undermined white support for progressive racial reforms.

The selection of Hubert "Rap" Brown as SNCC's new chair was meant to reduce SNCC's vulnerability. But Brown, seeking to provide guidance for leaderless urban blacks, soon became as notorious among whites and moderate blacks as Carmichael had been. Brown and other SNCC workers suffered not only because of their own activities but because they were singled out as scapegoats for many of the black rebellions. The addition of SNCC to the FBI's Counterintelligence Program (COINTELPRO) during the summer of 1967 was part of a concerted effort at all levels of government to crush black militancy through overt and covert means and through the more subtle techniques of co-optation and timely concessions.

One of SNCC's major goals at the beginning of 1967 was to rebuild its support on southern black campuses, which once supplied SNCC with most of its personnel. Indeed campus affiliates had previously selected members of SNCC's governing executive committee. But by 1966 SNCC affiliates at Howard, Fisk, Atlanta University, and other colleges either had weakened or disappeared. Carmichael's emergence as a spokesman for black power revived black student activism and SNCC staff members moved to tap the youthful energy Carmichael had aroused. Like earlier SNCC organizers in the rural South, they encouraged blacks to demand greater control over institutions affecting their lives, to gain confidence in their ability to confront existing authority, and to lead their own struggles. SNCC workers soon realized that the students were readily mobilized around campus concerns, such as restrictive college regulations and the lack of black studies courses. Black students required little encouragement to become more militant during a period when academic institutions everywhere were under attack. Indeed, staff members discovered that, just as students often faced harassment as a result of their association with SNCC, the militancy of the autonomous campus groups increased SNCC's notoriety.

This pattern was illustrated after SNCC's Campus Coordinator George Ware came to Nashville in the fall of 1966 to build support at southern black colleges. An Alabama native who had become active in SNCC while a graduate student in chemistry at Tuskegee Institute during 1965, Ware began speaking in the classes of sympathetic faculty members and soon encouraged students at Fisk to form a SNCC support group. He also convinced some to go to Alabama to assist local leaders of the LCFO. Ware had a low-key manner and was conscious of the dangers of attracting too much attention to himself with SNCC at the center of a nationwide controversy over black power. He hoped his work in Nashville would serve as a model for surviving police harassment and other forms of repression.[1]

Critical of Carmichael's tendency to speak at northern, predominantly white colleges, Ware arranged a speaking tour early in 1967 for Carmichael that included visits to black campuses in Nashville and other southern cities. He also organized a black power conference seeking to attract students from Fisk and nearby Tennessee A. & I. State University. Ware soon encountered opposition from Fisk officials, however, and had to move the conference to the Chapel of Saint Anselm, an Episcopal student parish directed by Father James Woodruff, a black clergyman who became a strong SNCC supporter.[2]

The conference caused concern among Nashville police and FBI officials, who placed informants among SNCC's supporters in the city. The police interpretation of SNCC's role in Nashville demonstrated little understanding of its organizational structure or ideological orientation. Viewing SNCC as a hierarchical group in which plans were formulated by national leaders after consultation with Communists, police decided that SNCC had formulated a conspiracy to instigate violence in Nashville at the three-day black power conference in March, which attracted about seventy people, among them "outsiders" such as Carmichael, Sellers, Ricks, and Rap Brown. Carmichael spoke at the conference and then, according to police, "left some of his top aides to finish setting up Operation Nashville." At a subsequent meeting on April 4, members of the Nashville SNCC chapter allegedly were given "assignments" by unidentified persons to carry out this operation. The head of the chapter, Fred Brooks, a Tennessee State student, and Willie Ricks were also alleged to have been instructed to "teach the Negro children hatred for the whites telling them that the white man has done nothing for them." Another student, Andrea Felder, was supposed to have been assigned to teach others how to manufacture Molotov cocktails.[3]

According to the police version, Communists and Communist sympathizers were involved in SNCC's conspiracy. Students at the March conference were shown a "propaganda" film of war damage in North Vietnam and listened to former SNCC leader Diane Nash Bevel, who recently had made an unauthorized trip there. When Carmichael returned to Nashville early in April to take part in a Vanderbilt University symposium he met "secretly" with Carl and Anne Braden and other members of SCEF, described by police as a Communist front group and SNCC's "parent organization."[4]

The police version accorded SNCC influence over its local affiliates that it did not possess and certainly exaggerated SNCC's ties to SCEF, but it was consistent with the widespread fears that existed among whites regarding SNCC and black militancy. Although some SNCC staff members and student supporters in Nashville may indeed have made preparations for violence, the local SNCC chapter was mainly concerned with campus issues similar to those raised by black students elsewhere. SNCC's Nashville supporters undoubtedly varied in their attitudes toward violence, as did SNCC itself. Fred Brooks later testified under oath that neither he nor anyone he knew had planned to stimulate racial violence. "Had a riot been planned or anticipated by SNCC or any other civil rights organization in Nashville, I feel that I would have known about it, since my contacts are considerably closer than any contacts the police may have had with these groups," he told a Senate subcommittee.[5]

Nonetheless, Carmichael's speeches had created a climate of suspicion, especially among whites, toward SNCC and anyone associated with it. Shortly before Carmichael's planned appearance at Vanderbilt in April, the *Nashville Banner* urged Vanderbilt officials to bar him from campus, a stand supported by Veterans of Foreign Wars and American Legion posts. The police department had prepared an emergency riot plan and placed heavily armed squads of police on "standby, around the clock" on the morning of April 7, a day before Carmichael's Vanderbilt appearance.[6]

A few hours after Carmichael spoke at Vanderbilt, an unplanned incident took place at the University Inn, across the street from the Fisk University campus and a few doors from SNCC's chapter headquarters. Early in the evening, the inn's black proprietor called police to remove a black man he found to be offensive from the premises. Police removed the man but did not arrest him. Shortly thereafter they also expelled a black soldier at the proprietor's request and turned him over to military police. The first man proceeded to SNCC headquarters and convinced about a dozen students to set up a picket line at the inn to protest the actions of the proprietor. When protesters attracted a crowd, police on the scene stopped traffic from entering a nearby busy intersection where people were standing in the street. A few blacks including Leroy Wilson of SNCC attempted to defuse the situation, but by 9:30 P.M. the crowd, now containing between 350 and 500 people, had become increasingly hostile toward police and whites who happened to be present.[7]

By this time, police were allowing only city buses to pass the intersection and the attempted passage of one of these buses prompted the first violent incident of the evening. A pro-SNCC account reported that the bus driver "forced his way through" the crowd and that people in the intersection reacted by "booing the bus driver and the cops." When a policeman rushed into the street and fired several shots into the air, "enraged and confused" students "began to throw rocks and bottles at the cops, who began to move on them with the first shots." Riot squads called to the scene forced people into Fisk dormitories by beating them with clubs and firing shots that struck several students. A federal court later provided a somewhat different account. After the bus incident, "agitators ran up and down the area urging Negro policemen to leave their posts and to join the agitators, spitting upon the officers, using obscene and abusive language." When rocks were thrown at the police, the court reported that police dispersed the crowd, firing shots into the air. "Three students while on the Fisk campus were struck by stray bullets, but there was no intentional firing on any students or any other person in the crowds," the court found.[8]

Battles between blacks and police continued during that and subsequent nights, spreading to the area near the Tennessee State campus and to parts of north Nashville. Although the role of SNCC workers and supporters in igniting the violence was disputed, resentment against living conditions and antagonism toward police was obviously already present among large numbers of blacks in Nashville, as it was in other cities that experienced similar racial violence. Despite the fact that no leaders of the SNCC chapter were arrested on the first night of violence, police blamed SNCC for the outbreak.

Before the initial clash with police, Carmichael and George Ware quickly departed from the demonstration, as an FBI agent following Carmichael later confirmed. According to Ware, they recognized the potential for violence and decided to depart to avoid being blamed. Ware, Carmichael, and Ernest Stephens, an SNCC field secretary, left Nashville early in the morning of April 9 to accompany Carmichael on a speaking engagement in Knoxville. When they returned to Nashville the following night, Ware and Stephens decided to leave Carmichael at a safe location—"he was a hot package" Ware recalled—while they went to Fred Brooks' house to pick up SNCC literature to use in another speaking engagement in New Orleans.

Off-duty Nashville police patrolling the area spotted their car and arrested Ware and Stephens on a charge of inciting a riot. Police found two guns when they searched the car, one in a briefcase belonging to Carmichael, and added a charge of possessing weapons.[9]

Almost simultaneous to the arrest of Ware and Stephens, police raided SNCC's Nashville headquarters, arresting seven people, including Leroy Wilson and Andrea Felder. Police reported that someone inside the headquarters threw six Molotov cocktails out a window as they arrived but that no explosives were found in the house. They also reported that Felder's fingerprints were found on one of the Molotov cocktails.[10]

When compared with other outbreaks of urban racial violence or with the bloody rebellions that would occur later that year in Detroit, Newark, and other cities, the Nashville episode was a relatively minor affair. Police jailed ninety-four people in connection with the disturbances; seventy-three of those arrested were students. Nonetheless, Nashville authorities reacted with shocked outrage, most of it directed against SNCC. Nashville Mayor Beverly Briley blamed Carmichael for the violence. The president of Fisk University charged that SNCC's "outside agitators" spearheaded the violence. The Tennessee House of Representatives quickly adopted a resolution asking that Carmichael, a United States citizen, be deported. The Interdenominational Ministerial Alliance almost alone resisted the tendency to blame SNCC workers, arguing that "the real causes of the recent turmoil were in existence long before Carmichael was born."[11]

SNCC representatives claimed that police provoked the Nashville violence and transformed a peaceful demonstration into a violent confrontation. Later in the month, SNCC filed suit against Nashville officials, claiming that they had conspired to deprive SNCC staff members and supporters of their constitutional rights. They asked for an injunction against Nashville officials to prevent prosecution of Ware, Stephens and others associated with SNCC. The suit ultimately failed, but it did postpone the trials of those arrested. To demonstrate that they were not intimidated by the arrests SNCC leaders announced that Nashville would become one of their "project areas" for the summer of 1967.[12]

\* \* \*

SNCC supporters at Texas Southern University in Houston, like those in Nashville, faced strong opposition from university officials, who forbade the "Friends of SNCC" chapter from meeting on campus and refused to renew the contract of the faculty advisor of the group. During March 1967 a growing number of students became involved in protests to reverse these decisions, to upgrade the quality of the school's curriculum, and to eliminate the 9 P.M. curfew for female students. Early in April about 150 students chained and padlocked entrances to a university building, while hundreds of other students expressed their dissatisfaction by sitting down on a campus street. Soon after this protest, Houston police arrested two leaders of the protest movement. Both were charged with threatening to kill a police officer. Another member of the SNCC chapter, Lee Otis Johnson, was suspended from school and arrested after he led a student protest in the cafeteria. The arrests strengthened student discontent, forcing the University's president to ask that charges be dropped, although the Houston district attorney continued to press charges. Student discontent finally exploded on the evening of May 16. During a massive assault against student demonstrators, police fired several thousand rounds of ammunition into the campus dormitories. After re-establishing control of the campus, police searched and, according to some accounts, vandalized the rooms and possessions of students. They arrested 481 people. During the police assault, one student and two policemen were shot, one of whom died. Although subsequent investigations suggested that the dead policeman may have been shot accidentally by his fellow officers, five students, all active in the SNCC chapter, were charged with his murder. Charges against students detained in the mass arrest were soon dropped for lack of evidence, but the murder charges against "the T. S. U. Five" were dropped only after months of support rallies and public outcry.[13]

The bloodiest of the clashes between students and police occurred early in 1968 at South Carolina State College in Orangeburg. Almost a year earlier former SNCC Program Secretary Cleveland Sellers had gone to the campus, a few miles from his hometown, after students had organized a successful boycott of classes to protest paternalistic campus rules and the nonrenewal of contracts for three politically active, white teaching fellows. Sellers worked closely with students who had organized a militant counterpart to the campus NAACP chapter, the Black Awareness Coordinating Committee (BACC). Early in February 1968, when police attacked a group of students protesting near a bowling alley whose owner refused to admit blacks, Sellers offered tactical advice to the students proposing that they block traffic along a street adjacent to the campus. Although students rejected Sellers' advice, white officials generally assumed that he had stimulated the protests. Sellers' involvement with BACC members had already attracted police and FBI surveillance.

Student anger increased when city officials refused to respond to their various demands. On the night of February 7, frustrated students pelted cars with rocks and bottles and took part in other scattered acts of vandalism. The escalating strife in Orangeburg reached a climax the following day when police called for a firetruck to extinguish a bonfire started by the students for warmth during the chilly evening. Backed by National Guards, police began their reoccupation of the campus. When a policeman was struck by a banister post thrown by a retreating student, his fellow officers, thinking that he had been shot, began firing on the students, many of whom held up their hands or fell to the ground. Thirty-three black demonstrators were shot by police during the barrage of gunfire. Three died of their wounds.

Initial news accounts suggested that the students had been killed in an exchange of gunfire, although actually no one had fired at police. Subsequent statements by city and state officials blamed Sellers, who was wounded during the incident. Henry Lake, the governor's official spokesman in Orangeburg, incorrectly claimed that it was Sellers who had thrown the banister that had injured the police officer. "He's the main man," Lake pronounced. "He's the biggest nigger in the crowd."[14] Sellers was later arrested and indicted on charges of inciting the riot, but he was never brought to trial. After a federal investigation of "the Orangeburg Massacre," nine members of the state patrol were indicted but later acquitted on a federal charge of depriving demonstrators of their constitutional rights.

The violence associated with attempts by SNCC members and supporters to instill a new militant consciousness among black students was only partly related to SNCC's black power rhetoric. Though some SNCC staff members were prepared by 1967 to use force to achieve their goals and to provoke violent clashes with police, their role in fomenting violence on college campuses was greatly exaggerated, for similar clashes occurred on campuses where they were not present. SNCC reflected rather than created the tide of black student militancy that would reach numerous campuses during the late 1960s. Police reaction to black student protest can be explained only by the climate of fear created by negative news articles on the meaning of the black consciousness phenomenon, by the stubborn insistence of police officials that student protest could be suppressed through the arrest of identifiable black militant leaders, and by white authorities' lack of concern for the safety and rights of black students.

The violent suppression of black student protest did not occur in a vacuum: black college campuses were a microcosm of American society. These campuses actually offered a relatively simple and benign environment for

SNCC organizers when compared to the complexities and dangers faced by other SNCC workers involved in the massive urban revolts of 1967.

Carmichael recognized the special risks associated with his highly visible role and SNCC's vulnerability during a period of extensive racial conflict. By the time of SNCC's annual staff meeting in the spring of 1967, he was eager to relinquish the chair. Staff members were then faced with finding someone capable of expressing the angry mood of urban blacks and of avoiding the role of scapegoat for the spreading black rebellion.

The excitement and camaraderie that once existed at SNCC gatherings was noticeably missing at the annual staff meeting in Atlanta. The remaining seventy-six staff members realized that affiliation with SNCC had acquired new meaning during the previous year, as arrests in Philadelphia, Atlanta, Nashville, and elsewhere demonstrated. Some staff members were themselves facing serious legal difficulties. By this time, most of the sixteen SNCC workers who had been drafted had decided to refuse induction, thereby risking a prison term. Only days before the staff meeting, Sellers had been indicted by a federal grand jury for refusing to submit to induction.[15] Ethel Minor recalled that the increasing risks associated with SNCC affiliation brought the staff close to a state of paranoia. The bitterness exhibited at the previous annual meeting was still evident when the staff was asked to ratify the decision to fire the Atlanta Project staff. Although the outcome of the vote was not in doubt, a member of the Atlanta staff, who had recently been released from jail, lambasted those who had betrayed his project and the cause of "blackness," charging that they had fallen under Forman's control. His outburst established a tone of hostility that permeated the rest of the meeting.[16]

Uncertain about SNCC's future direction or its long-term existence, staff members realized that SNCC's projects were in dire shape and that a period of circumspection and rebuilding was necessary. Most wanted to replace Carmichael with someone less likely to attract the attention of the press. Carmichael himself admitted that he may have taken SNCC "further than it wanted to go" with his speeches but explained that this was a "trap" for anyone who would take the chair since the staff had established no guidelines for its officers.[17] Staff members accepted the validity of Carmichael's comments but hoped nonetheless that they could find a leader who could remain sufficiently removed from the center of controversy to allow the organization to resolve its internal problems and to establish its bases of future support. Some believed that Ruby Doris Robinson could fulfill this role, but she had become debilitated with a rare form of cancer that would end her life in a few months. Other SNCC veterans such as Forman were exhausted by the demands placed on them during previous years. Most staff members also believed that the next chairperson should be someone who reflected SNCC's new urban emphasis rather than its roots in the southern protest movement. After considerable discussion, the staff chose a little known member of the Alabama field staff, Rap Brown, as the new chairman.

Born in Baton Rouge, Brown had spent most of his life in Louisiana, where his father worked for many years for a petroleum company. He did not become deeply involved in campus protest activities while attending Southern University. His political and intellectual acumen was still undeveloped when he traveled to Washington, D.C. in the summer of 1962 to visit his brother, Ed, who was a leader of NAG. Rap Brown was impressed with the political awareness of NAG members, recalling that they "talked some heavy shit and I could just catch some of the things they were saying 'cause I hadn't read all the books."[18]

Unlike previous SNCC chairmen, Brown acquired his views during a period when black activists were turning toward independent political activity and urban organizing. His involvement in the black struggle in Cambridge, Maryland during 1963 increased his awareness of the economic concerns that would become a major focus of the civil rights movement. He did not take part in civil rights efforts in the deep South until 1964 when he worked on a voter registration campaign in Holmes County, Mississippi. Following that summer, Brown decided not to finish his senior year in college and returned instead to Washington, where he continued to work with NAG, eventually becoming its chairman. During this period he acquired his nickname which derived from his ability to "rap" with poor black people. "His way of speaking, his whole style, has a grass-roots quality that gave him mass appeal," Jim Forman later wrote. As a NAG leader, he stressed the need for black college students to "identify with the brothers in the street" and "to begin to legitimatize the [street] brother's actions— begin to articulate his position, because the college student has the skills that the blood doesn't have."[19] When he became a full-time SNCC worker early in 1966, Brown went to Greene County, Alabama to help establish an independent black party modeled on the LCFO. A relatively new addition to the staff at the time of the 1967 annual staff meeting, some veteran staff members still thought of him as the "little brother" of Ed Brown, who had been a staff member much longer.

All officers chosen in 1967 were individuals whom the staff felt would exercise restraint in public statements and emphasize the development of effective urban programs. Robinson was replaced as executive secretary by Stanley Wise, a twenty-four year old North Carolina native who, like Brown, had been a leader of NAG during his years as a Howard University student. During 1964 Wise gained urban organizing experience working in the Cambridge movement. After joining SNCC's staff that same year, he became southern campus organizer and then worked closely with Forman,

Ivanhoe Donaldson, and later Carmichael, to evaluate and coordinate the work of the field staff. Ralph Featherstone, a former elementary school speech teacher, became SNCC's new program secretary, replacing Sellers. Featherstone came to Mississippi in 1964 to teach in the freedom schools and eventually became their coordinator. He also served as director of COFO's project in Noshoba County. Almost twenty-eight at the time of his election, Featherstone had gained the respect of other staff members through his quiet militancy and his forceful yet undogmatic advocacy of staff discipline.

The new officers attempted to establish the future tone for the organization in their initial contacts with reporters, who were barred from the meeting. They suggested that there should be fewer public speeches by SNCC leaders in the future. "SNCC is moving from rhetoric to program," Brown stated soon after the staff meeting. He announced that SNCC's main objective was to build Freedom Parties concerned with more than electoral politics. "The Freedom Organizations must be looked to by black people as a source of jobs, power and freedom." He confirmed that SNCC would continue its anti-draft activities, extending them to reach high school students. Featherstone added that greater emphasis would be placed on the goal of "establishing economic control by the black communities."[20]

Brown was doubtless sincere in his initial desire to avoid unnecessary controversy. After his first press conference, *Newsweek* confidently reported that Brown was "far less assured as an orator" than Carmichael "and far less flammable." Brown's wish to limit his contacts with white reporters was juxtaposed with an awareness of the inevitability of press coverage and its often useful role in building SNCC's support among blacks. In quieter times Brown might have avoided major controversy, but the year that he assumed the SNCC chair was one of exceptional social turmoil. Also Brown was less calculating, self-controlled, and purposely ambiguous in his public speeches than Carmichael had been and therefore less able than his predecessor to manipulate the press. Carmichael was probably more aware than Brown of the dangers that awaited the next national symbol of black militancy. At Brown's initial press conference, he remained in the background, telling reporters only that they would have to begin taking their "pop shots" at the new chair. "He'll take care of you all—he's a *bad* man," Carmichael bantered.[21]

Brown's attitude toward violence was predictably of major concern to the press. When asked at a San Francisco press conference about his opinion of that state's newly formed Black Panther Party for Self-Defense, Brown reasserted SNCC's position that black people had a right to defend themselves. But he added that "if black people are organized, they can seize power politically. At this point we are against the use of arms." Despite this cautious public stance, Brown's strong personal views regarding weapons and violence were shaped more by his own experiences than by political beliefs. He accepted the fact that nonviolent tactics were "correct at one time in order to get some sympathy for the Movement, but for me as an individual, [nonviolence] just never worked." Having hunted with his father, Brown, like other SNCC organizers in the rural South, often carried a gun for protection. In 1966 he was arrested in Alabama on a charge of carrying a concealed weapon and was disturbed that SNCC did not post his bond. "They could put me out of the organization," he later wrote, "but they weren't taking my gun . . . The only thing 'the man's' going to respect is that .45 or .38 you got."[22]

Brown believed that armed self-defense was necessary since more extensive racial violence was inevitable and he knew that unarmed blacks would lose in battles with heavily armed police and military forces. Even while SNCC's staff meeting was taking place, Ben Brown, a young black man who had worked with SNCC was killed when police fired into a crowd of demonstrators in Jackson, Mississippi. SNCC staff members went to the scene and urged students to defend themselves. Rap Brown later commented that SNCC workers felt that America was "headed toward a race war" and that SNCC's responsibility was "to make black people aware of this." In an oft-repeated phrase, he said that "if America chooses to play Nazis, black folks ain't going to play Jews."[23]

A few weeks after his election, Brown and other SNCC staff members exhibited their tendency to react impulsively when their militancy was challenged. They learned that Carmichael had been arrested in front of a church in Prattville, Alabama, for his refusal to stop shouting "black power." Black residents protested outside the jail where Carmichael was being held and later exchanged gunfire with local whites, including members of the Ku Klux Klan. During the following night, a white mob trapped Wise and a group of black residents in a house, and SNCC workers elsewhere heard rumors that Carmichael had been lynched. The following morning, after Wise and other black leaders were arrested and charged with inciting the violence, state police and National Guardsmen sent by Governor Lurleen Wallace assumed control of the Prattville black community, searching residents' homes and assaulting those who resisted. Later that day, Brown called a press conference to warn that SNCC would "no longer sit back and let black people be killed by murderers who hide behind sheets or behind the badge of the law." He described the incident as "a declaration of war" by "racist white America" and called "for full retaliation from the black community across America." Brown's statement was merely emotional bluster, however, for SNCC no longer was able to mobilize blacks to respond. "At another time in its history, SNCC would have flooded Prattville with organizers prepared to break the will of the white community," Cleveland Sellers noted. "Unfortunately, we were no longer in a position to launch such a campaign." SNCC was forced to use normal legal channels to gain the release of those arrested.[24]

A few days later, Brown attracted press attention when he arrived in Atlanta soon after police had killed one black man and wounded three others during a riot. While Ricks was announcing that SNCC militants in Atlanta would "make Vietnam look like a holiday," Brown reportedly stated at a press conference, "We came here to blow Atlanta up." He condemned black youngsters who had formed a youth patrol to keep order in the black community, saying that "any Negroes caught out there serving as patrol members will be dealt with as traitors."[25] SNCC workers did not participate in the Atlanta violence, but the eagerness of Carmichael, Ricks and Brown to offer support to violent blacks demonstrated their desire to become spokesmen for a nation-wide black rebellion over which they had little control. Despite their awareness of the consequences of their rhetoric, SNCC militants refused to allow the threat of external attacks to prevent them from carrying out their self-assigned role of preparing blacks for an impending racial revolution.

The most controversial incident involving Brown occurred after he accepted an invitation from the Cambridge Action Federation, composed of former members of SNCC's affiliate in Cambridge and black youngsters who were angered by the recent upsurge in anti-black activities by members of the Ku Klux Klan and the States Rights Party. Against a background of news reports of black guerilla warfare in Detroit, Brown made a forty-minute speech on July 25 to several hundred black residents. The speech repeated the themes of racial pride and racial assertiveness that were characteristic of Carmichael's speeches, but Brown went further than Carmichael in urging his listeners to take up arms against white society. "If America don't come around, we going burn it down, brother," he cried. "We are going to burn it down if we don't get our share of it." He warned that black people were faced with genocide as a result of poor living conditions and the drafting of young blacks to fight in Vietnam. He told blacks to take over white-owned stores. "You got to own some of them stores. I don't care if you have to burn him down and run him out." He also advised blacks to prevent whites from coming into their community. "Whenever you decide to fight the man, take it to his battleground. It's one thing that man respects. It's money. That's his god. When you tear down his store you hit his religion."[26]

No violence occurred during Brown's speech, but about an hour afterward gunshots were exchanged between black residents and police. According to police, Brown led a group of rioters to Cambridge's business district where they burned and looted stores. A black elementary school that Brown had derided as inferior to white schools was also burned. Brown claimed that he did not participate in the night of violence but had been

wounded by police as he was walking a woman home. He received medical
attention for his minor injury and left Cambridge early in the morning. By
this time, seventeen buildings had been damaged or destroyed, and recently elected governor Spiro T. Agnew sent the National Guard to the
city.[27]

Previously, Agnew had a reputation as a liberal. He had been elected
with considerable black support, and had supported new state civil rights
laws, but his response to the Cambridge violence signaled a change in his
political orientation. The following day he toured the black community
and charged that Brown was responsible for the destruction. "I hope they
pick him up soon, put him away and throw away the key," Agnew remarked.[28]

That Brown had already left the state proved no impediment for Maryland authorities. With no evidence that Brown himself had participated in
the burning of buildings in Cambridge, he was charged with arson and the
FBI entered the case. Believing that his life was endangered as the object of
a nationwide search, Brown arranged through an attorney close to SNCC,
William Kunstler, to surrender in New York. FBI officials denied making a
deal for Brown's surrender and arrested him at the Washington airport as
he attempted to board a plane bound for New York. Brown was taken to
the Alexandria, Virginia courthouse, where federal charges against him
were then dropped so that he could be rearrested for extradition to Maryland. Before being released on bond, he issued a statement declaring that
America stood "on the eve of a black revolution." Brown said that the
black masses were "fighting the enemy tit-for-tat" and that "neither imprisonment nor threats of death" would deter him. At a Washington, D.C.
press conference the following day he was even more aggressive in his rhetoric, calling President Johnson a "white honky cracker, an outlaw from
Texas" and charging that his arrest was the result of a conspiracy involving
Johnson, state authorities, and FBI director J. Edgar Hoover "to discredit
my organization and shift the blame for all the rioting from L. B. J. to
me."[29]

Within days of his release on bail, more charges were filed against
Brown. City officials in Dayton, Ohio charged him with "advocating criminal syndicalism" during an appearance that preceded a two-day outbreak
of rioting. Brown added to his legal troubles when he bought a rifle prior to
a visit to his family in Louisiana. Believing that he could exercise his right
to own such a weapon while under constant surveillance, he dutifully registered the gun in his name and gave it to an airplane stewardess when he
flew from New York to New Orleans and back. Unfortunately for Brown,
precisely at the time of his trip, a jury in Maryland was indicting him on
the charge of inciting to arson in the Cambridge violence. After arriving
back in New York, agents of the Alcohol and Tobacco Division of the Jus-

tice Department arrested Brown and charged him with violating a little-known law that makes it illegal to carry a gun across a state line while under indictment. Brown was held on a $25,000 bond and sent to New Orleans for arraignment. After he posted bond, a federal judge restricted his movements to the area under the jurisdiction of the federal court in New York City.[30]

The legal actions taken against Rap Brown decreased his ability to attract the support of urban blacks, but these actions had far greater significance than was immediately apparent in the summer of 1967. They established a pattern for the subsequent suppression of highly-publicized radical leaders. Brown encouraged alienated young blacks to rebel against white authority, but he also became a symbol for millions of white people who were prepared to strike out against the visible symbols of black militancy. Rather than building a strong black revolutionary force capable of overthrowing the established social order, Brown became an issue in the struggle between liberal and conservative factions of that order. The summer of 1967 revealed the power of black people to gain national attention through unfocused expressions of rage. The summer also revealed that a year of talk about black power had left SNCC militants more powerless than ever.

In 1964 Charles Sherrod wrote that SNCC workers still had "a little time before the giant awakens"; by the summer of 1967, their time had run out. Without fully understanding the consequences, SNCC willingly relinquished the undependable but nonetheless vital buffer of white liberal support that previously had restrained its opposition. Staff members' long-established tendency to publicly and forthrightly express their views regardless of the costs brought them closer to potential allies in black ghettoes and in the Third World, while also strengthening the hand of their critics in Congress and prompting more vigorous repression by the FBI. SNCC had survived attacks by southern sheriffs, but its existence was far more seriously threatened by opponents with access to the enormous power of the federal government. The effectiveness of local efforts to destroy SNCC chapters and to imprison individual SNCC activists was enhanced by the support local and state authorities received from federal agencies and national political leaders.

SNCC's strongest opposition at the national level still came from southern white Congressmen, many of whom had invariably opposed the organization, but who now had the support of many northern politicians who did not now wish to be associated publicly with black militancy. While many southern Democrats and conservative Republicans pressed for a national campaign to forcefully crush black militancy, other representatives urged support for social reform programs that would undermine black support for more radical alternatives. Thus, SNCC workers faced not only the iron

fist of repression but the velvet glove of co-optation and limited concessions.

Congressional debate on legislation that proposed to make the crossing
of state lines to incite riots a federal crime revealed the increasing ability of
conservative politicians to strengthen their popular support at the expense
of liberals over the issue of black militancy. During the House debate on
the anti-riot bill, southern Democrats proclaimed that Communists were
behind the violence. Gerald R. Ford, the House Republican leader, supported the conspiracy theory, asserting that Carmichael was the chief con-
spirator. The Republican Congressional Committee attacked President
Johnson for "unpardonable vacillation, indecision and even indifference"
in handling racial violence. Most Democrats were unwilling to appear
"soft" on the issue, and the House overwhelmingly passed the anti-riot
measure on July 19.[31]

Conservatives continued to hold the initiative when the anti-riot bill was
taken up early in August by the Senate Judiciary Committee, chaired by
Mississippi Democrat and plantation owner James O. Eastland. The initial
witnesses were police officials who generally urged the Senate to pass the
anti-riot bill, and they set the tone for the hearings. The Cambridge police
chief blamed Rap Brown for the violence that had occurred the previous
month in his city. The Cincinnati chief of police claimed that Carmichael's presence had ignited the rioting in his city. Captain John A. Sorace
of the Nashville police department asserted that SNCC workers had not
only played major roles in the violent outbreak in April but also mentioned
Carmichael's meetings with leaders of SCEF, which Eastland quickly identified as "a Communist organization." After making these charges, Sorace
suddenly announced that the Office of Economic Opportunity (OEO), the
federal anti-poverty agency, had given a grant to SNCC. Sorace claimed
that Fred Brooks, the head of SNCC's Nashville Office, had been given federal funds to conduct a "liberation school." He added that although the
ostensible purpose of the school was to teach young blacks about Afro-
American history, its actual function would be to teach "hatred for the
white man."[32]

Sorace's charges, which immediately became front-page news throughout the nation, brought into public view simmering conflicts between liberals and conservatives regarding both the usefulness and the administration
of federal anti-poverty programs. Although SNCC distrusted Johnson's
motives, there was much in the initial orientation of some of the early anti-
poverty programs that seemed to incorporate the democratic values inherent in SNCC's own projects. OEO officials were required by law to encourage "maximum feasible participation of the poor." Those who were conscientious in fulfilling this requirement often decided to recruit former civil
rights activists to undertake the task of mobilizing poor people to demand

services from local governments and to participate in the administration of programs established on their behalf. Civil rights activists typically were incorrigible employees, but some anti-poverty program administrators assumed the risk of hiring them, hoping that the activists could prove effective in reaching the more numerous legions of poor blacks who were even less corrigible and more threatening to the social order. Some former SNCC activists received substantial federal funds through private anti-poverty organizations which they helped establish. As an administrator of the Nashville anti-poverty agency told members of the Judiciary committee, officials had taken a "calculated risk" in hiring militants "to keep Nashville cool during the summer of 1967." He explained that the hiring of militants was part of a "rehabilitation" effort.[33]

Anti-poverty officials retreated quickly when confronted with congressional criticisms of the "hate school" they were alleged to have funded. The Rev. J. Paschall Davis, the surprised and embarrassed head of the Metropolitan Action Commission (MAC), quickly flew to Washington to deny that SNCC had been given federal funds or that Brooks had been hired, although he conceded that Brooks' application for the position of director of the summer program was under consideration. Davis' testimony was contradicted shortly afterward by the press. Meanwhile, Brooks added to the controversy at a news conference called to deny that the school would be used to teach hate when he readily admitted that black youngsters would be taught to protect themselves—"if a white man puts his hand on you, kill him before God gets the news."[34]

Soon after Davis' testimony, MAC reversed its earlier approval of the program. Brooks announced that the school would continue to operate in a Nashville city park although initially the City Parks Commission refused to grant a permit. Later in August, during a class at the park, George Ware reportedly applauded the recent Detroit black rebellion as "very good for the cause of black people" and announced that blacks would "burn this country to the ground" if they did not gain control of their communities. He was soon arrested and charged with sedition, although a grand jury later cleared him of the charges. Only in November, after many months of negative publicity, was Brooks able to answer criticisms when he testified before the Senate's Permanent Subcommittee on Investigations. Brooks denied that anyone connected with the school had participated in the April disturbance or that black students were taught to hate the white race, but he did not soften his own militant views. He was questioned relentlessly by the subcommittee's chairman, Senator John L. McClellan of Arkansas. At one point, Brooks told McClellan that he considered most whites his enemies. But he added that some of his best friends were white. "Don't include me," McClellan interjected. "I would not," Brooks replied. When McClellan asked Brooks to comment on Brown's statement that violence was as

"American as cherry pie," Brooks noted that the Vietnam War was "not being fought on love and morality." McClellan snapped, "I did not ask you about Vietnam."[35]

A few weeks before Brooks testified, a "Friends of SNCC" chapter in Houston became involved in a similar controversy. As in Nashville, the alleged role of chapter members in provoking campus violence during the spring prompted a federal inquiry that soon focused on the involvement of SNCC workers in anti-poverty programs. The Houston example reveals even more clearly the double-edged response to black militancy that occurred in many cities during the late 1960's. While some SNCC supporters encountered continued police surveillance and harassment after the spring of 1967, others were being recruited as employees of a federal Community Action Program (CAP) funded by the OEO and designed to prevent racial violence in the Houston area. According to later testimony by a poverty program official, the funds were earmarked "to actively involve the dissenters, the agitators, troublemakers, and the militants in constructive activities." The official noted that the hiring was timed to coincide with the trial of Muhammad Ali, who had refused induction into military service. OEO officials succeeded in recruiting ten "hard core 'Friends of SNCC' " and sixteen "sympathizers" to work as recreation guides. This attempt at co-optation did not entirely succeed, since some of those on the OEO payroll continued to agitate for black power. Ultimately, Congressional pressure forced the resignation of the director of the program, and the militants he had recruited were fired.[36]

An irony of the attempts by poverty program officials to channel the militancy of black activists by bringing them into reform institutions was that it could only work in instances where those involved had not gained notoriety for their militancy. A number of former SNCC staff members did manage to work in federally funded urban programs during this period, but for those who remained on the staff through the summer of 1967 such options were rarely available.

SNCC workers accepted the stigma that their association with SNCC brought. They knew that they were far more likely to encounter repression than co-optation as racial conflict intensified, but they could only imagine the lengths federal authorities would go to crush black radicalism. This would only be revealed years after the death of SNCC, when government repression was directed at liberal forces that were closer than SNCC to the political center and more able to fight back effectively.

Police actions against local SNCC chapters lessened the organization's chances of building durable bases of support, but SNCC's viability as a national organization was more seriously threatened by the increasing hostility of federal agencies, particularly the FBI. SNCC's relations with the Bureau always had been characterized by mutual suspicion. Workers publicly criticized the FBI for its cozy relationships with southern police and for its failure to protect civil rights workers. As early as 1964 SNCC had criticized FBI director J. Edgar Hoover for directing public attention away from the issue of black oppression in the South by suggesting that Communists had infiltrated the civil rights movement. Hoover continued to emphasize Communist infiltration, despite a paucity of evidence, just as he later suggested that SNCC militants, no matter how few, could control large numbers of pliable blacks.

When Hoover testified before a House appropriations subcommittee early in 1967, he modified his previous theme of Communist Party subversion by asserting that Stokely Carmichael had "been in frequent contact with Max Stanford, field chairman of the Revolutionary Action Movement (RAM), a highly secret all Negro, Marxist-Leninist, Chinese Communist-oriented organization which advocates guerilla warfare to obtain its goals." Carmichael and Stanford had known each other as teenagers in Harlem and both were products of the black student protest movement, but the implication that Stanford exercised a sinister influence over Carmichael missed the mark. Actually, RAM's influence within SNCC had been greatest among Atlanta Project separatists who were drawn to RAM's black nationalist rhetoric and who were engaged in a bitter struggle with Carmichael and other SNCC leaders at the time of Hoover's testimony.[37]

Hoover did not single out SNCC for inclusion in the FBI's Counterintelligence Program (COINTELPRO) until 1967, but concerted FBI surveillance of SNCC's activities had begun several years before. As early as October 1960 the FBI was receiving reports on SNCC meetings. The FBI's interest in SNCC increased in 1964, when FBI field offices began writing regular reports on the extent of Communist involvement in SNCC and its northern support groups. The FBI investigation intensified after southern newspaper articles asserted that Communists were involved in SNCC demonstrations in Atlanta. In March 1964 the FBI's Atlanta office wrote a report suggesting, erroneously, that a black woman sent from Philadelphia by the Communist Party had become SNCC's third in command—after Lewis and Forman. In 1965 Hoover received permission from Attorney General Nicholas Katzenbach to institute wiretaps on SNCC's phones.[38]

None of the FBI reports during the period from 1964 to 1967 presented evidence that any member of SNCC's staff was or had been a member of the Communist Party. Instead these reports simply asserted that individuals deemed to be subversive supported SNCC's activities and that SNCC personnel participated in events sponsored by leftist groups. After several years of investigation, an FBI study distributed in August 1967 admitted that, although SNCC did not exclude anyone because of his or her political background, "communists are not known to have gained any national leadership positions in SNCC to date." The study could cite only a few instances of local penetration, such as a communist in Los Angeles who was reported to have "worked on the SNCC publication in that city." In addition, the report stated that SNCC and the Communist Party "frequently cooperate in protest demonstrations and in exchanging speakers and sharing public platforms" and that "individuals with communist backgrounds" participated in the Mississippi Summer Project of 1964. SNCC was linked tenuously to the "Communist controlled" W. E. B. DuBois Clubs of America through the group's chairman, Franklin Alexander, a participant in the Texas Southern demonstrations. The "Trotskyite" Socialist Workers Party and its youth group, the Young Socialist Alliance, were said to have "collaborated" with SNCC by participating in "fund-raising ventures such as collecting trading stamps and holding a dinner." SNCC's ties with the SDS were demonstrated by the appearances of Featherstone and Cobb at SDS meetings.[39]

Such slim evidence of subversive influences in SNCC was apparently not sufficient, prior to 1967, to justify including SNCC in the FBI's counterintelligence program, created in 1956 to harass the Communist Party.[40] Only after the numerous black urban rebellions of 1967 did the FBI begin to use disruptive and often illegal tactics against militant black groups such as SNCC. Shortly after Hoover appeared on August 1, 1967 before the National Advisory Commission on Civil Disorders to condemn Carmichael, Brown, King, and McKissick as "vociferous firebrands," he ordered his subordinates to include SNCC militants and members of other organizations on a "Rabble Rouser Index." Persons on the index would become primary targets of the FBI's COINTELPRO.[41]

On August 25, Hoover ordered FBI field offices to begin a new effort "to expose, disrupt, misdirect, discredit, or otherwise neutralize the activities of black nationalist, hate-type organizations and groupings, their leadership, spokesmen, membership and supporters, and to counter their propensity for violence and civil disorder." Among the groups selected for "intensified attention" in this extension of COINTELPRO were the Deacons for Defense and Justice, Nation of Islam, CORE, SCLC, RAM, and SNCC. "No opportunity should be missed to exploit through counterintelligence techniques the organizational and personal conflicts of the leaderships of the groups and where possible an effort should be made to capitalize upon existing conflict between competing black nationalist organizations," the memorandum continued. FBI offices were instructed to "establish" the "unsavory backgrounds" of "key agitators" to discredit them and were reminded that the projects were to be kept secret and that no actions were to be initiated without prior Bureau authorization. "You are urged to take an enthusiastic and imaginative approach to this new counterintelligence endeavor and the Bureau will be pleased to entertain any suggestions or techniques you may recommend," the memorandum concluded.[42]

As the FBI expanded its counterintelligence program to control black militancy, it increased its surveillance of the activities of Carmichael, Brown and other SNCC staff members throughout the country. The FBI also worked closely with local police agencies, exchanging intelligence information with them. Captain Sorace of the Nashville police department testified, for example, that his department's files were open to the FBI. "We give all information that we feel they are interested in [regarding black militants] to them, and we deal with them almost daily," he commented.[43] By 1968 SNCC staff members and black militants had begun to face increasingly ruthless opposition from many sources. This opposition was not based simply on their actions but on their organizational ties and radical reputations.

An FBI memorandum written on February 29, 1968, bluntly stated the Bureau's intentions regarding "militant black nationalists." It announced that the goals of COINTELPRO were "to prevent the coalition of militant black nationalist groups, prevent the rise of a leader who might unify and electrify these violence-prone elements, prevent these militants from gaining respectability and prevent the growth of these groups among America's youth." To indicate the kind of activities FBI offices might undertake, the memorandum cited the tactics used the previous summer against RAM, a black militant group in Philadelphia. The group's leaders were "arrested on every possible charge until they could no longer make bail" and "as a result [the leaders] spent most of the summer in jail and no violence traceable to [the group] took place." The memo suggested that Rap Brown or Stokely Carmichael might become the " 'messiah' who could unify and electrify the militant black nationalist movement." The long-range goals of COINTELPRO were not only to prevent a coalition of militant black groups and violence on their part, but also to stop them "from gaining respectability," by discrediting them in "the responsible Negro community . . . the white community . . . and in the eyes of Negro radicals, the followers of the movement."[44]

This FBI memorandum indicated the agency's concern that black militant leaders would unite to give the urban black revolts the leadership they lacked. Yet the notion that the black struggle required a messiah or depended on organizations was one that contradicted the values that had once prevailed in SNCC. Hoover had consistently viewed black militancy as a result of the influence of leaders such as King, while paying less attention to the more radical SNCC activists. Not until SNCC abandoned its southern bases and shifted its focus from community organizing to speechmaking and alliance-building did it become a major target for COINTELPRO and other covert government programs.

Believing that Carmichael had the "necessary charisma" to be the new black messiah, the FBI concentrated on exploiting the tensions that existed between SNCC's former chairman and its current leadership and on undermining Carmichael's influence outside SNCC. FBI agents sought in particular to plant in the minds of SNCC staff and urban blacks the idea that Carmichael was motivated simply by a desire for power and wealth. Bureau officials tried to publicize reports that Carmichael and his wife were considering the purchase of an expensive home in Washington, D.C., for example, but these efforts ended when Carmichael failed to purchase such a home. On another occasion, FBI agents were encouraged to discredit Carmichael by spreading the rumor that he was a CIA agent. These and the more threatening FBI projects that would follow in 1968 and 1969 displayed the gradual loosening of legal restraints on the FBI as black militant rhetoric became linked with urban racial violence.[45] Ironically, however, SNCC workers encountered more government repression as they became less able to mobilize large numbers of blacks for sustained militant political action. Though they greatly expanded the range of their activities, many staff members abandoned the insights gained from earlier SNCC efforts to convince blacks that they could formulate their own political goals and create their own local institutions to respond to their needs.

Not always aware of the extent to which their new activities marked a crucial departure from the values on which SNCC had been built, staff members saw government interest in their activities as a measure of their importance and certainly of their radicalism. "What was surfacing was that we were revolutionaries, which meant that we actually had crossed the line of what we knew to be acceptable in this country," Ethel Minor recalled. Many staff members were not convinced, however, that they were prepared for the impending battles. "Neither this country nor this world is big enough for revolutionaries and reactionary forces," Julius Lester warned in 1967. "One has to be eliminated. The government's determination that we are the ones to be eliminated, by any means necessary, should never be underestimated."[46]

# 17. SEEKING NEW ALLIES

SNCC staff members encountered intense criticism during 1967 resulting from their ascribed role in urban racial violence and from their relationships with non-white radical groups in the United States and Third World revolutionary movements abroad. Reacting to the rapid decline in white support, SNCC attempted to transform the Afro-American struggle into an international movement against Western imperialism and capitalism. SNCC's ambitious ventures into foreign affairs were part of a gradual movement away from the organization's ideological roots in American pacifism and religious radicalism toward an international perspective based on secular ideologies of race and class.

SNCC's new perspective was revealed in its resistance to American involvement in Vietnam, trips to Third World nations, public expressions of solidarity with foreign radical and revolutionary groups, and the adoption by some staff members of Pan-Africanist or Marxian doctrines. SNCC's gradually expanding range of concerns had once placed it close to predominantly white New Left organizations. Now many SNCC workers suspected that alliances with American whites were improbable and unappealing, given the absence of significant white support for radical social change and the need for blacks to break with white-dominated racial reform movements and to determine their own future political course.

While most staff members agreed that American capitalism should be drastically changed or overturned, they usually stressed the overriding importance of racial rather than class struggle. Thus, during Carmichael's 1967 tour of Third World nations, he portrayed Afro-American urban rebellions as part of the international socialist movement but also suggested that they essentially were reactions to racial rather than class oppression. Carmichael's increasing emphasis on racial struggle prompted another group of staff members, led by Jim Forman, to insist that class analysis must remain a central aspect of black political strategy. SNCC's attempt to form an alliance with the most promising of potential domestic allies, the California-based Black Panther Party for Self Defense (BPP), brought these factional conflicts into the open.

Although severely weakened by police repression, loss of white financial

265

support, and internal dissension and disarray, SNCC workers undertook their search for new allies with characteristically brash confidence and forthrightness, quickly establishing more extensive international contacts than any other black organization. As in the past, SNCC expanded the boundaries of American political dialogue and assumed the risks inevitably borne by the most vigorous proponents of political dissent and innovation. Their ingrained determination to publicly air their views was restrained only by their growing awareness that important political divisions existed among even black militants seeking black power.

At the May 1967 meeting when staff members elected Rap Brown as chairman, they also declared SNCC a "Human Rights Organization" and announced that they would "encourage and support the liberation struggles against colonialism, racism, and economic exploitation" around the world. In addition, they proclaimed a position of "positive non-alignment" in world affairs, indicating their willingness to meet with Third World governments and liberation groups. They authorized an application for Non-Government Organization status on the United Nations Economic and Security Council.[1] To coordinate these activities an International Affairs Commission headed by Jim Forman was established.

At that meeting, Stokely Carmichael reportedly stated that SNCC was viewed "around the world and particularly the Third World" as the American organization that was most prepared "to lay the foundation for a revolution." He warned that SNCC would have to be "very, very careful," since individuals and groups would attempt to use SNCC for their own advantage and that SNCC would "begin to be infiltrated by agents who are black whose job it will be to disrupt and destroy this organization by any means necessary."[2] Carmichael's cautionary words were hardly the product of paranoia, since, despite the exclusion of all non-SNCC persons from the meeting, his remarks later were quoted verbatim before a Senate committee investigating SNCC. Nonetheless, staff members were unlikely to allow fear of surveillance to restrain the establishment of international contacts, for they saw these ties as necessary to compensate for SNCC's loss of domestic support and a means of convincing black people that they were not just a small minority within a white nation but part of the vast majority of the world's population that was non-white and the victim of white oppression. "This is a natural coalition—a coalition of those who know that they are dispossessed," wrote Julius Lester.[3]

SNCC workers varied in their indifference to the threat of greater repression and loss of backing at home caused by support for revolutionary movements abroad. They expressed increasing fatalism about continued loss of white support not only through the use of anti-white rhetoric but also through gratuitous statements on foreign policy issues that were designed to demonstrate SNCC's independence from its declining body of white financial supporters. Thus, shortly after Brown was arrested for his role in the Cambridge violence, a group of staff members enraged many of SNCC's white supporters by publishing an article clearly backing the Palestinian position in the Middle East conflict.

Although the press portrayed this article as an official SNCC policy statement, it was actually written to provoke discussion of the Middle East conflict by SNCC's staff and was distributed outside the organization without the approval of many of SNCC's leaders. Staff members probably would have agreed privately with the pro-Palestinian sentiments of the article, yet many were dismayed that once again SNCC would suffer because of the unauthorized actions of a few. The article was written after the Central Committee, meeting in the midst of Israel's six-day victory over Arab forces in June 1967, requested that SNCC's research and communications staff investigate the background of the Arab-Israeli conflict. Ethel Minor, editor of SNCC's newsletter, volunteered for this task, recalling that the committee wanted an "objective critique of the facts." Minor was not impartial on the issue, for she had been close friends with Palestinian students during her college years and had once been a member of the Nation of Islam. Central Committee members undoubtedly expected those exploring the issue to reach a conclusion in favor of the Palestinians. Nonetheless, Jim Forman, who, as head of SNCC's International Program, had recently met with Arab leaders, felt that SNCC should not take a stand on the issue until it had been discussed at a special staff meeting and the entire staff had been educated on the subject. He expressed concern about "SNCC's ability to withstand the external pressures" that would result from an anti-Israel stand. "I knew we would almost be united internally, but the external pressures would be fantastic, especially in New York," he later wrote.[4]

Since he was abroad during most of June and July 1967, Forman could do little to prevent the publication during July of the initial statements by SNCC workers regarding the Arab-Israeli conflict. Apparently without consulting other staff members, veteran SNCC worker Fred Meely wrote an article for a newsletter called *Aframerican News for You*. Meely's noncommittal essay suggested that black leaders should not take a stand on the crisis, which he said resulted from religious superstition, since they were "already under enough pressure" as a result of the black power controversy. "We black people neither need (nor) deserve the wrath of Arab or Jew, for we are even denied access to this debate that may well affect the future of all mankind," he wrote.[5]

Meely's essay was almost totally ignored outside of SNCC, but Minor's article in *SNCC Newsletter*, consisting of a listing of thirty-two "documented facts" regarding "the Palestine Problem," stimulated a sustained attack on SNCC by Jewish leaders and many others. Minor and her staff intended that the article would provide information otherwise unavailable to blacks through "the white American press." According to the article, the initial Arab-Israeli war was an effort to regain Palestinian land and that during the war "Zionists conquered the Arab homes and land through terror, force, and massacres." By itself, the *Newsletter* article would have provoked controversy, but accompanying photographs and drawings by SNCC artist Kofi Bailey heightened its emotional impact. The caption on one of the photographs, which portrayed Zionists shooting Arab victims who were lined up against a wall, noted "This is the Gaza Strip, Palestine, not Dachau, Germany."[6]

Although Minor later claimed that those who prepared the article did not anticipate such a response, other SNCC workers, particularly in the New York fund-raising office, realized immediately that the article would bring swift condemnations from Jewish liberals. Johnny Wilson, head of the office, called a press conference to announce that the article did not present SNCC's official position. Wilson's disclaimer went unnoticed in subsequent press reports, however, since workers at SNCC headquarters quickly called their own press conference to reiterate the anti-Israel position. Program Director Ralph Featherstone explained to reporters in Atlanta that the article did not indicate that SNCC was anti-Semitic, but he further inflamed the emotions of Jews by criticizing Jewish store owners in American black ghettoes. Forman, still out of the country when the newsletter was published, recalled that he publicly supported the article but privately expressed dismay that his counsel of caution had been ignored. He decided that SNCC should support the Arabs on the Palestinian question "regardless of how ragged the formation of our position" and concluded that "no formulation of our position would have satisfied the Zionists and many Jews."[7]

The article and the Atlanta press conference prompted an outpouring of condemnations of SNCC. The executive director of the American Jewish Congress labeled the article "shocking and vicious anti-Semitism." Similar criticisms came from the heads of other Jewish groups and from black leaders Whitney Young, A. Philip Randolph, and Bayard Rustin.[8] Although many staff members were disturbed by the manner in which the controversial article had been published, most believed that the stand would have been taken eventually in any case. Their desire for ideological consistency took precedence over any hope of retaining white support. Cleveland Sellers later acknowledged that afterward many donations "from white sources just stopped coming in," but he added: "Rather than breaking our will, this made us more convinced than ever that we were correct when we accused the majority of America's whites of being racists."[9]

The issue of whether or not SNCC staff members displayed anti-Semitic attitudes in their statements on the Middle East conflict was, of course, a crucial aspect of the controversy following publication of the pro-Palestinian article. SNCC spokespersons consistently denied that the organization was anti-Semitic, but some SNCC workers were willing to exploit anti-Jewish prejudices among blacks by offering Jews as a scapegoat for black oppression and singling out Jews for ridicule and condemnation. Even Minor herself was dismayed by the failure of some staff members, including SNCC's chairmen, to educate themselves regarding the background of the Middle East dispute so that they could discuss the issue intelligently.[10]

For many Jews the pro-Palestinian article was simply another of the accumulating signs that black militancy would be turned against them and constituted a betrayal since they saw black support for Israel as a reasonable quid pro quo for previous Jewish support for the civil rights movement. Yet it was the extensive involvement of Jews in previous racial reform efforts that made them potential targets for blacks demanding self determination. Given the background of increasing black-Jewish tensions resulting from the decision of CORE, which had a far higher level of Jewish involvement than did SNCC, to adopt black power policies and the onset of battles between black activists and Jewish teachers over community control of New York City schools, it is likely that the charge of anti-Semitism would have been levied against any SNCC pro-Palestinian statement, no matter how carefully formulated.[11]

The controversy over the pro-Palestinian article exposed a split within SNCC's ranks that would become increasingly important during 1967 and 1968. Most SNCC workers, especially Carmichael and staff members in Atlanta, continued to move toward racial separatist positions that discounted the possibility of future black-white coalitions and de-emphasized Marxian notions of class conflict. Yet other staff members, particularly concentrated around Forman's international affairs office in New York, were more open to working with white radicals and more willing to incorporate class analyses into their basically racial perspectives. The latter group had great difficulty attempting to avoid both the extremes of racial separatism and the traditional patterns of black dependence on white support. Anyone who argued at a SNCC meeting—or any other black gathering during this period—that the problems of black people resulted from class as well as racial oppression ran the risk of being attacked as insufficiently loyal to racial values or unduly influenced by whites. In November 1967, when speaking before a black audience in Los Angeles, Forman explained the basis of his concern about a singlemindedly separatist orientation. "A purely skin analysis . . . makes it very difficult to guard against reactionary nationalism," he warned, citing the historical examples of African leaders who had collaborated with European colonizers. He also mentioned black activists who had disrupted an anti-war demonstration by persuading blacks not to march with whites on the grounds that whites had started the war and therefore should end it. On another occasion, he said that a black man had objected to his use of the word Marxian. "He jumped up and pounded the table and yelled: 'But Motherfucker, Marx was not a black. He was not black, do you hear. He was a white writer.' "[12]

While Forman argued consistently within SNCC for a greater emphasis on class analyses, he was by no means a doctrinaire Marxist. He strongly opposed the efforts of Marxist groups to supply SNCC with a preconceived ideology. Thus, despite his belief in the ideal of open association, he apparently acquiesced in the expulsion of two known members of the Communist Party, Franklin Alexander and Angela Davis, from the Los Angeles SNCC chapter to ensure that the SNCC chapter remained independent of outside control.[13]

Forman revealed his ambivalent feelings about ties with predominantly-white leftist groups at the National Conference for a New Politics, held in Chicago on Labor Day weekend. By attending SNCC indicated a willingness to seek a national, interracial radical movement, but SNCC representatives were also determined to redefine relations with white liberals and radicals and insisted that the minority of black delegates be given voting power equal to that held by whites. Forman warned a caucus of black delegates of the dangers of "liberal-labor" allies, who, from SNCC's experience, had misled black people. Asserting that progressive whites could not fully understand the impact of racism on blacks, he argued that black people would have to lead struggles for social change. "This is our responsibility and anyone who does not like it can go to hell," he announced. Forman's dominant role at the conference gained him a reputation among many whites as a black separatist demagogue, but he was actually far more restrained than other black militants at the conference, including Rap Brown. After refusing to talk to white delegates at all, Brown reportedly told the black caucus that leadership of the American revolutionary struggle "should never be shared, it should always remain in the hands of the dispossessed."[14]

Although Forman won acceptance of the black demand for equal voting power—and indeed of almost all black demands—the Chicago conference was the last significant effort during the 1960's to forge a national, interracial, radical coalition. Forman and other SNCC workers who favored such a coalition found it difficult to resist the strong tendency of black militancy to move toward an emotional racial separatism that provided an outlet for black resentments against whites. "Putting a simple label of racism on all our problems and attacking individual whites had led many people astray," Forman later lamented, when writing about the convention. "Passionate arguments that our problem was purely racism had to be fought in the arena of ideas."[15]

The difficulty of resisting this separatist tendency became painfully apparent to Johnny Wilson, the head of SNCC's National Black Anti-War Anti-Draft Union (NBAWADU), when he tried to moderate bitter conflicts within the fledgling draft resistance movement. Wilson believed that blacks should maintain a separate identity within the anti-war movement while cooperating with white anti-war activists whenever possible. He was disturbed that black militants at a Pentagon demonstration in October 1967 refused to engage in joint protests with white activists and instead held a meeting while violent confrontations were taking place. "I don't think that we can any longer sit and talk about how black we are because if we haven't learned at this stage how black we are, then there's no need to discuss it." Yet, Wilson also advised white leftists that it did "no good for white people to sit around and patronize black people and to continuously say, 'Well, we understand why you act like that.' "[16]

As Wilson's comment suggests, SNCC workers who struggled against black racial chauvinism were placed in a difficult position in their attempts to moderate conflicts between black militants who saw their oppression in purely racial terms and white or black Marxists who attempted to sway blacks toward their particular class strategy. Although nearly all major socialist groups in the United States expressed verbal support for SNCC and black power, SNCC leaders were cautious in their relations with such groups. While hoping to acquire financial and political support from socialist organizations, they were aware that the CPUSA, Socialist Workers Party, Progressive Labor Party, and other groups had dramatically stepped up their efforts to recruit blacks during the mid-1960s and therefore had become a source of competition for SNCC. SNCC workers were more convinced than ever that they should work only with groups that scrupulously avoided even the appearance of ideological interference in the black struggle and preferably that did not attempt to organize black people. A consistent theme in the public statements of SNCC leaders was that interracial coalitions would be possible only after white leftist organizations had begun to acquire a base of power in white communities.

In specific instances, SNCC workers found that doctrinal infighting of the Left caused unnecessary divisions among blacks, since they were based on schisms within the Left of no relevance to the black struggle. Wilson, for example, was enraged by the role of black Trotskyists who became involved in the NBAWADU, recalling that they undermined the position of SNCC workers who had already gone to prison rather than be drafted by arguing that the correct policy should have been to join the military and organize from within.[17]

As SNCC workers found it difficult to reconcile their own unique political values with those of existing leftist organizations in the United States, they also found that their singular experiences complicated relations with socialist nations and Third World revolutionary organizations. Staff members believed that SNCC should develop international ties—in part as a means of overcoming isolation in the United States—but they were willing to establish these relations only on their own terms. Some SNCC leaders, particularly Forman, had adopted political views that placed them close to the main currents of Third World revolutionary thought, but SNCC did not speak with a unified voice in its foreign relations. Indeed, SNCC's ventures into the international political arena were characterized by the same types of impulsive, uncoordinated staff activity that generally prevailed in SNCC's domestic activities.

With Carmichael's election to the chair in 1966, SNCC already had become widely known abroad, and it began to receive numerous invitations from groups in many nations, including North Vietnam, Cuba, the Dominican Republic, Japan, the Soviet Union, and Israel. With the exception of Israel, SNCC workers visited all of these nations during 1966 and 1967. Increasingly convinced that racial violence in the United States was moving toward a stage of revolutionary struggle, staff members sought inspiration from Third World revolutionaries who had forcefully and sometimes successfully resisted European domination. Although many of SNCC's critics saw its foreign activities as part of an international communist conspiracy, SNCC representatives abroad generally remained skeptical of Marxism, which did not seem to offer an adequate means of understanding their own experiences as Afro-Americans.

Fay Bellamy's report of her 1966 trip to the Soviet Union with three other staff members indicated how the backgrounds and experiences of SNCC workers influenced their relations with representatives of foreign governments. Bellamy had difficulty explaining to her hosts from the Komsomol—the youth group of the Soviet Union's Communist Party— why SNCC did not work with the CPUSA, since the Russians were unaware of the differences between SNCC's racial radicalism and the doctrinaire Marxism of the American party. Although impressed by some aspects of Russian life, especially the treatment accorded women, she reported that many African students experienced discrimination and poor treatment, and complained about the latent racial prejudices of the Russian people. "Everywhere we go, people follow us and stare. Some with friendliness, others out of curiosity and some with hatred." In rewriting her report for distribution to the staff, Bellamy added a negative assessment of the veracity of her hosts: "It is very interesting being in the Soviet Union, but they lie just about as much as our government."[18]

SNCC workers' ingrained scepticism and distrust of whites was again evident in the course of their involvement with the War Crimes Tribunal, called by philosopher Bertrand Russell to investigate American military activities in Vietnam. Despite the intense criticism they knew would result, SNCC leaders quickly accepted an invitation to participate in the tribunal, but when Lester joined a group of tribunal members on a trip to North Vietnam to gather evidence of American war crimes, he expressed fear that he and the other SNCC representative, Cobb, might be "used." He mentioned that the two deliberately kept other members of the delegation "off balance" through their comments to ensure that their assent would not be taken for granted. Despite these concerns, Lester thought that participation in the tribunal was an important, though dangerous, step in SNCC's movement "into the international arena." He added: "No longer are we watched by the cracker cops in the South alone. Cracker cops the world over now watch. . . . revolution is a total kind of commitment and way of seeing and there is no plea you can cop if caught."[19]

Lester was disturbed by the failure of European members, particularly philosopher Jean Paul Sartre, to acknowledge the racial dimension of the Vietnam war that was so clearly evident to SNCC workers. "Yet the fact remains that at the present time the world is polarizing into West (white) versus everybody else (colored, black, and yellow) and that the war in Vietnam is only a rehearsal for what the U.S. must do if it is to protect its interest in Latin America, other parts of Asia, Africa, and at home,"[20] he wrote.

Through their contacts with potential allies abroad, staff members hoped to convince blacks across the nation to reject the Cold War orthodoxy of anti-communism and begin to explore alternative strategies of struggle. The most highly publicized foreign trip by a staff member during 1967 was Stokely Carmichael's unauthorized (by the government and by SNCC) tour of Third World nations. This tour demonstrated SNCC's lack of a common set of political principles to guide its efforts to build alliances and also illustrated one of the many forms SNCC's radicalism could take in the arena of international politics.

Stokely Carmichael's foreign travels during 1967 came as a surprise not only to most SNCC staff members but even to Carmichael himself. After finishing his term as chairman, he publicly announced that he was "going back to the field to organize,"[21] but he soon discovered that he was still in great demand as a black militant spokesman.

In July he went to London for the Congress on the Dialectics of Liberation, where he announced to an enthusiastic audience that the fight "to save the humanity of the world" would bring forth "new speakers" from the Third World. "They will be Ché, they will be Mao, they will be Fanon," he asserted.[22] After incurring the wrath of British officials through his speech at the Congress and his meetings with black militant leaders in England, Carmichael then accepted an invitation from Ralph Schoenman of the Bertrand Russell Peace Foundation to attend the Organization of Latin-American Solidarity (OLAS) meeting in Havana, Cuba.

Carmichael's arrival in Havana on July 25 was reported in the United States along with accounts of the bloody racial rebellion in Detroit. American newspapers quoted from an interview published by the Cuban news agency in which Carmichael asserted: "We are preparing groups of urban guerillas for our defense in the cities." He added that American blacks looked to the Cuban revolution and to Ché Guevara for inspiration. During the next few days Carmichael made numerous similar statements to reporters in an obvious effort to convince his hosts that Afro-Americans were already engaged in a revolutionary struggle against American capitalism. During an extended press conference on August 1 he made numerous statements seemingly designed to enrage government officials in the United States. While deriding the CPUSA as "the party of the rich," he applauded Cuban communism as "the system we like best" of existing communist societies.[23] Carmichael's most controversial statement was an implied threat against American political leaders: "If one of us should be killed, it is important that Negroes of the United States know that the CIA is responsible. Vengeance must be taken against the leaders of the United States."[24]

Carmichael's outspoken advocacy of armed revolution in the United States and sympathy for Cuban communism brought him considerable attention from reporters in Havana and apparently endeared him to the Cuban government. Although he was invited to attend the OLAS conference only as an observer, he was quickly elected by acclamation as an honorary delegate, giving him an opportunity to deliver a major address to the plenary session.[25]

Carmichael's main objective in his address was to convince delegates that Afro-Americans should be included in their plans for revolutionary struggle against "white Western imperialist society." Explaining that SNCC still encouraged white radicals in the United States to organize their own communities, he insisted that blacks would not "wait for this to happen, or despair if it does not happen." Instead, he asserted, black people recognized that their struggle was international. "Because our color has been used as a weapon to oppress us, we must use our color as a weapon of liberation, just as other people use their nationality as a weapon for their liberation." He insisted that a "two-pronged attack" against racism and exploitation was necessary. "Black Power not only addresses itself to exploitation, but to the problem of cultural integrity," which he asserted was an "important fight in the Third World," where Western society "has imposed her culture through force." He concluded that it was necessary "to root out our corrupt Western values" and that "our resistance cannot prevail unless our cultural integrity is restored and maintained."[26]

Although some segments of Carmichael's address emphasizing the importance of racial struggle did not coincide with the policies of the Cuban government, Cuban Premier Fidel Castro apparently was pleased with Carmichael's performance. Castro wanted OLAS delegates to support his plans to encourage revolution in the Americas, and Carmichael provided evidence that support for revolution existed even within the United States. The Cuban press played down Carmichael's implied threat against American leaders, but otherwise Cuban officials ensured that Carmichael's statements received wide coverage. Reacting to Congressional demands for Carmichael's imprisonment when he returned to the United States, Castro announced that Carmichael could remain in Cuba if he wished and that "revolutionary movements all over the world must give Stokely their utmost support as protection against the repression of the imperialists, so that it will be very clear that any crime committed against the leader will have serious repercussions throughout the world."[27]

Carmichael remembered Castro as "very open and very beautiful" during a weekend they spent together in the Sierra Maestra mountains. As they drove around the area in a jeep, Castro repeatedly grabbed Carmichael's shoulder to point out the sites of battles in the struggle against the Batista regime. Later reporting that he was satisfied with Castro's responses to his questions about the position of Afro-Cubans, Carmichael related that the Cuban leader described Cuban racism as the result of the "legacy of colonialism" and said that the government was "doing everything possible to fight it." Julius Lester, who coincidentally was in Cuba for a folksong festival and was enlisted to handle Carmichael's press relations, later wrote a somewhat different account of the Cuban episode that was distinctly hostile to Carmichael. Lester admitted that he "never learned the gist of Stokely's conversation with Fidel" but recounted that Carmichael "would only say that Fidel did not understand racism." Castro probably viewed Carmichael's political attitudes as undeveloped but certainly worthy of support. During his speech at the end of the conference, Castro suggested as much when he defended the black movement in the United States against the charge that it lacked a program. "What is happening is that the Negro sector of the population of the United States at this moment, overwhelmed by daily repression, has concentrated its energies on defending itself, on resisting, on struggle," he explained. He added that a "revolutionary movement" would arise within the United States "not for racial reasons, but for social reasons, reasons of exploitation and oppression, because this sector is the most long suffering and oppressed."[28]

Carmichael's remarks in Cuba produced an expected storm of criticism within the United States. The Johnson administration came under intense pressures to take strong action against Carmichael, although administration officials soon concluded that there was little they could do other than seize Carmichael's passport upon his return to the states. Carmichael reacted to government criticism by insisting that he had "never asked any-one's permission to go anywhere, at any time, for any reason." This com-ment also could have been applied to Carmichael's relations with SNCC's central committee, for the Cuban speeches revived resentment toward Carmichael by other staff members. Bellamy, like other SNCC leaders, was disturbed that Carmichael once again had prompted criticisms of SNCC through unauthorized public statements. "Ain't no one person going to call for no revolution," Bellamy commented. Ironically, consid-ering Carmichael's later political statements, the criticisms of SNCC staff members stemmed in part from Carmichael's apparent identification of the black struggle with white Marxist movements and with communism. SNCC leaders placed a phone call to Carmichael to convey their criticisms. "All of us got on the phone and ordered him to shut up and told him that no one understood what he was saying back here," Ethel Minor recalled.[29]

Despite the rebuke, Carmichael was convinced that he should continue to establish the revolutionary credentials of Afro-Americans in the eyes of Third World revolutionaries. Promising that black people would no longer fight in "U.S. racist and imperialist wars," he said that when blacks took up arms again, it would be to fight in Guinea against the Portuguese or in Zimbabwe against Great Britain and the United States or in American cities. "Our struggle will be one and the same," he advised potential Third World allies. "Our struggles should be coordinated."[30]

While in Cuba, Carmichael accepted an invitation to visit North Viet-nam. Traveling by way of Moscow, he flew first to China, meeting briefly with exiled black activist Robert F. Williams. He also met Shirley Graham DuBois, widow of the scholar and Pan-Africanist leader W. E. B. DuBois, who suggested that he go to Guinea to confer with President Sekou Touré and exiled Ghanian leader Kwame Nkrumah. In Vietnam, Carmichael talked with Ho Chi Minh, who told the SNCC leader of his stay in New York during the heyday of Marcus Garvey, stimulating Carmichael's growing interest in Pan-Africanism by asking why Afro-Americans did not return to Africa, since America was not their true home. The question re-mained on Carmichael's mind.[31]

Carmichael then flew by way of Algeria to Guinea where he was wel-comed as an official guest of the government. He traveled extensively while in Africa and talked privately with Touré and Nkrumah, becoming con-vinced that Pan-Africanism, especially as it was formulated in the writings of Nkrumah, was the appropriate ideology for the Afro-American struggle. Touré invited Carmichael to make his home in Guinea and Nkrumah of-fered him a position as his personal secretary. By this time pessimistic about his chances for long-term survival in the United States and con-vinced that Afro-Americans needed a land base in Africa, Carmichael eventually accepted both offers.[32]

While establishing a close relationship with Touré and Nkrumah, Carmichael acquired the lasting enmity of some African revolutionaries. In Tanzania he reportedly questioned the commitment and racial loyalties of South African "freedom fighters" who were "too interested in big cars and white women" and who exaggerated their military successes, prompting the African National Congress to charge that Carmichael "excelled . . . in meaningless and arrogant demagoguery."[33]

Despite SNCC workers' criticisms of Carmichael during his four-month tour of the Third World, he returned to the United States with greater prestige than ever among militant blacks. He strengthened his reputation as the most outspoken black leader on the national scene by publicly condemning the United States, calling for revolutionary violence, associating himself with Third World leaders, and still managing to avoid prosecution for his actions. (Johnson administration officials apparently had decided that any attempt to prosecute Carmichael might not succeed and, in any case, would have the unacceptable effect of making Carmichael a martyr.)[34] Yet Carmichael's personal popularity would produce few benefits for SNCC. He returned confident that he could build a unified and powerful black movement—a goal shared by other SNCC staff members—but his activities on behalf of Pan-Africanism were often at cross-purposes with the efforts of SNCC's new leadership to build domestic Third World alliances.

Carmichael's personal popularity contributed to the decline of his influence within SNCC, for some staff members believed that he had separated himself from the rest of the staff by departing from the values that had been developed during the early 1960s. "We didn't like the fact that Stokely was creating a leader-type image," Bellamy recalled. "It was a false image for SNCC; it was only real for Stokely."[35]

In some respects, such criticisms of Carmichael were unfair, since he was not alone in having abandoned SNCC's previous emphasis on indigenous, local leadership. He was singled out for criticism not only because he allowed himself to become more well-known in the North than SNCC itself but also because he was an effective advocate of political ideas different from those that came to prevail in SNCC. Although all staff members placed themselves in the struggle to end racial oppression, some were not as willing to adopt a form of Pan-Africanism that ignored or de-emphasized the existence of class divisions or that appealed for black support purely on the basis of a common African heritage. Forman, for example, though himself a Pan-Africanist who retained ingrained skepticism of interracial alliances, was more willing than Carmichael to accept the Marxian doctrines shared by most socialist nations and revolutionary movements with which SNCC hoped to establish ties. Forman prevailed within SNCC over Carmichael's faction, largely because he continued to seek his political objectives by working within SNCC's organizational structure. But Carmichael's personal popularity gave him important advantages over Forman when the two competed for influence in the organization that, at the beginning of 1968, seemed to be SNCC's closest counterpart and most promising potential domestic ally: the Black Panther Party.

SNCC workers' involvement in the Black Panther Party grew from their previous contacts with other militant groups, especially those representing racial minorities. These contacts usually led to verbal statements of mutual support that contributed few tangible benefits to SNCC and in fact made it more vulnerable to government repression. Nonetheless, most SNCC staff members were willing to assume risks in order to forge a Third World revolutionary alliance in the United States. Thus, in January 1967, SNCC publicized the efforts of Puerto Rican nationalists to bring their cause before the United Nations by sending Carmichael to San Juan to sign a statement of support.[36] In October 1967, a SNCC delegation—Featherstone, Minor, Ricks, and Freddie Greene—went to Albuquerque to sign a treaty with Hopi leader Tomas Banyaca and Reies Tijerina, head of a group seeking the return of land taken from the ancestors of Spanish-speaking residents of the southwest.[37]

Though they were eager to build ties with all non-white militant groups, SNCC staff members believed that the BPP was the most appealing potential domestic ally, since the Party seemed to have a following among young urban blacks similar to that once possessed by SNCC among southern black college students. Despite the attractions of the BPP for SNCC workers, however, relations between the two groups were hampered from the outset by mistrust and misunderstanding. These relations brought into sharp focus both the values that still distinguished SNCC from other organizations seeking social change and the serious differences that existed among SNCC workers regarding their future course.

The founders of the BPP, Huey Newton and Bobby Seale, later asserted that they were inspired by SNCC's accomplishments in the deep South, but their evolving attitudes about SNCC revealed little understanding of its history. After reading a pamphlet about "how the people in Lowndes County had armed themselves," Newton and Seale adopted the black panther symbol of the LCFO as the name for their organization in Oakland, California. The two formulated a ten-point program in the fall of 1966 and began to monitor police conduct with armed patrols. A few months after the party was formally established early in 1967, it gained national attention and many new recruits by sending an armed contingent to the state capitol in Sacramento to protest a proposed gun-control law.

Soon afterward, Newton, the BPP's defense minister, took the first step toward establishing ties with SNCC by "drafting" Carmichael to serve as the party's field marshal with authority "to establish revolutionary law, order and justice" in the eastern United States. Newton recognized that Party members lacked "the bourgeois skills" needed to administer a large organization and looked to SNCC as a source of assistance and political guidance for the BPP as it expanded from its base in Oakland. Apparently unaware of SNCC's own organizational problems, he thought that SNCC leaders "could do a good job of administering the Party because they were all committed people and highly skilled." Believing that SNCC was "headed for a decline, because the thrust of the movement was diminishing in the South and moving into the cities of the North and West," he concluded "that SNCC and the Black Panther Party needed each other, and Black people needed us both."[38]

Newton's description of his motives stressed his own selfless willingness to accept SNCC leadership. Yet, he did indicate more mundane reasons for joining forces with SNCC, such as the fact that he would gain "access to their duplicating equipment and other sorely needed materials." Newton also mentioned that his contacts were with SNCC leaders—"those who spoke publicly for SNCC"—suggesting that he assumed SNCC was organized along an hierarchical model similar to that of the BPP. Assuming that SNCC's leaders spoke for the group, Newton claimed that BPP representatives made clear to SNCC leaders, particularly Carmichael, that the Party's goal was a merger of the two groups.[39] Newton, however, was not directly involved in the crucial contacts of late 1967 and early 1968, as he was imprisoned on the charge of murdering an Oakland police officer. As Newton awaited trial, the BPP concentrated its efforts on building mass support for his successful legal defense, and Eldridge Cleaver emerged as the BPP's major spokesman and the central figure in its relations with SNCC.

Cleaver was a forceful leader whose strongly held attitudes were developed while serving a nine-year sentence at Soledad Prison and during his periods of involvement in the Nation of Islam and Malcolm X's Organization of Afro-American Unity. A staff writer for *Ramparts*, Cleaver attracted white radical support for the BPP, allying it with the newly established Peace and Freedom Party. In 1967, he expressed great admiration for Carmichael as a leading representative of a new generation of black intellectuals "who have thrown off the shackles of the slave and are willing to put their talents and genius selflessly to work for the masses."[40] While preparing the article on Carmichael, he also met Kathleen Neal, a SNCC worker in Nashville who later married Cleaver and became the BPP's communications secretary. Yet, despite his regard for Carmichael and personal ties with SNCC staff members, Cleaver felt that the BPP had eclipsed SNCC as the leading black militant organization, and thus was more concerned with obtaining Carmichael's appearance at a planned series of "Free Huey" rallies than with gaining SNCC's organizational backing.

When Cleaver and Seale met with Carmichael in Washington, D.C. shortly after the latter's return from Africa, the BPP leaders ignored signs that Carmichael's political perspective was different from their own, even when Carmichael criticized the BPP's ties with the Peace and Freedom Party. "He told us that many people . . . didn't want him to speak in Oakland because there were going to be white people on the platform," Seale later wrote. "We told Stokely that there was going to be a Peace and Freedom Party member speaking from the platform and we thought it was very necessary that he speak."[41] Although Carmichael decided to accede to the request to speak on behalf of Newton, particularly after Cleaver and Seale offered him the post of prime minister of the Afro-American nation, he had serious doubts about the BPP's leadership and tactics. He later commented that they "didn't understand anything about organizing" and "camouflaged" their lack of organized strength through their cultivation of white leftist support.[42]

Carmichael held no SNCC office, but Seale and Cleaver assumed that he would be the crucial figure in their relations with SNCC. Only after meeting with Carmichael did the Panther leaders seek the participation of other SNCC staff members. They quickly discovered a major gulf between Carmichael and SNCC's current officers. "There was Rap Brown running on one end with James Forman directing things and Stokely on the other end, directing his own thing,"[43] Seale observed. When Forman learned that Carmichael would be the BPP's prime minister, he immediately objected, but Seale and Cleaver made it clear to Forman that they placed a higher value on Carmichael's support. Thus Carmichael's personal popularity allowed him to gain an advantage over the leaders of SNCC. He later stated candidly that he saw the BPP as an organization sorely in need of ideological leadership—"up for grabs"—and that he and Forman were engaged in a battle to control it.[44]

Black Panther leaders made no attempt to elicit the approval of SNCC's central committee for their planned merger with SNCC. When Forman mentioned the idea of an alliance to other staff members, most responded negatively. Lester later noted, however, that since SNCC "lacked the ability to discipline its members," nothing was done to stop Forman from proceeding with plans for an alliance.[45] In short, the actions of both Carmichael and Forman were further indications that SNCC remained torn between the ideals of group leadership and hierarchical authority.

Forman was eager to counter Carmichael's apparent influence in the BPP, believing that the new black militant group was the organization most likely to become the kind of "broadly based party" that he had hoped SNCC would become and could avoid the problems that had led to SNCC's decline, which he attributed to the middle-class backgrounds of many SNCC staff members. "The emphasis on recruiting street brothers, young people from the 'ghettos,' rather than college students, gave it a large base and eliminated some of the class tensions which we had experienced." Despite Forman's growing awareness that he would play a subordinate role to Carmichael, he agreed to help with preparations for the California rallies in support of Newton, using his numerous California contacts. While in Los Angeles Forman cleared the way for the expansion of BPP operations in southern California by arranging for the dissolution of a competitor, the SNCC-inspired Black Panther Political Party.[46]

Forman also mediated in the simmering dispute between the Panthers and the Los Angeles-based US organization, headed by Ron Karenga. Members of the two groups had narrowly avoided violent clashes as they competed for dominance among Los Angeles black militant groups. Karenga had attempted to establish a relationship with SNCC as he expanded his influence outside California, once calling SNCC "the greatest" and anticipating that he would help SNCC "set up cultural and educational programs wherever they need them."[47] Karenga's flamboyance and authoritarian leadership style alienated some SNCC staff members who were not used to leaders as "rigidly regimented" as they believed Karenga to be. Forman recognized, however, that the disciplined US members were a major force in the Black Congress, a coalition of Los Angeles black organizations, and that Karenga's backing was vital to the success of the Newton support rally planned for that city. Fearing that it would be "easy" for competing black groups "to point the gun at one another rather than at the oppressor," Forman succeeded in convincing Seale and Cleaver to enter negotiations with Karenga to enable the Black Congress to sponsor the rally.[48]

Although Cleaver utilized Carmichael's name and Forman's organizing talents during the weeks before the rallies, he angered the two leaders when he told an audience of white Panther supporters that SNCC was "composed virtually of black hippies ... of black college students who have dropped out of the black middle class." Asserting that SNCC workers had been unable to mobilize "the black brother on the block," he claimed that SNCC workers had decided to make "their apparatus" available to the BPP. He then suggested that Carmichael's and Brown's militant rhetoric had been adopted only after they had "come to the West Coast and spent a little time with the Black Panthers out here."[49]

Despite the complex tensions evident in the relations among leaders of SNCC, BPP, and US, the Huey Newton rallies displayed a degree of unity among California black militants that never again existed. At the first rally at the Oakland Auditorium on the evening of February 17, over five thousand people gathered to celebrate Newton's birthday and to demand his release from prison. Carmichael, Forman, and Brown (who made a surprise appearance, ignoring court restrictions on his movements) joined Cleaver and Seale on the stage.[50]

While announcing the naming of SNCC leaders to positions in the BPP, Cleaver also proclaimed that the action constituted a merger with SNCC. Forman was surprised by this announcement, since it was "the first time the term had been used, although we had not decided definitely on another." Speaking at the rally, Forman attempted to redefine the relationship between SNCC and the BPP as an alliance, but most members of the audience listened more to his bombastic statements calling for retaliation in the event of the assassination of black leaders. He urged the destruction of war factories, police stations, and power plants and the death of southern governors and mayors should he, Brown, or Carmichael be assassinated. He then announced that if Newton were killed "the sky is the limit."[51]

The emotional high point of the evening was Carmichael's speech, which displayed the oratorical qualities that accounted for his appeal to the BPP leaders and also revealed his ideological differences with the Party. Carmichael clearly indicated his acceptance of a formulation of racial separatism that left no place for white allies or for "white" doctrines such as Marxism. He told the audience, which included a substantial number of white radicals, that Afro-Americans were concerned primarily with survival in a hostile society. Putting forward the slogan "every Negro is a potential black man," he asserted that all blacks should be enlisted in the fight against the "honky" and his racist institutions.

Contradicting some of his statements while abroad, Carmichael announced: "Communism is not an ideology suited for black people, period, period. Socialism is not an ideology fitted for black people, period, period." Explaining that neither communism nor socialism addressed the issue of racism, Carmichael insisted that blacks must be provided with "an African ideology which speaks to our blackness—nothing else. It's not a question of right or left, it's a question of black." He then concluded that blacks were "going to build a concept of peoplehood in this country or there will be no country." In a rousing finish, he proclaimed, "Brother Huey P. Newton belongs to us. He is flesh of our flesh, he is blood of our blood . . . Brother Huey will be set free—or else."[52]

Seale and Cleaver undoubtedly strongly disagreed with parts of Carmichael's speech, which left many of the Panther's white supporters with feelings of "confusion, betrayal, anger, and exclusion." In his own speech, Seale pointedly rejected the notion that the BPP was anti-white, stating "that's the Ku Klux Klan's game."[53] Nonetheless, Panther leaders were determined to retain Carmichael as a national spokesman for the BPP and as the primary attraction for subsequent fund-raising rallies.

In the days after the Oakland rally, there were signs that the unity of black militant forces would not last. Shortly before a February 18 rally in

Los Angeles, Cleaver and Karenga argued over the necessity of removing Los Angeles police who were providing security at the rally. Carmichael backed Cleaver's insistence that the BPP provide its own security, as had been the case in Oakland. Rap Brown and Karenga eventually prevailed with the view that a confrontation with police would be pointless and futile.[54] Although Karenga's differences with BPP leaders were contained long enough to ensure the success of the Los Angeles event, members of his organization would soon be engaged in bloody battles with the Panthers, culminating early in 1969 with the killing of two Panthers by US members on the UCLA campus.

While publicly ignoring Carmichael's departures from Party policy, BPP leaders privately expressed their criticisms during subsequent weeks as Carmichael continued to speak at meetings organized by the Party. Ethel Minor, who stayed at Cleaver's home while handling arrangements for Carmichael's appearances, recalled that Cleaver and his wife tried to talk to Carmichael "about moderating his anti-socialism thing." She concluded that the Panthers leaders "could see that even though they were using Stokely, Stokely was also trying to use them, and Eldridge wasn't going to stand for anyone trying to use him." She claimed that Carmichael "didn't realize that some of those guys were at the point where they were going to move on him physically," but added that Cleaver was even more hostile toward Forman and Brown, who were seen as less useful to the Panthers.[55]

Some SNCC workers were uneasy with the Panthers' militaristic ways and with the arbitrary manner in which a merger between SNCC and the BPP had been announced, but most were hopeful that the two organizations could cooperate. They admired the Panthers' brash militancy, which was much like their own. As Willie Ricks commented: "They were saying that SNCC people were the bad niggers in town, and then the Panthers jumped up and starting saying, 'We are badding you out.'" To Cleveland Sellers, the BPP appeared to have "the ear of militant young blacks in the ghettos, a group with which SNCC had never really managed to develop any significant rapport."[56] Some SNCC workers, typically Carmichael supporters, decided to join the BPP. Carver (Chico) Neblett, a Tennessee sharecropper's son who had joined SNCC's staff in 1962, became the BPP field marshal for the western states; Donald Cox, a recent addition to SNCC's staff, assumed similar responsibilities for the eastern states; and Bob Brown, who had worked in SNCC's Chicago office, became head of BPP operations in that city.

Staff members who supported Forman remained more skeptical about the idea of a merger with Panthers, although they viewed the BPP as an organization worthy of support. Some female members were disturbed by Cleaver's disparaging remarks about black women in his best-selling book of essays, *Soul on Ice*, published during 1968. Other staff members objected to the Panther leaders' demand that SNCC adopt their ten-point program without change, seeing the program as reformist rather than revolutionary. At a staff meeting in June 1968, they adopted a vague resolution promising to assist the BPP, but news accounts of the meeting stressed their failure to explicitly approve the ten-point program or the merger idea. At a meeting the following month with BPP leaders, SNCC representatives were criticized for failing to comply with previous understandings. Forman recalled feeling "that not only the integrity of SNCC but also my own political integrity had been challenged."[57]

Later in the summer Newton made public his feelings that SNCC's failure to accept the alliance with the Black Panther Party was due to its history of relations with white liberals. He asserted that SNCC previously had been controlled by "the omnipotent administrator, the white person." Proceeding from this dubious assessment of SNCC's past, he concluded that SNCC workers had developed an unreasonable fear of white radicals that was not shared by the BPP, which he claimed was never controlled by whites.[58]

The adamant tone of the Panther leadership was a response to their preoccupation with police harassment that intensified during the weeks after the February rallies. On February 25, Seale was arrested after a raid on his home. On April 6 police killed the teenage treasurer of the BPP, Bobby Hutton, after they cornered him and Cleaver in an Oakland house. Cleaver was wounded in the battle and was forced to return to prison after his parole was rescinded. In Los Angeles, the BPP's ranks were decimated during the spring as a result of a police raid on the Party's headquarters which resulted in many arrests and a purge of the membership to expel those thought to be police agents.

FBI agents were also eager to exploit the tensions that surfaced between the BPP and SNCC. The FBI contributed to Forman's fears about Panther violence directed against himself by making anonymous phone calls threatening that the Panthers would "get him." Further FBI efforts directed against Forman were not carried out only because the SNCC leader had already been hospitalized due to stress. Carmichael was the target of numerous FBI plots, including an anonymous call to his mother warning her that BPP members would kill her son and various efforts to create suspicions about Carmichael's motives and sincerity among BPP members.[59] These COINTELPRO efforts probably hastened a rupture of SNCC-BPP relations, but the FBI's success was due in part to the lack of basic trust and understanding in those relations. As each organization tried to exploit the other, the problems that resulted were exploited to the detriment of both.

The final break in relations between SNCC and the BPP came in July when BPP accused Forman of dragging his feet in organizing New York rallies to protest the upcoming trial of Huey Newton. Forman later insisted that he worked strenuously to build support for Newton and had scheduled a press conference at the United Nations, but he admitted that his health had deteriorated due to his numerous travels and the tensions resulting from his efforts to gain approval of the BPP alliance from SNCC's wary staff. According to Forman's account, BPP representatives failed to appear at the United Nations press conference. "Later, some Panthers spread the lie that I had simply refused to go into the UN, and also that I had called off the press conference all on my own, not because of their actions," Forman recounted. Sellers' account suggested that Forman had become debilitated by paranoid fears and that Panther leaders, angered by Forman's lack of progress in organizing the rallies, demanded that Forman explain his actions, including his insistence at one point that BPP representatives communicate with him only in writing. "The meeting ended with the Panthers threatening to extract physical retribution if Jim didn't get himself together for the press conference scheduled for the following morning," Sellers recounted. Subsequent newspaper accounts stated that an empty gun was placed into Forman's mouth and the trigger squeezed three times, but both Forman and Sellers deny that this happened.[60] A few days after the bungled press conference at the United Nations, SNCC's central committee voted to terminate the alliance with the Panthers.

SNCC leaders had allowed themselves to be drawn into the alliance because they believed that the younger, more dynamic organization could bring new vitality to SNCC. They discovered, however, that BPP leaders did not understand SNCC's history or the important lessons that SNCC workers had learned during their earlier struggles. SNCC workers themselves had become less confident that their distinctive style of organizing, which relied on the development of local leadership, could be applied in urban areas. SNCC's support network and its national and international contacts had once been by-products of its organizing activities in the deep South, but by 1968 SNCC's projects had deteriorated and its most effective community organizers had departed. What remained was a withering institution waiting to be picked clean by the urban black militants seeking to expand their influence, by police agents and informers seeking to undermine black militancy, and by staff members more concerned with institutional control than with the painstaking work of building mass struggles out of black discontent.

Staff members would not have succeeded in reviving the black struggle even if the alliance with the BPP had survived, because both organizations were losing touch with the social realities that had brought them into existence. SNCC staff members had long acknowledged the need for greater staff discipline, for systematic staff education, for a more effective organizational structure, but many of them, especially those who had not been part of the southern struggles of the mid-1960s, lost sight of the initially unarticulated and widely-shared desire among blacks to express discontent through mass struggle. This desire had been the source of SNCC workers' commitment, the basis of their unique insights, and the sole reason for SNCC's creation.

Although the increasing popularity of black militant rhetoric gave the appearance of racial unity, serious differences emerged during the spring of 1968 as black leaders attempted to formulate programs to achieve the goal of black power. Even the militants disagreed about whether the goal of the black struggle should be black capitalism or African communalism, whether the strategy should emphasize electoral politics or revolution. The major line of cleavage within the black militant community was between cultural nationalists, who urged blacks to unite around various conceptions of a black cultural ideal, and self-defined political revolutionaries who were more likely than the cultural nationalists to advocate armed struggle to achieve political or economic goals. SNCC's staff included adherents of each of the two major trends, but by 1968 both factions increasingly doubted whether SNCC would remain the principal vehicle to reach their goals.

*Party headquarters, 1966*

*Election night, Lowndes County, 1966*

*H. Rap Brown speaking in Cambridge, Maryland, shortly before being shot by police, 1967*

*Bob Zellner, Ella Baker, and Charles Sherrod at civil rights conference in Jackson, Mississippi, 1979*

# 18.  DECLINE OF BLACK RADICALISM

The spontaneous urban uprisings of 1968 ended an era of black struggle, for unlike earlier rebellions involving SNCC and southern blacks, they dissipated quickly when confronted by powerful institutions. White political leaders responded to violent black challenges with deadly repression and anesthetizing palliatives. The uprisings failed to foster a strong enough sense of collective purpose to override the endemic selfish and vindictive motives that emerged in outbursts of racial spite. Black urban rebellions were too short-lived to transform personal anger and frustration into a sustained political movement.

The remaining SNCC staff members competed for roles as leading ideologues of the black liberation movement, but could not arouse and guide black militancy through exemplary action. Few staff members were willing to attempt to gain the trust of residents of particular communities, develop indigenous leadership, and build strong local institutions. Increasingly preoccupied with internal factional disputes and external repression, they isolated themselves from the everyday realities of the black people in whose name they acted. Staff members who set themselves apart from other blacks lacking "correct" political ideals replaced dedicated community organizers. The skills required for destructive organizational infighting supplanted those that had enabled SNCC to inspire thousands of people outside the group during its years of greatest influence. Rather than utilizing the creative energy released in the new upsurge of black militancy, SNCC joined the ranks of social movement organizations throughout history which sought to impose their worldview on people who were struggling to think for themselves.

Throughout the decade SNCC staff members had tried to achieve a balance between personal rebellion and collective political action, but during the late 1960s a succession of leaders who saw individualism as the source of SNCC's problems took control. In their desperate efforts to revive the organization, these leaders—many of them recent additions to SNCC's staff— tried to sever SNCC's ties with the past by purging veteran staff members who refused to obey new rules of conduct or accept dogmatic "revolutionary" principles. Individualistic values remained in SNCC, however, for its new leaders' advocacy of revolutionary discipline often merely expressed intellectual arrogance and justified arbitrary use of authority.

Optimism among blacks that racial unity was possible eroded quickly during the tumultuous year of 1968. Although many of the controversial ideas that once had defined SNCC's radicalism were widely accepted, events in the spring and summer of 1968 suggested that black unity was an illusive goal. Covert government programs such as COINTELPRO were partly responsible for divisiveness between black militant groups. There is considerable evidence that the FBI succeeded in creating distrust among black militants, most notably by provoking deadly clashes between members of the BPP and Ron Karenga's US organization.[1] While the full extent to which SNCC was undermined by informers, agents provocateurs, and illegal police activities cannot yet be determined, SNCC's opposition was not solely responsible for the breakdown of its alliance with the BPP or Carmichael's failure to build Black United Fronts. SNCC workers expected strong opposition from the white-controlled system, but their attempt to survive repression by becoming even more concerned with internal security and ideological purity caused them to engage in sterile political cant and abandon their roles as catalysts of black militancy.

The assassination of Martin Luther King in April 1968 revealed to the SNCC staff both the depth of black discontent and the vulnerability of black leaders. They often had disagreed with the nonviolent tactics King advocated, but they joined other black Americans in expressing their outrage over his murder. Although no longer part of SNCC's leadership, Stokely Carmichael probably expressed the sentiments of many other staff members when he publicly warned "white America" that it had made a mistake by killing King. He called King "the one man of our race that this country's older generations, the militants and the revolutionaries and the masses of black people would still listen to." Some observers expected Carmichael's influence to increase with King' death, but, rather than conveying a sense of confidence, Carmichael displayed a curious tone of fatalism when he predicted a violent struggle in which black people would "stand up on our feet and die like men. If that's our only act of manhood, then Goddammit we're going to die."[2]

After delivering these remarks, Carmichael, along with millions of other black people, went into the streets to express their anger. In a unique display of nationwide racial unity, blacks in numerous cities burned and looted white property and battled the police and military forces sent to suppress them. Over forty blacks were killed and more than twenty thousand arrested throughout the nation. Carmichael was blamed for the destruction in Washington, but actually no leader was capable of exerting much control over the spontaneous activities.[3] White fears and black fantasies to the contrary, the uprisings after King's death demonstrated the absence of political coordination or even communication among black militants.

Staff members choosing to remain in SNCC had in common a willingness to endure continued repression rather than accommodate to the existing American political order. Though they must have felt some sense of satisfaction as moderate black leaders began to jump on the black power bandwagon, they bitterly condemned leaders who used militant rhetoric while pursuing reformist goals or personal aggrandizement. Citing Whitney Young's announcement in 1968 that the Urban League would henceforth pursue black power through black capitalism Rap Brown complained that the concept of Black Power had been "diluted and prostituted to the point where even the most conservative negroes are now for Black Power."[4] Some former SNCC workers benefited from the efforts of the federal government and private foundations to sponsor black self-help projects, but those who remained realized that the taint of association with SNCC or, more accurately, with its outspoken leaders, was daily becoming more and more eradicable.

SNCC workers knew the many arms of the legal system constantly stifled their activities. As the most visible staff member, Brown's legal difficulties attracted more attention, yet his experiences and his reaction to them typified the response of SNCC workers to their predicament.

Early on February 21, 1968, federal law enforcement officers broke into a New York apartment where Brown was staying and arrested him on the charge of violating conditions of his bond by traveling to California for the Huey Newton rally. The House Un-American Activities Committee had alerted the Justice Department to Brown's planned trip. After failing to convince a federal judge that he went to California to meet with his lawyer, William Kunstler, Brown was returned to New Orleans where another judge set a new bond of $50,000. While waiting for his appearance in the New Orleans courtroom, Brown exchanged words with a black FBI agent who then complained that Brown had threatened him. (Brown claimed that he said, "I hope your children don't grow up to be a Tom like you are.") Unable to post bond of $100,000 after being charged with threatening the agent, Brown spent more than a month in jail waiting for his trial on the federal firearms charge.[5]

Instead of acquiescing in the face of governmental power, Brown became even more resolute in his defiance. He began a hunger strike, explaining in a public letter that "one loses a bit of manhood with every stale compromise to the authority of any power in which one does not believe." Although he had been forced to use a nonviolent protest tactice to call attention to his situation, Brown called upon black people to find other ways of escaping "from slavery and oppression . . . We must move from resistance to aggression, from revolt to revolution," he announced. In a note to white America, he proclaimed that "if it takes my death to organize my people to revolt against you . . . then, here is my Life!"[6]

Rather than mobilizing blacks through his sacrifice, Brown unwittingly reinforced the increasingly popular belief among blacks that overt resistance to white authority was futile and meaningless. "A lot of Black people . . . couldn't understand what I was doing,"[7] Brown later admitted. Brown was taken to Maryland for further legal proceedings and then required to return to New Orleans in May for his trial. His conviction on the charge of carrying a rifle from New Orleans to New York while under indictment surprised few people, but his severe sentence shocked some. Judge Lansing Mitchell sentenced Brown to the maximum term of five years in jail and imposed a $2000 fine. It was later revealed that Judge Mitchell said prior to the trial that he was going to take care of his health so that he could "get that nigger." Testimony at the trial also revealed that Brown's telephone conversations had been bugged by the FBI and other agencies even before he became SNCC's chairman.[8]

Brown's experiences were only part of a pattern of government repression that SNCC condemned but could not effectively resist. SNCC workers refused to soften the tone of their rhetoric even while recognizing that outspoken militancy often unified whites in support of police repression while dividing blacks. Unable to instill the optimism required to sustain the black struggles of the 1960s, they instead encouraged an enervating pessimism among blacks through their talk of racial genocide and their premature calls for armed revolt. Caught up in a self-reinforcing process of racial polarization, SNCC workers hastened the demise of their organization by focusing attention on their setbacks.

SNCC workers attending the annual staff meeting that began on June 11, 1968, recognized that they had to select new leadership to rebuild SNCC. Rap Brown, too preoccupied with his own legal problems to attend the meeting, was not a candidate to succeed himself as chairman. Although staff members sympathized with Brown's travail, they also were determined to prevent the seemingly inexorable process through which SNCC's recent chairmen had attracted press attention and become targets for federal, state, and local law enforcement agencies.

Recognizing the difficulty of predicting whether the person they selected could avoid publicity, staff members altered SNCC's structure and elected nine deputy chairmen to replace Brown. The new collective leadership consisted of veteran staff members, including Forman, Stanley Wise, George Ware, Johnny Wilson, Donald Stone, and Bob Smith, and more recent additions to the staff such as Brother Crook (Ronald LeRoy Wilkins) of Los Angeles and Charles Koen of St. Louis. This attempt to reduce the importance of SNCC's chair only partly alleviated SNCC's problems, however, since little was done at the meeting to deal with the underlying weakness of the organization: the lack of significant local programs that would divert attention from unbridled leaders to mass struggles. Moreover, staff members could not prevent the press from identifying whomever was chosen to speak for the group as SNCC's new leader. Thus, reporters predictably responded to SNCC's election by identifying the newly elected program secretary, Phil Hutchings, as the new leader.[9]

Although Hutchings did not actually have much control over other staff members' activities, his election to a major post and his emergence as SNCC's principal spokesperson reflected the respect he had gained from other staff members. His most appealing quality was his quiet, thoughtful manner and his proven effectiveness as a northern, urban organizer. He led a battle in Newark against the building of a state medical college in the black ghetto and succeeded in gaining concessions by state officials. As was the case in the election of Brown, SNCC staff members hoped that Hutchings would avoid public statements and concentrate on developing effective programs, but the fact that the press saw him as SNCC's spokesman led Hutchings to try to moderate SNCC's image. He was quoted as saying that SNCC's goal was to go beyond calls for blacks to arm themselves. "The man wants riots and black people in the streets . . . We've got to move on all levels and all fronts—angry but smart," he said.[10]

Hutchings attracted less press attention than did Brown, but this was mainly because reporters were more interested in militants such as Cleaver, who shocked the sensibilities of white listeners with obscenities and calls for violent retaliation against white officials, than in reporting Hutchings' unemotional, thoughtful statements about programs. Hutchings' goal was to encourage blacks to form a national black political party that would deal with the problems of both racial and class oppression. "If you are talking about really going for power, and not simply some kind of cultural faddism," he told an interviewer, "you have to talk about overturning the capitalist power system." He believed that it was possible to build class alliances between poor blacks and other groups. "We think that because of the unique role of black people in this country, they will always be in the vanguard of the revolutionary struggle," he explained. "But that does not necessarily mean that they have to be the only group that is revolutionary."[11]

Most staff members were still undecided regarding whether SNCC itself should attempt to become a national black political party. The prevailing view of staff members, which Hutchings shared, was that SNCC should remain a group of organizers seeking to create black-controlled institutions without becoming part of them. SNCC workers at the June meeting were involved in diverse, uncoordinated efforts that were only loosely linked to SNCC. For many staff members, SNCC was no longer the central focus of their activities; for some, association with SNCC had become a hindrance.[12]

Their inability to attract support at the local level frustrated staff members and tempted some to blame SNCC for their failures. SNCC's lack of ideological consistency troubled staff members competing with representatives of other militant groups. Tolerance declined as SNCC workers became increasingly concerned with staff desertions and police infiltration. Since few staff members could display success as organizers, conformity to changing policies became the principle criteria for evaluating their performances.

Stokely Carmichael was the first of SNCC's former leaders to be expelled for failure to conform to the organization's constantly shifting ideological stance. Hutchings announced the expulsion at a New York press conference on July 27, explaining that the decision, made "with regret and no pleasure," was necessary because SNCC and Carmichael "were moving in different directions." SNCC leaders charged Carmichael with "engaging in a power struggle" with Forman that had "almost resulted in physical harm to SNCC personnel and threatened the existence of the organization"—a reference to the previous week's clash between Forman and Panther party members. Carmichael was saddened but not surprised by the decision, since he had endured increasingly personal attacks in the years since his election as chairman. He had not attended a staff meeting since his return from Africa in 1967, and most of his supporters were no longer active in SNCC affairs. Moreover, he had continued to work with the BPP despite the rupture of its relations with SNCC. He responded with a restrained statement indicating his own regret that his differences with other staff members were being aired in public and offering to work with SNCC again in the future if the differences could be resolved.[13]

Carmichael was far more concerned about using the BPP as a base for building black united fronts across the nation. He soon discovered, however, the tenuousness of his standing within the BPP, based as it was more on his own usefulness as an internationally-known spokesman for the party than as a source of ideological guidance. His statements in Africa in favor of racial rather than class unity prompted increasingly harsh and personal criticisms from Panther leaders. In July 1969 Carmichael accepted the inevitable and announced his resignation from the party in an open letter that condemned the alliance that existed between the BPP and white radicals.[14]

Staff members who had expelled Carmichael saw their action as necessary to build a disciplined, revolutionary organization, but SNCC's staff could not agree on an inclusive set of policies that would attract new support and instead adopted doctrines that narrowed their base of support and resulted in further staff purges. Newcomers sought to displace veterans by pointing to the extensive evidence of SNCC's decline. Following the life-cycle of other social movement organizations that began to splinter as they lost their ability to mobilize large numbers of people, SNCC came under the control of ever smaller factions of its staff. An organization that had long had a policy of open association became a group of dogmatists who were suspicious of everyone outside the organization and many within it. Many staff members were willing to participate in SNCC's affairs only as long as they could prevail in its internal disputes.

SNCC's December 1968 staff meeting in Atlanta provided further indications of internal conflicts. Recognizing that there was little to be gained from continued association with a dying organization, some staff members simply drifted away while those who remained became even more determined to rid the organization of personnel who were deemed responsible for SNCC's decline. Staff members who lacked local bases of support were among those most likely to cling desperately to their positions in SNCC. SNCC workers once had avoided leadership roles, but SNCC was becoming a group of self-appointed leaders seeking a following.

Veteran staff members who might have provided SNCC with a degree of continuity were exhausted by years of constant external and internal pressures. Forman, previously the strongest leader in SNCC, was on the verge of complete nervous collapse after the breakup of the alliance with the Black Panthers, and he spent much of the fall resting and traveling in the Caribbean. Although he arrived at the December meeting with renewed strength, some staff members had begun to see him as paranoid and doubted his capacity for continued leadership. Certainly Forman had good reason to distrust some of the staff members since at least two of those present at the meeting were FBI informers.[15] Moreover, Forman found that some staff members who previously had supported him were now mobilizing support against him. A leader of the anti-Forman faction was Irving Davis, who had replaced Forman as SNCC's International Affairs Director. Hutchings, who was caught in the middle of the factional infighting, found that his position as program secretary gave him little actual authority since few programs remained to supervise.

The most notable occurrence of the meeting was the debate over the expulsion of two veteran staff members, Cleveland Sellers and Willie Ricks. Sellers only recently had been an officer of SNCC; yet, even as he faced the prospect of a long prison term for his Orangeburg activities and his refusal to be drafted, he suddenly found himself an outsider in the organization in which he had spent nearly all of his adult life. He recalled that when he and Ricks arrived at the meeting, he recognized few of the people in attendance. "Although they were acting as if they were old SNCC veterans, the majority had joined the organization after Stokely was fired," Sellers later

wrote. Indeed, of the twenty-eight attendees identified by the FBI's observ-
ers, only six—Ricks, Sellers, Forman, Stanley Wise, Courtland Cox and
Charles Cobb—had been members of the staff prior to 1966. Forman
joined the newcomers in criticizing Sellers and Ricks for maintaining contact with Carmichael and for refusing to dissassociate themselves from the
Black Panther Party. The two were asked to demonstrate their loyalty to
SNCC by helping organize the St. Louis paramilitary group called the
Black Liberators, but they refused. "We took the position that if we were
going to organize Panthers we'd organize Panthers, but we weren't going to
organize no imitation Panthers," Ricks recalled. Sellers and Ricks tried to
divert the criticisms by questioning whether SNCC should be associated
with any paramilitary groups, but their accusers became increasingly hostile and the two were fired.[16]

Shocked and dismayed by the action, Sellers and Ricks protested bitterly, but they knew that there was little chance that SNCC's central committee would reverse the decision. Soon after leaving the meeting, Sellers
reported that he was attacked by several SNCC staff members who claimed
that he was trying to destroy SNCC. Sellers recalled that this was the first
time he had seen SNCC workers resort to "gangsterism tactics" to force
other staff members to conform. When he pulled out a pistol to frighten off
his attackers, Sellers realized that, for him, SNCC was dead. It was a painful end to a period of his life. "I felt kind of strange not being in the organization I had grown up in," he recalled.[17]

Sellers felt especially betrayed by Forman, who might have been able to
pursuade the staff not to expel the two veterans, but Forman's own vulnerability in SNCC's factional warfare was soon evident. Perhaps recognizing
that SNCC was no longer of much value as a base for his activities, Forman
hoped to spread his influence through other organizations. In April 1969,
for example, he took control of the National Black Economic Development
Conference, held in Detroit under the sponsorship of the Interreligious
Foundation for Community Organization (IFCO), which was established
by Protestant church organizations to fund reform projects in minority
communities. Forman was ambivalent about such efforts to divert blacks
from revolutionary strategies, complaining that many black nationalists
had become the "pimps" of black militancy and had "been the first to
jump on the bandwagon of black capitalism,"[18] but the proposal he offered
to the conference was hardly revolutionary. Presenting his ideas in a Black
Manifesto, he demanded that white Christian churches pay a half billion
dollars to blacks as reparation for previous exploitation that had been
"aided and abetted" by white religious institutions. Forman acknowledged
that the call for reparations "did not represent any kind of long-range
goal," but he defended it by explaining that the money would be used to
establish new black-controlled institutions. He did not explain how he

would ensure that the reparations would be used in ways that would equitably benefit all black people. Moreover, he found it difficult to argue convincingly that his proposal was different from other attempts by black militants to gain monetary concessions for themselves and their organizations by using black oppression as a rationale.[19]

Forman did attract a great deal of publicity for the manifesto when he interrupted a service on May 4, 1969, at New York's Riverside Church and presented his demands to shocked parishioners. Forman later described his brash act as simply another stage in the black struggles of the 1960s. "I felt my action as one more rebellion against the vast system of controls over black people and their minds, of which the church and religion stood as a prime example," he later wrote. Yet, despite the enormous amount of press coverage he received after the invasion of Riverside and other churches, disruptions of white religious activities were destined to be an ineffectively short-term, small group activity. The reparations idea did bring, however, an increase of church support for minority development projects. Forman later wrote of his dismay that little of this money went to the group that started the campaign, the Black Economic Development Conference. He claimed that "greedy black churchmen" diverted money for their own programs. Of the reparations money that did end up in the hands of the BEDC, a major proportion was used to establish Black Star publications, which distributed black militant writings, including several by Forman.[20]

Indicative of the lack of black support for Forman's reparations campaign was the fact that SNCC itself refused to adopt it as a project. This decision was taken at the last staff meeting of the Student Nonviolent Coordinating Committee, which was held in June 1969 in facilities provided, somewhat ironically, by New York's Washington Square Episcopal Church. Like preceding staff meetings, the New York gathering was characterized by rancor and confusion. It culminated in the victory of a faction that repudiated an organizational name that had once been a source of pride. Rap Brown, identifying himself with staff members who wished to break decisively with SNCC's past, entered the meeting with a group of supporters and strongly condemned the failures of the existing SNCC leadership. He demanded control of the organization for his faction and insisted that the organization become a paramilitary group to be called the Black Revolutionary Action Party. Since few staff members cared enough firmly to resist the takeover, Brown and his supporters prevailed. Realizing that he no longer had significant influence in the organization of which he was the senior staff member, Forman resigned.[21]

At a press conference on July 22, Brown announced that he was once again in charge of SNCC and that the new SNCC leadership had decided to change the name of the organization. Rather than dropping the former name completely, Brown said that they would keep the "SNCC" acronym, which was still well known throughout the nation, but it would henceforth refer to the Student National Coordinating Committee. While Brown became the titular head of SNCC, actual control over what was left of the organization was vested in the hands of Irving Davis and Muhammad (William) Hunt, who became head of SNCC's Revolutionary Political Council, which replaced the Central Committee as SNCC's policy making body. Jimmy Johnson, formerly of a group of military anti-war protesters called the "Ft. Hood 3," replaced Johnny Wilson as head of SNCC's anti-draft organization.[22]

After leaving SNCC, Forman had difficulty finding a place in the increasingly variegated black struggles of the 1970s. He became an officer in the League of Revolutionary Black Workers, formed by dissident members of the United Automobile Workers Union in Detroit. Forman also devoted much of his time during the early 1970s to writing his massive account of SNCC's development, *The Making of Black Revolutionaries,* in which he concluded that SNCC's decline resulted from its failure to organize black workers "and put them at the center of decision making" and to "hold the power [it] had acquired in the rural South."[23]

SNCC survived for several years after Forman's departure, but was of significance mainly for those few militants who continued to struggle for control of it and for the FBI informers who slowly recognized that it no longer posed a threat to the social order. SNCC used part of a room in the Rectory of St. Peter's Episcopal Church in New York as its national headquarters, but had no telephone nor full-time personnel. The only active SNCC chapters outside of New York at the end of the decade were in Atlanta and Cincinnati. Police in Texas had decimated the chapters in that state. The New York office occasionally published a newspaper to promote the concept of "revolutionary nationalism," but it had only a small readership and no coherent ideological viewpoint. Unlike the *Student Voice,* which once had reported on the activities of hundreds of SNCC workers throughout the deep South, the new publication was primarily a forum for the opinions of staff members who no longer mobilized black people.

A few staff members tried to launch projects but had only modest success. The only SNCC project during the early 1970s that gave any evidence of success was a feminist group called the Third World Women's Alliance, headed by Frances Beal. Even the steady growth of the alliance did not stem SNCC's decline, however, since Beal obtained independent means of financial support for the group and operated autonomously.[24]

Staff members witnessing the disintegration of their organization continued to purge others who were blamed for SNCC's ineffectiveness. During 1969 the central conflict was between Hunt and Davis. Having displaced Forman, the two were unable to agree on the future direction of the organization. Hunt criticized Davis for spending much of his time meeting with African representatives at the United Nations and traveling to friendly socialist countries rather than developing programs of his own. Hunt also charged Davis with using funds contributed to SNCC without gaining the approval of the staff and further undermined Davis' position by winning adoption at the November 1969 staff meeting of new rules of staff conduct that called for the expulsion of staff members who did not submit to the authority of the Revolutionary Political Council, which Hunt headed. All staff members were also required to spend at least half of each month working on community projects.[25] These and numerous other rules of conduct were intended to turn SNCC into a revolutionary organization, but Davis recognized that they were designed to be used against him. Early in 1970 when Davis was charged with violating the new rules, he resigned from SNCC.

After Davis' departure, Hunt and Brown were the dominant figures in SNCC, but they could not hold the organization together. Brown was too preoccupied with his upcoming trial in Maryland to devote much attention to SNCC's internal affairs. During 1969 he published a personal account of his political development called *Die, Nigger, Die!*, a book written in the profane vernacular of urban black militancy. The book sold well, but Brown could not benefit from his literary success since he faced a federal prison sentence and the probability of a long prison term in Maryland.

Brown never appeared at his trial, which was transferred from the volatile Cambridge community to the small town of Bel Air. On March 9, 1970, the day before the trial was scheduled to start, two of his associates in SNCC, Ralph Featherstone and William H. (Che) Payne, were killed by an explosion that ripped apart their car as they drove away from Bel Air. The bodies of the two were unrecognizable, resulting in early reports that Brown himself had been one of the victims. FBI agents and Maryland state police who investigated the explosion concluded that the car had contained a time bomb. They speculated that the two SNCC workers may have gone to Bel Air to plant a bomb at the courthouse and then abandoned the attempt due to the heavy security around the building. SNCC spokesmen charged that the bomb had been planted in the car and called for "massive retribution and revenge."[26] Whatever the reason for the explosion, the death of the two men marked another stage in SNCC's decline. Featherstone in particular had been one of SNCC's most dedicated staff members and the only remaining veteran of the pre-1965 period. In accordance with his wishes, Featherstone's body was taken to Africa for burial. In Lagos, Nigeria, thousands of Africans joined his wife and a few close friends in paying their respects to the "brother from across the seas who came to rest in the soil of his ancestors."[27]

Brown went into hiding in Canada after the death of his close friends. While in exile, he carefully stayed away from public view, except for one interview he granted to an underground newspaper. On that occasion, he expressed the wish to go to Africa to participate in the African liberation movement.[28] On October 16, 1971, he was wounded in a shootout with New York police following a robbery of a Manhattan cocktail lounge. The motive for the holdup remains unclear, although some former SNCC members speculated that Brown and three associates who were also arrested may have been attempting to rob drug pushers in the lounge. Brown spent several months in a hospital and then was tried and convicted in March 1973 of armed robbery and assault with a deadly weapon. He was sentenced to a term of five to ten years in prison.[29]

After the death of Featherstone and Payne, SNCC workers grew more distrustful of those around them and more ineffectual as an organization. Indicative of the atmosphere that existed inside the organization was a letter written by Muhammad Hunt in August 1970 in which he told staff members that they must "destroy ALL vestiges of certain bourgeois ideas, attitudes and behavior patterns of certain individuals within the organization." He blamed "reactionary ideas and attitudes" for the steady decline of SNCC. "It must be very clearly understood by those workers within the organization that we are in the process of rebuilding the organization, and any acts we interpret as being detrimental to the organization will be dealt with according to the severity of the crime against us."[30]

Hunt's attempt to impose discipline was meaningless since there was no one left on the staff who would accept his authority. Still, the FBI continued to observe SNCC's corpse. In May 1971 an FBI report stated that in the previous months SNCC had "not staged or participated in any demonstration or disruptive activity, and it is believed incapable of accomplishing same in view of the limited membership, lack of funds and internal dissension." Despite this bleak judgment, the FBI continued to report on SNCC for more than two years afterward. Finally, on December 11, 1973, the Bureau acknowledged the futility of their surveillance. The New York office reported: "In view of the fact that SNCC has no national office, no national officers, has engaged in no significant activites for several years, and that future prospects for such are exceedingly faint, NY is closing this case."[31]

SNCC's rise and fall coincided with the evolution of the black struggles of the 1960s. Emerging from the black student sit-in movement of 1960, SNCC initially had drawn inspiration and ideas from the American tradition of religious radicalism, a tradition influenced by Mahatma Gandhi and intertwined with previous, isolated civil rights protests. As SNCC workers became deeply involved in an expanding social movement in the South, they acquired a distinctive style of rebellious activism and of community organizing that enabled them to mobilize large segments of black communities under indigenous leadership. SNCC workers epitomized the militant mood of black people, particularly those in the most racially repressive regions of the Black Belt, who were suddenly released from the psychological burdens of cultural and political conformity. As SNCC workers came together to form an activist community in the midst of an awakening black populace, they were transformed by their experiences. Their openness to new ideas, their brash willingness to challenge powerful institutions, their experimental approach to life allowed staff members to express the changing mood of the southern struggle. SNCC "freedom fighters" acquired a singular mystique based on their rebelliousness and their commitment to humanistic ideals. They became models for a generation of young activists, inside and outside the South, who challenged many of the assumptions that made possible the continued existence of injustice and oppression in American society.

By the mid-1960s, however, SNCC staff members had begun to question some of the assumptions underlying their own radicalism. As the focus of the southern black struggle changed from desegregation to political and economic concerns, SNCC's radicalism assumed a secular rather than religious tone, although the theme of moral outrage remained evident in SNCC's public criticisms of the federal government and of Cold War liberalism. Disillusioned with the prevailing values of American society, SNCC workers articulated the implicit, emergent ideas of the southern struggle. They expressed the sense of racial pride and potency that had developed among southern blacks as they overcame determined segregationist opposition and built institutions of their own. Although some staff members identified themselves as black nationalists and Atlanta Project staff members put forward explicit black separatist doctrines during 1966, SNCC workers initially derived their racial consciousness from their experiences in the southern struggle rather than from existing nationalist or separatist ideologies. Veteran SNCC workers rejected the use of white organizers in black communities on the grounds that this hindered the development of feelings of self-confidence among blacks. They affirmed the legitimacy of a long-standing tradition of armed self-defense among blacks in the rural deep South. They saw the black power slogan as a logical outgrowth of SNCC's previous attempts to instill in the minds of black people the notion that they could create a better world for themselves. SNCC workers underwent a difficult and painful process of learning through struggle while also confronting a dilemma that was not unique to them: the problem of reconciling their anti-authoritarian values with the need to place restraints on personal freedom in order to achieve greater social justice.

Prompted by the black urban rebellions of the mid-1960s, SNCC workers brought to northern cities the unifying racial ideals that had emerged from the southern struggle, but ironically they soon experienced divisive competition with other black militant groups and many internal ideological disputes. Although police harassment and covert repression exacerbated divisions among black militants, SNCC hastened its own decline by losing touch with its roots in the deep South. Propagandists and ideologues who pursued the illusive goal of finding doctrines that would unify increasingly intractable urban blacks supplanted community organizers whose attitudes had reflected the changing character of the southern struggle. SNCC became one of many black militant groups offering black people the doctrinal residues of previous struggles while failing to fully comprehend the novel ideological implications of the new black urban revolt against white domination and existing black leadership. SNCC's previous qualities of openness and fluid organizational structure became liabilities rather than distinctive assets when outspoken SNCC radicals gave unwitting support to a notion they once had discarded: that leaders and organizations were responsible for massive black insurgencies. During the final years of SNCC's existence, staff members became increasingly dogmatic and isolated. Formerly controversial ideas became cant and posturing. SNCC's demise as a national organization merely confirmed the earlier death of its singular spirit and of the black struggles that had produced that spirit.

SNCC workers failed to resolve the enduring dilemmas that had perplexed earlier radicals and revolutionaries, but they provided a surviving legacy. This legacy is most evident among black people in the deep South communities where SNCC became enmeshed in strong local struggles. Local black leaders who gained new conceptions of themselves as a result of SNCC's work carried on political movements after SNCC workers departed and the excitement of protest subsided. "People that were sharecroppers and tenant farmers are now running for office," remarked John Lewis, who maintained close contact with these leaders while serving as head of VEP during the early 1970s. Lewis mentioned in particular blacks in Lowndes County, a place that typified the worst of southern racial oppression when Stokely Carmichael launched SNCC's project there in 1965. John Hullet and Charles Smith could not register to vote when SNCC workers arrived, but with SNCC's encouragement, Hullet and Smith became leaders of the Lowndes County Christian Movement for Human Rights, the parent organization of the Lowndes County Freedom Organization—the first Black Panther party. In 1970, after blacks in the county decided to merge with a new statewide Democratic organization, Hullet was elected sheriff of Lowndes County. A few years later Smith became a county commissioner. In 1978, Hullet and Smith headed a slate of eight black candidates who won every county office for which they contended. "SNCC did an excellent job," Smith concluded in 1978. "SNCC did not say that this and this must be the thing; they suggested things. The people in the county accepted or rejected and then did what was best suited for the local conditions of Lowndes County."[32]

In other areas of the South where SNCC was active, the evidence of success is less dramatic, but there is no doubt that an important and irreversible change occurred among black people during the 1960s. Marion Barry credits SNCC with "awakening the simmering feelings of blackness that black people had but had not expressed." Black nationalist leaders articulated these feelings, but their most profound expression came in the massive black struggle in the South. Leaders and organizations did not initiate these struggles; SNCC and its best organizers were produced by them. Stokely Carmichael's call for black power reflected his own experiences in southern black movements that had begun to acquire power. If many black people in the South and elsewhere remain poor and powerless, if many black youngsters have turned to self-destructive behavior when they no longer can look to the exemplary actions of dedicated civil rights workers, they nonetheless now have an unprecedented opportunity to launch future struggles on a foundation SNCC helped to build. Dewey Greene of Greenwood, Mississippi, the father of two SNCC workers and a person who made his own contribution to the struggle, spoke for many black people who realize the importance of the partial gains of the 1960s when he commented that whites could no longer beat a black man with impunity. "That Negro won't take no beating," he said. "So, I guess it's coming little by little, but I know it's come that far."[33]

Black people who never participated in the collective struggles of the 1960s have also benefited from them. Indeed, blacks who chose not to participate in black struggles and who are primarily concerned with pursuing personal goals rather than assuming social responsibilities are the ones most likely to gain the rewards of American society. As Willie Ricks commented, "Black folks walking around in suits and ties, having jobs, that's an outgrowth of SNCC."[34] Purposeful amnesia about recent Afro-American history has enabled many contemporary blacks to ignore the fact that they enjoy the benefits of sacrifices made by earlier generations and to see their personal success as solely the result of their own efforts. Black youngsters who have greater educational opportunities open to them, who can take black studies courses, who can find high-paying jobs are not more able than their parents and grandparents, but they are certainly more fortunate to live at a time when their abilities are more likely to be rewarded.

SNCC's legacy survives not only in the deep South but also in the sexual, ethnic, and class consciousness movements that adopted ideas and tactics from SNCC. Many of the participants in these contemporary movements have little awareness of the extent to which they are the progeny of SNCC, for the early leaders of these movements who recognized SNCC's importance have departed—sometimes to be replaced by leaders who believe their struggles began when they became aware of them. "A whole thought pattern, a whole culture has been influenced by SNCC," Lewis concluded. "People in SNCC may never receive the credit—maybe people never really wanted credit—but a lot of the good things that are happening not just to black people but to the whole society can be attributed to SNCC."[35] Former SNCC staff members do not always agree on the nature of SNCC's contribution to later movements, since SNCC's internal conflicts foreshadowed many of the political controversies that still divide progressive forces in the 1980s, but they are convinced that their role was seminal. SNCC workers had lived through the same experiences that shaped Tom Hayden before he became a nationally known leader of the New Left or Casey Hayden and Mary King before they wrote one of the early manifestos of the modern feminist movement or Mario Savio before he became a spokesman for the Berkeley Free Speech Movement. SNCC had been at the center of an experiment based on the belief that people of every social status could play significant roles in determining their destiny, and people associated with it had learned lessons that were of lasting value for anyone who shared the belief.

SNCC workers have continued in various ways to live their lives on the basis of this radical belief. Some regret that SNCC no longer provides a setting for their activities; others have concluded that SNCC was not suited for survival in the social climate of the 1970s. Some have found roles in reform institutions or in government at the federal, state, and local levels; others have joined political organizations such as the All African Peoples Revolutionary Party, which they see as the successors of SNCC; others have avoided institutional ties altogether. Some have achieved considerable success according to the prevailing standards of American society; others have been unwilling or unable to adjust to life outside a social struggle. Whatever they have made of their lives since leaving SNCC, the process of self-discovery that took place during the 1960s remains a special part of their lives. Bob Zellner spoke for many when he said that SNCC "was the greatest thing that ever happened in my life and I'm sure in the lives of everybody else that was connected with it."[36]

Johnny Wilson was in many respects representative of the staff members who never acquired national prominence but nonetheless gained a new self-confidence as a result of their association with SNCC. He recalled that when he became a SNCC worker in 1962 he "had no political philosophy," but as the result of his associations with other SNCC workers, he grew along with SNCC. One of the last of the SNCC veterans of the early 1960s to leave the organization, he was deeply hurt by the disintegration of the SNCC "family." He recalled: "It might have been more emotional with me than it was for a lot of other people, but I think it was emotional with everybody. Even today, when one of us is doing something, all of us are doing it."[37]

SNCC left many different legacies, because it was composed of people from different backgrounds who drew different conclusions from their lives in SNCC. Many of the activists who came together during a brief and exceptional period of history have continued to confront basic issues of human freedom, and they have continued to offer partial answers based on their particular experiences during the 1960s and afterward. Jim Forman, who remained on SNCC's staff longer than any other person, represents a dimension of SNCC's legacy in his continuing efforts to build a powerful revolutionary organization in the United States. He symbolizes SNCC workers' attempts during the late 1960s to achieve radical social change by disciplining the rebellious qualities that were strengthened by years of protest and agitation. Forman is driven by his awareness both of SNCC's accomplishments as a civil rights group and its limitations as a revolutionary organization. "We must organize and learn from black workers, constantly summarize our total experiences,discover laws of revolution in the United States, unite with sincere anti-imperialist forces and always give class leadership, resting ourselves in the particular historical forces that have shaped our people."[38]

Forman's belief that revolutionary movements require strong institutions was an outgrowth of an ideological tendency that always conflicted with the deeply rooted belief of many SNCC workers that their role was to stimulate social struggles rather than provide institutionalized leadership for them. Bob Moses symbolized the latter orientation, which was the most singular part of SNCC's legacy.

SNCC departed from Moses' organizing approach during the late 1960s, but it was this approach that set SNCC's radicalism apart from most other reform or revolutionary organizations. Moses recognized how easily the creative potential of people can be crushed by leaders and institutions, and thus he removed himself from the southern struggle at a crucial turning point. Always fearful that his faith in free people would be transformed by others into an enslaving deification of personal freedom, he escaped from the worshipful cult that had gathered around him. More recently he has again expressed his vision of SNCC's complex legacy. "Leadership is there in the people," he affirmed. "You don't have to worry about that. You don't have to worry about where your leaders are, how are we going to get some leaders. The leadership is there. If you go out and work with your people, then the leadership will emerge . . . We don't know who they are now; we don't need to know. But the leadership will emerge from the movement that emerges."[39]

# EPILOGUE

SNCC workers scattered like seeds in a wind after their radicalism could no longer find fertile ground in the southern struggle. Some are still rootless, having left behind much of their spirit in the 1960s, but others have thrived anew in different settings. For most, the years in SNCC brought important accomplishments, personal growth, and warm friendships. More than the bitterness and sadness that sometimes accompanied leaving SNCC, these attributes were evident when former SNCC workers gathered on November 6, 1976, for a reunion.

There were serious matters to be discussed at the gathering in Atlanta, including a plan to file suit against the federal government because of its covert activities against SNCC. But most of the 150 people who attended were attracted mainly by the opportunity to reestablish contact after years apart. The passage of years had softened painful memories; the joy of SNCC's activism survived and found expression in late-night partying, accompanied by freedom songs.

Few of those at the reunion lived in the rural southern communities where SNCC had once concentrated its personnel. More than half were living in large cities, mainly Atlanta, New York, and Washington, D.C. Undoubtedly many former staff members in the Black Belt could not afford to attend the reunion. Those who did attend were typically former college students who had achieved a measure of affluence due to skills for which SNCC had paid them as little as $10 a week. Most were still in some way engaged in promoting social change; as individuals, they still sought the goals for which they had once struggled together.

Some had become prominent in their chosen fields. SNCC's first chairman, Marion Barry, was then a member of the Washington, D.C., Board of Education; later, with the help of his principal adviser Ivanhoe Donaldson, he would be elected mayor of the city. John Lewis had failed in his bid to succeed Andrew Young as a Congressman from Georgia; he would soon be appointed by President Jimmy Carter as associate director of Action, joining another ex-SNCC worker, Mary King, Action's deputy director. Julian Bond, who had achieved national prominence when he was nominated for the Vice-Presidency at the 1968 Democratic convention, has continued to

305

win re-election to his seat in the Georgia Senate. Charles Sherrod became an Albany city commissioner while also seeking to create an agricultural cooperative in southwest Georgia. Johnny Wilson was elected to Washington's city council.

Many former SNCC workers at the reunion had returned or would return to academic lives that had been interrupted by their involvement in the southern struggle. James Forman enrolled at Cornell to work for his doctorate in Pan-African studies. Bob Moses did not attend the reunion, since he was living in Tanzania with his family, but he subsequently returned to Harvard to complete work for his doctorate in philosophy. Stokely Carmichael, who had lived in Guinea since 1968, also did not attend the reunion, as he was traveling abroad at the time. The All African Peoples Revolutionary Party with which he is affiliated was represented, however, by a number of former SNCC workers, including Cleveland Sellers, Willie Ricks, and Bill Hall. Rap Brown, who had adopted the Muslim faith and the name Jamil Abdullah Al-Amin, also did not attend, although he had recently been paroled from prison and was living quietly in Atlanta. Ruby Doris Robinson, Ralph Featherstone, and Fannie Lou Hamer were also not there; they had died while still engaged in struggle.

The reunion offered an unexpected opportunity to talk with staff members I had not previously interviewed. I also gained information about where to find other former SNCC workers living across the country. SNCC's spirit remains vibrant in many places among participants in the struggle who never received much recognition for their sacrifices. Dewey Greene was living in the Greenwood, Mississippi, home that had been a target of bombings and had served as a resting place for numerous SNCC workers, including Greene's children, Freddie and George. Bob Mants owned a farm in Lowndes County, Alabama, where he was attempting to reverse the pattern of black abandonment of southern agricultural lands. Jessie Morris was working for the same objective in Mississippi, a state to which he had gone from California almost two decades before as a college student planning to spend a few weeks aiding the MFDP. In Atlanta, Fay Bellamy was devoting much time to maintaining contact with former SNCC workers. In Mississippi, Jean Wiley was making a film about the southern struggle, and Worth Long was trying to preserve a record of the disappearing musical heritage of southern rural blacks. Maria Varela was working at the medical clinic she had helped organize in a Spanish-speaking community of New Mexico. Phil Hutchings was involved in radical political work in Oakland. Bob Zellner was engaged in labor organizing near his home in New Orleans. Stanley Wise was a leader in the movement to support the African liberation struggle. These and many other people carried on a struggle that did not begin with SNCC's emergence and did not end with its demise.

# NOTES

## ABBREVIATIONS

All sources for which no location is given are in author's files.

FOF    Facts on Film, Southern Education Reporting Service, Nashville, Tennessee

HU    Civil Rights Documentation Project, Howard University, Washington, D.C.

JFK    John F. Kennedy Library, Boston, Massachusetts

*KLM*    *Key List Mailing: Selected Documents of Current and Lasting Interest in the Civil Rights Movement,* San Francisco Regional Office of SNCC, 1965–67

LBJ    Lyndon Baines Johnson Library, Austin, Texas

NL-SU    New Left Collection, Hoover Institution on War, Revolution and Peace, Stanford University, Stanford, California

PS-SU    Project South Collection, Stanford University Archives, Stanford University, Stanford, California

SC-SU    Lorna Smith-Stokely Carmichael Collection, Stanford University Archives, Stanford University, Stanford, California

SHSW    Civil Rights Collection, State Historical Society of Wisconsin, Madison, Wisconsin

UCLA    Civil Rights Movement in the United States Collection, Special Collections, University Research Library, University of California, Los Angeles, California

## INTRODUCTION

1. See e.g. Howard Zinn, *SNCC: The New Abolitionists* (Boston: Beacon Press, 1964; rev. 1965); Julius Lester, *Look Out, Whitey! Black Power's Gon' Get Your Mama!* (New York: Dial Press, 1968); H. Rap Brown, *Die Nigger Die!* (New York: Dial Press, 1969); James Forman, *The Making of Black Revolutionaries* (New York: Macmillan, 1972); Cleveland Sellers, with Robert Terrell, *The River of No Return: The Autobiography of a Black Militant and the Life and Death of SNCC* (New York: William Morrow, 1973). See also Emily Schottenfeld Stoper, "The Student Nonviolent Coordinating Committee: The Growth of Radicalism in a Civil Rights Organi-

zation" (Ph.D. diss., Harvard University, 1968); Stoper, "The Student Nonviolent Coordinating Committee: Rise and Fall of a Redemptive Organization," *Journal of Black Studies* 8 (Sept. 1977): 13–34; Allen J. Matusow, "From Civil Rights to Black Power: The Case of SNCC, 1960–1966," in Barton J. Bernstein and Allen J. Matusow, eds., *Twentieth Century America: Recent Interpretations* (New York: Harcourt Brace & World, 1969), pp. 531–566.

## 1. SIT-INS

1. Albert L. Rozier, Jr., "Students Hit Woolworth's for Lunch Service," (North Carolina A. & T.) *Register*, Feb. 5, 1960; Wilma Dykeman and James Stokely, "Sit Down Chillun, Sit Down!" *Progressive*, June 1960, p. 8; Miles Wolff, *Lunch at the Five and Ten, The Greensboro Sit-ins: A Contemporary History* (New York: Stein and Day, 1970), p. 16.

2. *Greensboro Daily News*, Feb. 8, 1960.

3. James Howard Laue, "Direct Action and Desegregation: Toward a Theory of the Rationalization of Protest" (Ph.D. diss., Harvard University, 1965), pp. liii–lviii, 113–114. See also "The Student Protest Movement, Winter 1960," mimeograph (Atlanta: Southern Regional Council, 1960), pp. xix–xxv; Martin Oppenheimer, "The Genesis of the Southern Negro Student Movement (Sit-in Movement): A Study in Contemporary Negro Protest" (Ph.D. diss., University of Pennsylvania, 1963), pp. 63–65; Paul Ernest Wehr, "The Sit-down Protests . . . A Study of a Passive Resistance Movement in North Carolina" (M.A. thesis, University of North Carolina, 1960); Clarence H. Patrick, *Lunch-Counter Desegregation in Winston-Salem, North Carolina* (Winston-Salem: Department of Sociology, Wake Forest, 1960); Donnie L. Everette and Kennell A. Jackson, Jr., *The Hampton Sit-ins and the Southern Society* (n.p., 1960).

4. Frederick Solomon and Jacob R. Fishman, "The Psychosocial Meaning of Nonviolence in Student Civil Rights Activities," *Psychiatry* 27 (May 1964): 94–95. See also James W. Vander Zanden, "The Nonviolent Resistance Movement against Segregation," *American Journal of Sociology* 68 (Mar. 1963): 544–550.

5. Ted Dienstfrey, "A Conference on the Sit-ins," *Commentary*, June 1960, p. 527; *Student Voice*, Oct. 1960, p. 4.

6. Wehr, "Sit-down Protests," pp. 100, 103; Michael Walzer, "A Cup of Coffee and a Seat," *Dissent*, Summer 1960, p. 114.

7. E. Franklin Frazer, *Black Bourgeoisie* (New York: Collier Books, 1962), p. 76; Ruth Searles and J. Allen Williams, "Negro College Students Participation in Sit-ins," *Social Forces* 40 (Mar. 1962): 219.

8. John Orbell, "Protest Participation among Southern Negro College Students," *American Political Science Review* 61 (June 1967): 554–555; cf. Anthony M. Orum, *Black Student in Protest: A Study in the Origins of the Black Student Movement* (Washington, D.C.: American Sociological Association, n.d.); Thomas E. Pettigrew, *A Profile of the Negro American* (Princeton: D. Van Nostrand, 1964), p. 191.

9. "Protest at Charlotte Is Guided by Student," *Greensboro Daily News*, Feb. 10, 1960; Bill Lamkin, "U.S. Misunderstood—Jones," *Register*, Feb. 12, 1960. See also U.S., Congress, House, Committee on Un-American Activities, *Hearings,*

86th Cong., 2d sess., Feb. 5, 1960, pp. 1451–1461; "Charlotte Negro Shows American Way of Life," *Charlotte Observer,* Aug. 6, 1959.

10. "Fisk Coed Tells of Day in Jail," *Nashville Tennessean,* Aug. 25, 1960.

11. *Atlanta Constitution,* Mar. 9, 1960; "Statement Submitted by the Student Nonviolent Coordinating Committee to the Platform Committee of the National Democratic Convention, June 7, 1960, Los Angeles, California."

12. Eisenhower, in Lester A. Sobel, ed., *Civil Rights, 1960–66* (New York: Facts on File, 1967), p. 11; *News Leader* editorial, Feb. 22, 1960.

13. David Richmond interview, April 10, 1972, in Greensboro; Frederic Solomon and Jacob R. Fishman, "Youth and Social Action: II, Action and Identity Formation in the First Student Sit-in Demonstration," *Journal of Social Issues* 20 (April 1964): 39.

14. Cleveland Sellers, with Robert Terrell, *The River of No Return: The Autobiography of a Black Militant and the Life and Death of SNCC* (New York: William Morrow, 1973), p. 17.

15. Lewis W. Johns, in "Southern Negro Students Termed Angry Youth," *Washington Post,* Mar. 6, 1960; Wehr, "Sit-down Protests," p. 21; Helen Fuller, "We Are All So Very Happy," *New Republic,* April 25, 1960, p. 13.

16. Walzer, "Cup of Coffee," p. 114; Laue, "Direct Action," pp. 115, 116.

17. Diane Nash, "Inside the Sit-ins and Freedom Rides: Testimony of a Southern Student," in Mathew H. Ahmann, ed., *The New Negro* (New York: Biblo and Tannen, 1969), pp. 49–50; Anne Braden, "Student Movement: New Phase," *Southern Patriot,* Nov. 1960, p. 4; Walzer, "Cup of Coffee," p. 120; Ben H. Bagdikian, "Negro Youth's New March on Dixie," *Saturday Evening Post,* Sept. 8, 1962, p. 15.

## 2. GETTING ORGANIZED

1. Youth Leadership Meeting, box 2, folder 1, Atlanta Project Papers, SHSW.

2. Ella Baker, "Bigger than a Hamburger," *Southern Patriot,* May 1960, p. 4; Gerda Lerner, "Developing Community Leadership: Ella Baker," in Lerner, ed., *Black Women in White America: A Documentary History* (New York: Vintage Books, 1973), p. 352.

3. See "Report of the Raleigh Conference," SNCC mimeograph in box 26, CORE Archives, Community Relations Department, SHSW; "Delegates to Youth Leadership Conference, Shaw University—Raleigh, N.C., April 15–17, 1960," SCLC mimeograph, June 2, 1960.

4. "The Nashville Sit-in Story," Folkways Records recording, 1960.

5. Diane Nash, "Inside the Sit-ins and Freedom Rides: Testimony of a Southern Student," in Mathew H. Ahmann, ed., *The New Negro* (New York: Biblo and Tannen, 1969), pp. 44, 45, 48, 49.

6. Archie E. Allen, "John Lewis: Keeper of the Dream," *New South,* Spring 1971, p. 18.

7. "Nonviolent Discipline of the 1960 Nashville Student Sit-in Movement," in folder on Nonviolent Student Sit-in Movement, Student Nonviolent Coordinating Committee, Chicago SNCC Freedom Center Collection, University of Illi-

nois at Chicago Circle Library. Lawson background in "Special Report—the Lawson Case," *Contact,* May 1, 1960, pp. 11–14.

8. Gun Munger, "Students Begin Strategy Talks on Integration," *Greensboro Daily News,* April 16, 1960. See also Helen Fuller, "Southern Students Take Over: 'The Creation of the Beloved Community,' " *New Republic,* May 2, 1960, p. 16; and James Howard Laue, "Direct Action and Desegregation: Toward a Theory of the Rationalization of Protest" (Ph.D. diss., Harvard University, 1965), p. 125.

9. James M. Lawson, "From a Lunch-Counter Stool," reprinted in August Meier, Elliott Rudwick, and Francis L. Broderick, eds., *Black Protest Thought in the Twentieth Century,* 2d ed. (Indianapolis: Bobbs-Merrill, 1971), pp. 308–315.

10. Ted Dienstfrey, "A Conference on the Sit-ins," *Commentary,* June 1960, p. 526.

11. Recommendations passed by Student Nonviolent Coordinating Committee Conference, Atlanta, Georgia, Oct. 14–16, 1960, box 47, folder 3, Braden Papers, SHSW.

12. Howard Zinn, *SNCC: The New Abolitionists* (Boston: Beacon Press, 1965), pp. 33, 34; Baker interview, May 5, 1972, in New York City; Baker, "Bigger Than a Hamburger," p. 4; John Lewis interview, April 17, 1972, in Atlanta.

13. "Racial Problems Put to President," *New York Times,* April 18, 1960, and *Greensboro Daily News,* April 18, 1960.

14. See materials on first meeting of the temporary SNCC in CORE Archives, series 2, Southern Regional office, box 13, Louisiana office, SHSW.

15. *Student Voice,* June 1960, p. 4.

16. Statement submitted by SNCC to Platform Committee of National Democratic Convention, July 7, 1960, Los Angeles, California.

17. Aug. 23 address in box 32, folder 4, Braden Papers, SHSW.

18. "Report from the Office of SNCC," *Student Voice,* Oct. 1960, p. 4; Anne Braden, "Student Protest Movement Taking Permanent Form," *Southern Patriot,* Oct. 1960, p. 4.

19. "Nonviolence and the Achievement of Desegregation," box 62, folder 2, Braden Papers, SHSW. See also "SNCC Conference," *Student Voice,* Oct. 1960, p. 1; Anne Braden, "Student Movement: New Phase," *Southern Patriot,* Nov. 1960, p. 4; Martin Oppenheimer, "The Genesis of the Southern Negro Student Movement (Sit-in Movement): A Study in Contemporary Negro Protest" (Ph.D. diss., University of Pennsylvania, 1963), pp. 92–97; Laue, "Direct Action," pp. 129–130, 346–347.

20. "Student Movement: New Phase," *Southern Patriot,* Nov. 1960, p. 4; James M. Lawson, "Eve of Nonviolent Revolution?" *Southern Patriot,* Nov. 1961, p. 1.

21. Bond interview by Gwen Gillan, tape 497, SHSW.

22. See "SNCC Visits Fayette," *Student Voice,* Jan. 1961, p. 1; "April Meeting of SNCC," *Student Voice,* April-May 1961, p. 3.

23. "November Meeting of SNCC," *Student Voice,* Dec. 1960, p. 1.

### 3. FREEDOM RIDES

1. See Thomas Gaither, *Jailed-In* (New York: League for Industrial Democracy, 1961); James Peck, *Freedom Ride* (New York: Grove Press, 1962), chap. 7;

August Meier and Elliott Rudwick, *CORE: A Study in the Civil Rights Movement 1942–1968* (New York: Oxford University Press, 1973), pp. 117–119; Howard Zinn, *SNCC: The New Abolitionists* (Boston: Beacon Press, 1965), pp. 38, 39; "Three Protest Groups Elect Jail; Call Comes from Rock Hill for Help," *Student Voice*, Feb. 1961, p. 1; "Students Prefer Jail-Ins to Bail-Outs," *Southern Patriot*, March 1961, pp. 1, 3.

2. Fred Sheheen, "South's Negroes to Focus on 'Jail-ins' at Rock Hill," *Charlotte Observer*, Feb. 7, 1961.

3. Ibid.

4. Charlotte Devree, "The Young Negro Rebels," *Harper's Magazine*, Oct. 1961, pp. 134–135.

5. See Meier and Rudwick, *CORE*, pt. 1; George M. Houser, *Erasing the Color Line* (New York: Fellowship Publications, 1947); Carleton Mabee, "Two Decades of Sit-ins: Evolution of Non-violence," *Nation*, Aug. 12, 1961, pp. 78–81.

6. Devree, "Young Negro Rebels," p. 138.

7. On freedom rides, see Zinn, *SNCC*, chap. 3; Meier and Rudwick, *CORE*, chap. 5; Peck, *Freedom Ride*, chap. 8; Louis E. Lomax, *The Negro Revolt* (New York: Harper & Row, 1963), chap. 11; "Freedom Ride, 1961," *Student Voice*, April-May 1961; Southern Regional Council, *The Freedom Ride: May 1961* (Atlanta, 1961).

8. See Peck, *Freedom Ride*, pp. 98–99. For the complicity of Birmingham police and possibly FBI officials in the violence, see U.S., Congress, Senate, Select Committee to Study Governmental Operations with Respect to Intelligence Activities, *Intelligence Activities: Hearings on Senate Resolution 21*, 94th Cong., 1st sess., Dec. 2, 1975, pp. 116–118.

9. Bill Mahoney, "In Pursuit of Freedom," *Liberation*, Sept. 1961, p. 7; Diane Nash, "Inside the Sit-ins and Freedom Rides: Testimony of a Southern Student," in Mathew H. Ahmann, ed., *The New Negro* (New York: Biblo and Tannen, 1969), p. 53.

10. Nash, "Inside the Sit-ins and Freedom Rides," pp. 53–54; Zinn, *SNCC*, pp. 44–45.

11. Cf. Carl M. Brauer, *John F. Kennedy and the Second Reconstruction* (New York: Columbia University Press, 1977), chap. 4; Arthur M. Schlesinger, Jr., *A Thousand Days: John F. Kennedy in the White House* (Boston: Houghton Mifflin, 1965), pp. 847–892; Theodore C. Sorensen, *Kennedy* (New York: Harper & Row, 1965), pp. 528–569.

12. Brauer, *John F. Kennedy*, p. 100. See also Burke Marshall interview by Louis Oberdorfer, May 29, 1964, JFK; John Patterson interview by John Steward, May 26, 1967, JFK; "Untold Story of the 'Freedom Rides,' " *U.S. News and World Report*, Oct. 23, 1961, pp. 76–79; "More Light on the 'Freedom Rides,' " *U.S. News and World Report*, Oct. 30, 1961, pp. 70–71.

13. Marshall interview, p. 19.

14. Lucretia Collins, in James Forman, *The Making of Black Revolutionaries*, (New York: Macmillan, 1972), p. 156. See also Brauer, *John F. Kennedy*, pp. 102–103.

15. Larry A. Still, "A Bus Ride through Mississippi," *Ebony*, Aug. 1961, p. 23.

16. Brauer, *John F. Kennedy*, pp. 106, 108.

17. *Student Voice,* March 1961, p. 1; "SNCC Wires President Kennedy," *Student Voice,* April-May 1961, p. 1.

18. Doar interview, May 5, 1972, in New York City.

19. Memo, Wofford to Kenneth O'Donnell, June 12, 1961, box 804, White House Central Subject Files, JFK.

20. Carmichael interview by Howard Zinn, Summer 1963, in Mississippi.

21. Frank Holloway, "Travel Notes from a Deep South Tourist," *New South 17* ( *July-August 1961*): 8; Forman, *Black Revolutionaries,* p. 157; Mahoney, "In Pursuit of Freedom," p. 11.

22. Meier and Rudwick, *CORE,* p. 173; Brauer, *John F. Kennedy,* p. 114; Victor Navasky, *Kennedy Justice* (New York: Atheneum, 1971), pp. 118–119.

23. Baker interview, May 5, 1972, in New York City. See also U.S., Congress, House, Committee on Un-American Activities, *Hearings,* 86th Cong., 2d sess., Feb. 5, 1960, pp. 1451–1461; "U.S. Misunderstood—Jones," *Register* (North Carolina A. & T.), Feb. 12, 1960; "Charlotte Negro Shows American Way of Life," *Charlotte Observer,* Aug. 6, 1959.

24. Report of Harry Belafonte Committee to SNCC, Aug. 11, 1961, box 62, folder 3, Braden Papers, SHSW.

25. Minutes of SNCC meeting, July 14–16, 1961, box 62, folder 4, Braden Papers, SHSW.

26. "SNCC Office Report," box 62, folder 3, Braden Papers, SHSW.

27. James Howard Laue, "Direct Action and Desegregation: Toward a Theory of the Rationalization of Protest" (Ph.D. diss., Harvard University, 1965), pp. 167, 168.

28. Emily Schottenfeld Stoper, "The Student Nonviolent Coordinating Committee: The Growth of Radicalism in a Civil Rights Organization" (Ph.D. diss., Harvard University, 1968), p. 131; Laue, "Direct Action," p. 172.

29. Baker interview.

30. Baker interview; Marion Barry interview, April 7, 1972, in Washington, D.C.; Zinn, *SNCC,* pp. 58, 59; Forman, *Black Revolutionaries,* pp. 221, 222; David L. Lewis, *King: A Critical Biography* (Baltimore: Penguin Books, 1970), pp. 136–137.

31. Forman, *Black Revolutionaries,* p. 20.

32. "Report on Monroe," *Southern Patriot,* Oct. 1961, p. 2. See also Robert F. Williams, *Negroes with Guns* (New York: Marzani & Munsell, 1962), p. 75; Robert Carl Cohen, *Black Crusader* (Secaucus, New Jersey: Lyle Stuart, 1972), chap. 8.

33. James Forman, "What Is the Student Nonviolent Coordinating Committee; 'A Band of Brothers, a Circle of Trust,'" paper prepared for SNCC staff retreat, Nov. 1964, box 8, UCLA.

## 4. RADICAL CADRE IN McCOMB

1. Robert Penn Warren, *Who Speaks for the Negro?* (New York: Random House, 1965), p. 95.

2. Ben H. Bagdikian, "Negro Youth's New March on Dixie," *Saturday Evening Post,* Sept. 8, 1962, p. 16.

3. Bob Moses, "Mississippi: 1961–1962," *Liberation* 14 (Jan. 1970): 8 (transcript of a tape recording made in 1962). See also Howard Zinn, *SNCC: The New Abolitionists* (Boston: Beacon Press, 1965), chap. 4; Tom Hayden, *Revolution in Mississippi* (New York: Students for a Democratic Society, 1962); James Forman, *The Making of Black Revolutionaries* (New York: Macmillan, 1972), chap. 30; Janet Feagans, "Voting, Violence and Walkout in McComb," *New South,* Oct. 1961, pp. 3, 4, 11.

4. Moses, "Mississippi," p. 10.

5. Ibid., pp. 12, 13; Julian Bond, "Death of a Quiet Man: A Mississippi Postscript," *Rights and Reviews,* Winter 1967, pp. 15–17; "Witness Murdered," *Student Voice,* Feb. 3, 1964, p. 1. See also John Doar and Dorothy Landsberg, *The Performance of the FBI in Investigating Violations of Federal Laws Protecting the Right to Vote— 1960–1967* (n.p., 1971), pp. 32–39.

6. Hayden, *Revolution in Mississippi,* p. 4; Moses, "Mississippi," pp. 14, 15.

7. Robinson interview, April 26, 1972, in Washington, D.C.

8. Forman, *Black Revolutionaries,* p. 220; Minutes of SNCC Executive Committee meeting, Dec. 28, 1963.

9. Braden to Dombrowski, March 9, 1961, box 62, folder 3, Braden Papers, SHSW; Anne Braden, "What is White Person's Place in Current Struggle?" *Southern Patriot,* Sept. 1960, p. 4.

10. See Braden to Barry, Nov. 22, 1960; Braden to Baker, Nov. 22, 1960; Braden to Dombrowski, March 9 and Aug. 8, 1961; box 62, folder 3, Braden Papers, SHSW.

11. Zellner to Dombrowski, June 11, 1961, box 85, Myers G. Lowman Collection, Hoover Library, Stanford University. See also Robert Zellner, "Repression Keeps White Students Silent," *Southern Patriot,* Jan. 1964, pp. 1, 3; Edgar A. Love, "Claiming the Right to Choose: A Profile," *Motive,* Nov. 1962; Zinn, *SNCC,* pp. 168–171.

12. Report by Zellner, May 19, 1962, box 62, folder 3, Braden Papers, SHSW.

13. Hayden to Robert [Al] Haber, "Re: SNCC meeting, Jackson, Mississippi, September 14–17, 1961." See also Kirkpatrick Sale, *SDS* (New York: Random House, 1973), p. 36.

14. Forward to Hayden, *Revolution in Mississippi,* p. 2; James M. Lawson, "Eve of Nonviolent Revolution?" *Southern Patriot,* Nov. 1961, p. 1.

15. "Julian Bond: The Movement, Then and Now," interview by Bob Hall and Sue Thrasher, *Southern Exposure* 3, No. 4 (1976): 10; Forman, *Black Revolutionaries,* p. 238.


5. THE ALBANY MOVEMENT

1. Howard Zinn, *SNCC: The New Abolitionists* (Boston: Beacon Press, 1965), pp. 125–126.

2. David L. Lewis, *King: A Critical Biography* (Baltimore: Penguin Books, 1970), p. 143.

3. Sherrod to Davis, n.d., folder 9, Sherrod Papers, SHSW; Charlotte Devree, "The Young Negro Rebels," *Harper's Magazine,* Oct. 1961, p. 135.

4. Zinn, *SNCC*, p. 125; James Howard Laue, "Direct Action and Desegregation: Toward a Theory of the Rationalization of Protest" (Ph.D. diss., Harvard University, 1965), p. 174.

5. Ibid., pp. 350, 174.

6. Fred Powledge, *Black Power/White Resistance: Notes on the New Civil War* (Cleveland: World Publishing, 1967), p. 39.

7. Zinn, *SNCC*, p. 126.

8. Laue, "Direct Action," p. 176. See also Howard Zinn, *Albany: A Study in National Responsibility* (Atlanta: Southern Regional Council, 1962); James Forman, *The Making of Black Revolutionaries* (New York: Macmillan, 1972), pp. 247-262; Vincent Harding and Staughton Lynd, "Albany, Georgia," *Crisis*, Feb. 1963.

9. Zinn, *SNCC*, p. 128.

10. Forman, *Black Revolutionaries*, p. 247.

11. Bernice Reagon, "In Our Hands: Thoughts on Black Music," *Sing Out!* 24 (Jan.-Feb. 1976), p. 2; Pat Watters, *Down to Now: Reflections on the Southern Civil Rights Movement* (New York: Random House, 1971), p. 158.

12. Laue, "Direct Action," p. 178; Zinn, *SNCC*, p. 130.

13. Zinn, *SNCC*, p. 130.

14. Ibid., p. 131.

15. Lewis, *King*, p. 159.

16. Zinn, *SNCC*, p. 135.

17. Watters, *Down to Now*, pp. 222-223, 206.

18. Zinn, *Albany*, p. 19. See also Reese Cleghorn, "Epilogue in Albany: Were the Mass Marches Worthwhile?" *New Republic*, July 20, 1963, pp. 15-18.

19. Laue, "Direct Action," p. 189. Emphasis in original.

20. Ibid., p. 380; Powledge, *Black Power*, p. 47.

21. Claude Sitton, "Negro Groups Split on Georgia Protest," *New York Times*, Dec. 24, 1961; Lewis, *King*, pp. 152, 163.

22. Reagon, "In Our Hands," p. 1.

23. Josh Dunson, *Freedom in the Air: Song Movements of the 60's* (New York: International Publishers, 1965), p. 62, see also p. 43.

24. Fred Powledge, "Civil Rights Youth Study Strategy," *Atlanta Constitution*, April 14, 1963.

25. Reagon, "In Our Hands," p. 2.

26. See *Songs of the Southern Freedom Movement: We Shall Overcome!*, comp. Guy and Candie Carawan (New York: Oak Publications, 1963).

27. Powledge, *Black Power*, pp. 39-40.


## 6. SUSTAINING THE STRUGGLE

1. See box 62, folders 3 and 4, Braden Papers, SHSW; "Southern Students Leap Forward," *Southern Patriot*, June 1962, pp. 1, 4; Lucy Komisar, "SNCC Challenges Racist Power," *New America*, May 25, 1962, p. 4; James Howard Laue, "Direct Action and Desegregation: Toward a Theory of the Rationalization of Protest" (Ph.D. diss., Harvard University, 1965), p. 344.

2. Laue, "Direct Action," pp. 56, 57, 199, xvii, xli. The persons interviewed

were Julian Bond, Diane Nash Bevel, Paul Brooks, Bernard Lafayette, Charles McDew, Robert Zellner, James Monsonis, Charles Sherrod, Lester McKinnie, Cordell Reagon, Charles Jones, James Forman, and Robert Moses.

3. "Student Charged with Anarchy," *Southern Patriot*, March 1962, pp. 1, 3. SNCC workers' public expressions of determination were sometimes accompanied by private doubts. Psychiatrist Robert Coles commented that an unidentified activist being held on criminal anarchy charges in Louisiana "was afraid of losing his gritty, tough, daring ways and dissolving in tears of panic and confusion, if not disorientation and delusion." See Coles, *Farewell to the South* (Boston: Little, Brown and Co., 1972), p. 211; Major Johns and Ronnie Moore, *It Happened in Baton Rouge, U.S.A.: A Real Life Drama of Our Deep South Today* (New York: CORE, 1962).

4. SCEF news release, April 30, 1962, box 47, folder 12, Braden Papers, SHSW; "Miss[issippi] Judge Halts Expectant Mother's Jail Try," *Student Voice*, June 1963, p. 1.

5. James Forman, *The Making of Black Revolutionaries* (New York: Macmillan, 1972), p. 236; Laue, "Direct Action," pp. 313, 317.

6. Carl M. Brauer, *John F. Kennedy and the Second Reconstruction* (New York: Columbia University Press, 1977), p. 115 fn.

7. Forman, *Black Revolutionaries*, pp. 244, 245.

8. Ibid., p. 237; SNCC audit for 1963, submitted by Jesse B. Blayton, CPA, April 17, 1964.

9. Financial report Jan. 1 to June 1, 1962; SNCC audit for 1963. In 1963 SNCC still received almost half of its income (more than $142,000) from institutional sources (primarily religious organizations, labor unions, and foundations). Personal contributions accounted for $74,000.

10. Bill Hall interview, Nov. 7, 1976, in Atlanta.

11. John Perdew interview, Nov. 7, 1976, in Atlanta.

12. John Wilson interview, April 26, 1972, in Washington, D.C.

13. Fannie Lou Hamer et al., *To Praise Our Bridges: An Autobiography* (Jackson, Mississippi: KIPCO, 1967), pp. 11–12; "Story of Greenwood, Mississippi," Folkways Records. See also Hamer interview, PS-SU; *SNCC Newsletter*, Jan. 21, 1963, p. 2; Jerry DeMuth, "Tired of Being Sick and Tired," *Nation*, June 1, 1964, pp. 548–551.

14. Forman, *Black Revolutionaries*, pp. 267–268.

15. "Report on Terrell County," box 62, folder 3, Braden Papers, SHSW.

16. Forman, *Black Revolutionaries*, p. 276.

17. Pat Watters and Reese Cleghorn, *Climbing Jacob's Ladder: The Arrival of Negroes in Southern Politics* (New York: Harcourt Brace and World, 1967), pp. 165–167.

18. Anne Braden, "The Images Are Broken; Students Challenge Rural Georgia," *Southern Patriot*, Dec. 1962, p. 1.

19. Ibid., p. 3.

20. Perdew interview; Pat Watters, *Down to Now: Reflections on the Southern Civil Rights Movement* (New York: Pantheon Books, 1971), p. 192.

21. Braden, "Students Challenge," p. 3; John Perdew, "Difficult to Organize

the Poorest and the Wealthiest among Negroes . . . ," *I. F. Stone's Bi-Weekly*, Dec. 9, 1963, p. 3; Perdew interview.

22. Watters and Cleghorn, *Climbing Jacob's Ladder*, p. 21.

23. "Survey: Current Field Work, Spring 1963," reprinted in U.S., Congress, House, Committee on the Judiciary, *Civil Rights: Hearings*, 88th Cong., 1st sess., May 28, 1963, p. 1278.

24. Anne Cooke Romaine, "The Mississippi Freedom Democratic Party through August, 1964" (M.A. thesis, University of Virginia, 1970), p. 54; Bob Moses, "Mississippi: 1961–1962," *Liberation* 14 (Jan. 1970): 14–15.

25. See Mississippi Voter-Education Report by Bernice Robinson of the Highlander Center, July 19, 1962, box 3, Braden Papers, University of Tennessee.

26. "Interview with SNCC Leader: Voter Registration Drive Moves Forward Painfully," *New America*, Feb. 6, 1963, p. 5.

27. Moses to "Northern Supporters," Feb. 27, 1963, reprinted in Joanne Grant, ed., *Black Protest: History, Documents, and Analyses: 1619 to the Present* (Greenwich, Conn.: Fawcett, 1968), p. 300; Ernest Nobles interview, Sept. 19, 1968, in McComb.

28. Forman, *Black Revolutionaries*, p. 283.

29. Watters and Cleghorn, *Climbing Jacob's Ladder*, pp. 159–160. See also "Registration Efforts in Mississippi Continue Despite Violence and Terror," *Student Voice*, Oct. 1962, p. 2.

30. Moses, "Mississippi," p. 17.

31. "Surplus Food Denied to Registrants," *Student Voice*, Dec. 19, 1962, p. 2.

32. *Civil Rights: Hearings*, p. 1292; Larry Still, "Step Up Drive to Aid Hungry Mississippi Negroes," *Jet*, Feb. 21, 1963.

33. John Fisher, "A Small Band of Practical Heroes," *Harper's Magazine*, Oct. 1963, p. 24; Grant, *Black Protest*, p. 300.

34. Grant, *Black Protest*, pp. 300–301.

35. Forman, *Black Revolutionaries*, p. 295.

36. Ibid., pp. 300–301.

37. "Civil Rights Youths Study Strategy Here," *Atlanta Constitution*, April 1, 1963. See also "The Students: A New Look," *Southern Patriot*, May 1963, p. 1.

38. Forman, *Black Revolutionaries*, pp. 305, 306, 307. See also, "Only the Literate?" *Southern Patriot*, May 1963, pp. 1, 3; Moses testimony before House Judiciary Committee, in *Civil Rights: Hearings*, p. 1256.

39. Forman, *Black Revolutionaries*, p. 307.

## 7. MARCH ON WASHINGTON

1. "NAG Plans May 17 Demonstrations in D.C.," *Student Voice*, April 1962, p. 3; Carl M. Brauer, *John F. Kennedy and the Second Reconstruction* (New York: Columbia University Press, 1977), p. 156.

2. "SNCC Staffers Sentenced in Mississippi, Kennedy Asked to Witness Trials," *Student Voice*, June 1962, pp. 1, 4; "Police Invade Federal Property," *Student Voice*, June 1962, p. 2.

3. SNCC news release, July 26, 1962, FOF, 1962–63, N21-5643; SNCC news release, n.d. FOF, 1962–63, N21-5644; "Albany Leaders, NAG Protest in Washington," *Student Voice*, Dec. 19, 1962, p. 2.

4. SNCC news release, Aug. 29, 1962, FOF, N21-5658; SNCC news release, Sept. 13, 1962, FOF, N21-5665.

5. McLaurin to Kennedy, Sept. 21, 1962, box 368, White House Subject Files, JFK.

6. SNCC news release, Jan. 26, 1963.

7. "Voter Registration Drive Moves Forward Painfully," *New America*, Feb. 6, 1963, p. 5. See also Neil R. McMillen, "Black Enfranchisement in Mississippi: Federal Enforcement and Black Protest in the 1960s," *Journal of Southern History* 43 (Aug. 1977): 357–358; Alexander M. Bickel, "Impeach Judge Cox," *New Republic*, Sept. 4, 1965, p. 13.

8. See U.S., Congress, House, Committee on the Judiciary, Subcommittee No. 5, *Civil Rights: Hearings*, 88th Cong., 1st sess., pt. 2, p. 1282.

9. Doar interview, May 5, 1972, in New York City.

10. White to McDew, Sept. 18, 1962; White to McDew, Oct. 1, 1962, box 368, White House Subject Files, JFK (emphasis added).

11. John Doar later argued that the Justice Department did not have sufficient evidence of Mississippi voting rights violations to justify intervention in 1962, but that the evidence collected over many years in the case of *United States vs. Mississippi* was crucial in gaining congressional support for the voting rights legislation passed in 1965. When he filed the case in 1962, "no one on the floor of the Senate, no members of the civil rights organizations spoke up and said that every fact in that complaint is accurate—we know it to be true. And the country at large didn't know. Whereas . . . two years later after the evidence had been put in before the Congress . . . there was no question by then as to what were the facts in the South. The facts were the same, but the proof of the facts was different." Doar interview.

12. See Marshall to McDew, April 5, 1963, box 369, HU 2/St 24, White House Subject Files, JFK; memo to President Kennedy, April 8, 1963, box 23, White House Staff Files, Lee White Papers, JFK.

13. Doar interview. Doar added that in rural Mississippi "a complete law enforcement network" would have been necessary to protect "even a handful of civil rights workers . . . And you couldn't protect them then, because the SNCC kids were going to feel that they had a right to come and go anywhere they pleased . . . How do you protect a person in that situation? . . ." See also Brauer, *John F. Kennedy*, chap. 6; Victor Navasky, *Kennedy Justice* (New York: Atheneum, 1971), chap. 3.

14. *Civil Rights: Hearings*, p. 1250, 1253–1254, 1256, 1259.

15. See "Gloria Richardson: Lady General of Civil Rights," *Ebony*, July 1964, pp. 23, 24, 25, 28, 30.

16. See James Forman, *The Making of Black Revolutionaries* (New York: MacMillan, 1972), pp. 326–331.

17. Southern Regional Council, "Civil Rights: Year-End Summary," Dec. 31, 1963.

18. Arthur M. Schlesinger, Jr., *A Thousand Days: John F. Kennedy in the White House* (Boston: Houghton Mifflin Company, 1965), pp. 884–885.

19. "Negro Leader Takes Issue with Kennedy's Remarks," *Roanoke Times*, July 19, 1963; SNCC news release, FOF, 1963–64, J7 3598, June 15, 1963.

20. Cf. Jane Lee J. Eddy, Executive Director of the Taconic Foundation, to author, April 16, 1971; *Taconic Foundation Report, December 1965*; Reese Cleghorn, "The Angels Are White: Who Pays the Bills for Civil Rights?" *New Republic*, Aug. 17, 1963, pp. 12–14; Lerone Bennett, Jr., *Confrontation: Black and White* (Baltimore: Penguin Books, 1965), pp. 241–248.

21. "Federal Jury Indicts Nine," *Student Voice*, Oct. 1963, p. 3; Navasky, *Kennedy Justice*, pp. 121–123; Brauer, *John F. Kennedy*, p. 289.

22. Original text reprinted in Joanne Grant, ed., *Black Protest: History, Documents, and Analyses, 1619 to the Present* (Greenwich, Conn.: Fawcett, 1968), pp. 375–377.

23. Lewis interview, April 17, 1972, in Atlanta.

24. Lewis interview; Cox interview, April 8, 1972, in Washington, D.C.; Forman, *Black Revolutionaries*, pp. 334–335; Emily Schottenfeld Stoper, "The Student Nonviolent Coordinating Committee: The Growth of Radicalism in a Civil Rights Organization" (Ph.D. diss., Harvard University, 1968), pp. 70–72. A conflicting account of the meeting at the Statler Hotel is provided by Closter B. Current, NAACP administrator (letter to author, Jan. 10, 1977): "John Lewis as I recall it was reasonable, but Cox was not. Also, the next day, [Lewis] had some difficulty with James Forman who seemed to exercise undue influence over the SNCC ideology."

25. Cleveland Sellers, with Robert Terrell, *The River of No Return: The Autobiography of a Black Militant and the Life and Death of SNCC* (New York: William Morrow, 1973), p. 66.

26. *Student Voice*, Oct. 1963, pp. 1, 3, 4.

## 8. PLANNING FOR CONFRONTATION

1. "Moses of Mississippi Raises Some Universal Questions," *Pacific Scene* 5 (Feb. 1965): 4; Branton to Moses, in Pat Watters and Reese Cleghorn, *Climbing Jacob's Ladder: The Arrival of Negroes in Southern Politics* (New York: Harcourt Brace and World, 1967), pp. 213–214.

2. Lowenstein interview, May 16, 1977, in Stanford, California.

3. Executive Committee minutes Sept. 6–9, 1963; Leslie Burl McLemore, "The Mississippi Freedom Democratic Party: A Case Study of Grass-Roots Politics" (Ph. D. diss., University of Massachusetts, 1971), p. 102.

4. Donaldson in James Forman, *The Making of Black Revolutionaries* (New York: Macmillan, 1972), p. 356; Lawrence Guyot and Mike Thelwell, "The Politics of Necessity and Survival in Mississippi," *Freedomways* 6 (Spring 1966): 132.

5. "Three Hundred Attend SNCC Conference," *Student Voice*, Dec. 9, 1963, p. 2; I. F. Stone, *In a Time of Torment* (New York: Random House, 1967), p. 361.

6. Howard Zinn, *SNCC: The New Abolitionists* (Boston: Beacon Press, 1965), pp. 187–189. See also "Notes on Mississippi Staff Meeting, Greenville, November

14–16, 1963"; Len Holt, *The Summer That Didn't End* (London: Heinemann, 1966), p. 36; Mary Aickin Rothschild, "Northern Volunteers and the Southern 'Freedom Summers,' 1964–1965: A Social History" (Ph.D. diss., University of Washington, 1974), pp. 26–29; Anne Cooke Romaine, "The Mississippi Freedom Democratic Party through August, 1964" (M.A. thesis, University of Virginia, 1970), pp. 88–89.

7. Bob Robertson, "Militant Plan to Create Crisis in Mississippi," *San Francisco Chronicle*, Dec. 7, 1963.

8. Minutes of SNCC Executive Committee meeting, Dec. 30, 1963.

9. Romaine, "Mississippi Freedom Democratic Party," pp. 71, 73.

10. "The Students: A New Look," *Southern Patriot*, May 1963, p. 3.

11. Zinn, *SNCC*, pp. 185, 222, 235.

12. Robert Penn Warren, *Who Speaks for the Negro?*, (New York: Random House, 1965), pp. 95–97.

13. Lewis interview in *Dialogue Magazine* 4 (Spring 1964), reprinted in August Meier, Elliott Rudwick, and Francis L. Broderick, eds., *Black Protest Thought in the Twentieth Century*, 2d ed. (Indianapolis: Bobbs-Merrill, 1971), p. 357.

14. Minutes of SNCC Executive Committee meeting, Dec. 29, 1963.

15. Untitled manuscript by Anne Braden, box 62, Braden Papers, SHSW.

16. Executive Committee meeting, Dec. 29, 1963.

17. Braden to Continuations Committee of SSOC, April 17, 1964, box 61, folder 3, Braden Papers, SHSW.

18. Minutes of SNCC Executive Committee meeting, April 19, 1964.

19. James Howard Laue, "Direct Action and Desegregation: Toward a Theory of the Rationalization of Protest" (Ph.D. diss., Harvard University, 1965), p. 377.

20. "Wallace Sparks Cambridge Protests," *Student Voice*, May 19, 1964, p. 2.

21. Cleveland Sellers, with Robert Terrell, *The River of No Return: The Autobiography of a Black Militant and the Life and Death of SNCC* (New York: William Morrow, 1973), p. 61.

22. Carmichael interview by Howard Zinn, summer 1963, in Mississippi. See also Kirkpatrick Sale, *SDS* (New York: Random House, 1973), p. 102.

23. Brochure regarding conference and report of the Resolutions Committee in box 62, folder 4, Braden Papers, SHSW; Elizabeth Sutherland, "SNCC Takes Stock: Mandate from History," *Nation*, Jan. 6, 1964, pp. 30–33; Eleanor Holmes, "Conway and Rustin Praise Negro Youth on the March," *New America*, Dec. 27, 1963, p. 4; "SNCC Conference: Affirm Continued Rights Battle," *News & Letters*, Dec. 1963, FOF, 1963–64, K16 2634.

24. Minutes of SNCC Executive Committee meeting, Dec. 27, 1963.

25. Ruby Doris Robinson, "The SNCC Explosion," Spring 1964, mimeograph.

26. King stated that although there was no evidence that O'Dell was still a Communist party member, SCLC could not risk the impression "that SCLC and the Southern Freedom Movement are Communist inspired." See King to O'Dell, July 3, 1963, box 8, Martin Luther King folder, Burke Marshall Papers, JFK; David Wise, "The Campaign to Destroy Martin Luther King," *New York Review of Books*, Nov. 11, 1976, pp. 38–42.

27. Carmichael interview by Howard Zinn, 1963.

28. Theodore H. White, "Power Structure, Integration, Militancy, Freedom Now!" *Life,* Nov. 29, 1963, pp. 86–87.

29. Minutes of SNCC Executive Committee meeting, Dec. 28, 1963.

30. Minutes of SNCC Executive Committee meeting, April 19, 1964, Atlanta; Lewis in "SNCC Charges Hoover, FBI, Aid Racists," SNCC news release, April 30, 1964; William M. Kunstler, "Journey to Understanding: Four Witnesses to a Mississippi Summer," *Nation,* Dec. 28, 1964. During the summer of 1964 Moses established the COFO Legal Advisory Committee, comprised of SNCC supporters R. Hunter Morey, Arthur Kinoy, William Kunstler, and Benjamin Smith. Kinoy and Smith were members of the Lawyers Guild, a fact that drew criticism of COFO from NAACP officials and Arthur Schlesinger, Jr. See Forman, *Black Revolutionaries,* pp. 367, 381–382.

31. Forman, *Black Revolutionaries,* p. 365; Reese Cleghorn, "The Angels Are White: Who Pays the Bills for Civil Rights?" *New Republic,* Aug. 17, 1963, pp. 12–14.

32. Minutes of SNCC Executive Committee meeting, April 10, 1964.

33. See "Meeting," *New Yorker,* April 11, 1964, pp. 33–36; Holt, *Summer That Didn't End,* p. 157.

34. Zinn, *SNCC,* chap. 6; "Freedom Day in Hattiesburg," *Student Voice,* Jan. 27, 1964, p. 2; "Ministers Arrested, Demonstrations Banned," *Student Voice,* Feb. 3, 1964, p. 3; "Miss[issippi] Freedom Days Spur Registration," *Student Voice,* Mar. 3, 1964, p. 2.

35. Minutes of COFO Convention, Feb. 9, 1964, JoAnn O. Robinson Papers, "Mississippi: Madison County COFO Staff Minutes and Reports, 1964–1965," SHSW.

36. Holt, *Summer That Didn't End,* pp. 155–156.

37. Ibid., p. 158; Romaine, "Mississippi Freedom Democratic Party," p. 26; and McLemore, "Mississippi Freedom Democratic Party," pp. 107–108.

38. "Prospectus for a Summer Freedom School Program," and memo from Cobb to SNCC Executive Committee, Jan. 14, 1964, box 9, UCLA.

39. Viola M. Brooks, *Freedom Schools* (Los Angeles: California State Association of Colored Women's Clubs, 1965), p. 31.

40. Memo from Mississippi Summer Project Staff to Mississippi Freedom School Teachers, May 5, 1964, box 9, UCLA; "Notes on Teaching in Mississippi," in Holt, *Summer That Didn't End,* p. 325.

41. Text in Holt, *Summer That Didn't End,* pp. 197–198; James Forman, "Freedom Push in Mississippi," *Los Angeles Times,* June 14, 1964.

## 9. MISSISSIPPI CHALLENGE

1. "Criteria for Screening Applications for Work with COFO in Mississippi," box 3, UCLA.

2. James Atwater, " 'If We Can Crack Mississippi . . . ',' " *Saturday Evening Post,* July 25, 1964, p. 16. See also Mary Aickin Rothschild, "Northern Volunteers and the Southern 'Freedom Summers,' 1964–1965: A Social History" (Ph.D. diss., University of Washington, 1974), chap. 2.

3. Cleveland Sellers, with Robert Terrell, *The River of No Return: The Autobiography of a Black Militant and the Life and Death of SNCC* (New York: William Morrow, 1973), p. 82.

4. Bill Hodes to "Folks," ca. June 16, 1964, in Hodes Papers, University of Tennessee.

5. Elizabeth Sutherland, ed., *Letters from Mississippi* (New York: McGraw-Hill, 1965), p. 4; Muriel Tillinghast interview, Nov. 7, 1976, in Atlanta.

6. Bill Hodes to "Folks."

7. Sally Belfrage, *Freedom Summer* (New York: Viking Press, 1965), pp. 81, 9–11. See also Sellers, *River of No Return*, pp. 83–84.

8. "A Chronology of Violence and Intimidation in Mississippi since 1961," SNCC, 1964.

9. Len Holt, *The Summer That Didn't End* (London: Heinemann, 1966), pp. 189–194.

10. Belfrage, *Freedom Summer*, pp. 25–26.

11. "Chairman Requests Federal Marshalls," *Student Voice*, June 30, 1964, p. 2. See also Hoover to Walter Jenkins, July 13, 1964, HU 2/ST 24, White House Central Files, JFK; Lester A. Sobel, ed., *Civil Rights, 1960–66* (New York: Facts on File, 1967), p. 244; Memo from Moses to Mississippi Summer Project Contacts, June 27, 1964, FOF, 1963–64, N17 451.

12. See William Bradford Huie, *Three Lives for Mississippi* (New York: New American Library, 1968).

13. Sellers, *River of No Return*, pp. 95–96.

14. Jerry DeMuth, "Summer in Mississippi; Freedom Moves in to Stay," *Nation*, Sept. 14, 1964, p. 109; Sutherland, *Letters*, p. 43.

15. Belfrage, *Freedom Summer*, pp. 50, 75.

16. Paul Good, *The Trouble I've Seen: White Journalist/Black Movement* (Washington, D.C.: Howard University Press, 1975), pp. 143–144; Polly Greenberg, *The Devil Has Slippery Shoes: A Biased Biography of the Child Development Group of Mississippi* (London: Macmillan, 1969), pp. 89–90.

17. Atwater, " 'If We Can Crack Mississippi . . . ,' " pp. 17–18.

18. Neil R. McMillen, "Black Enfranchisement in Mississippi: Federal Enforcement and Black Protest in the 1960s," *Journal of Southern History* 43 (Aug. 1977): 367. See also Leslie Burl McLemore, "The Mississippi Freedom Democratic Party: A Case Study of Grass-Roots Politics" (Ph.D. diss., University of Massachusetts, 1971), pp. 110–111.

19. Memo from Bruce Maxwell to COFO staff, Sept. 7, 1964.

20. Bruce Maxwell, "We Must Be Allies . . . Race Has Led Us Both to Poverty," (mimeograph, 1964).

21. Ed Hamlett, "White Folk's Project," (mimeograph, 1964), Maxwell to COFO staff.

22. Maxwell, "We Must Be Allies."

23. Maxwell to COFO staff.

24. Sutherland, *Letters*, p. 104.

25. Holt, *Summer That Didn't End*, p. 113.

26. Sutherland, *Letters*, pp. 100, 97.

27. "Freedom School Data," (COFO mimeograph, Aug. 1964), box 9, UCLA;

Ralph Featherstone quoted in "Freedom Schools Mississippi," *Student Voice*, Aug. 5, 1964, p. 2.

28. Staughton Lynd, "The Freedom Schools: Concept and Organization," *Freedomways* 5 (Spring 1965): 306. See also Holt, *Summer That Didn't End*, pp. 116–122.

29. Howard Zinn, "Schools in Context: The Mississippi Idea," *Nation*, Nov. 23, 1964, p. 10.

30. John Doar and Dorothy Landsberg, *The Performance of the FBI in Investigating Violations of Federal Law Protecting the Right to Vote—1960–1967* (n.p., 1971), p. 47, photocopy at JFK. See also Steven F. Lawson, *Black Ballots: Voting Rights in the South, 1944–1969* (New York: Columbia University Press, 1976), p. 302.

31. Belfrage, *Freedom Summer*, pp. 55, 164.

32. "Mississippi Summer Project, Running Summary of Incidents," SNCC, 1964, box 4, folder 22, UCLA; "Bombings in McComb, Mississippi," box 8, presidential folder, Burke Marshall Papers, JFK. Another source lists the following statistics for the summer: "A thousand arrests; 35 shooting incidents, with three persons injured; 30 homes and other buildings bombed; 35 churches burned; 80 persons beaten; at least six persons murdered." See Pat Watters, *Encounter with the Future* (Atlanta: Southern Regional Council, 1965), p. 3.

33. Howard Zinn, *SNCC: The New Abolitionists* (Boston: Beacon Press, 1965), p. 222; Tillinghast interview; Sutherland, *Letters*, pp. 44–45.

34. Belfrage, *Freedom Summer*, p. 183.

35. James Millstone, "Better Police Protection Called Most Important Gain in Summer of Rights Work in Mississippi," *St. Louis Post Dispatch*, Aug. 13, 1964.

36. "Over 800 Meet at MFDP Convention," *Student Voice*, Aug. 12, 1964, p. 1.

37. Holt, *Summer That Didn't End*, p. 167; "Demo Convention Faces Showdown," *Student Voice*, Aug. 19, 1964, pp. 1, 4.

38. Holt, *Summer That Didn't End*, p. 165.

39. See transcript of George Reedy news conference, Aug. 19, 1964, National Security File, Civil Rights, vol. 1, LBJ; U.S., Congress, Senate, Select Committee to Study Government Operations with Respect to Intelligence Activities, *Intelligence Activities: Hearings on Senate Resolution 21*, 94th Cong., 1st sess., vol. 6, pp. 174–177, 495–510; *Final Report: Supplementary Detailed Staff Reports on Intelligence Activities and the Rights of Americans*, Book II, 94th Cong., 2d sess., April 26, 1976, pp. 117–199.

40. Rauh interview in Anne Cooke Romaine, "The Mississippi Freedom Democratic Party through August, 1964" (M.A. thesis, University of Virginia, 1970), pp. 311, 315. Johnson had been informed of the idea of seating both delegations in an August 10 memo from Bill Moyers. See Fred Dutton to Moyers, Aug. 10, 1964, box 368, White House Subject Files, PL 1/ST 24, LBJ; "Presidential Neutrality Urged on Mississippi," *Los Angeles Times*, Aug. 19, 1964.

41. See *Congressional Record*, Aug. 20, 1964, pp. 20712–20713.

42. James Forman, *The Making of Black Revolutionaries* (New York: Macmillan, 1972) p. 387.

43. Theodore H. White, *The Making of the President 1964* (New York: New American Library, 1965), p. 333.

44. Romaine, "Mississippi Freedom Democratic Party," pp. 335–336.

45. Charles Sherrod, "Mississippi at Atlantic City," *Grain of Salt* (Union Theological Seminary), Oct. 12, 1964, p. 6.

46. Sherrod, "Mississippi at Atlantic City," p. 9; Forman, *Black Revolutionaries*, pp. 391–395.

47. Lyndon Johnson, *The Vantage Point: Perspectives of the Presidency, 1963–1969* (New York: Holt, Rinehart and Winston, 1971), p. 101. See also Professor Walter Adams (who was supervising the sergeants-at-arms on the convention floor) to Walter Jenkins, Sept. 1, 1964, White House Central Files, PL 1/ST 24, LBJ.

48. "The Convention Challenge," mimeograph sent to Friends of the MFDP; condensed as "MFDP Gives Live Lesson in Democracy," in Nov. 1964 newsletter of Bay Area Friends of SNCC.

49. Lewis interview, April 17, 1972, in Atlanta; Romaine, "Mississippi Freedom Democratic Party," p. 248.

50. Sherrod, "Mississippi at Atlantic City," pp. 9–11.

51. Stokely Carmichael and Charles V. Hamilton, *Black Power: The Politics of Liberation in America* (New York: Random House, 1967), p. 96; Lawrence Guyot and Mike Thelwell, "The Politics of Necessity and Survival in Mississippi," *Freedomways* 6 (Spring 1966): 132.

52. "Moses of Mississippi Raises Some Universal Questions," *Pacific Scene* 5 (Feb. 1965): 4.

53. Mario Savio, "An End to History," in Massimo Teodori, ed., *The New Left: A Documentary History* (Indianapolis: Bobbs-Merrill, 1969), p. 159.

## 10. WAVELAND RETREAT

1. James Forman, *The Making of Black Revolutionaries* (New York: Macmillan, 1972), p. 427.

2. "Brief Report on Guinea," mimeograph, Sept. 26, 1964, p. 10.

3. Fannie Lou Hamer et al., *To Praise Our Bridges: An Autobiography* (Jackson, Mississippi: KIPCO, 1967), p. 21.

4. John Neary, *Julian Bond: Black Rebel* (New York: William Morrow, 1971), p. 73. Staughton Lynd wrote that Moses, during a 1965 visit to Africa, saw his and Hamer's picture in a magazine published by the United States Information Agency "over some such caption as: 'Bob Moses and Mrs. Hamer leading delegates of the [MFDP] to their seats at the Democratic party convention.' Bob felt . . . that the magazine had used him, and those who had died in Mississippi . . . to convey to the rest of the world that democracy still existed in a country which could produce Bob Moses." See Lynd, "A Radical Speaks in Defense of S. N. C. C.," *New York Times Magazine*, Sept. 10, 1967, p. 152.

5. John Lewis and Don Harris, "The Trip," report to SNCC staff, Dec. 14, 1964, pp. 5–6.

6. Ibid., pp. 3, 8. See also George Breitman, *The Last Year of Malcolm X: The Evolution of a Black Revolutionary* (New York: Schocken Books, 1968), p. 79.

7. George Breitman, ed., *Malcolm X Speaks: Selected Speeches and Statements* (New York: Merit, 1965), pp. 151–152; "Interview with John Lewis," *Militant*, April 5, 1965.

8. Rowland Evans and Robert Novak, "Civil Rights—Danger Ahead," *Washington Post*, Dec. 2, 1964; mimeographed text of Lewis' speech, Feb. 1965.

9. Moses in "Two Hundred Volunteers to Stay in Mississippi This Winter," *New Orleans Times-Picayune*, Aug. 20, 1964; Evans and Novak, "Freedom Party Postscript," *Washington Post*, Sept. 3, 1964. See also Joseph Alsop, "An Unhappy Secret" *Washington Post*, April 15, 1964.

10. Transcript by Mendy Samstein of SNCC, "Rough Minutes of a Meeting Called by the National Council of Churches to Discuss the Mississippi Project," Sept. 18, 1964. See also Forman, *Black Revolutionaries*, pp. 399–405; transcript in box 13, CORE, Southern Regional office, series 2, Louisiana office, SHSW; Current to author, Jan. 10, 1977.

11. See "Outline for Projected Black Belt Program," Aug. 1964; Forman, *Black Revolutionaries*, p. 416; memo from Moses to COFO workers, Aug. 11, 1964, box 3, folder 11, UCLA.

12. Cleveland Sellers, with Robert Terrell, *The River of No Return: The Autobiography of a Black Militant and the Life and Death of SNCC* (New York: William Morrow, 1973), p. 112; Robert Coles, *Farewell to the South* (Boston: Little, Brown, 1972), p. 253; Forman, *Black Revolutionaries*, p. 416.

13. Forman, *Black Revolutionaries*, p. 417.

14. Ibid., pp. 425, 424, 366; Forman, "What Is the Student Nonviolent Coordinating Committee: 'A Band of Brothers, a Circle of Trust,' " box 8, UCLA, p. 21.

15. Forman, *Black Revolutionaries*, pp. 423, 420.

16. Memo to SNCC staff, "Re: SNCC Staff Retreat." This paper and most other Waveland position papers are in folder 23, Sherrod Papers, SHSW.

17. Untitled, unsigned paper. See also Forman, *Black Revolutionaries*, p. 432.

18. "From Sherrod," n.d., folder 23, Sherrod Papers, SHSW.

19. "Some Basic Considerations for the Staff Retreat," n.d., folder 23, Sherrod Papers, SHSW.

20. Howard Zinn, memo to planners of staff meeting, n.d.; "Introduction: Semi-Introspective" (author's name withheld by request), n.d., folder 23, Sherrod Papers, SHSW.

21. "From Sherrod"; Maria Varela, "Training SNCC Staff to Be Organizers," n.d.; "What Is SNCC?" n.d., folder 23, Sherrod Papers, SHSW.

22. "What Is SNCC? What Should It Be to Accomplish Its Goals?" n.d.; James Pittman, untitled paper, n.d., folder 23, Sherrod Papers, SHSW.

23. Frank Smith, "Position Paper #1," n.d., folder 23, Sherrod Papers, SHSW.

24. R. Hunter Morey, quoted in Mary Aickin Rothschild, "Northern Volunteers and the Southern 'Freedom Summers,' 1964–1965: A Social History" (Ph.D. diss., University of Washington, 1974), p. 94; Liz Fusco, "To Blur the Focus of What You Came Here to Know: A Letter Containing Notes on Education, Freedom Schools and Mississippi," mimeograph (Siden, Mississippi, 1966), p. 1.

25. "Moses of Mississippi Raises Some Universal Questions," *Pacific Scene* 5 (Feb. 1965): 4.

26. Silas Norman, "What Is the Importance of Racial Considerations in the SNCC Staff?" n.d., folder 23, Sherrod Papers, SHSW.

27. "From Sherrod"; Rev. Tom Brown, "Position Paper"; "Introduction: Semi-Introspective," n.d., folder 23, Sherrod Papers, SHSW; Mike Miller, memo to SNCC national staff, "Re: Questions Raised for National Staff Meeting."

28. Mimeographed text of Forman's address, Nov. 6, 1964.

29. "Summary of Staff Retreat Minutes," Nov. 10, 1964.

30. Sellers, *River of No Return*, p. 115.

31. "SNCC Position Paper," n.d. Authorship of this paper has erroneously been attributed to Ruby Doris Robinson, but Sara Evans has recently concluded that Hayden and King were the principal authors. See Evans, *Personal Politics: The Roots of Women's Liberation in the Civil Rights Movement and the New Left* (New York: Alfred A. Knopf, 1979), p. 85.

32. Forman address, Nov. 6, 1964; Stokely Carmichael interview (telephone), Oct. 18, 1977; Muriel Tillinghast interview, Nov. 7, 1976 in Atlanta; Cynthia Washington, "We Started from Different Ends of the Spectrum," *Southern Exposure* 4 (Winter 1977): 15. Carmichael asserted that those who raised the issue of sexual discrimination were trying "to stop the movement from going towards nationalism, because they [white women] thought that they were going to be put out of the movement."

33. Sandra Hayden and Mary E. King, "Sex and Caste," *Liberation*, April 1966, pp. 35–36.

34. Marion Barry interview, April 7, 1972, in Washington, D.C.

35. "Mississippi: A Man and a Movement," *Southern Patriot*, Nov. 1966, p. 7.

36. See Debbie Louis, *And We Are Not Saved: A History of the Movement as People* (Garden City, N.Y.: Doubleday, 1970), pp. 215–216.

37. Apparently, Kunstler and Smith also forced the resignation of moderate Henry Aronson as COFO's staff counsel by refusing to provide promised financial support for Aronson's office. See Aronson to COFO staff, Jan. 19, 1964, box 1, Benjamin E. Smith Collection, SHSW.

38. "Holly Springs Project—Letters from Cleveland Sellers," box 3, folder 11, UCLA.

39. Forman *Black Revolutionaries*, p. 437.

40. "Statement by John Lewis, Chairman," mimeograph, Feb. 1965. See also Howard Zinn, *SNCC: The New Abolitionists* (Boston: Beacon Press, 1965), p. 268; materials regarding meeting in box 8, UCLA.

41. "SNCC Programs for 1965," mimeograph, Feb. 23, 1965.

## 11. BREAKING NEW GROUND

1. Transcript of address at SSOC conference, Mar. 20, 1965, in Atlanta. See also Jimmy Garrett, "Who Decides?" *Movement*, April 1965, p. 2.

2. Charles Cobb, "What We Have Discovered," *Freedomways* 5 (Spring 1965): 340–341.

3. Anonymous white female SNCC volunteer, interview #405, PS-SU, pp. 4–5.

4. Liz Fusco, "To Blur the Focus of What You Came Here to Know: A Letter Containing Notes on Education, Freedom Schools and Mississippi," mimeograph (Sidon, Mississippi, 1966), p. 1; Jane Stembridge, "Some Notes on Education," box 6, NL-SU.

5. Cleveland Sellers, with Robert Terrell, *The River of No Return: The Autobiography of a Black Militant and the Life and Death of SNCC* (New York: William Morrow, 1973), p. 131. Cobb distinguished between two groups of "floaters"—the "freedom highs" who were "essentially white intellectuals and some southern black staff members who tended to go off to do 'irresponsibility.'" See Charles Cobb, "On Snick/Revolution/and Freedom," box 6, NL-SU.

6. Sellers, *River of No Return*, pp. 131, 134.

7. James Forman, *The Making of Black Revolutionaries* (New York: Macmillan, 1972), p. 422.

8. Lerone Bennett, Jr., "SNCC: Rebels with a Cause," *Ebony*, July 1965, p. 148.

9. Sellers, *River of No Return*, pp. 135–137.

10. Cobb, "On Snick/Revolution/and Freedom."

11. Cf. minutes of Executive Committee, Mar. 5–6, 1965, in Atlanta; SNCC's narrative of events of Mar. 7–9 in section 48, Lucy Montgomery Papers, SHSW; "Bloody Sunday," special supplement to *Student Voice* entitled "March through Selma," Mar. 1965; James Forman, *Sammy Younge, Jr.: The First Black College Student to Die in the Black Liberation Movement* (New York: Grove Press, 1968), p. 75; Forman, *Black Revolutionaries*, p. 441; "The Southern Movement," *Mt. Adams Review* 2 (1966): 13.

12. Earl and Miriam Selby, *Odyssey: Journey through Black America* (New York: G. P. Putnam's Sons, 1971), p. 68; David L. Lewis, *King: A Critical Biography* (Baltimore: Penguin Books, 1970), p. 275.

13. Sellers, *River of No Return*, pp. 122–123.

14. Lewis, *King*, p. 281.

15. Forman, *Sammy Younge*, pp. 91, 100–101; "Dr. King May Be White South's Best Friend," *Nashville Banner*, Mar. 24, 1965.

16. Paul Good, "Odyssey of a Man—and a Movement," *New York Times Magazine*, June 25, 1967, p. 46.

17. SSOC conference, Mar. 20, 1965. See also Martin Luther King, *Where Do We Go from Here: Chaos or Community?* (Boston: Beacon Press, 1967), p. 34.

18. Transcript of Executive Committee meeting, April 12, 1965, p. 11; Penny Patch, Chris Williams, Elayne Delatt, Louis Grant, Ed Brown to "SNCC Folk," Mar. 19, 1965, box 6, NL-SU.

19. Carmichael interview by Howard Zinn, 1963; Carmichael interview, Feb. 15, 1973, in Los Angeles; Carmichael interview (telephone), Oct. 18, 1977.

20. See Sally Belfrage, *Freedom Summer* (New York: Viking Press, 1965), p. 134.

21. Stokely Carmichael, "Who Is Qualified?" *New Republic*, Jan. 8, 1966, p. 22.

22. Alabama State staff meeting, April 22, 1965, p. 6; Carmichael interview, Oct. 18, 1977. See also Stokely Carmichael and Charles V. Hamilton, *Black Power: The Politics of Liberation in America* (New York: Random House, 1967), pp. 98–103.

23. Jack Shepherd, "A Worker Hits the Freedom Road," *Look,* Nov. 16, 1965, p. 46.

24. Transcript of executive committee meeting, April 11, 1965, in Holly Springs, Miss.; Carmichael interview, Feb. 15, 1973. Cf. Julian Bond interview in Howell Raines, *My Soul Is Rested: Movement Days in the Deep South Remembered* (New York: G. P. Putnam's Sons, 1977), p. 267.

25. "Tense Lowndes Erupts as Minister Is Slain," *Southern Courier,* Aug. 25, 1965, p. 1.

26. Frank Miles in "Lowndes County Freedom Organization Leaders Talk about Their Party," *The Movement,* June 1966, p. 3.

27. Ibid.

28. Stokely Carmichael, " 'Integration Is Completely Irrelevant to Us: What We Want Is Power for People Who Don't Have It,' " *The Movement,* June 1966, p. 4.

29. Courtland Cox, "What Would It Profit a Man. . . . A Report on Alabama," SNCC pamphlet, 1966. See also transcript of SNCC staff meeting, Nov. 25, 1965.

30. Gwen Gillan interview, July 6, 1967, tape 497, SHSW. See also John Neary, *Julian Bond: Black Rebel* (New York: William Morrow, 1971), pp. 77–79.

31. Charles Cobb, "A Reflective Look," May 7, 1965, mimeograph. Reprinted as "Atlanta: The Bond Campaign," *Studies on the Left* 5 (Spring 1965): 79–82.

32. Ibid., pp. 80, 81, 82.

33. SNCC Executive Committee meeting, April 12–14, 1965, Holly Springs, Mississippi, p. 2.

34. Ibid., April 12, p. 3.

35. Ibid., April 12, p. 9; April 13, p. 15.

36. Ibid., April 12, pp. 11, 12; April 13, p. 23.

37. Ibid., April 12, p. 12.

38. "SNCC Summer Program" mimeograph, April 1965.

39. Minutes of Alabama State staff meeting, April 21–23, 1965.

40. Mimeographed report of Fifth District COFO staff meeting, April 14–17, 1965, Waveland, Mississippi.

41. Ibid.

42. See "Poor Peoples Group Aids Co-ops," *The Voice,* Dec. 20, 1965, p. 4; memo from Margaret Lauren to northern office (1965), box 3, UCLA; "Mississippi Freedom Labor Union, 1965 Origins," in Joanne Grant, ed., *Black Protest: History, Documents, and Analyses, 1619 to the Present* (Greenwich, Conn.: Fawcett, 1968), pp. 498–500; "Agricultural Workers Strike, Freedom Labor Union Formed," *The Movement,* June 1965, p. 1; " 'They Said We Couldn't Have a Union'; Militancy in the Delta," *The Movement,* July 1965, p. 1. In 1966 the MFLU led an occupation of barracks at the inactive Greenville Air Force Base to dramatize the desperate situation of blacks in rural Mississippi. See *KLM* 154–158, April 17, 1966.

43. Polly Greenberg, *The Devil Has Slippery Shoes: A Biased Biography of the Child Development Group of Mississippi* (London: Macmillan, 1969), p. 61. See also Jean Smith, "I Learned to Feel Black," in Floyd B. Barbour, ed., *The Black Power Revolt* (Boston: Porter Sargent, 1968), pp. 214–216.

44. Minutes of SNCC general staff meeting, Nov. 26, 1965, Atlanta, box 8, UCLA. See John Lewis to Executive Committee of the MFDP, Dec. 1965, Sherrod Papers, SHSW.

45. Memo from Finance Committee to SNCC staff, Dec. 2, 1965. The memo did not indicate the source of the loan. Although SNCC had optimistically planned to raise more than one million dollars during 1965, its actual income was less than half that amount. Income for the three months for which reports were located (June, Nov., and Dec.) were $37,997.84, $33,615.69, and $40,705.24. Of this total ($112,318.77), $65,006.53 (57.9 percent) came from Friends of SNCC, $15,324.46 (13.6 percent) from personal contributions to the Atlanta office, and only $8,570.00 (7.6 percent) from other institutions, including foundations and labor unions.

## 12. THE NEW LEFT

1. *The Port Huron Statement* (Chicago: SDS, 1962), p. 3, reprinted in part in Massimo Teodori, ed., *The New Left: A Documentary History* (Indianapolis: Bobbs-Merrill, 1969), pp. 163–172.

2. Hayden to Haber, "Re: SNCC meeting, Jackson, Mississippi, September 14–17, 1961."

3. *Port Huron Statement*, pp. 5, 7.

4. See Hayden to Davis, Feb. 10, 1964; Davis to Hayden, Feb. 21, 1964 and June 20, 1964; Davis to Forman, Aug. 16, 1964; Davis memo, "SNCC-ERAP Relations"; Gitlin to Prathia Hall, Dec. 9, 1964, SDS Papers, series 2B, section 139, SHSW.

5. Kirkpatrick Sale, *SDS* (New York: Random House, 1973), p. 137.

6. Staughton Lynd, "SNCC: The Beginning of Ideology," *The Activist,* Fall 1964, p. 12; Lynd, "Coalition Politics or Nonviolent Revolution?" *Liberation,* June-July 1965, pp. 19–20; Bayard Rustin, "From Protest to Politics: The Future of the Civil Rights Movement," *Commentary,* Feb. 1964, pp. 25–31.

7. Jack Newfield, *A Prophetic Minority* (New York: New American Library, 1967), pp. 71, 90.

8. Howard Zinn, *SNCC: The New Abolitionists* (Boston: Beacon Press, 1965), p. 237; Tom Hayden, "SNCC: The Qualities of Protest," *Studies on the Left* 5 (Winter 1965): 119.

9. Norm Fruchter, "Mississippi: Notes on SNCC," *Studies on the Left* 5 (Winter 1965): 77.

10. Tom Hayden, Norm Fruchter, and Alan Cheuse, "From the Editors: Up from Irrelevance," *Studies on the Left* 5 (Spring 1965): 6; "Reply" by Weinstein et al., Ibid., p. 11; Victor Rabinowitz, "An Exchange on SNCC," Ibid., pp. 83–91.

11. See Eastland's remark in the *Congressional Record,* Senate, Feb. 3, 1965, vol. 3, pt. 2, pp. 1948–50.

12. "Waving the Red Flag," *Newsweek,* April 12, 1965, p. 31.

13. See Rowland Evans and Robert Novak, "Danger from the Left," *Washington Post,* Mar. 18, 1965; Evans and Novak, "A Long Look at Snick," April 9, 1965.

14. "SNCC Head Denies Control by Reds," *Washington Post,* Mar. 28, 1965;

SNCC Executive Committee meeting, Holly Springs, Mississippi, April 14, 1965, SHSW, p. 31; "Waving the Red Flag."

15. Andrew Kopkind, "New Radicals in Dixie: These 'Subversive' Civil Rights Workers," *The New Republic,* April 10, 1965, p. 13; Lerone Bennett, Jr., "SNCC: Rebels with a Cause," *Ebony,* July 1965, pp. 146, 152; C. Vann Woodward, "After Watts—Where is the Negro Revolution Headed?" *New York Times Magazine,* Aug. 29, 1965, p. 82; Pat Watters, *Encounter with the Future* (Atlanta: Southern Regional Council, 1965), pp. 16, 20.

16. Gallup Poll released on Nov. 19, 1965.

17. James Forman, *The Making of Black Revolutionaries* (New York: Macmillan, 1972), p. 445.

18. James Petras et al., eds., *We Accuse* (Berkeley: Diablo Press, 1965), pp. 150–151.

19. "A Talk with Bob Parris. . . . One Freedom Worker's Views," *Southern Patriot,* Oct. 1965, p. 3. See also Rowland Evans and Robert Novak, "The Moses Rally," *Washington Post,* July 27, 1965.

20. *Congressional Record,* House of Representatives, July 28, 1965, pp. 18649–18650; Evans and Novak, "The Moses Rally."

21. Leslie Burl McLemore, "The Mississippi Freedom Democratic Party: A Case Study of Grass-Roots Politics" (Ph.D. diss., University of Massachusetts, 1971), pp. 234–242. See also *Congressional Record,* House of Representatives, Aug. 3, 1965, pp. 19232–19244.

22. Cf. August Meier and Elliott Rudwick, *CORE: A Study in the Civil Rights Movement, 1942–1968* (New York: Oxford University Press, 1973), pp. 329–373, 413–414.

23. Cf. David L. Lewis, *King: A Critical Biography* (Baltimore: Penguin Books, 1970), chap. 9. See also N. J. Demerath III, Gerald Marwell, and Michael T. Aiken, *Dynamics of Idealism: White Activists in a Black Movement* (San Francisco: Jossey-Bass, 1971).

24. See Lewis' statement before the Equal Rights Subcommittee, Oct. 6, 1965, and memo from Lewis and Barry to A. Philip Randolph, Morris Abrams, and William Coleman, Dec. 14, 1965, box 8, UCLA; Julian Bond interview in James Finn, *Protest: Pacifism and Politics: Some Passionate Views on War and Nonviolence* (New York: Vintage Books, 1967), p. 305; Howard Zinn, "Should Civil Rights Workers Take a Stand on Vietnam?" *Voice,* Aug 30, 1965.

25. Dona Richards to SNCC staff, Sept. 1965.

26. SNCC staff meeting, Nov. 29, 1965, pp. 19–25.

27. See SNCC news release, Jan. 5, 1966, box 1, UCLA; James Forman, *Sammy Younge, Jr.: The First Black College Student to Die in the Black Liberation Movement* (New York: Grove Press, 1968), pp. 185–196.

28. *Movement,* Jan. 1966, p. 2. See also Teodori, *New Left,* pp. 251–252.

29. See memo from Clifford L. Alexander to President Johnson, Jan. 7, 1966, White House Central Files, King name file, LBJ; Roy Wilkins, "SNCC Does Not Speak for Whole Movement," *Los Angeles Times,* Jan. 17, 1966.

30. Hubert Humphrey to Joseph Califano, Jan. 22, 1966, White House Central Files, SNCC name file, LBJ.

31. See "King Defends Bond's Right to Views," *Atlanta Journal-Constitution,* Jan. 9, 1966.

32. Lillian Smith, letter in *Atlanta Constitution,* Jan. 14, 1966.

### 13. RACIAL SEPARATISM

1. William Ware interview, Nov. 8, 1976, in Atlanta.

2. "Prospectus for an Atlanta Project," and "The Necessity for Southern Urban Organizing," box 1, folder 1, Atlanta Project Papers, SHSW.

3. See "Purpose of the Atlanta Project," SNCC News Service, box 2, UCLA, reprinted in *KLM* 169, May 1, 1966.

4. Ware interview; "The Nitty-Gritty: The Reasons Why," box 1, folder 1, Atlanta Project Papers, SHSW.

5. "An Analysis of the Civil Rights Movement," box 1, folder 5, Atlanta Project Papers, SHSW.

6. Donald Stone interview in Atlanta, April 19, 1972; Ware interview, Nov. 8, 1976; text in Atlanta Project Papers, box 1, folder 5, SHSW; "Excerpts from Paper on Which the 'Black Power' Philosophy Is Based," *New York Times,* Aug. 5, 1966.

7. Julius Lester, *All Is Well* (New York: William Morrow, 1976), p. 129; Willie Ricks interview, May 10, 1976, at Stanford.

8. Stokely Carmichael interview (telephone), Oct. 18, 1977.

9. Carmichael in "Negro Split Endangers Vote Success in South," *Los Angeles Times,* April 24, 1966. Cf. Carmichael and Charles V. Hamilton, *Black Power: The Politics of Liberation in America* (New York: Random House, 1967), pp. 106–108. See telegram from Carmichael to John Doar, April 27, 1966, and SNCC release, "Report on Alabama Elections," May 6, 1966, box 1, UCLA; "Lowndes County Negroes Work to Take Over County," *Movement,* June 1966, p. 1; "Lowndes Third Party Attracts 900, Nominates Logan to Face Sheriff," *The Southern Courier,* May 7–8, 1966, p. 6; Julius Lester, *Look Out, Whitey! Black Power's Gon' Get Your Mama!* (New York: Dial Press, 1968), pp. 29–30.

10. Ware and James Forman interviews, Nov. 8, 1976, in Atlanta.

11. A possible explanation for the changes in Parris was later provided by SNCC worker Stanley Wise: when Parris was in Africa in 1965, "it was a traumatic experience. What I gathered from him was that he saw how the USIA and the American propaganda apparatus in Africa was using the whole question of blacks and whites together. Saying, look, we can work with [blacks in America] so let us work with you here. He was very disappointed and quite upset by that. He came back very angered and decided he had to change his relationship to a great number of people, especially white people. Many of the people he broke relationships with and refused to speak to any more had been very close friends of his. Not only intellectual, but personal friends. These were people he cut away in one fell swoop." Wise interview, April 19, 1972, in Atlanta.

12. Stone interview.

13. Transcript of talk, "A Review of the Direction of SNCC—Past and Future," released by SNCC News Service, May 31, 1966, box 8, UCLA.

14. "Assumptions Made By SNCC," mimeograph, May 11, 1966, box 62, folder 4, Braden Papers, SHSW.

15. See "Suggestions for Direction of SNCC" and "Programs," May 11, 1966, Braden Papers, box 62, folder 4, SHSW. Cf. James Forman, *The Making of Black Revolutionaries* (New York: Macmillan Company, 1972), pp. 447–456; Cleveland Sellers, with Robert Terrell, *The River of No Return: The Autobiography of a Black Militant and the Life and Death of SNCC* (New York: William Morrow, 1973), pp. 158–159; Jack Newfield, *A Prophetic Minority* (New York: New American Library, 1966), pp. 75–76; Pat Watters, *Down to Now: Reflections on the Southern Civil Rights Movement* (New York: Random House, 1971), pp. 349–351.

16. John Lewis interview, April 17, 1972, in Atlanta; Worth Long interview, Nov. 7, 1977, in Atlanta; Jack Minnis interview, Dec. 28, 1977, in New Orleans.

17. Worth Long interview.

18. Forman, *Black Revolutionaries*, pp. 452–453.

19. Jack Minnis interview.

20. Lewis interview.

21. Bill Shipp, "SNCC's Lewis, Forman Replaced; Views Blamed," *Atlanta Constitution*, May 17, 1966; Jack Nelson, "Two Veteran Rights Leaders Ousted by SNCC," *Los Angeles Times*, May 17, 1966; Gene Roberts, "New Leaders and New Course for 'Snick'," *New York Times*, May 22, 1966.

22. "What's Happening in SNCC?" special bulletin from New York office, June 3, 1966, box 8, UCLA; "Rights Unit Quits White House Parley," *New York Times*, May 24, 1966.

23. Rowland Evans and Robert Novak, "The New Snick," *Washington Post*, May 25, 1966; "Thinking Big," *Time*, May 27, 1966, p. 22.

24. William A. Price interview, *National Guardian*, June 4, 1966, pp. 1, 8, 9. See also " 'We Don't Need or Want Moderation,' Says SNCC Leader," *The Afro-American*, May 20, 1966.

25. "What's Happening in SNCC?"

26. "Behind the Hostile Press Campaign Unleashed by the Election of Stokely Carmichael; SNCC Does Not Wish to Become a New Version of the White Man's Burden," *I. F. Stone's Weekly*, June 6, 1966; Anne Braden, "The SNCC Trends: Challenge to White America," *Southern Patriot*, May 1966.

27. "What's Happening in SNCC?"

28. Wise interview, April 18–19, 1972, in Atlanta. Cf. Sellers, *River of No Return*, pp. 160–161; Martin Luther King, *Where Do We Go from Here: Chaos or Community?* (Boston: Beacon Press, 1967), pp. 23–25; David L. Lewis, *King: A Critical Biography* (Baltimore: Penguin Books, 1970), pp. 322–323; James M. Lawson, Jr., "Black Power and the Mississippi March," *Fellowship*, Sept. 1966, pp. 18–19.

29. Minutes of Central Committee meeting, June 10, 1966, box 8, UCLA; Sellers, *River of No Return*, pp. 161–162.

30. Sellers, *River of No Return*, p. 164.

31. Minutes of Central Committee meeting, June 10, 1966.

32. Ricks interview.

33. Cf. Sellers, *River of No Return*, pp. 166–167; Gene Roberts, "Mississippi Reduces Police Protection for Marchers," *New York Times*, June 17, 1966; King, *Where Do We Go*, p. 29.

34. King, *Where Do We Go,* pp. 30–31; Lewis, *King,* pp. 325–326.

35. Paul Good, *The Trouble I've Seen: White Journalist/Black Movement* (Washington, D.C.: Howard University Press, 1975), pp. 259–260; Lester A. Sobel, ed., *Civil Rights, 1960–66* (New York: Facts on File, 1967), pp. 394–395.

36. Good, *Trouble I've Seen,* p. 261.

37. Sobel, *Civil Rights,* p. 396.

## 14. BLACK POWER

1. Paul Good, "The Meredith March," *New South* 21 (Summer 1966): 8; Carmichael interview for Associated Press by Don McKee, *Miami Herald* and other newspapers, July 8, 1966.

2. Stokely Carmichael, "What We Want," *New York Review of Books* 7 (Sept. 22, 1966): 5, 6, 8; Carmichael, "Toward Black Liberation," *Massachusetts Review* 7 (Autumn 1966): 639–651.

3. Carmichael, "Black Liberation," p. 647.

4. Carmichael, "What We Want," p. 6.

5. Ibid., p. 8.

6. Carmichael, "Black Liberation," pp. 650–651; Carmichael, "What We Want," p. 6; transcript of debate with Randolph Blackwell at Spelman College, Atlanta; "Black Power: The Widening Dialogue," *New South* 21 (Summer 1966): 71.

7. Transcript of Watts speech by Clayborne Carson.

8. Carmichael, "Black Liberation," p. 642; Columbia Broadcasting System, "Face the Nation," June 19, 1966, pp. 10, 11.

9. Carmichael, "What We Want," p. 5.

10. Transcript of Watts speech.

11. "Where We Stand," address at 57th annual convention of NAACP at Los Angeles, July 5, 1966, reprinted in *KLM* 327, Jan. 27, 1967. See also Roy Wilkins column, *Los Angeles Times,* June 6, 1966.

12. Hubert Humphrey, Lyndon Johnson, Robert F. Kennedy, and Whitney Young in " 'Black Power'—How Powerful?" *Christian Science Monitor,* July 11, 1966.

13. Bayard Rustin, " 'Black Power' and Coalition Politics," *Commentary* 42 (Sept. 1966): 35–36.

14. Text of telegrams in Central Committee minutes, Aug. 1–4. Approved by 7 to 2 vote.

15. See Stokely Carmichael, "It Seems to Me," *Movement,* Aug. 1966, p. 4; Lester A. Sobel, ed., *Civil Rights, 1960–66* (New York: Facts on File, 1967), pp. 370–372.

16. See "A 'Black Power' Speech That Has Congress Aroused," *U.S. News and World Report,* Aug. 22, 1966, p. 6.

17. "New Racism," *Time,* July 1, 1966, p. 11; " 'Black Power': Politics of Frustration," *Newsweek,* July 11, 1966, p. 31; editorial, *Saturday Evening Post,* Sept. 10, 1966.

18. I. F. Stone, "Why They Cry Black Power," *I. F. Stone's Weekly,* Sept. 19,

1966; Tom Wicker column, *New York Times,* July 21, 1966; "Distorted Cry?" *Newsweek,* Aug. 8, 1966, p. 54. See also Paul Good, "A White Look at Black Power," *Nation,* Aug. 8, 1966.

19. Lerone Bennett, Jr., "Stokely Carmichael: Architect of Black Power," *Ebony,* Sept. 1966, p. 32; William Brink and Louis Harris, *Black and White: A Study of U.S. Racial Attitudes Today* (New York: Simon and Schuster, 1967), pp. 264–265.

20. Joyce Ladner, "What 'Black Power' Means to Negroes in Mississippi," *TRANS-action* 5 (Nov. 1967): 7–15, 20–22.

21. See Sobel, *Civil Rights,* p. 389; " 'Black Power'—How Powerful?"; Martin Luther King, *Where Do We Go from Here: Chaos or Community?* (Boston: Beacon Press, 1967), pp. 33, 36, 38, 44.

22. See August Meier and Elliott Rudwick, *CORE: A Study in the Civil Rights Movement 1942–1968* (New York: Oxford University Press, 1973), pp. 414–415.

23. " 'Black Power': Statement by National Committee of Negro Churchmen," *New York Times,* July 31, 1966.

24. See Cleveland Sellers, "Organization Report," n.d., box 10, UCLA; Action Taken on Policy Questions and Reports Submitted to the Central Committee, Aug. 1–4, 1966; Minutes of Central Committee meeting, Oct. 22, 1966; Sellers, Report of Program Secretary, Dec. 2, 1966; James Forman, *The Making of Black Revolutionaries* (New York: Macmillan, 1972), p. 470.

25. Cleveland Sellers, with Robert Terrell, *The River of No Return: The Autobiography of a Black Militant and the Life and Death of SNCC* (New York: William Morrow, 1973), pp. 170, 183.

26. See Paul Good, "A Tale of Two Cities," *Nation,* Nov. 21, 1966, pp. 535–536; "Philadelphia Report," box 4, UCLA, mimeograph; "Report: The Preliminary Hearing, in the Case of Arrested SNCC Worker in Philadelphia, Pennsylvania, on August 22, 1966," *KLM,* 270, Sept. 18, 1966; *Aframerica News for You,* Oct. 12, 1966; "A Thousand Cops with Machine Guns 'Find' 2½ Sticks of Dynamite in Philadelphia, Try to Pin It On SNCC," *Movement,* Sept. 1966, p. 1; Forman, *Black Revolutionaries,* chap. 56.

27. See Good, "Two Cities"; "Classic Frame-up; SNCC Unit Dies," *National Guardian,* May 27, 1967, p. 11.

28. "Snick March Squelched, 10 Seized at Riot Scene," *Atlanta Constitution,* Sept. 8, 1966; Good, "Two Cities," pp. 537–538; Sellers, *River of No Return,* pp. 174–176; "Eye Witnesses to the Atlanta 'Riots,' " *Movement,* Dec. 1966, p. 10; William Ware interview, Nov. 8, 1976, in Atlanta.

29. "SNCC's Version of What Sparked the Racial Outbreaks in Atlanta," *I. F. Stone's Weekly,* Sept. 19, 1966, p. 4. See also "One Thousand Riot after Arrest in Atlanta: Mayor Is Felled Pleading with Mob," *Washington Post,* Sept. 7, 1966.

30. See "Atlanta Report: Slums Cause Outbreak," *Southern Patriot,* Oct. 1966; "Atlanta Mayor Says SNCC Provoked Riot," *Washington Post,* Sept. 8, 1966; "Snick March Squelched," and "Text of Summit Statement Condemning Violence Here," *Atlanta Constitution,* Sept. 8, 1966; Ralph McGill, "The Story of Two 'Snicks,' " *Atlanta Constitution,* Sept. 9, 1966; "Behind the Image," *Newsweek,* Sept. 19, 1966, p. 32.

31. See "Carmichael Arrested on Riot Charges in Raid on Snick Office," *Atlanta Constitution,* Sept. 9, 1966; Sellers, *River of No Return,* p. 177; "Atlanta Riot

Act Voided by Court," *New York Times,* Dec. 14, 1966; Sobel, *Civil Rights,* pp. 446–447.

32. Stokely Carmichael and Charles V. Hamilton, *Black Power: The Politics of Liberation in America* (New York: Random House, 1967), pp. 181, 184.

33. Harold Cruse, *The Crisis of the Negro Intellectual* (New York: William Morrow, 1967), p. 556, 560, 548. See also Christopher Lasch, "The Trouble with Black Power," *New York Review of Books,* Feb. 29, 1968, p. 11; Martin Duberman, "Black Power in America," *Partisan Review* 35 (Winter 1967): 34–38; "Black Power: A Discussion," *Partisan Review* 35 (Spring 1968): 195–232; James E. Jackson, "The Meaning of 'Black Power,'" *Political Affairs* 47 (Feb. 1968): 1–97; Claude M. Lightfoot, *Ghetto Rebellion to Black Liberation* (New York: International Publishers, 1968).

34. Robert L. Allen, *Black Awakening in Capitalist America: An Analytic History* (New York: Doubleday, 1969), p. 247.

35. Ethel Minor interview, May 11, 1978, in Washington, D.C.

## 15. INTERNAL CONFLICTS

1. Ruby Doris Robinson, Organization Report to SNCC Central Committee, Oct. 21, 1966.

2. Fay D. Bellamy, "A Little Old Report," Nov. 1966, box 8, UCLA.

3. Muriel Tillinghast interview, Nov. 7, 1976, in Atlanta.

4. Minutes of Central Committee meeting, Oct. 23, 1966, pp. 6–7.

5. Statistics derived from comparison of personnel list in Robinson's Organization Report and various lists for the period prior to 1965.

6. Minutes of Central Committee meeting, June 11, 1966; "Ex-Chief Lewis Quits SNCC," *Atlanta Constitution,* July 1, 1966; "Black Power in the Red," *Time,* July 8, 1966, p. 21; "Ousted Chairman Tells of New Setup in SNCC," *Los Angeles Times,* July 29, 1966; John Lewis interview, April 17, 1972, in Atlanta.

7. Julian Bond interview by Gwen Gillan, July 6, 1967, tape 497, SHSW; "Julian Bond Gets Out of Snick," *Atlanta Constitution,* Sept. 9, 1966; "Julian Bond Keeps SNCC Ties Although He Quit Organization," *Miami Herald,* Sept. 18, 1966.

8. Motions, recommendations, mandates of SNCC Central Committee, May 14–17, 1966; "Black Power Idea Long in Planning," *New York Times,* Aug. 5, 1966; Charles Sherrod interview, Oct. 31, 1979, in Jackson, Mississippi.

9. Excerpts from minutes of Arkansas staff meeting, June 9, 1966; Jim Jones interview, Nov. 7, 1976, in Atlanta; Sellers, Organization Report, n.d., box 10, UCLA; Bill Hansen interview, Nov. 6, 1976, in Atlanta; "State SNCC Chief Attacks New Policy, Threatens to Resign," *Arkansas Gazette,* May 25, 1966; "Director of SNCC Resigns and Joins Relations Council," *Arkansas Gazette,* July 1, 1966.

10. Minutes of Central Committee meetings, June 11, Oct. 23, 1966; Sellers, Organization Report; Sid Walker to Central Committee, Aug. 20, 1966; Robinson to Central Committee, Oct. 21, 1966.

11. See "Lowndes County; Candidates Lose, but Black Panther Strong," and "Carmichael's Speech at Mt. Moriah Church in Lowndes," *Movement,* Dec. 1966,

pp. 1, 8; "Freedom Party Wins Legal Ballot Status in Lowndes County Vote," *Militant*, Nov. 21, 1966, p. 1.

12. Minutes of Central Committee meetings, June 11, Oct. 23, 1966, Jan. 20–23, 1967. See also Clayborne Carson, "Black Power Proposed for Watts," *Los Angeles Free Press*, July 8, 1966, p. 3.

13. Report, Free D.C. Movement to Central Committee, July 1966; Actions Taken on Policy Questions and Reports Submitted to the Central Committee, Aug. 1–4, 1966; Sellers, Report of the Program Secretary, Dec. 2, 1966, p. 9; Decisions of the Central Committee meeting, Jan. 20–23, 1967, Atlanta Project Papers, box 2, SHSW; "Barry Quits SNCC Post to Aid Poor," *Washington Post*, Jan. 19, 1967.

14. Bill Hall interview, Nov. 7, 1976, in Atlanta; minutes of Central Committee meeting, Oct. 23, 1966.

15. Minutes of Central Committee meeting, Oct. 23, 1966; decisions of Central Committee, Jan. 20–23, 1967; James Forman, *The Making of Black Revolutionaries* (New York: Macmillan, 1972), p. 470; Bob Brown interview (telephone), Oct. 18, 1977.

16. Sellers, Organization Report; Report of Program Secretary; Robinson, Organization Report.

17. Robinson, Organization Report. Robinson reported that the New York office raised about $100,000 during the period from May to Sept. 1966, but $52,000 of it went toward office expenses. In addition to New York, only the San Francisco Bay Area and Boston provided significant financial support for SNCC.

18. Sellers, Organization Report; Sellers, Report of Program Secretary; minutes of Central Committee meeting, Aug. 1–4, 1966; minutes of meeting on internal education program, Aug. 29, 1966, Atlanta.

19. James Forman, "Rock Bottom," reprinted in Black Star Publishing, ed., *The Political Thought of James Forman* (Detroit: Black Star Publishing, 1970), p. 138–140, 142, 144, 146.

20. Alvin F. Poussaint, "A Negro Psychiatrist Explains the Negro Psyche," *New York Times Magazine*, Aug. 20, 1967, pp. 75–76. See also Poussaint, "How the 'White Problem' Spawned 'Black Power,'" *Ebony*, Aug. 1967, pp. 88–90, 92, 94; Poussaint, "The Negro American: His Self-Image and Integration," *Journal of the National Medical Association* 58 (Nov. 1966): 419–423.

21. Julius Lester, "The Angry Children of Malcolm X," *Sing Out!* 16 (Oct.–Nov. 1966): 22, 24, 25.

22. Julius Lester, *Look Out, Whitey! Black Power's Gon' Get Your Mama!* (New York: Dial Press, 1968), pp. 137–138; text of Chicago leaflet in August Meier et al., eds., *Black Protest Thought in the Twentieth Century* (Indianapolis: Bobbs-Merrill, 1971), pp. 484–490.

23. Julius Lester, *All Is Well* (New York: William Morrow, 1976), pp. 134, 131.

24. William Ware interview, Nov. 8, 1976, in Atlanta.

25. "SNCC Sound Truck Assails 'White Jesus' in Vine City," *Atlanta Constitution*, July 7, 1966. See also "White Jesus," *Newsweek*, July 25, 1966.

26. See SNCC publication, *Atlanta's Black Paper*, Aug. 25, 1966, Atlanta Project Papers, box 1, SHSW.

27. Ware letter in *The Vine City Voice*, Sept. 23, 1966, Atlanta Project Papers, box 1, SHSW.

28. Freddie Greene interview, May 11, 1978, in Washington, D.C.

29. Carmichael interview (telephone), Oct. 18, 1977; Ethel Minor interview, May 11, 1978, in Washington, D.C.; Jack Minnis interview, Dec. 28, 1977, in New Orleans; Robert Zellner interview, Sept. 19, 1978, in New Orleans; Fay Bellamy interview, Sept. 23, 1978, in Atlanta. See also Andrew Kopkind, "The Future of 'Black Power'; A Movement in Search of a Program," *New Republic*, Jan. 7, 1967; Forman, *Black Revolutionaries*, pp. 475–477.

30. Mimeographed untitled text in Atlanta Project Papers, box 1, SHSW.

31. Forman, *Black Revolutionaries*, pp. 475–477; Kopkind, "Future of 'Black Power,'" p. 17; Minor and Jean Wiley interview, May 11, 1978, in Washington, D.C.; Minnis interview.

32. Minor interview.

33. Transcript of Central Committee meeting, March 4, 1967; Ware and Bellamy interviews; Cleveland Sellers, with Robert Terrell, *The River of No Return: The Autobiography of a Black Militant and the Life and Death of SNCC* (New York: William Morrow, 1973), pp. 185–187.

34. William Ware interview. See also Central Committee Rules and Decisions, Jan. 1967–Dec. 1967, pp. 7–9. When Ware and Forman confronted each other at end of Ware interview, Ware stated that Forman had threatened to use force to prevent the Atlanta separatists from presenting their case. Forman denied this, but restated his conviction that the expulsion was necessary. "There's a limit to how much a serious organization can allow people to disrupt the normal functioning of their business," he told Ware.

35. Bob and Dottie Zellner, "A Statement to Our Brothers and Sisters in SNCC," mimeograph, n.d.

36. Sellers, *River of No Return*, pp. 194, 197. See Rules and Decisions, pp. 13–14.

## 16. WHITE REPRESSION

1. George Ware interview, Nov. 7, 1976, in Atlanta. See also "North Nashville Project Begins Community Works," *Southern Patriot*, Aug. 1966; Ware's reports in U.S., Congress, Senate, Permanent Subcommittee on Investigations, Committee on Government Operations, *Riots, Civil and Criminal Disorders* [hereafter cited as *Criminal Disorders*], 91st Cong., 1st sess., pt. 19, June 25, 1969, pp. 4019-31.

2. *Criminal Disorders*, pt. 2, Nov. 7-8, 1967, pp. 682-683.

3. See testimony of Nashville police in U.S., Congress, Senate, Committee on the Judiciary, *Anti-riot Bill—1967*, Hearings on H.R. 421, 90th Cong., 1st sess., p. 1, Aug. 3-4, 1967, esp. pp. 137-138, 160-162, and in *Criminal Disorders*, pt. 2, Nov. 21, 1967, esp. pp. 642, 682-685; Stokely Carmichael interview (telephone), Oct. 18, 1977.

4. *Criminal Disorders*, pt. 2, Nov. 21, 1967, pp. 683-684, 686-691; Diane Nash Bevel, "Journey to North Vietnam," *Freedomways* 7 (Spring 1967): 118-128.

5. See Brooks' testimony in *Criminal Disorders*, pt. 2, Nov. 22, 1967, p. 710.

6. Steven D. Price, comp., *Civil Rights, Volume 2, 1967-68* (New York: Facts on File, 1973), p. 81; *Criminal Disorders*, pt. 2, Nov. 21, 1967, pp. 643, 644.

7. *Criminal Disorders,* pt. 2; "Frederick Brooks, et al. v. Beverly Briley, Mayor, etc., et al.," *Race Relations Law Reporter* 12 (Winter 1967): 1784–97; "Black Students in Nashville Victims of Police Set-up," SNCC press release, April 10, 1967, *KLM* 368, April 2, 1967; "Cops Attack Black Students," *Movement,* May 1967, pp. 1, 10; "SNCC Linked to Costly '67 Rioting," *Birmingham News,* June 2 and 4, 1969: "Riot Review," *Newsweek,* June 9, 1969.

8. "Cops Attack Black Students," p. 1; *Criminal Disorders,* pt. 2, Nov. 7, 1967, pp. 416–417.

9. Ware interview; *Criminal Disorders,* pt. 2, Nov. 21, 1967, pp. 677–780.

10. *Criminal Disorders,* pt. 2, Nov. 21, 1967, pp. 672–673.

11. *Criminal Disorders,* pt. 2, Nov. 21, 1967, p. 674; "A Call to Deport Carmichael Made," *New York Times,* April 11, 1967; "Nashville Peaceful after Strife," *New York Times,* April 12, 1967.

12. The suit was dismissed on Oct. 9, 1967. Ware and Stephens later pleaded guilty to the charges against them and were sentenced to pay small fines. See "Two Carmichael Aides Fined Here," *Nashville Banner,* Sept. 25, 1968.

13. Testimony in *Criminal Disorders,* pt. 1, Nov. 1–3, 6, 1967; "Black Power Revolt at Texas Southern," *Movement,* May 1967, p. 1, 10; "Five Charged in TSU Riot Fatal to Young Officer," *Houston Post,* May 18, 1967; Frederick Kirkpatrick, "A First-hand Report: The Police Attack at Texas Southern," *Militant,* June 26, 1967, p. 8; "Will They Die?" *Movement,* Sept. 1967, p. 10; SAC, Houston to Director, FBI, "Communist Infiltration of SNCC," Nov. 30, 1967; "Texas Southern University: Five Fight for Their Lives," *Movement,* May 1968, pp. 4, 15.

14. Jack Nelson and Jack Bass, *The Orangeburg Massacre* (New York: World Publishing, 1970), p. 63; Cleveland Sellers, with Robert Terrell, *The River of No Return: The Autobiography of a Black Militant and the Life and Death of SNCC* (New York: William Morrow, 1973), pp. 216–227. See also "Slaughter in South Carolina," *Movement,* April 1968, p. 12.

15. See "SNCC's Cleveland Sellers vs. the Draft," *SNCC Newsletter,* Mar. 15, 1967, reprinted as *KLM* 401, May 14, 1967.

16. Ethel Minor interview, May 11, 1978, in Washington, D.C.

17. Carmichael's report, "The Structure of SNCC," in *Criminal Disorders,* pt. 19, June 25, 1969, p. 4041.

18. H. Rap Brown, *Die Nigger Die!* (New York: Dial Press, 1969), p. 59. See also Bernard Z. Conn, "H. Rap Brown," *Boston Globe,* Sept. 24, 1967; "Angry Rights Leader: Hubert Gerold Brown," *New York Times,* July 18, 1967.

19. James Forman, *The Making of Black Revolutionaries* (New York: Macmillan, 1972), p. 504; Brown, *Die Nigger Die!,* pp. 66–67.

20. Brown in "We Are Going to Build," *Movement,* June 1967, p. 1; Charlotte Featherstone in "Negro Student Group to Push Economic Goals," *St. Louis Post Dispatch,* May 21, 1967. See also "Carmichael Successor 'Meaner' Than He Is," *Southern Courier,* May 20–21, 1967, p. 6.

21. "The Man from SNCC," *Newsweek,* May 22, 1967; "Carmichael Out as Head of SNCC," *Atlanta Constitution,* May 13, 1967; "Another SNCC Militant Replaces Carmichael," *Los Angeles Times,* May 13, 1967.

22. "Meet Rap Brown—SNCC's New Head," *People's World,* June 3, 1967, p. 9; Brown, *Die Nigger Die!,* pp. 81, 84.

23. See Price, *Civil Rights*, pp. 82–83; "New SNCC Chief Speaks His Mind," *National Guardian*, June 10, 1967, pp. 1, 5.

24. Cf. testimony of Prattville police in *Anti-riot Bill—1967*, Aug. 4, 1967, pp. 294–300; "White Cops, Klan, Guard Attack Blacks in Alabama," *SNCC Newsletter*, June-July 1967, p. 6; "Statement to Afro-Asian Missions to the United Nations on Events in Prattville, Alabama," press release of New York SNCC office, June 13, 1967; "Carmichael Arrested: The Siege at Prattville," *Movement*, July 1967, pp. 4–5; Sellers, *River of No Return*, p. 199.

25. "Atlanta Hit by New Violence, Gunfire Kills Negro, Wounds 3," *Los Angeles Times*, June 21, 1967.

26. "Patrolman, SNCC Head, Wounded in Cambridge," *Washington Post*, July 25, 1967; transcript of tape recording of Brown's speech, *Anti-riot Bill—1967*, Aug. 2, 1967, pp. 31–36.

27. See *Anti-riot Bill—1967*, Aug. 2, 1967, pp. 37; Brown, *Die Nigger Die!*, pp. 100–101.

28. "Blazes Level Negro Area of Shore City," *Washington Post*, July 26, 1967.

29. SNCC press release, July 26, 1967; "Rap Brown Denounced Johnson as 'Mad Dog,'" *Los Angeles Times*, July 28, 1967. See also "Sporadic Gunfire Mars Detroit Lull, Cambridge Riot Figure Seized Here" and "Cambridge Riot Beautiful, Brown Says," *Washington Post*, July 1967. Bob Woodward, then a reporter for the *Montgomery County Sentinel*, reported that the Maryland prosecutor in Brown's case admitted that the arson charge was "fabricated" in order to involve the FBI. The prosecutor was subsequently found guilty of contempt for violating a court order prohibiting pre-trial publicity. He later remarked that he meant to say that "the charge lacked substantial evidence." See "Attorney Explains Rap Brown Story," *Washington Post*, Oct. 20, 1971; "Maryland Seen Adding to Rap Brown Charges," *Washington Post*, Oct. 22, 1971; "Honky Harassment of Chairman Rap," SNCC press release, Mar. 3, 1968.

30. "Rap Brown Seized on Arms Charge by Federal Agents," *New York Times*, Aug. 19, 1967; Brown, *Die Nigger Die!* pp. 109–110.

31. "Bills Offered for Probe of Urban Riots," *Washington Post*, July 26, 1967; "House GOP Labels LBJ a Vacillator in Crises," *Washington Post*, July 29, 1967.

32. See *Anti-riot Bill—1967*, Aug. 2, 1967, p. 36, 108; Aug. 3, 1967, p. 142, 163; "U.S.-Aided School Held Antiwhite," *New York Times*, Aug. 4, 1967.

33. *Criminal Disorders*, pt. 2, Nov. 9, 1967, p. 590.

34. *Anti-Riot Bill—1967*, Aug. 3–4, 1967, pp. 163, 334–352.

35. See *Criminal Disorders*, pt. 2, Nov. 22, 1967, pp. 722–723. See also "Carmichael Aide at 'Hate School,'" *Chattanooga Times*, Aug. 22, 1967; "Carmichael Aide Cleared by Nashville Grand Jury," *Arkansas Gazette*, Aug. 30, 1967.

36. See testimony of Samuel L. Price in *Criminal Disorders*, pt. 1, Nov. 1, 1967, pp. 63, 102, 104, 114.

37. In 1964 Hoover announced that "the number of Communist Party recruits which may be attracted from the large Negro racial group in the nation is not the important thing" but nonetheless concluded that, since some Communist influence did "exist in the Negro movement," this influence was "vitally important." Hoover's testimony in *Criminal Disorders*, June 25, 1967, pp. 4096–97. See also "J. Edgar Hoover Speaks Out on Reds in the Negro Movement," *U.S. News*

*and World Report,* May 4, 1964; "Carmichael Tied to Left Group," *New York Times,* May 17, 1967.

38. SAC, Atlanta to Director, FBI, "Communist Infiltration of SNCC," Mar. 20, 1964; U.S., Congress, Senate, Select Committee to Study Governmental Operations with Respect to Intelligence Activities, *Supplementary Detailed Staff Reports on Intelligence Activities and the Rights of Americans* [hereafter cited as *Intelligence Activities*], 94th Cong., 2d sess., April 23, 1976, Book III, p. 318, 334. According to documents obtained through the Freedom of Information Act, the FBI's investigation entitled "Communist Infiltration of SNCC," began late in 1963, although later summary reports include references to information obtained from informants as early as Oct. 1960.

39. "Student Nonviolent Coordinating Committee," Aug. 1967, monograph prepared by research-satellite section of FBI's Central Research Unit (accompanied by memo from R. W. Smith to W. C. Sullivan, Aug. 8, 1967), pp. 8–13.

40. See *Intelligence Activities,* Book III, pp. 15–20; David Wise, *The American Police State: The Government against the People* (New York: Random House, 1976), pp. 314–315; Morton H. Halperin et al., *The Lawless State: The Crimes of the U.S. Intelligence Agencies* (New York: Penguin Books, 1976), pp. 112–114.

41. See *Intelligence Activities,* Book III, pp. 491, 492, 510, 511.

42. Exhibit 15 in U.S., Congress, Senate, Select Committee to Study Government Operations with Respect to Intelligence Activities, *Intelligence Activities, Senate Resolution 21,* 94th Cong., 1st sess., vol. 6, pp. 383–383, and testimony of Dec. 3, 1975, pp. 245–246; *Intelligence Activities,* Book III, pp. 20, 187. See also Cathy Perkus, ed., *COINTELPRO: The FBI's Secret War on Political Freedom* (New York: Monad Press, 1975), pp. 22–23. In Sept. 1967 Attorney General Ramsey Clark authorized the FBI to develop more informants in SNCC and other groups. See *Intelligence Activities,* Book II, p. 84.

43. *Anti-riot Bill—1967,* Aug. 3, 1967, p. 217.

44. *Intelligence Activities, Senate Resolution 21,* vol. 6, Dec. 3, 1975, pp. 245, 386–390; *Intelligence Activities,* Book III, pp. 21–22.

45. Quote from Director, FBI to SAC, Albany, Mar. 4, 1968, p. 3 in *Intelligence Activities, Senate Resolution 21,* vol. 6, pp. 386–390. See also the following: Director to SAC, WFO [Washington Field Office], "Counterintelligence Program, Black Nationalists-Hate Groups, Racial Intelligence" [hereafter cited as "COINTELPRO"], Mar. 18, 1968; SAC, New Orleans to Director, FBI, "COINTELPRO," Mar. 28, 1968; SAC, New York to Director, FBI, "COINTELPRO," April 1, 1968; SAC, WFO to Director, FBI, "COINTELPRO," April 4, 1968; SAC, Albany to Director, FBI, "COINTELPRO," April 5, 1968; G. C. Moore to W. C. Sullivan, "COINTELPRO," April 26, 1968; Director FBI to SAC, WFO, "COINTELPRO," June 6, 1968; Director, FBI to SAC, WFO, "COINTELPRO," July 1, 1968; SAC, New York to Director, FBI, "COINTELPRO," July 10, 1968; SAC, Chicago to Director, FBI, "COINTELPRO," Sept. 18, 1968.

46. Minor interview; Julius Lester, *Revolutionary Notes* (New York: Grove Press, 1969), p. 37.

### 17. SEEKING NEW ALLIES

1. "May Staff Meeting," undated newsletter issued by New York SNCC office. See also SNCC press release, May 12, 1967, SC-SU; U.S., Congress, Senate, Committee on Government Operations, Permanent Subcommittee on Investigations, *Riots, Civil and Criminal Disorders*, 91st Cong., 1st sess., pt. 19, June 25, 1969, pp. 3962–63.

2. *Criminal Disorders*, June 25, 1969, pp. 4013–14.

3. Julius Lester, *Look Out, Whitey! Black Power's Gon' Get Your Mama!* (New York: Dial Press, 1968), p. 139.

4. Ethel Minor interview, May 11, 1978, in Washington, D.C.; Forman to Wise, June 7, 1967, in James Forman, *The Making of Black Revolutionaries* (New York: Macmillan, 1972), p. 496.

5. Fred Meely, "The Chicken or the Egg of the Middle East," *Aframerican News for You*, July 1967, pp. 1, 4.

6. "Third World Round Up; The Palestine Problem: Test Your Knowledge," *SNCC Newsletter*, June-July 1967, pp. 4–5.

7. Forman, *Black Revolutionaries*, p. 496; Jean Wiley interview, May 11, 1978, in Washington, D.C. See also "S.N.C.C. Charges Israel Atrocities," *New York Times*, Aug. 15, 1967; "Zionism Assailed in Newsletter of SNCC," *Los Angeles Times*, Aug. 15, 1967; "SNCC and the News," *Newsweek*, Aug. 28, 1967.

8. See "SNCC Criticized for Israel Stand," *New York Times*, Aug. 16, 1967; "SNCC Attack on Jews Is Strongly Protested," *Washington Post*, Aug. 16, 1967; "Bikel Scores Attack on Jews by S.N.C.C. and Quits the Group," *New York Times*, Aug. 17, 1967; "Golden Criticizes S.N.C.C. and Quits," *New York Times*, Aug. 22, 1967.

9. Cleveland Sellers, with Robert Terrell, *The River of No Return: The Autobiography of a Black Militant and the Life and Death of SNCC* (New York: William Morrow, 1973), p. 203. See also Julius Lester column, "SNCC and the Israeli-Arab War," *Guardian*, Oct. 14, 1967, reprinted in Julius Lester, *Revolutionary Notes* (New York: Grove Press, 1969), pp. 27–29.

10. In her interview, Minor recalled that on one occasion Carmichael and Brown drove through a black neighborhood shouting, "Guns for the Arabs, Sneakers for the Jews."

11. Cf. Robert G. Weisbord and Arthur Stein, *Bittersweet Encounter: The Afro-American and the American Jew* (New York: Schocken Books, 1970), pp. 101–105.

12. Black Star Publishing, ed., *The Political Thought of James Forman* (Detroit: Black Star Publishing, 1970), pp. 24–25.

13. See *Angela Davis: An Autobiography* (New York: Bantam, 1974), pp. 183–185; *Criminal Disorders*, pt. 19, June 25, 1969, p. 4101.

14. *Political Thought of Forman*, p. 110; Forman, *Black Revolutionaries*, p. 501; transcript of Brown's speech in SAC, Chicago to Director, FBI, Dec. 6, 1967, p. 26.

15. Forman, *Black Revolutionaries*, p. 503.

16. Lamar Hoover interview, "Blacks and the Antiwar Movement," *Liberation*, Nov. 1967, pp. 29, 30.

17. Johnny Wilson interview, April 26, 1972, in Washington, D.C. Cf. U.S.,

Congress, Senate, Committee on the Judiciary, Subcommittee to Investigate the Administration of the Internal Security Act and Other Internal Security Laws, *Testimony of Gerald Wayne Kirk,* Hearings, 91st Cong., 2d sess., pt. 3, Mar. 11, 1970, pp. 230-231, 234, 327-328.

18. Fay Bellamy, "Soviet Union Report," Aug. 1, 1966, reprinted in slightly altered form in *Aframerican News for You,* Oct. 12, 1966, pp. 31, 35.

19. Letters in "SNCC Workers on War Crimes Mission; Letters from Hanoi," *Movement,* May 1967, p. 5. See also Julius Lester, *All Is Well* (New York: William Morrow, 1976), pp. 136-139.

20. Lester, *Revolutionary Notes,* p. 16.

21. "Carmichael Out as Head of SNCC," *Atlanta Constitution,* May 13, 1967.

22. David Cooper, ed., *The Dialectics of Liberation* (Middlesex England: Penguin Books, 1968), p. 168; Ethel N. Minor, ed., *Stokely Speaks: Black Power Back to Pan-Africanism* (New York: Random House, 1971), pp. 93-94.

23. See "Carmichael Turns Up in Havana, Calls for U.S. Guerilla Warfare," *Washington Post,* July 26, 1967; "Stokely Calls for 'War' in U.S.," *Washington Post,* July 28, 1967; "Carmichael Lauds Cuban Communism," *Washington Post,* Aug. 2, 1967; "Carmichael Joins Vietnam Reds in Anti-U.S. Chorus," *Los Angeles Times,* Aug. 2, 1967; George Ware interview, Nov. 7, 1976, in Atlanta.

24. From *Le Monde* Aug. 3, 1967, in "Reportage and Comment on Stokely Carmichael's Activities and Statements Abroad," special memo of Foreign Broadcast Information Service, Aug. 9, 1967, p. 49, National Security File, Subject File: Civil Rights and Anti-war Personalities, LBJ.

25. See Julius Lester, "Black Revolution Is Real: Stokely in Cuba," *Movement,* Sept. 1967, pp. 1, 4.

26. Minor, *Stokely Speaks,* pp. 101-110.

27. "Castro on Stokely and Black Revolution," *Movement,* Sept. 1967, p. 4, 10.

28. Carmichael interview (telephone), Oct. 18, 1977; Lester, *All Is Well,* p. 143; "Castro on Stokely and Black Revolution," p. 10.

29. Carmichael in "Carmichael Joins Vietnam Reds in Anti-U.S. Chorus"; Fay D. Bellamy interview, Sept. 23, 1978, in Atlanta; Minor interview. See also Jack Anderson, "SNCC Votes Carmichael Reprimand," *Washington Post,* Aug. 18, 1967.

30. "Carmichael Calls for Unified Struggle," *National Guardian,* Sept. 9, 1967.

31. Carmichael interview, Feb. 1975, Pacifica Tape Library, Los Angeles.

32. "Exclusive: Stokely Carmichael Breaks Silence" *Baltimore Afro-American,* Oct. 14, 1969.

33. Steven D. Price, comp., *Civil Rights, Volume 2, 1967-68* (New York: Facts on File, 1973), p. 124.

34. See Jack Anderson column, "Carmichael Critics Urge Treason Charge," *Washington Post,* Aug. 9, 1967; James Kilpatrick, "Looks Like Carmichael's Home Free," *Miami Herald,* Jan. 1, 1968.

35. Bellamy interview.

36. See "Stokely Carmichael on Puerto Rico, Cities, the Draft, Blackness and More," *Movement,* Feb. 1967, pp. 1, 4; Carmichael texts and Joint Statement of SNCC and the Movement for Puerto Rican Independence, New York Branch, *KLM* 336-338, Feb. 5, 1967; Decisions of Central Committee meeting, Jan.

20–23, 1967, box 2, Atlanta Project Papers, SHSW; U.S. Congress, Senate, Committee on the Judiciary, Subcommittee to Investigate the Administration of the Internal Security Act and Other Internal Security Laws, Hearing, *Testimony of Stokely Carmichael,* 91st Cong., 2d sess., Mar. 25, 1970, pp. 8–13.

37. Ethel Minor and Freddie Greene interviews, May 11, 1978, in Washington, D.C.; Maria Varela interview, Sept. 1, 1977, in Bracos, N.M.; Forman, *Black Revolutionaries,* p. 503; U.S., Congress, Senate, Committee on the Judiciary, Subcommittee to Investigate the Administration of the Internal Security Act and Other Internal Security Laws, Hearings, *Extent of Subversion in the "New Left": Testimony of Robert J. Thoms,* 91st Cong., 2d sess., pt. 1, Jan. 20, 1970, appendix A.

38. See Executive Mandate No. 2, June 29, 1967, in Huey P. Newton, *To Die for the People: The Writings of Huey P. Newton* (New York: Vintage Books, 1972), pp. 9–10; Newton, *Revolutionary Suicide* (New York: Harcourt Brace Jovanovich, 1973), pp. 113, 154, 155.

39. Newton, *Revolutionary Suicide,* pp. 155, 156.

40. Robert Scheer, ed., *Eldridge Cleaver: Post-prison Writings and Speeches* (New York: Random House, 1969), p. 52.

41. Bobby Seale, *Seize the Time: The Story of the Black Panther Party and Huey P. Newton* (New York: Random House, 1970), p. 219.

42. Carmichael interview (telephone), Oct. 18, 1977. See also "Carmichael Jars New Negro Unity," *New York Times,* Jan. 16, 1968; "Carmichael Briefs Negro Leaders on Unity Drive," *Washington Post,* Jan. 10, 1968; "D.C. Leaders Work to Maintain Uneasy Coalition," *Washington Post,* Jan. 12, 1968; "Negro Coalition Leadership Rift Brews," *Washington Post,* Jan. 13, 1968; Rowland Evans and Robert Novak, "Carmichael To Be No. 1 Negro Leader?" *Washington Post,* Feb. 22, 1968.

43. Seale, *Seize the Time,* p. 221.

44. Carmichael interview. See also Forman, *Black Revolutionaries,* pp. 529–530. Eldridge Cleaver responded that neither Carmichael nor Forman had much success in controlling SNCC: "We were pulling them . . . They tried everything . . . but we rebuffed them . . . There were people ready to snuff Stokely. The troops in the BPP related more to Rap." Cleaver interview, May 2, 1980, at Stanford.

45. Lester, *Revolutionary Notes,* p. 147.

46. Forman, *Black Revolutionaries,* pp. 524, 526, 527. See also Earl Anthony, *Picking Up the Gun: A Report on the Black Panthers* (New York: Dial Press, 1971), pp. 103–104.

47. See Clayborne Carson, "A Talk with Ron Karenga, Watts Black Nationalist," *Los Angeles Free Press,* Sept. 2, 1966. See also Clyde Halisi and James Mtume, eds., *The Quotable Karenga* (Los Angeles: US, 1967).

48. See Forman, *Black Revolutionaries,* p. 524; Anthony, *Picking Up the Gun,* pp. 103–104.

49. Gene Marine, *The Black Panthers* (New York: New American Library, 1969), pp. 122–123. Cf. Lester, *Revolutionary Notes,* pp. 148–149.

50. See "The Man Doesn't Have Us Outnumbered, He Has Us Out Organized," *Movement,* April 1968, pp. 2, 3; "SNCC, Panthers Announce Merger," *National Guardian,* Feb. 24, 1968; "Huey Newton's Birthday Party," *San Francisco Express Times,* Feb. 22, 1968; "Black Leaders Declare Huey Must Go Free," *Berke-*

*ley Barb*, Feb. 23–29, 1968; Reginald Major, *A Panther Is a Black Cat* (New York: William Morrow, 1971), pp. 95–96; *Criminal Disorders*, June 18, 1969, pp. 3722–3732, 3833.

51. Forman, *Black Revolutionaries*, p. 531; Lester, *Revolutionary Notes*, p. 148; "The Man Doesn't Have Us Outnumbered," p. 2.

52. Carmichael in *San Francisco Express Times*, Feb. 22, 1968. Reprinted with deletions in Minor, *Stokely Speaks*, pp. 111–130.

53. "Where It's At," and "Bobby Seale Speaks," *Movement*, April 1968, pp. 2, 11.

54. Karenga interview, Oct. 4, 1977, at Stanford.

55. Minor interview. See also Major, *Panther Is a Black Cat*, pp. 70–71.

56. Willie Ricks interview, May 10, 1977, at Stanford; Sellers, *River of No Return*, p. 247.

57. Forman, *Black Revolutionaries*, p. 534, Cf. Lester, *Revolutionary Notes*, p. 144.

58. "Huey Newton Talks to the Movement about the Black Panther Party, Cultural Nationalism, SNCC, Liberals and White Revolutionaries," *Movement*, Aug. 1968, p. 9.

59. See esp. SAC New York to Director, FBI, "COINTELPRO," June 26, 1968; SAC, New York to Director, FBI, "COINTELPRO," Sept. 9, 1968; Director, FBI to SAC, WFO, "COINTELPRO," Oct. 24, 1968. The FBI also formulated a plan to forge a letter of expulsion from BPP officials to Carmichael, but Carmichael left the Panthers before the plan could take effect. See esp. Director, FBI to SAC, San Francisco, "COINTELPRO," June 17, 1969; SAC, San Francisco to Director, FBI, "COINTELPRO," June 30, 1969.

60. Forman, *Black Revolutionaries*, pp. 537–538; Sellers, *River of No Return*, p. 249. See also C. Gerald Fraser, "SNCC in Decline after 8 Years in Lead; Pace-Setter in Civil Rights Displaced by Panthers," *New York Times*, Oct. 7, 1968; Lester, *Revolutionary Notes*, p. 144; Chuck Moore, *I Was a Black Panther* (New York: Doubleday, 1970), p. 101.

## 18. DECLINE OF BLACK RADICALISM

1. U.S., Congress, Senate, Select Committee to Study Government Operations with Respect to Intelligence Activities, *Final Report: Supplementary Detailed Staff Reports on Intelligence Activities and the Rights of Americans*, Book III, 94th Cong., 2d sess., April 23, 1976, pp. 189–195; R. Rogers, "Black Guns on Campus: Black Panthers and US," *Nation*, May 5, 1969, pp. 558–560; Maulana Ron Karenga, *The Roots of the US-Panther Conflict: The Perverse and Deadly Games Police Play* (San Diego: Kawaida Publications, 1976).

2. "Stokely on King," *Los Angeles Free Press*, April 12, 1968; "Carmichael's News Conference—Inciting to Violence?" *U.S. News and World Report*, April 22, 1968, pp. 49–50.

3. See Ben W. Gilbert, *Ten Blocks from the White House: Anatomy of the Washington Riots of 1968* (New York: Praeger, 1968).

4. H. Rap Brown, *Die Nigger Die!* (New York: Dial Press, 1969), p. 142.

5. "Rap Brown Arrested Here for Violation of Bail," *New York Times*, Feb. 21,

1968; "Brown Ordered to Appear Here," *New Orleans Times-Picayune*, Feb. 21, 1968; "Brown Is Held on New Charge," *New Orleans Times-Picayune*, Feb. 22, 1968; Brown, *Die Nigger Die!*, pp. 112–113.

6. Brown, *Die Nigger Die!*, pp. 114–115.

7. Ibid., p. 117.

8. See "Bugged Rap Brown, but Accidentally, U.S. Says," *Los Angeles Times*, May 11, 1968; "Racism Exposed in H. Rap Brown Case," *Guardian*, July 7, 1974; "Court Hits Judge's Bias in Rap Brown Case," *Guardian*, Feb. 12, 1975.

9. "SNCC Reorganizes," press release of Los Angeles SNCC office, June 17, 1968; U.S., Congress, Senate, Committee on the Judiciary, Subcommittee to Investigate the Administration of the Internal Security Act and Other Internal Security Laws, Hearings, *Extent of Subversion in the "New Left": Testimony of Robert J. Thoms*, 91st Cong., 2d sess., pt. 1, Jan. 20, 1970, p. 6; "SNCC Here Denies Report of Hutchings as Chairman," *Atlanta Journal*, June 20, 1968; "New S.N.C.C. Chief Quiet Organizer," *New York Times*, June 22, 1968.

10. "S.N.C.C. Sets a Negro Party in the Nation as Its Major Goal," *New York Times*, June 10, 1968.

11. Derick Morrison, "Interview with Phil Hutchings of SNCC: 'For a Mass Black Revolutionary Party,' " *Militant*, Oct. 4, 1968, p. 8.

12. See "SNCC Reorganizes."

13. "Carmichael Is Expelled by SNCC in Dispute," *Washington Post*, Aug. 22, 1968. See also "S.N.C.C. Breaks Ties with Stokely Carmichael," *New York Times*, Aug. 23, 1968; "Bigger BUF Role Seen for Carmichael," *Washington Post*, Aug. 24, 1968; Reginald Major, *A Panther Is a Black Cat* (New York: William Morrow, 1971), p. 99.

14. "Carmichael Quits Post in Panthers," *Los Angeles Times*, July 4, 1969. See also "Carmichael Condemns Panthers, Resigns Post," *Washington Post*, July 4, 1969; "Carmichael Tells of Meeting Cleaver in Algiers," *New York Times*, July 25, 1969; Eldridge Cleaver, "Open Letter to Stokely Carmichael," *The Black Panther*, Aug. 16, 1969, p. 5; Major, *Panther Is a Black Cat*, pp. 100–102; Daniel H. Watts, "The Carmichael Cleaver Debate," *Liberator*, Sept. 1969, pp. 3, 5.

In an attempt to capitalize on the animosity between Carmichael and Panther leaders, the FBI proposed that news items featuring Carmichael's anti-BPP statements "be furnished to a cooperative news media source on a confidential basis." See exhibit 69–15 in U.S., Congress, Senate, Select Committee to Study Government Operations with Respect to Intelligence Activities, *Intelligence Activities: Hearings on Senate Resolution 21*, 94th Cong., 1st sess., Dec. 2, 1975, pp. 788–789.

15. SAC, Atlanta to Director, FBI, "Student Nonviolent Coordinating Committee," Mar. 10, 1969.

16. Cleveland Sellers, with Robert Terrell, *The River of No Return: The Autobiography of a Black Militant and the Life and Death of SNCC* (New York: William Morrow, 1973), p. 250; SAC, Atlanta to Director, FBI, "SNCC," Mar. 10, 1969, pp. 13–14; Willie Ricks interview, May 10, 1976, at Stanford.

17. Sellers interview, Dec. 13, 1978, in Greensboro; Sellers, *River of No Return*, pp. 221–267; Ricks interview.

18. Text of speech in Black Star Publishing, ed., *The Political Thought of James Forman* (Detroit: Black Star Publishing, 1970), pp. 59, 62. See also James Forman,

*The Making of Black Revolutionaries* (New York: Macmillan, 1972), pp. 543–545.

19. See text of manifesto in *Political Thought of Forman*, pp. 63–69. See also Murray Kempton, "The Black Manifesto," *New York Review of Books*, July 10, 1969; Arnold Schucter, *Reparations: The Black Manifesto and Its Challenge to White Churches* (Philadelphia: Lippincott, 1970).

20. Forman, *Black Revolutionaries*, pp. 547–549.

21. Ibid., p. 550. According to an FBI account of the meeting, Brown told staff members "that it was obvious that the present SNCC leadership has done nothing during the past year and that he and eight members present at the meeting saw fit to declare a standing takeover . . . He declared the meeting to be under a dictatorial chairmanship with all powers of recommendation delegated to himself." SAC Atlanta to Director, FBI, "SNCC," Aug. 1, 1969, p. 16. See also H. Rap Brown, "Racism and Revolution!" *SNCC Monthly*, Mar. 1970, pp. 10–14.

22. " 'Nonviolent' Deleted from Name of SNCC," *Washington Post*, July 23, 1969; SAC, New York to Director, FBI, "SNCC," Oct. 16, 1969.

23. Forman, *Black Revolutionaries*, p. 551. See James A. Geschwender, *Class, Race, and Worker Insurgency: The League of Revolutionary Black Workers* (Cambridge: Cambridge University Press, 1977).

24. See "Women Strike But Equal to What?" *SNCC Monthly*, Sept.-Oct. 1969, p. 2; "Women" [Statement of Third World Women's Alliance], *SNCC Monthly*, Mar. 1970, pp. 8–9.

25. SAC, New York to Director, FBI, "SNCC," Jan. 21, 1970.

26. SNCC press release, Mar. 16, 1970, reprinted in SAC, New York to Director, FBI, "SNCC," May 25, 1970, p. 17. See also "Mystery and Distrust over Bombings Grow," *National Observer*, Mar. 23, 1970; Sellers, *River of No Return*, pp. 363–364; Forman, *Black Revolutionaries*, p. 542.

27. "Charlotte Featherstone Reveals Doubts, Fears," *Chicago Defender*, May 14, 1970.

28. Brown interview in *Guerilla* (Toronto), 1973, reprinted in *Los Angeles Free Press*, undated copy in *FOF*, 1972–73, J1 682.

29. "H. Rap Brown and 3 Convicted of Robbery and Assault," *New York Times*, Mar. 30, 1973; "Brown Is Given 5-to-15 Year Term," *New York Times*, May 10, 1973; Robert Daley, "The Men Who Shot Rap Brown," *New York*, Oct. 23, 1972, pp. 35–42; "Police Says Brown Planned to Rob Pusher," *Baltimore Afro-American*, Dec. 5, 1972; "The Jury's Verdict: Guilty," *New York Times*, April 1, 1973; "The 'Street Story' of H. Rap Brown's Arrest," *Washington Post*, April 30, 1973.

30. Hunt to SNCC staff, Aug. 13, 1970 in SAC, New York to Director, FBI, "SNCC," May 10, 1971, p. 47.

31. SAC, New York to Director, FBI, "SNCC," Dec. 11, 1973, p. 6.

32. John Lewis interview, April 17, 1962, in Atlanta; Charles Smith interview, Sept. 14, 1978, in Haynesville, Alabama.

33. Marion Barry interview, April 7, 1972, in Washington, D.C.; Dewey Greene interview, Sept. 16, 1978, in Greenwood, Miss.

34. Ricks interview.

35. Lewis interview.

36. Bob Zellner interview, Sept. 19, 1978, in New Orleans.

37. Johnny Wilson interview, April 26, 1972, in Washington, D.C.

38. Forman, *Black Revolutionaries*, p. 551.

39. Moses' address at Ella J. Baker 75th birthday celebration, Dec. 9, 1978, in New York City.

# INDEX

Abernathy, Ralph, 36, 60, 61, 93
Abolitionism, 141, 147
Action, 27, 45, 54, 69, 140
Aelony, Zev, 92
Africa, 24; independence movements in, 16; Lawson on, 23; identification with, 94, 101; SNCC trip, 134–136; Atlanta Project and, 197, 198; Carmichael visit, 276–277; Moses visit, 330n. *See also* Pan-Africanism
African National Congress, 277
Afro-American Festival, 201
Agnew, Spiro T., 256
Alabama: SNCC project, 150; before 1965, 157–158; staff meeting, 170–172; SCOPE project, 187. *See also* Lowndes County; Selma protests
Al-Amin, Jamil Abdullah, 306. *See also* Brown, H. Rap
*Albany Herald,* 57, 59
Albany Movement, 56–65, 84, 92–93
Albany State College, 56, 59
Alexander, Clifford, 189
Alexander, Franklin, 262, 270
Ali Muhammad, 260
All African Peoples Revolutionary Party, 302, 306
Allen, Ivan, 226
Allen, Louis, 48–49
Allen, Ralph, 76, 92
Allen, Robert, 228
American Baptist Theological Seminary, 21–22
American Friends Service Committee, 46, 67
Americans for Democratic Action, 109
Amos, Mr. and Mrs., 116
Anderson, William G., 58, 60, 61
Anti-poverty program, 258–260

Anti-riot legislation, 221, 224–225, 257–258
Anti-Semitism, 268–269
Aptheker, Herbert, 104
Arkansas SNCC, 150, 232
Aronson, Henry, 325n
Atlanta, 166–168, 225–226, 255
Atlanta Committee on Appeal for Human Rights, 67
*Atlanta Constitution,* 204
Atlanta Project, 189–201, 206, 216–217, 225, 228, 229, 236–242, 251, 261, 299
Atlanta Summit Leadership Conference, 226
Atlanta University, 245

Bailey, John, 124
Bailey, Kofi, 268
Baker, Ella Jo, 70, 71, 182, 346n; and SNCC founding, 19–20, 24–26; on group leadership, 20, 24, 30; overcomes split, 31, 41–42; and SCLC, 71; and MFDP, 109, 123; and SCEF, 182; and education program, 202, 235
Bankhead, Lee, 170
Banyaca, Tomas, 278
Baptist Ministerial Alliance, 58
Barry, Marion: on sit-ins, 17; background, 21, 22; as chairman, 24, 25; at 1960 party conventions, 26; and funding, 41–42; in McComb, 48; in Knoxville, 90; and Mississippi Summer Project, 99, 100, 149; on economic programs, 104; and MFDP, 123; against arming, 164; in Washington, D.C., 168, 187, 233, 305; on Atlanta police, 226; on SNCC legacy, 301
Bates, Daisy, 15
Bates, "Peg Leg," 239

Baton Rouge, La., 53, 68, 83
Beal, Frances, 296
Belafonte, Harry, 39, 70, 134
Belfrage, Sally, 113, 116, 121–123
Bellamy, Fay, 164, 169, 230, 306; in So-
    viet Union, 272; on Carmichael, 276,
    277
Beloved community, 21, 23–24, 101, 145
Bennett, Lerone, Jr., 182–183, 222
Berkeley Free Speech Movement, 3, 202
Bevel, Diane Nash, 68, 94, 246. *See also*
    Nash, Diane
Bevel, James, 22, 68, 78, 165–166; in jail,
    38; and Nashville seminar, 41; as
    SCLC militant, 186
Biloxi, Miss., 118–119
Birmingham, Ala. 34–35, 36, 90
Black, Hector, 238–239
*Black Awakening in Capitalist America,* 228
Black Awareness Coordinating Commit-
    tee (BACC), 249–250
Black Belt Program, 138–139
*Black Bourgeoisie,* 12
Black churches, 58, 223
Black Congress, 281
Black consciousness, 3, 77, 176, 215, 244,
    299; freedom songs and, 63–64; and
    whites, 100–103; and Waveland re-
    treat, 144; Lewis on, 151; and Atlanta
    Project, 192, 193–195, 196–200; Car-
    michael on, 206, 211; Forman on, 236.
    *See also* Black nationalism; black sepa-
    ration
Black Liberators, 294
Black Manifesto, 294–295
Black nationalism, 192, 286, 301; Moses
    and, 137; Donaldson on, 201; Carmi-
    chael on, 204–205, 217; in SNCC, 299.
    *See also* Black consciousness; Black sep-
    aratism
Black Panther Party (Alabama), 153,
    162. *See also* Lowndes County Freedom
    Organization
Black Panther Party (California), 253,
    265, 278–286, 284, 288
Black Panther Political Party, 281
Black power, 3, 4, 127–129, 209–211,
    215–228, 233, 235–242, 244, 274, 286,
    289, 299
*Black Power: The Politics of Liberation in
    America,* 227
Black Revolutionary Action Party, 295

Black separatism, 141, 166, 180, 186,
    189–211, 217–221, 236–242, 265,
    269–271, 282, 299. *See also* Black con-
    sciousness; Black nationalism
Black Star publications, 295
Black United Fronts, 288, 292
Blackwell, Randolph, 81
Blair, Izell, 9, 16–17
Blake, Eugene Carson, 93
Block, Sam, 77–79, 80, 86
Bond, Horace Mann, 166
Bond, H. Julian, 25, 29; on SNCC, 54;
    on Albany Movement, 62; as commu-
    nications director, 69–70; in Africa,
    134–135; legislative campaigns,
    166–168, 231–232; Vietnam war, 187;
    barred from seat, 189–190, 192–195,
    231; subsequent career, 305–306
*Boston Herald,* 222
Braden, Anne, 52–53, 67, 76, 102,
    205–206, 246
Braden, Carl, 51–52, 67, 246
Branton, Wiley, 97
Briley, Beverly, 248
Britt, Travis, 48
Brooks, Fred, 246, 248, 258, 259–260
Brooks, Paul, 22, 43, 69, 84
Brown, Ben D., 28
Brown, Ben, 254
Brown, Bob, 234, 283
Brown, Ed, 252
Brown, Hubert (Rap), 157, 233, 235,
    246; as chairman, 244, 252–256,
    258–260, 266; legal actions against,
    256–257, 289–290, 298; and FBI, 262,
    263; at National Conference for a New
    Politics, 270; and Black Panthers,
    281–282, 283; on government re-
    pression, 289–290; SNCC takeover,
    295–296, 297, 345n; subsequent career,
    306; on Arabs and Jews, 340n
Brown, Joyce, 234
*Brown* vs. *Topeka Board of Education,* 15
Bryant, C. C., 46

California Democratic Council, 109
Cambridge, Md., 72, 90, 252, 255–256,
    258
Cambridge Action Federation, 255
Camus, Albert, 2, 46, 114, 140, 156, 175,
    235

Carmichael, Stokely (Kwame Touré),
3–4, 17, 72, 157, 253; on jail, 38; Nashville seminar, 41; on socialism, 104; on
Communists, 105, 106; on federal officials, 121; on armed self-defense, 122,
123; on MFDP, 128; on women, 148,
325n; on local leadership, 154; on
Sellers, 156; at Selma, 161; in Lowndes
County, 162, 163–166, 199, 200, 206,
233, 300; on new programs, 170, 171,
235; elected chairman, 199–204, 242,
272; on whites, 205, 206, 217, 240; and
Mississippi marches, 206–211; and
black power, 209–210, 211, 215–219,
221–224, 227–228, 244, 274; on race
vs. class, 217, 227, 265, 269, 274–278,
280, 282, 283, 292; Summerhill incident, 225–226; *Black Power*, 227; criticism of, 229–230, 276; and Atlanta
Project, 241; appeal of, 244, 245; Vanderbilt speech, 246–248; replaced, 251;
and press, 253; in Prattville, 254; and
Atlanta riots, 255, 258; and FBI, 261,
262, 263, 264, 284; on surveillance,
266; in Third World, 273–277; on Pan-
Africanism, 276, 277–278, 282; and
Black Panther Party, 277–279, 280,
281–282, 283, 284, 292; and Black
United Fronts, 228, 292; expelled, 292;
subsequent career, 306; on Arabs and
Jews, 340n
Carter, Jimmy, 305
Cason, Sandra, 28. *See also* Hayden,
Casey
Caston, Billy Jack, 47–48
Castro, Fidel, 275
Chaney, James, 114–115
Cheuse, Alan, 179
Chicago SNCC, 234, 238
Christianity, 21, 23–24
*Christian Science Monitor,* 222
Churchville, John, 195
Civil Rights Act: of 1964, 142; of 1965,
235
Clark, Jim, 159
Clark, Kenneth, 41
Class. *See* Race
Cleaver, Eldridge, 279–280, 281,
282–284, 291
Cleaver, Kathleen, 279, 283
Cloud, John, 159

Cobb, Charles, 78, 79–80, 262, 294; and
Mississippi Summer Project, 99; and
freedom schools, 109, 110; and MFDP,
124; on resistance, 154; on idealism,
157; and Bond, 167, 168; and War
Crimes Tribunal, 273; on floaters,
326n
Coffin, William Sloane, 37
Coles, Robert, 138, 315n
Collins, Lucretia, 38
Collins, Norma, 59, 69
Columbus, Ohio, 168
*Commentary,* 220
Communists: and SNCC, 105–107,
180–183; and red-baiting, 136–137,
180–183, 185, 187, 189, 245–246,
261–262; and Carmichael, 162; and
SDS, 180; in Nashville Black Power
Conference, 246; in Los Angeles
SNCC, 270; blacks recruited by, 271
Community Action Program (CAP), 260
Congress of Racial Equality (CORE), 2,
16, 34, 67, 234; and SNCC founding,
21; and Rock Hill protests, 31–32; and
freedom rides, 33–34, 36; and March
on Washington, 92; and Mississippi
Summer Project, 108; radicalization
in, 186; on black power, 223; and FBI,
262; black-Jewish tensions in, 269
Connor, Eugene "Bull," 35
Council of Federated Organizations
(COFO), 78; and VEP funding, 97; on
whites, 98–99; and Mississippi Summer Project, 100, 111–114; and freedom schools, 119, 120–121; independence of, 149, 150; problems in,
171–173
Council on United Civil Rights Leadership, 186
Cox, Courtland, 93, 220, 294; on Sherrod, 101; on SSOC, 102–103; and economic programs, 104; defends SNCC,
137; on LCFO, 166; on Central Committee, 204; opposes Mississippi march,
207
Cox, Donald, 283
Crook, Brother, 290
Cruse, Harold, 227–228
Cuba, 273–275
Current, Gloster, 137
Currier, Stephen, 92
Curry, Constance, 25

Dammon, Peggy, 76
Daniels, Carolyn, 75
Daniels, Jonathan, 165
Davis, Angela, 270
Davis, Benjamin, 15, 162
Davis, Irving, 293, 296–297
Davis, J. Paschall, 259
Davis, Rennie, 177
Dawson, Barry, 225
Dawson, Charles, 125
Deacons for Defense and Justice, 164, 207–208, 262
Delany, Martin, 215
Democratic party: MFDP challenge, 3, 14, 26–27, 97, 123–129
Dennis, David, 78
Dennis, Gene, 162
Devine, Annie, 123, 125–126
Diamond, Dion, 68
*Die, Nigger, Die!*, 297
Direct action. *See* Nonviolent direct action
Discipline, 2, 4, 69, 133, 137–141, 143–144, 153, 155–157, 159, 161–162, 169–170, 173–174, 230, 232, 234–235, 276, 285–286, 299, 303
Doar, John, 36, 38, 41, 47; and Moses, 85, 87; on federal protection, 88, 121
Donaldson, Ivanhoe, 80, 157, 253; in Danville, 90; on freedom vote, 98; and Mississippi Summer Project, 116; and MFDP, 124, 127; at Selma protest, 162; and Bond, 166–167; urban organizing, 168; assessment of, 170; and new strategy, 201; on Central Committee, 204; and education program, 235; subsequent career, 305
Draft resistance, 183, 188, 251, 271
Drake, St. Clair, 193
Duberman, Martin, 120
DuBois, Shirley Graham, 276
DuBois, W.E.B., 15, 262, 276
Dulles, Allan, 115

Eastland, James O., 78, 181, 258
Edwards, Len, 117
Eisenhower, Dwight D., 14, 15, 24
Ellender, Allen J., 83
Evans, Rowland, 136–137, 181–182, 185, 205
Evans, Sara, 325n

Evers, Charles, 149
Evers, Medgar, 97, 193

Fanon, Franz, 192, 198, 235
Farmer, James, 36
Featherstone, Ralph, 230, 262, 278; on freedom schools, 120; in Central Committee, 204; in Lowndes County, 233; as program secretary, 253; and Arab-Israeli issue, 268; death, 297, 306
Federal Bureau of Investigation (FBI), 105; suspicions of, 49; and Mississippi Summer Project, 114, 115, 121–122; and MFDP, 124; COINTELPRO (Counterintelligence Program), 244, 261, 262–264, 284, 288, 290, 305; and Sellers, 250; and Brown, 256; surveillance and repression of SNCC, 257, 260–264, 298. *See also* Hoover
Federal government: protection by, 1, 81, 83–89, 91, 96, 200; disillusionment with, 2, 37–38, 87, 92–95, 115, 127–129, 159, 161, 183, 184, 208; positive attitude to, 13–14; and freedom ride campaign, 35–37; and voter registration, 38–39, 41; complicity of, 83–85, 92–94, 115, 184; and Mississippi Summer Project, 96, 98–100, 110, 111, 114–115, 121–123, 128, 129; and MFDP, 127–129; and black image abroad, 134–135, 323n. *See also* Federal Bureau of Investigation; Johnson, Lyndon; Kennedy, John and Robert; Vietnam
Federation of Women's Clubs, 58
Felder, Andrea, 246, 248
Fellowship of Reconciliation (FOR), 2, 21, 22
Feminism, 141, 147–148, 301, 302
Field Foundation, 70
Fisk University, 21, 245, 247–248
Ford, Gerald R., 258
Forman, James, 31, 46, 51, 73, 81, 200, 251, 261; background, 42–43; administrative skills, 43–44, 66, 69–71; on discipline and organization, 54, 82, 138, 139, 140, 145–146, 156, 169, 170, 303; and Albany Movement, 59; and Greenwood protests, 86; and March on Washington, 92–94; on whites, 99–100, 101, 240; on economic programs, 103; in United Civil Rights Leadership

Council, 107; on Mississippi Summer Project, 110; and MFDP, 124, 126; in Africa, 134; on staff weariness, 138; and Black Belt Program, 138–139; and factionalism, 139, 293, 294; and Waveland retreat, 140; on leave, 146; on sexual discrimination, 148; on field staff, 150–151; in Secretariat, 151; on local leadership, 156; at Selma, 159, 160, 162; and SCLC, 163–164; on new issues, 169; Eastland on, 181; on Vietnam war, 184; and Atlanta Project, 192, 196, 241, 336n; resigns as executive secretary, 202; and Lewis, 203; in Central Committee, 204; and black power, 224; and Philadelphia police raid, 225; and education program, 235–236; on class, 236, 265, 269–270, 277, 303; and Zellners, 242; and Brown, 252; in International Affairs Commission, 266; on Middle East, 267, 268; international views of, 272; and Black Panther Party, 278, 280–285, 292, 293; in collective leadership, 290; and reparations, 294–295; subsequent career, 296, 306
Frazier, E. Franklin, 12, 41
Free D.C. Movement, 233
Freedom: vs. authority, 2, 4, 28, 66, 137–140, 142–143, 145, 154, 155, 157, 170–174, 211, 277, 299; groups, 153, 155–157, 169–170, 326n; parties, 253
Freedom Riders Coordinating Committee, 36, 38
Freedom rides, 1, 31–38, 43–44, 73
Freedom schools, 109–111, 119–121, 129, 149, 171, 172
Freedom Singers, 64, 135
Freedom songs, 49, 59, 63–64, 75, 81, 305
Free Southern Theater, 120
Free Speech Movement, 3, 302
Friendship Junior College, 31–32
Fruchter, Norm, 179, 180
Fusco, Liz, 144, 155

Gaither, Tom, 32
Gallup poll, 183
Gandhian influence, 2, 16, 21, 298
Garmen, Betty, 70, 175
Garrett, Jimmy, 182
Garvey, Marcus, 215, 276

Georgia, 73–77, 84, 85, 101–102. *See also* Albany movement
Ginsberg, Allen, 175
Gitlin, Todd, 177
Gober, Bertha, 59
Goldwater, Barry, 123, 127
Good, Paul, 116, 210, 216
Goodman, Andrew, 114–115
Goodman, Paul, 175
Gray, Jesse, 209
Gray, Victoria, 109
Green, Edith, 126
Greenberg, Jack, 107
Greene, Dewey, 86, 301, 306
Greene, Freddie, 239, 278, 306
Greene, George, 306
Greensboro, N.C., 9–11, 215
Greenwood, Miss., 77–81, 86–87
Gregory, Dick, 108
Grinnage, Ben, 169, 232
Guinea, 134–135, 276
Guyot, Lawrence, 98–99, 123, 128, 139, 232

Hall, Bill, 72, 160, 168, 234–235, 306
Hall, Blanton, 59
Hall, Prathia, 85, 134
Hamer, Fanny Lou, 73–74; on whites, 99; and MFDP, 109, 123, 125–126; in Africa, 134; and Malcolm X, 135; on Executive Committee, 151; black separatists on, 240; death, 306
Hamilton, Charles V., 227, 235
Hamlett, Ed, 102, 103, 118–119
Hansen, Bill, 61, 83–84, 134, 150, 164, 169, 232
Hardy, John, 47, 48, 88
Harris, Donald, 92, 134, 135
Harris poll, 222
Harvard University, 26, 46
Hattiesburg Freedom Day, 108
Hayden, Casey, 53–54, 70, 157, 302; on women, 147–148, 325n; criticism of, 170; in SDS, 175. *See also* Cason, Sandra
Hayden, Tom, 53, 67, 176, 178–179, 302
Hayes, Curtis, 48, 77
Henry, Aaron, 78, 97–98, 125
Higgs, William, 86
Highlander Folk School, 28, 41, 50–52, 77
Hill, Herbert, 41

Ho Chi Minh, 276
Hodes, Bill, 113
Holloway, Frank, 38
Holt, Len, 67, 109
Hoover, J. Edgar: SNCC suit against, 86; on Communists, 107, 261; and Mississippi murders, 115; and Brown, 256; and surveillance of SNCC, 262–264. *See also* Federal Bureau of Investigation
House Committee on Un-American Activities (HUAC), 13, 51–52, 106, 163, 181, 289
Howard University, 21, 30, 103–104, 163, 245. *See also* Nonviolent Action Group
Hulett, John, 165–166, 300
Humphrey, Hubert, 124, 126, 127, 189, 220
Hunt, Muhammad (William), 296–298
Hurst, E. H., 48
Hutchings, Phil, 291–293, 306
Hutton, Bobby, 284

Institute for Policy Studies, 105
Interdenominational Alliance, 58
Interdenominational Ministerial Alliance, 248
Interracialism, 3, 75–77, 100. *See also* Whites
Interreligious Foundation for Community Organization, 294
Interstate Commerce Commission, 37, 58, 60
*In White America,* 120

Jackson, Goldie, 59
Jackson, Jimmy Lee, 158, 160, 161, 184
Jenkins, Herbert, 226
Jenkins, Timothy, 28, 39, 40, 52, 54
Jews, 268–269, 340n
Johnson, Frank, 159
Johnson, Jimmy, 296
Johnson, Lee Otis, 249
Johnson, Lyndon B.: and Mississippi murders, 115; and MFDP, 123–127, 149; and Selma protests, 158, 160, 161; on antiwar position, 188–189; on black power, 220; civil rights legislation of, 221; Brown on, 256; attacks on, 258; and Carmichael, 275–277
Johnson, Paul B., 124

Johnson, Robert, 67
Jones, Charles, 13; Rock Hill protest, 32; on voter registration, 39–40, 42, 51, 52; at Nashville seminar, 41; and Albany Movement, 59–63
Jones, Matthew, 134

Kahn, Tom, 163, 180
Karenga, Ron, 281, 283, 288
Katzenbach, Nicholas, 159, 261
Kelley, Asa, 59
Kennedy, John F.: and freedom rides, 1, 35–38; election of, 29; and voter registration, 38–39, 41; and Albany demonstrations, 61; criticism of, 83; and civil rights, 87–89; and March on Washington, 91
Kennedy, Robert F.: and 1960 election, 29; and freedom rides, 35, 36; and voter registration, 39; and SNCC, 83–84, 86; and Cambridge demonstration, 90; on black power, 220
Kilpatrick, James, 14
King, C.B., 61
King, Edward, 27, 30, 32, 33, 37–38, 43
King, Edwin, 97–98, 125
King, Marion, 61, 62, 84
King, Martin Luther, 3, 4, 15, 67, 121–122, 220; and SNCC, 19, 20, 22–23, 28, 186–187; Lewis on, 21; arrest, 29; freedom rides, 36; and Albany Movement, 60, 61, 63; and March on Washington, 93, 94; and Communists, 105; and MFDP, 125, 126; and Selma protests, 157–161; Carmichael on, 163–164, 219; opposes Vietnam war, 187, 189; and Mississippi marches, 207–210; on black power, 210, 223; Hoover on, 262; assassination, 288
King, Mary E., 70, 147–148, 302, 305, 325n
King, Slater, 58, 60, 61
Kinoy, Arthur, 150
Koen, Charles, 290
Kopkind, Andrew, 182
Ku Klux Klan, 36, 85, 255
Kunstler, William, 150, 256, 289, 325n

Labor unions, 104, 172
Ladner, Joyce, 222–223
Lafayette, Bernard, 22, 106, 150, 157
Lafayette, Colia, 157

Lake, Henry, 250
Landsburg, Dorothy, 121
Lane, Mark, 37
Lawrence, David, 124
Lawson, James, 29, 46, 67, 207; as Nashville leader, 22; impact on SNCC, 23–25; on jail, no bail, 28; and freedom rides, 36; on revolution, 54
Leadership: local, 3, 150, 171–174, 193–195, 201, 207, 211, 264, 287–288, 291–292, 299–303; group, 20, 24, 30, 112–113, 138, 179
League for Industrial Democracy, 163, 180
League of Revolutionary Black Workers, 296
Lee, Herbert, 48, 49
Lee, Mrs. Herbert, 94
Lester, Julius, 199, 237–238, 264, 266, 273, 275
Levin, Tom, 172
Lewis, David, 63, 160
Lewis, Ike, 49
Lewis, John, 57, 181, 238, 261; background, 21–22; on Baker, 24; in freedom rides, 33, 35, 36, 38; at Nashville seminar, 41; becomes full-time staffer, 67; in Nashville demonstration, 90; and March on Washington, 91–95; on nonviolence, 94–95, 200; on Mississippi Summer Project, 99; on racial consciousness, 101; on Communists, 106, 107, 182; on federal protection, 115; and President Johnson, 124; on MFDP, 127; in Africa, 134, 135; on Malcolm X, 136; on local leadership, 139; on black-led civil rights movement, 151; and Selma protests, 158–159, 161, 162; on arming, 164; on discipline, 169, 170; Evans and Novak on, 182; and White House Conference on Civil Rights, 187, 200, 203, 204; unseated as chairman, 199–204; resigns, 231, 232; on SNCC legacy, 300, 302; subsequent career, 305
Liberals, 92–94, 96, 127–128, 146, 151–152, 184, 270
Lincoln, C. Eric, 41
Liuzzo, Viola, 161, 162
Logan, Rayford, 41
Long, Worth, 157, 202–203, 306

Look Out, Whitey! Black Power's Gon' Get Your Mama, 237–238
Love, John, 157
Lowenstein, Allard, 97–100, 137
Lowndes County, Ala., 162–166, 199, 200, 206, 233, 300–301
Lowndes County Christian Movement for Human rights, 165–166, 300
Lowndes County Freedom Organization (LCFO), 153, 164–166, 200, 233, 245, 278, 300
Lynd, Staughton, 109, 120, 177–178

McCain, Franklin, 9, 10, 15, 17
McClellan, John L., 259–260
McComb, Miss., 45–56, 84, 184–185
McDew, Charles, 28–30, 49–50, 54, 68, 84–85
McGhee, Silas, 122, 151
McGill, Ralph, 226
McKissick, Floyd, 207–210, 262
McLaurin, Charles, 78–80, 85, 123
McNeil, Joseph, 9, 17
Mahoney, Bill, 34, 38, 67, 72, 104
Making of Black Revolutionaries, The, 296
Malcolm X, 2, 4, 100, 103, 135–136, 192, 215, 279
Mants, Robert, 158–159, 163, 204, 306
March on Washington, 83, 91–95, 136
Marshall, Burke, 36, 84
Martin, Louis, 189
Marxism, 265, 270, 271, 276, 277, 282
Massachusetts Review, 216
Mathews, Z.T., 75
Matthews, Carl, 10–11
Maxwell, Bruce, 118, 119
Medical Committee for Human Rights, 108
Meely, Fred, 204, 225, 267
Meredith, James, 207
Middle East Conflict, 267–269
Miller, Dottie, 70. See also Zellner, Dottie
Miller, Michael, 145
Mills, C. Wright, 175
Minnis, Jack, 165, 181, 203–204, 235–236, 240–241
Minor, Ethel, 228, 241, 251, 264, 267–269, 276, 278, 283
Mississippi: community organizing in, 74, 77–81; federal protection in, 84–89; marches in 1966, 206–211; black power in, 222–223; SNCC weakened

in, 232–233. *See also* McComb; Mississippi Summer Project
Mississippi Child Development Group, 172–173
Mississippi Freedom Democratic Party (MFDP), 3, 137, 171, 172, 306; organized, 108–109; and voter registration, 117; and White Folk's Project, 119; challenge by, 123–129, 185–186; morale problem, 149; and COFO, 149–150; and SNCC, 149–151, 173, 232–233
Mississippi Freedom Labor Union, 172, 327n
Mississippi Summer Project, 2–3, 111–129; proposal for, 96; whites in, 96, 98–103, 111–114, 118–119; plans for, 98–100, 107–110; and freedom schools, 109–111, 119–121, 129; and black control, 110, 111, 119, 123–129; orientation for, 111–114; violence during, 114–115, 121–122; acceptance of, in black community, 115–117; and White Folk's Project, 118–119; and armed self-defense, 122–123; aftermath, 133, 136, 138, 141–142, 146, 148–149; Carmichael in, 163; FBI on, 262
Mitchell, Clarence, 189
Mitchell, Lansing, 290
Mitford, Jessica, 70
Monsonis, Jim, 53–54, 175
Montgomery, Ala., 4, 35–36
Moore, Amzie, 26, 46
Morris, Jesse, 151, 172, 306
Morrisroe, Richard, 165
Moses, Dona. *See* Richards, Dona
Moses, Robert (Bob), 4, 51, 73, 74, 84, 238; and sit-ins, 17; joins SNCC, 26; background, 46; in McComb, 46–50, 77–78; and Mississippi Summer Project, 96–97, 114–115, 138; on food drives, 80; on one man, one vote, 81–82, 89; seeks federal protection, 85–89, 115; on whites, 96–100, 112, 201, 330n; on racial animosities, 101, 114, 144; on economic programs, 103–105; on Communists, 106–107; arrested, 108; and Rauh, 109; and MFDP, 126, 128; in Africa, 134, 330n; Evans and Novak on, 136–137; on freedom vs. structure, 138–141, 303; and Black Belt Program, 138, 139; re-

sists personal following, 139–140, 242; withdraws from leadership role, 140, 156–157, 303; and field staff, 150–151; changes surname, 156; on local leadership, 170–171, 303; on revolution, 178; Eastland on, 181; on Third World, 184; opposes Vietnam war, 184–185; on SNCC legacy, 303; subsequent career, 306
Muhammad, Elijah, 135

Nash, Diane, 13, 38; on sit-ins, 17; background, 21, 22; in Atlanta, 28; and Rock Hill protest, 32; and freedom rides, 34–36; and Nashville seminar, 41; and direct action, 42, 51. *See also* Bevel, Diane Nash
Nashville, Tenn., 41, 42, 245–248, 258–259
Nashville group, 21–25, 29, 34–35
Nation of Islam, 14, 17, 135, 192, 262, 279
National Association for the Advancement of Colored People (NAACP), 14, 67, 71; Lawson on, 23; and Rock Hill protests, 31–32; in Monroe, N.C., 42–43; and Albany Movement, 58, 59, 60; and March on Washington, 92; and Mississippi Summer Project, 108; and SNCC, 137, 181, 186, 189
National Black Anti-War Anti-Draft Union, 271
National Black Economic Development Conference, 294, 295
National Conference for a New Politics, 270
National Council of Churches, 99, 108
*National Guardian*, 205, 228
National Lawyers Guild, 67, 107, 137, 182
National Student Association (NSA), 21, 25
National Student Christian Federation, 21
Neblett, Carver (Chico), 283
Negro Voters League, 58
Nelson, Jack, 204
Newfield, Jack, 178
New Left, 175–180, 184, 190–191, 265, 269–272, 301–302. *See also* Students for a Democratic Society
*Newsweek*, 181, 221, 222, 253

Newton, Huey, 278–279, 280–285
New World Foundation, 41
*New York Review of Books*, 216
*New York Times*, 204
*Nitty Gritty*, 194
Nixon, Richard, 29
Nkrumah, Kwame, 139, 276, 277
Nobles, Ernest, 78
Nonviolence: in sit-ins, 11–12; at SNCC's founding, 19, 23–25; and Nashville group, 21–23, 25; as a tactic, 38, 61, 65, 68, 164, 237. *See also* Nonviolent direct action
Nonviolent Action Group (NAG), 30, 72, 83–84, 103–104, 162, 163, 252
Nonviolent direct action, 2, 3; as new political consciousness, 12; jail, no bail, 22–24, 28, 32, 36–37, 60; vs. voter registration, 26, 31, 39–42; jail-in movement, 32–33; and freedom rides, 33–37; in McComb project, 45, 48–51; in Albany Movement, 56–65; in 1963, 89–95; and Selma protests, 159–162
Norman, Silas, 144, 157, 161–162, 170, 171, 196
North Carolina Agricultural and Technical College, 9, 10, 12, 16
North Carolina College, 11
North Vietnam, 272–273, 276
Novak, Robert, 136–137, 181–182, 185, 205

Oberlin College School of Theology, 22
O'Dell, Jack, 105
Odinga, Oginga, 134
Office of Economic Opportunity (OEO), 258–259, 260
Ogelsby, Carl, 1978
O'Neal, John, 120
One man, one vote, 82, 89, 94, 143
Orangeburg, S.C., 249–250, 293
Orbell, John, 13
Organization of Afro-American Unity, 135, 279
Organization of Latin-American Solidarity, 274–276

Pan-Africanism, 193, 265, 276–278, 282
Parks, Rosa, 15
Parris, Bob. *See* Moses
Patterson, John, 35, 36
Payne, William H. (Che), 297

Peace and Freedom Party, 279, 280
Peace Corps, 141, 193
Peacock, Willie, 78, 86
Peck, Jim, 33, 34
People's Conferences, 170–171
Perdew, John, 72–73, 76, 92
Pettigrew, Thomas F., 13
Philadelphia, Miss., 114, 115
Philadelphia, Pa., 225
Pittman, James, 143
Police: and Moses, 47–48; in Albany Movement, 56, 61, 62; in Mississippi, 79, 80; and Selma protests, 159; and SNCC, 225, 234, 243, 244, 260–264, 288–290, 296, 300; and Carmichael, 225–226; in Nashville, 245–248; at Texas Southern University, 249; at South Carolina State College, 249–250; and Black Panther Party, 284. *See also* Federal Bureau of Investigation
Poor People's Corporation, 172
Port Huron Statement, 175, 176
Pouissant, Alvin, 237
Poverty, 2, 82, 94–95, 141–144, 146–147, 152, 155–156, 227, 300–303
Powell, Adam Clayton, 209, 223–224
Prattville, Ala., 254–255
Price, Cecil, 210
Pride, Inc., 233
Pritchett, Laurie, 59, 60, 61, 64
Progressive Labor Party, 271
Project Awareness, 103–104
Puerto Rican nationalists, 278
Pullum, D.U., 75

Rabinowitz, Joni, 181
Rabinowitz, Victor, 179–180
Race: appeals to, 166, 191, 194, 196, 201; vs. class, 227, 265, 269–271, 277, 291
Raines, "Mama Dolly," 75
Randolph, A. Philip, 91, 93, 94, 220, 268
Randolph, E. Harlan, 41
Rauh, Joseph, 109, 124–126, 137, 150
Reagon, Bernice, 59, 63, 64
Reagon, Cordell, 56–58, 60
Reeb, James, 160, 161, 184
Republican party, 26–27
Reuther, Walter, 126
Revolutionary Action Movement (RAM), 196, 261–263

Richards, Dona, 134, 156–157, 170, 172, 187
Richardson, Gloria, 72, 94
Richardson, Judy, 163
Richmond, David, 9, 15, 17
Ricks, Willie, 246, 278; at Selma protests, 160; on Atlanta Project, 199; background, 208–209; and black power, 209, 210; and Atlanta violence, 255; on SNCC-Black Panther merger, 283; expelled, 293–294; on SNCC legacy, 301; subsequent career, 306
Rizzo, Frank, 225
Robeson, Paul, 15, 209
Robinson, Reginald, 47, 50, 73, 83–84, 123, 182
Robinson, Ruby Doris, 70, 234, 239, 325n; on economic programs, 105; in Africa, 134; on floaters, 169, 170; elected executive secretary, 202–204; on Carmichael, 229–230; on Mississippi staff, 232–233; death, 251, 306; replaced, 252. See also Smith, Ruby Doris
Rock Hill, S.C., 31–33, 39
Rollins, Avon, 90
Romilly, Constancia (Dinky), 70
Roosevelt, Eleanor, 51
Roosevelt, Franklin D., 91
Ruleville, Miss., 78, 79, 85
Russell, Bertrand, 272–273
Rustin, Bayard, 93; invitation withdrawn, 29, 105; and Moses, 46; on whites, 102; and Malcolm X, 103; and MFDP, 126; and Carmichael, 163; criticism of, 178; on black power, 220; on Mideast, 268

Samstein, Mendy, 194–195
Sartre, Jean Paul, 273
Saturday Evening Post, 221
Savio, Mario, 129, 182, 302
Schoenman, Ralph, 273–274
Schwerner, Michael, 114–115
Seale, Bobby, 278, 280–282, 284
Searles, Ruth, 12–13
Seigenthaler, John, 35–36
Sellers, Cleveland, 232, 246; background, 15–16; on NAG, 104; after Mississippi Summer Project, 138; on Waveland retreat, 147; on COFO, 150; as program secretary, 151, 200, 202–204; on discipline, 155–157, 159, 204, 234; and Kingston Springs meeting, 202; and Mississippi march, 207; on weakening of SNCC, 224, 254–255; and education program, 235; and Atlanta Project, 241; on Zellners, 242; at South Carolina State College, 249–250, 293; indictment for draft evasion, 251; on whites, 268; on Black Panther Party, 283, 285; expelled, 293–294: subsequent career, 306
Selma protests, 133, 135, 153, 157–162
Sharpe, Monroe, 234
Shaw University, 19, 20
Sherrod, Charles, 51, 238, 257; Rock Hill protest, 32–33; at Nashville seminar, 41; on nonviolent protest, 48, 57, 58, 65; and Albany Movement, 56–58, 62, 63; background, 57; on freedom songs, 64; in Southwest Georgia, 74–77; on whites, 75–77, 101, 144; on local leaders, 81; and Robert Kennedy, 83–84; on Kennedy administration, 85; on Mississippi Summer Project, 99; criticism of, 104; and MFDP, 125–128; at Waveland retreat, 141, 142; at Union Theological Seminary, 150; resigns, 232; subsequent career, 306
Shields, Roy, 164
Shirah, Sam, 101–103, 177
Simmons, Michael, 239
Sit-ins, 1, 4, 215, 216; psychological importance of, 9, 11–12, 15–18; outgrowth of, 9, 18–20, 27; spread of, 10–11; explanations of, 12–18; and Barry, 21; and Nashville group, 22; and Rock Hill protests, 31, 32; in McComb, 48; in Albany Movement, 58, 59, 60
Smiley, Glenn, 22
Smith, Benjamin, 150, 325n
Smith, Bob, 204, 290
Smith, Charles, 300–301
Smith, Frank, 104, 112, 138, 143, 172–173
Smith, Lillian, 189
Smith, Ruby Doris, 32, 41, 67. See also Robinson, Ruby Doris
Smith, Scott B., 163
Snellings, Roland, 196
Socialists, 28, 29, 51
Socialist Workers Party, 262, 271

Sorace, John A., 258, 263
*Soul on Ice,* 283
South Carolina State College, 249–250
Southern Christian Leadership Conference (SCLC), 2, 16, 67, 234; and SNCC founding, 19–21, 25; and freedom rides, 36; in Albany Movement, 62–63; relations with SNCC, 70–71, 137, 163–164, 181, 186–187; and March on Washington, 92; and Mississippi Summer Project, 108; and FBI, 262
Southern Conference Educational Fund (SCEF), 28, 51–53, 67, 105–106, 182, 246, 258
*Southern Patriot,* 52
Southern Regional Council, 67
Southern Students Organizing Committee (SSOC), 102–103, 119, 177
Southwest Georgia Independent Voters Project, 232
Soviet Union, 272
Stanford, Max, 261
Stanford University, 98
Stembridge, Jane, 25–26, 27, 155
Stennis, John, 109
Stephens, Ernest, 248, 337n
Steptoe, E.W., 123
Stern Family Fund, 70
Stone, Donald, 196, 201, 241, 290
Stone, I.F., 205–206
Strickland, R.L., 164
Student National Coordinating Committee, 296
Student Nonviolent Coordinating Committee (SNCC): appeal of, 1, 3, 53, 71–74, 100, 154–155, 175–180, 299; on authority and individual freedom, 2, 4, 28, 66, 137–140, 142–143, 145, 154, 155, 157, 170–174, 211, 277, 299; as "shock troops," 2, 45, 47, 68–69, 136; shift from civil rights to economic goals, 2, 82, 94–96, 103–105, 141–144, 146–147, 152, 155–156, 227, 300–303; stages of development, 2–3, 128–129, 133–134, 211, 298–300; and other civil rights groups, 19, 20, 24, 27, 52, 96, 105, 107, 136–137, 173–174, 180, 181, 186–187, 189, 219–221, 289; founding of, 19–25; conferences, 19–25, 27–29, 66–67, 81–82, 104; religious ideas, 21–23, 29–31, 38, 56, 76, 77, 81, 95,

265, 298; statement of purpose, 23–24; moral orientation, 23–25, 31, 32, 37, 64–65, 94–95, 229; factions, 31, 39–42, 104, 139–141, 146, 152, 153, 155–157, 161–162, 169–171, 180, 199, 204, 229–230, 238, 240–241, 277, 287–288, 290–298, 300; and jail, 32–33, 38; international ties, 37–38, 136, 265–266, 271–278; finances, 39–41, 70–71, 108, 173, 187, 234, 315n, 328n, 335n; revolutionary élan, 45, 51, 54–55, 264, 299; education programs, 54, 105, 140, 204, 235–236; critical of liberal allies, 92–94, 96, 127–128, 146, 151–152, 184, 270; economic programs, 96, 103–105; freedom-high faction, 153, 155–157, 169–170, 326n; as catalyst for local activity, 153, 160, 163, 171, 172; on urban projects, 166–168, 189–195, 231, 233–235, 251–252, 299–300; ideological conformity, 191, 198, 287–288, 292–298; leadership shift (1966), 191–192, 202–204, 231–232; decline, 224, 232–235, 285–287, 292, 296, 300; as scapegoat, 242–244, 247–248, 250, 251, 258, 260; new role as ideologues, 287, 288, 292–294, 296, 298, 300; legacy, 300–303; reunion, 305–306
—Coordinating Committee, 29–30, 45, 50, 66–68, 145, 151
—Executive Committee, 67, 100–101, 145, 151, 167, 204; meetings, 97, 99–100, 102–107, 158, 164, 169–170, 182
—Organizing techniques: and local leadership, 2, 4, 28–30, 55, 58, 62–64, 75, 77, 81, 139, 142–144, 149–152, 154, 155, 158, 163, 170–171, 285, 299–303; in difficult areas, 2, 45, 47, 68–69; and religion, 56, 58, 75; and fear of white authority, 57–58, 62, 75, 78–79; living with people, 57–58, 74–75, 81, 116, 118; and freedom songs, 63–64, 81; common elements in, 74, 81; food drive, 80; and racial appeals, 166, 191, 194, 196, 201; debate about (1966), 201–202
—Staff: full-time organizers, 1, 31, 42–44, 50, 54–55, 66–68, 145; identity in McComb, 45, 49–51, 54; and Coordinating Committee, 50, 66–68; wages,

71, 305; radicalization of, 71–74; conflicts, 143, 150–152; and local people, 154–156, 171–172; evaluation in 1965, 169–170; changes in 1966, 231–236; focus no longer on SNCC, 291–292
—Staff meetings: May 1960, 25; February 1961, 32; August 1961, 41–42; fall 1961, 50–51; October 1964, 137–140; November 1964, 140–148; February 1965, 151–152; November 1965, 187–188; March 1966, 196–200; May 1966, 200–204; December 1966, 239–241; spring 1967, 251–253, 266; June 1968, 290–291; December 1968, 293; June 1969, 295–296
—Structure: initial, 28–29; under Forman, 66, 69–71; reorganization (1962), 67; northern offices, 70–71, 108; Communications Department, 117–118; Secretariat, 151; Central Committee, 204; collective leadership, 290–291; Revolutionary Political Council, 296
*Student Voice*, 25, 29, 37, 70, 296
Students for a Democratic Society (SDS), 67, 163, 262; and SNCC, 21, 28, 175–178, 180; and black southern student movement, 53–54; and SSOC, 103; on poor and blacks, 177, 179; isolation, 180; opposes Vietnam war, 184
*Studies on the Left*, 179–180
Summer Community Organizing and Political Education (SCOPE), 187
Summerhill, 225–226

Taconic Foundation, 41–42, 70, 92
Talbert, Robert, 49
Tanzania, 277, 306
Tate, John, 225
Taylor, Benjamin, 80
Teach-ins, 184
Texas Southern University, 249
Thelwell, Mike, 98, 128
Third World: SNCC and, 151, 184, 198, 201, 257, 265–266, 271–278; black power and, 227, 274; Carmichael in, 273–277
Third World Women's Alliance, 296
Thomas, Henry, 33, 34, 38
Thomas, Norman, 104
Thrasher, Sue, 102
Tijerina, Reies, 278
Till, Emmett, 84

Tillinghast, Muriel, 112–113, 122, 148, 230
*Time*, 221
Touré, Sekou, 134, 276, 277
Travis, Brenda, 48, 49
Travis, Jimmy, 81, 86, 113
Turnbow, Hartman, 89, 123

United Civil Rights Leadership Council, 92, 107
*United States* vs. *Mississippi*, 88
Urban League, 92, 186, 189, 289
Urban rebellions, 4, 219, 287–289, 299–300
US, 281, 283, 288

Varela, Maria, 119, 142–143, 175, 306
Vaughs, Cliff, 233
Vaugn, Willie, 163
Vietnam war: SNCC opposes, 174, 176, 183–189, 220–221, 246, 260, 265; Brown on, 255; and War Crimes Tribunal, 272–273
Vine City Project. See Atlanta Project
Violence: in sit-ins, 11; in McComb project, 47–49; in Albany Movement, 60–61, 64–65; in Mississippi, 79–81, 210; in 1963 demonstrations, 90–91; in Mississippi Summer Project, 114–115, 122–123; in Selma protests, 159–161; and armed self-defense, 164, 166, 200, 253–255, 259, 299; blamed on SNCC, 226, 247–248, 250, 255–256, 258, 288. *See also* Police
VISTA, 141
Voter Education Project (VEP), 70, 78, 97, 300
Voter registration: and Amzie Moore, 26; vs. nonviolent direct action, 26, 31, 39–42; and Kennedy administration, 38–39, 41; in McComb project, 45–51; and fund-raising, 70; in Mississippi, 74–81; Sherrod on, 75; and federal nonprotection, 84–89; adequacy of, 103; in Mississippi Summer Project, 117; in Alabama, 157–158; in Lowndes County, 165
Voting Rights Act, 165

Waggoner, Joe, 185
Walker, Johnnie Mae, 171
Walker, Sid, 232

Walker, Wyatt T., 61, 63
Wallace, George, 159, 161, 165
Wallace, Lurleen, 254
Walton, Bobby, 225–226
Walzer, Michael, 17
War Crimes Tribunal, 272–273
War on Poverty, 169. *See also* Office of
  Economic Opportunity
Ware, Bill, 225–226; at Selma protests,
  160; and Atlanta Project, 192–196,
  201; background, 193; on whites,
  238–240; and SNCC leadership, 241,
  336n
Ware, George, 235, 245, 247–248, 259,
  290, 337n
Washington, Cynthia, 148
Washington, D.C., 233
Watkins, Hollis, 48, 49, 77
Watters, Pat, 61, 75, 183
White, Lee, 87
White, Theodore H., 106
White Folk's Project, 118–119
White House Conference on Civil
  Rights, 187, 200, 204–205
Whites: in SNCC, 52–53, 72–73, 299; at
  Atlanta conference (1962), 67; in
  southwest Georgia project, 75–77, 101;
  Moses on, 77, 80, 81, 96, 98–99, 100,
  112; in Mississippi Summer Project,
  96, 98–103, 111–114, 118–119; and ra-
  cial hostility, 101, 141; in white com-
  munities, 102–103, 118–119, 197, 198,
  201, 204–206, 217, 271, 274; influx of,
  137; Waveland retreat on, 144–145;
  and freedom-high and floater groups,
  155, 326n; COFO on, 171–172; and
  Atlanta Project, 194–200; Kingston
  Springs meeting on, 201; final debate
  on, 229, 236–242; and class vs. race,
  269–272
Wicker, Tom, 222
Wiley, Jean, 306
Wilkins, Ronald LeRoy, 290
Wilkins, Roy, 189, 207, 219–220
Williams, Bob, 119
Williams, Hosea, 158–159
Williams, J. Allen, 12–13

Williams, Robert F., 42–43, 181, 196,
  276
Wilson, Johnny, 73, 239, 296; on Arab-
  Israeli issue, 268; and racial sep-
  aratism, 271; in collective leadership,
  290; impact on, 302–303; subsequent
  career, 306
Wilson, Leroy, 247, 248
Wise, Stanley, 202, 235, 254, 294, 330n;
  and Mississippi march, 207; back-
  ground, 252–253; in collective leader-
  ship, 290; subsequent career, 306
Wofford, Harris, 38
Women, 147–148, 283
Woodruff, James, 245
Woodward, C. Vann, 183
*Wretched on the Earth, The,* 192
Wright, Nathan, 224
Wright, Richard, 209

Yale University, 98, 99
Young, Andrew, 137, 165–166, 186, 189,
  305
Young, Whitney, 189, 220, 268, 289
Young Militants, 225
Young People's Socialist League, 28
Young Socialist Alliance, 262
Younge, Sammy, 188
Youth Marches for Integrated
  Schools, 16

Zellner, Bob, 51, 52–54, 70, 101–102; in
  McComb project, 49; in Albany Movement, 59; arrests, 68; in Danville demonstration, 90; in SDS, 175; expelled,
  241–242; on SNCC, 302; subsequent
  career, 306
Zellner, Dottie, 241–242. *See also* Miller,
  Dottie
Zinn, Howard, 107; on SCLC ties, 24; on
  Albany Movement, 62; on whites, 98;
  on interracial ideal, 100; on freedom
  schools, 121; and armed self-defense,
  122; and Waveland retreat, 142; history of SNCC, 178–179; on anti-war
  position, 187